STOP!

This is the back of the book.
You wouldn't want to spoil a great ending!

This book is printed "manga-style," in the authentic Japanese right-to-left format. Since none of the artwork has been flipped or altered, readers get to experience the story just as the creator intended. You've been asking for it, so TOKYOPOP® delivered: authentic, hot-off-the-press, and far more fun!

DIRECTIONS

If this is your first time reading manga-style, here's a quick guide to help you understand how it works.

It's easy… just start in the top right panel and follow the numbers. Have fun, and look for more 100% authentic manga from TOKYOPOP®!

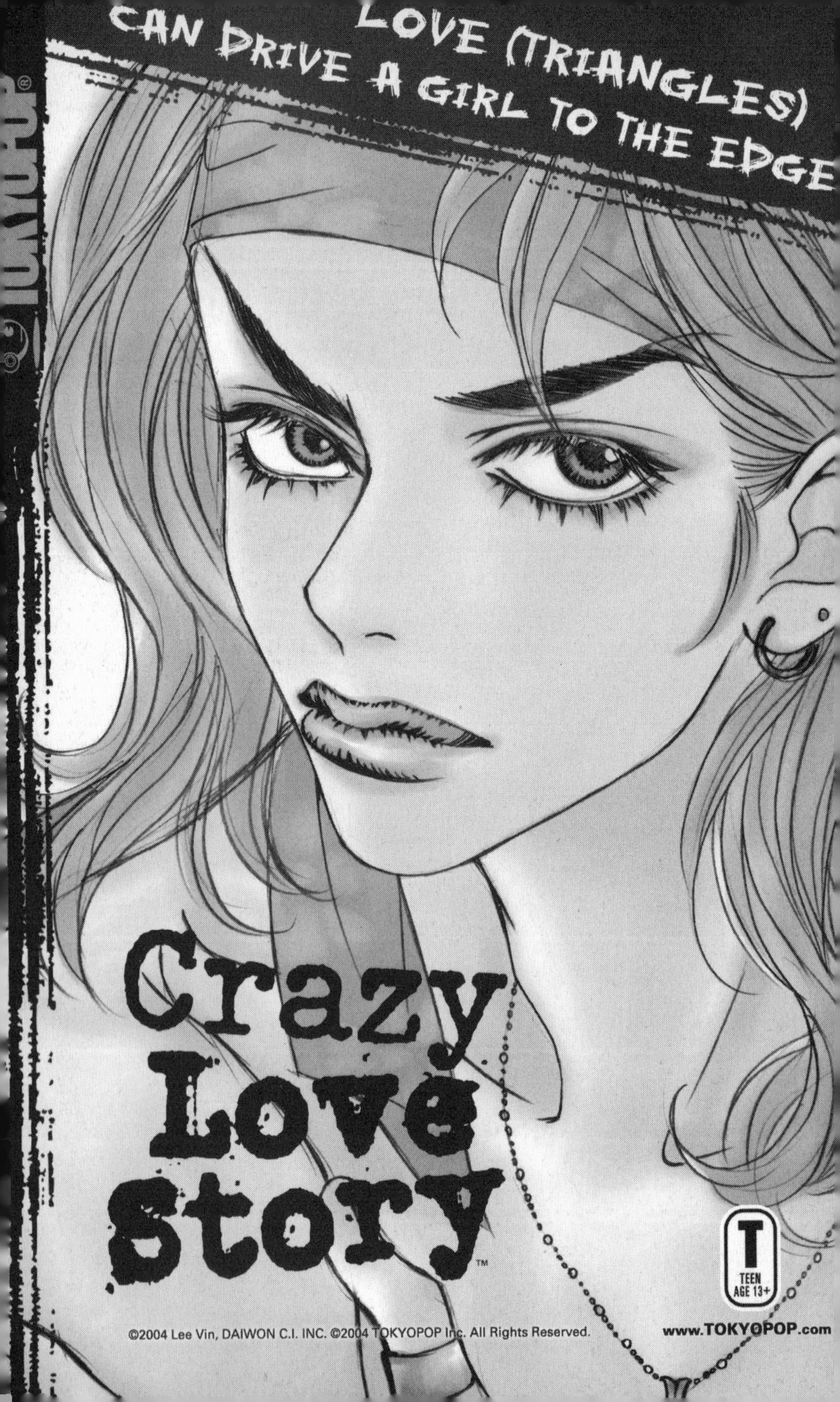
LOVE (TRIANGLES)
CAN DRIVE A GIRL TO THE EDGE
Crazy Love Story™
T TEEN AGE 13+
©2004 Lee Vin, DAIWON C.I. INC. ©2004 TOKYOPOP Inc. All Rights Reserved.
www.TOKYOPOP.com

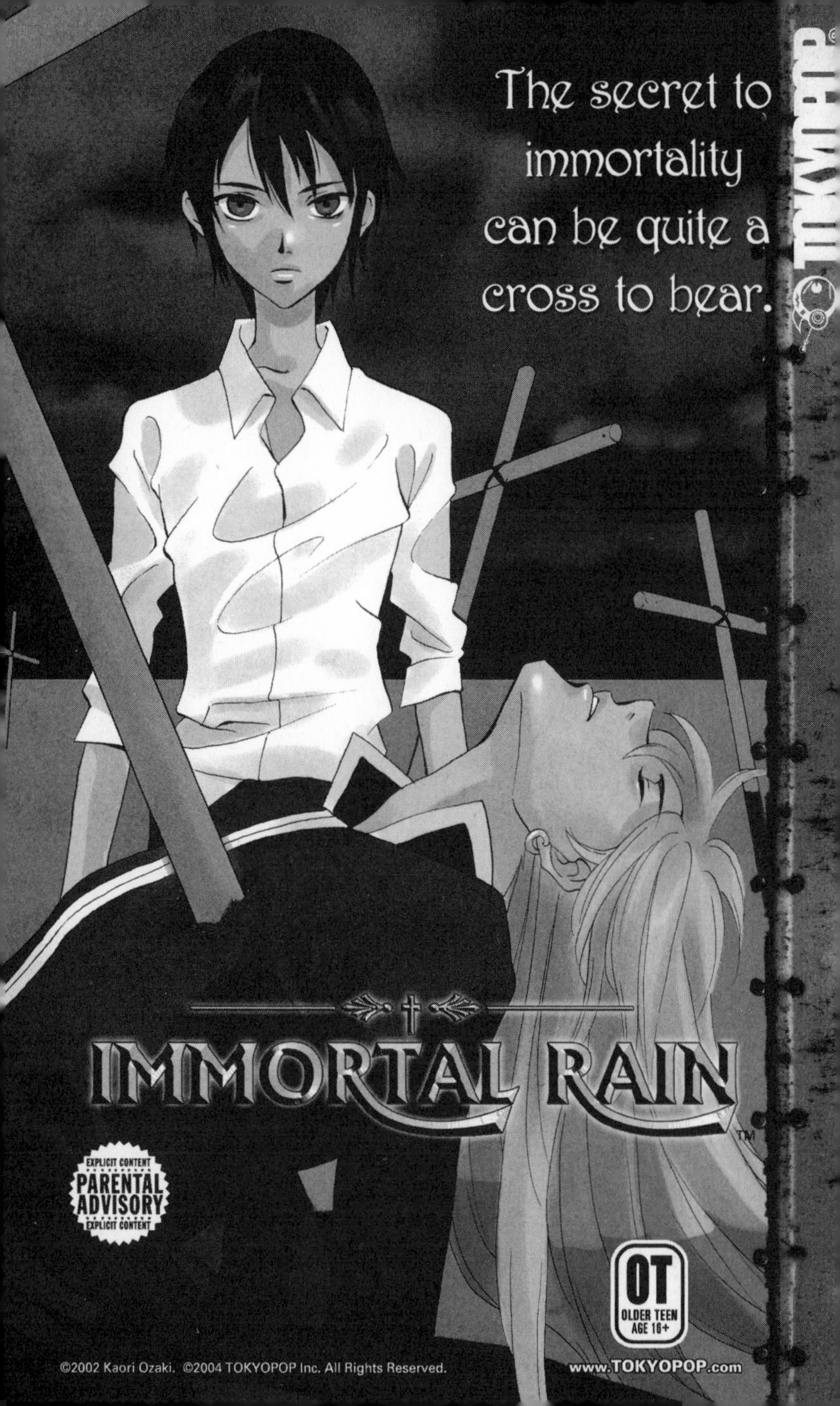
TOKYOPOP
The secret to immortality can be quite a cross to bear.
IMMORTAL RAIN™
EXPLICIT CONTENT PARENTAL ADVISORY EXPLICIT CONTENT
OT OLDER TEEN AGE 16+
©2002 Kaori Ozaki. ©2004 TOKYOPOP Inc. All Rights Reserved.
www.TOKYOPOP.com

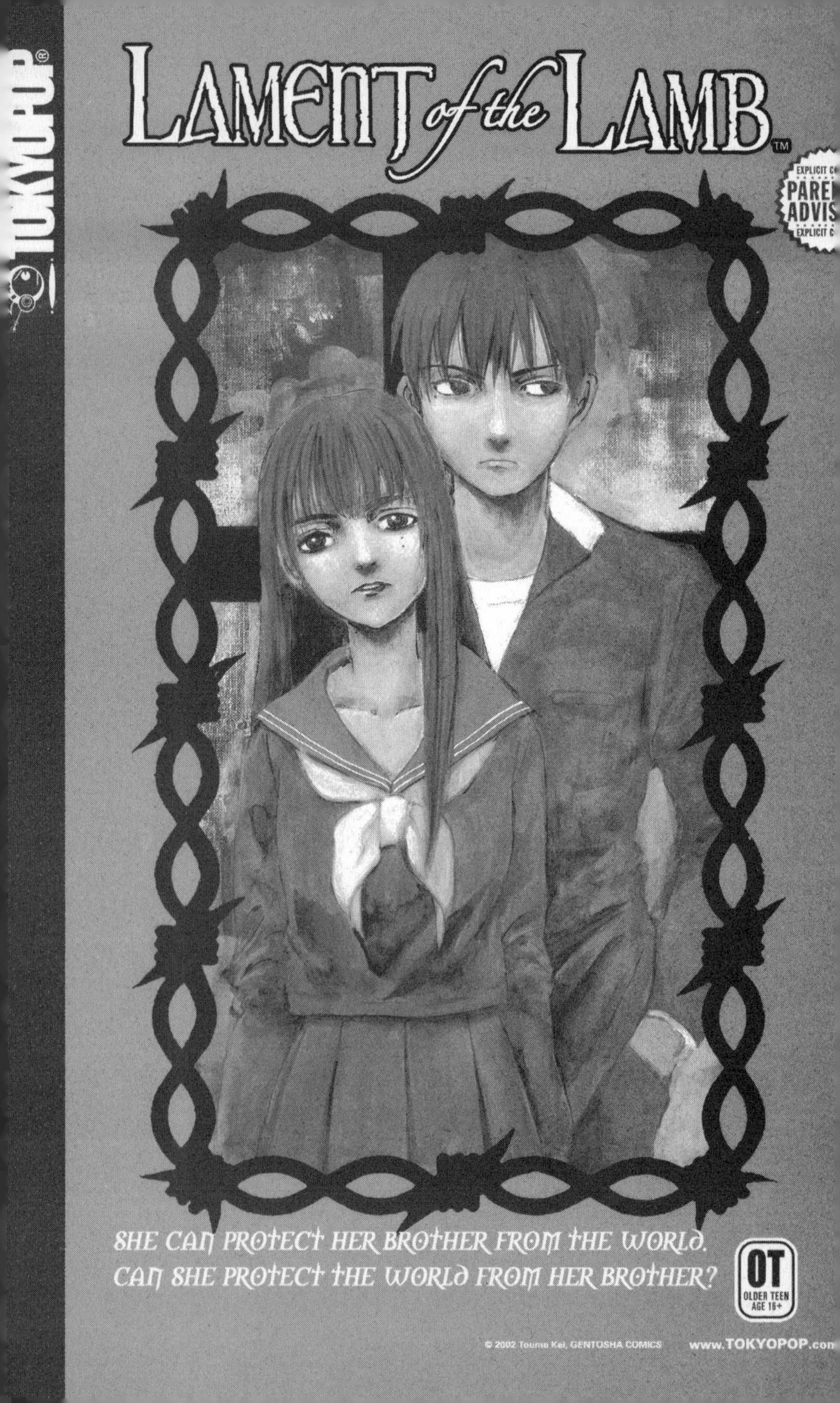
TOKYOPOP®
LAMENT of the LAMB™
SHE CAN PROTECT HER BROTHER FROM THE WORLD.
CAN SHE PROTECT THE WORLD FROM HER BROTHER?
OT
OLDER TEEN AGE 16+
© 2002 Toume Kei, GENTOSHA COMICS
www.TOKYOPOP.co

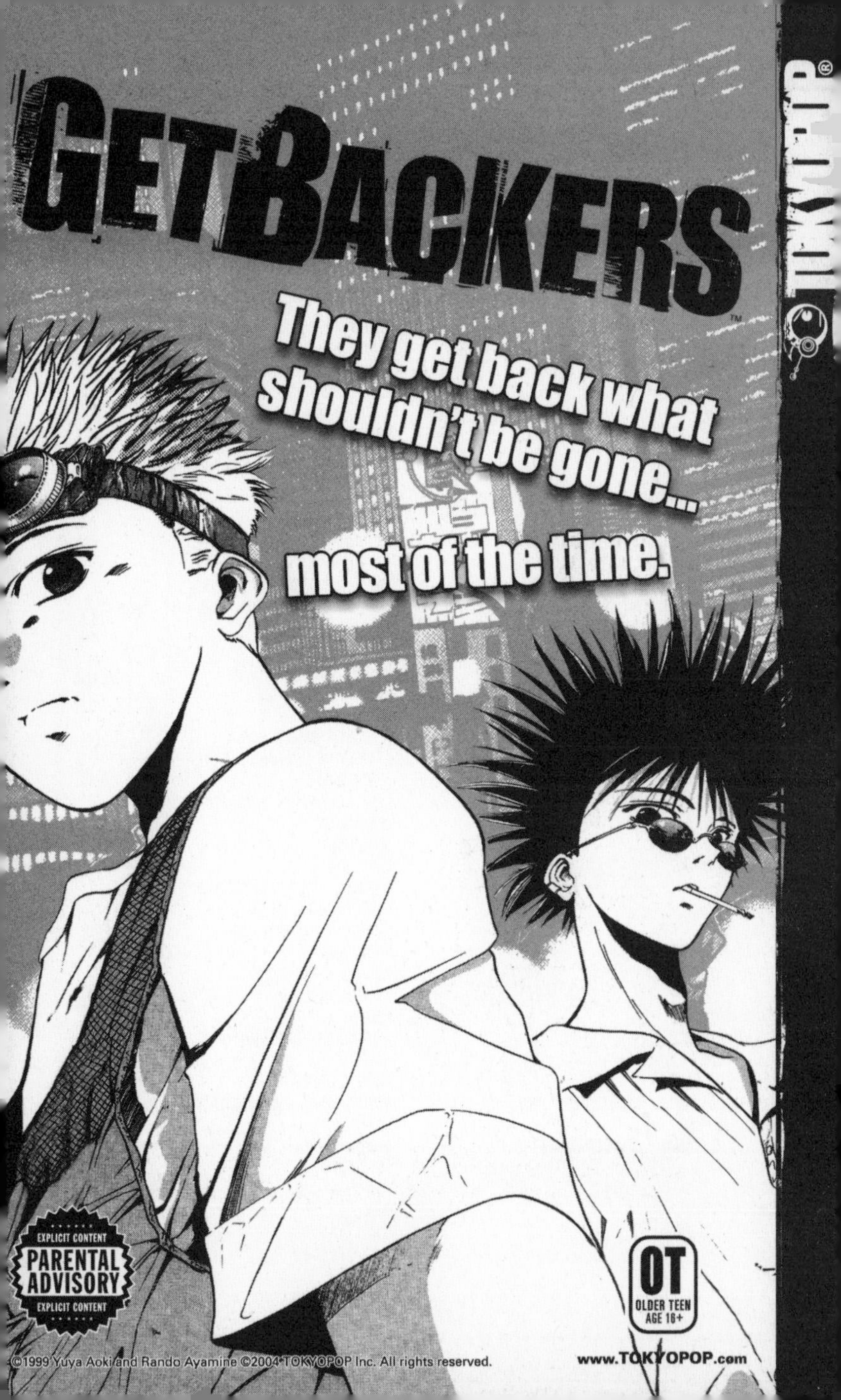
GETBACKERS™
They get back what shouldn't be gone... most of the time.
TOKYOPOP®
EXPLICIT CONTENT
PARENTAL ADVISORY
EXPLICIT CONTENT
OT
OLDER TEEN AGE 16+
©1999 Yuya Aoki and Rando Ayamine ©2004 TOKYOPOP Inc. All rights reserved.
www.TOKYOPOP.com

ALSO AVAILABLE FROM ✪ TOKYOPOP®

MANGA

.HACK//LEGEND OF THE TWILIGHT
@LARGE
ABENOBASHI: MAGICAL SHOPPING ARCADE
A.I. LOVE YOU
AI YORI AOSHI
ANGELIC LAYER
ARM OF KANNON
BABY BIRTH
BATTLE ROYALE
BATTLE VIXENS
BOYS BE...
BRAIN POWERED
BRIGADOON
B'TX
CANDIDATE FOR GODDESS, THE
CARDCAPTOR SAKURA
CARDCAPTOR SAKURA - MASTER OF THE CLOW
CHOBITS
CHRONICLES OF THE CURSED SWORD
CLAMP SCHOOL DETECTIVES
CLOVER
COMIC PARTY
CONFIDENTIAL CONFESSIONS
CORRECTOR YUI
COWBOY BEBOP
COWBOY BEBOP: SHOOTING STAR
CRAZY LOVE STORY
CRESCENT MOON
CROSS
CULDCEPT
CYBORG 009
D•N•ANGEL
DEMON DIARY
DEMON ORORON, THE
DEUS VITAE
DIABOLO
DIGIMON
DIGIMON TAMERS
DIGIMON ZERO TWO
DOLL
DRAGON HUNTER
DRAGON KNIGHTS
DRAGON VOICE
DREAM SAGA
DUKLYON: CLAMP SCHOOL DEFENDERS
EERIE QUEERIE!
ERICA SAKURAZAWA: COLLECTED WORKS
ET CETERA
ETERNITY
EVIL'S RETURN
FAERIES' LANDING
FAKE
FLCL
FLOWER OF THE DEEP SLEEP
FORBIDDEN DANCE
FRUITS BASKET

G GUNDAM
GATEKEEPERS
GETBACKERS
GIRL GOT GAME
GIRLS EDUCATIONAL CHARTER
GRAVITATION
GTO
GUNDAM BLUE DESTINY
GUNDAM SEED ASTRAY
GUNDAM WING
GUNDAM WING: BATTLEFIELD OF PACIFISTS
GUNDAM WING: ENDLESS WALTZ
GUNDAM WING: THE LAST OUTPOST (G-UNIT)
HANDS OFF!
HAPPY MANIA
HARLEM BEAT
HYPER RUNE
I.N.V.U.
IMMORTAL RAIN
INITIAL D
INSTANT TEEN: JUST ADD NUTS
ISLAND
JING: KING OF BANDITS
JING: KING OF BANDITS - TWILIGHT TALES
JULINE
KARE KANO
KILL ME, KISS ME
KINDAICHI CASE FILES, THE
KING OF HELL
KODOCHA: SANA'S STAGE
LAMENT OF THE LAMB
LEGAL DRUG
LEGEND OF CHUN HYANG, THE
LES BIJOUX
LOVE HINA
LUPIN III
LUPIN III: WORLD'S MOST WANTED
MAGIC KNIGHT RAYEARTH I
MAGIC KNIGHT RAYEARTH II
MAHOROMATIC: AUTOMATIC MAIDEN
MAN OF MANY FACES
MARMALADE BOY
MARS
MARS: HORSE WITH NO NAME
MINK
MIRACLE GIRLS
MIYUKI-CHAN IN WONDERLAND
MODEL
MOURYOU KIDEN
MY LOVE
NECK AND NECK
ONE
ONE I LOVE, THE
PARADISE KISS
PARASYTE
PASSION FRUIT
PEACH GIRL
PEACH GIRL: CHANGE OF HEART

06.21.04T

It didn't take long at all. You cracked *The Demon Ororon* vol. 1 and in no time heard the truth rattling around inside of it. The two main characters, Chiaki and Ororon, spoke smartly. They lived fully in evocative glances rendered minimally. The story sang with little effort. Here came the Devil, flying in low on attitude and hipster vulnerability. James Dean from Hell. The woman (well, the girl) was crafted out of spacey half-formed soliloquies and soft-lens supernatural dramas. Her wide eyes perpetually wet with crystallized innovations in innocence. They fell in love. That's what happens in these things. They built each other mansions in their hearts, but never handed out the keys. Then, through conflicting natures and unstated feelings, they started to tear those unlived-in mansions down. Familiar story. Age-old. But still... still, you believed it. You wanted them to be real and strong and to overcome differences and enemies and find peace in each other's arms. And when that first volume was done, you wondered "will they ever learn how--or even just find the time--to love?" You cracked that Ororon story, the one that started on a rainy Monday, and you ate that shit up from page one. Now, here you are. At the end. Page one far, far behind.

You think Hakase Mizuki is a bad ass. Of this, there is no doubt. She's relentless and satirical, brutal and chaste, chipper and dejected. She crafts, here, not just an adventure fantasy love story for teens, but a work that is obsessed with the inherent cruelty of the universe and the paper thin logic of our collective cosmologies. In her work, the cry in the dark is always louder than the wonder at the light. At this point you've probably tripped through more than 600 pages of her philosophical missives, manga goofiness and hyper-violence, and never once did it seem burdensome, or exploitive. Every page came from her heart/mind. She spilled herself out. You gladly soaked her up.

On the other side of this rambling page of praise, the paladins of revenge, ambition and ego surround our crystal-eyed angel and her Jimmy Dean Devil. Our protagonists have been worn down by the relentlessness of their world. Blood comes in buckets. Ororon's seemingly ever-present wound grows deeper and deeper. And you, dear reader, are about to go full steam ahead towards their final fate. But in the midst of your reading experience, if you think about it, take a pause. Breathe. Close your eyes and think back to those dawning pages of that original volume. To that rainy Monday. Things were lighter then. From there, our couple could've built any kind of future. But I guess Romeo and Juliet will always end up riding black horses into the sunset. That's the way the cookie crumbles. Mizuki knows this, and she channels her frustrations into Chiaki in the form of a central question that the little angel poses over and over again... why? Why is this the way the story goes?

There are no answers. No one's heard from God in some time. The architect of it all has packed up its things and caught a train to a better hood. This is just the way of things. The trick is to love through the pain.

I had an amazing time helping transmit this book across cultural boundaries. If you made it to Volume 4, then you and I have something in common. We've both fallen in love with a half-breed angel and her sulky devil King...

... and we're sad to see their story end.

Peace,
Joshua Dysart
Venice Beach, Ca.
(The writer of *Violent Messiahs*, *The Demon Driven Out* and *Swamp Thing* is proud to have adapted *The Demon Ororon* books 1–4 for the English language).

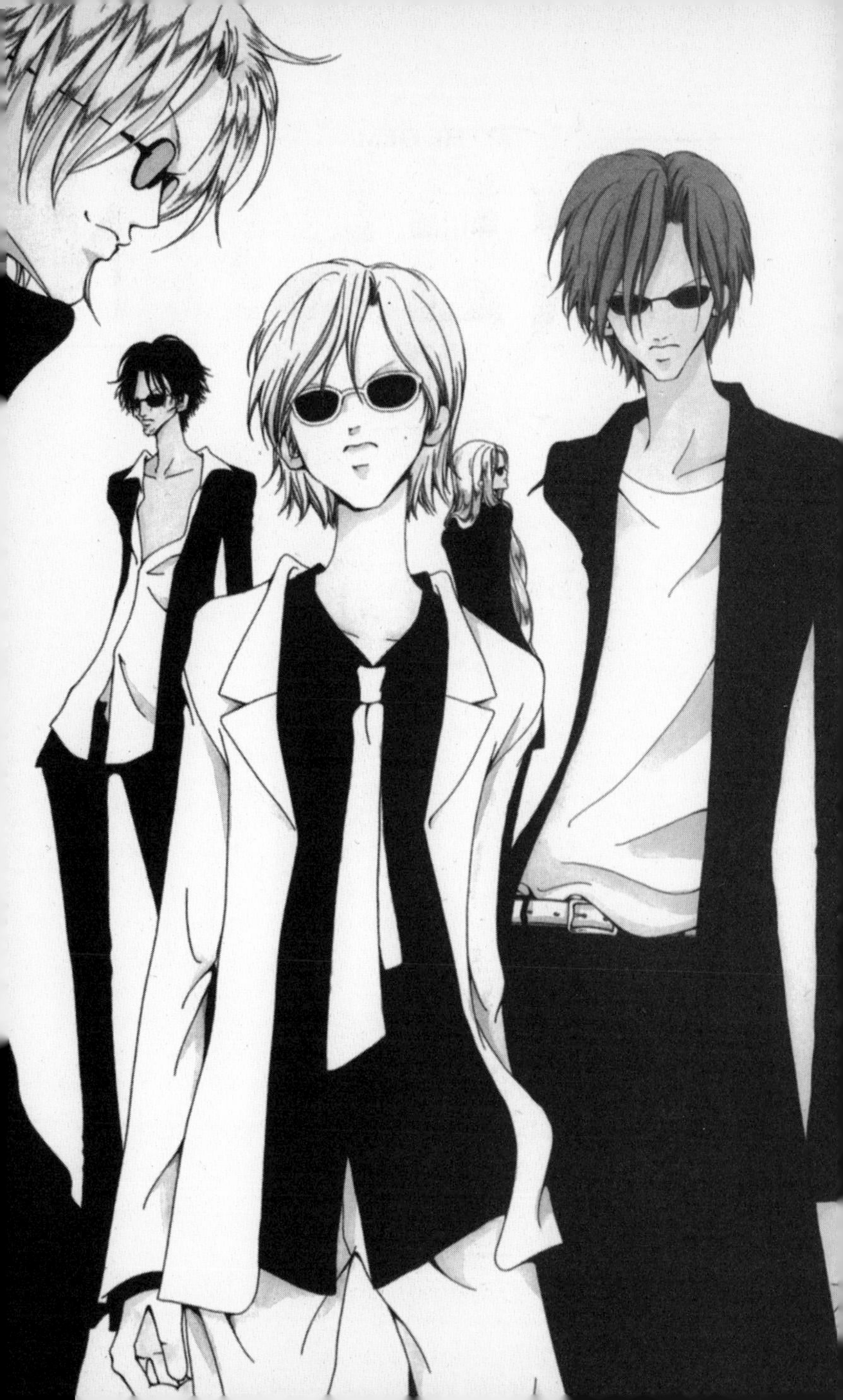

THE DEMON ORORON

VOLUME 4

BY HAKASE MIZUKI

TOKYOPOP®

HAMBURG // LONDON // LOS ANGELES // TOKYO

The Demon Ororon Vol. 4
Created by Hakase Mizuki

Translation - Tomoko Kamimoto
English Adaptation - Josh Dysart
Retouch and Lettering - Keiko Okabe
Production Artist - Sophia Hong
Cover Layout - Ray Makowski

Editor - Luis Reyes
Digital Imaging Manager - Chris Buford
Pre-Press Manager - Antonio DePietro
Production Managers - Jennifer Miller and Mutsumi Miyazaki
Art Director - Matt Alford
Managing Editor - Jill Freshney
VP of Production - Ron Klamert
President and C.O.O. - John Parker
Publisher and C.E.O. - Stuart Levy

A  Manga

TOKYOPOP Inc.
5900 Wilshire Blvd. Suite 2000
Los Angeles, CA 90036

E-mail: info@TOKYOPOP.com
Come visit us online at www.TOKYOPOP.com

ISBN: 1-59182-728-0

First TOKYOPOP printing: October 2004
10 9 8 7 6 5 4 3 2 1
Printed in the USA

THE DEMON ORORON

The Story Thus Far

CHIAKI IS A RARE GIRL INDEED. SHE'S THE HALF-BREED CHILD OF AN ANGEL AND A MORTAL, AND SHE'S FALLEN IN LOVE WITH THE KING OF THE DEMONS, A.K.A. SATAN, A.K.A. ORORON...THE DEVIL.

AS YOU MIGHT IMAGINE, THE RELATIONSHIP HASN'T BEEN ALL ROSES AND CANDLELIGHT DINNERS. NOT ONLY DOES THE COUPLE HAVE THEIR CONFLICTING NATURES TO RECONCILE, BUT ORORON IS APPARENTLY AWOL FROM THE THRONE OF HELL. HAVING LEFT THE SAFETY OF HIS REALM, ORORON, AND THEREFORE CHIAKI, HAS BECOME THE CENTER OF A DELUGE OF DEMONIC ASSASSINS HIRED BY FACTIONS OF ORORON'S OWN FAMILY TO INSURE THAT HE NEVER RETURNS. CHIAKI'S ONCE QUIET LIFE HAS BECOME AWASH IN DEATH.

A SHORT TIME AGO, DRIVEN TO THE END OF HER ROPE AND PSYCHOLOGICALLY EXHAUSTED FROM THE STRUGGLE, CHIAKI UNCONSCIOUSLY RELEASED AN EXTRAORDINARILY DESTRUC-TIVE POWER SHE DIDN'T EVEN KNOW SHE POSSESSED. WHEN THE BLOOM OF HER PSYCHIC BLAST HAD SUBSIDED, AN ENTIRE CITY LAY IN RUINS.

SINCE THE INCIDENT, ORORON, CHIAKI, AND THE REST OF THEIR STRANGE FAMILY, HAVE GONE ON THE RUN, EVADING NOT ONLY COUNTLESS HATCHET MEN AT EVERY TURN, BUT ALSO A BAND OF COOL CATS LED BY ORORON'S BROTHER, OTHELLO, WHO'S DETERMINED TO PUT THE YOUNG RUNAWAY KING BACK ON THE THRONE. OF COURSE, ONE OF ORORON'S OTHER BROTHERS, OSCAR, HAS JUST CRASHED THE SCENE INTENT ON KEEPING HIS YOUNGER BROTHER OFF THE THRONE.

NOW ORORON HAS BEEN INJURED, ENEMIES WHO WOULD GLAD-LY SEE HIM DEAD CLOSE IN FROM ALL SIDES AND OTHELLO'S ARMY SEARCHES FOR THE KING IN AN EFFORT TO KEEP HIM ALIVE.

OH, THE SUSPENSE IS JUST KILLING ME. HOW 'BOUT YOU?

CONTENTS

16 LONG NIGHT

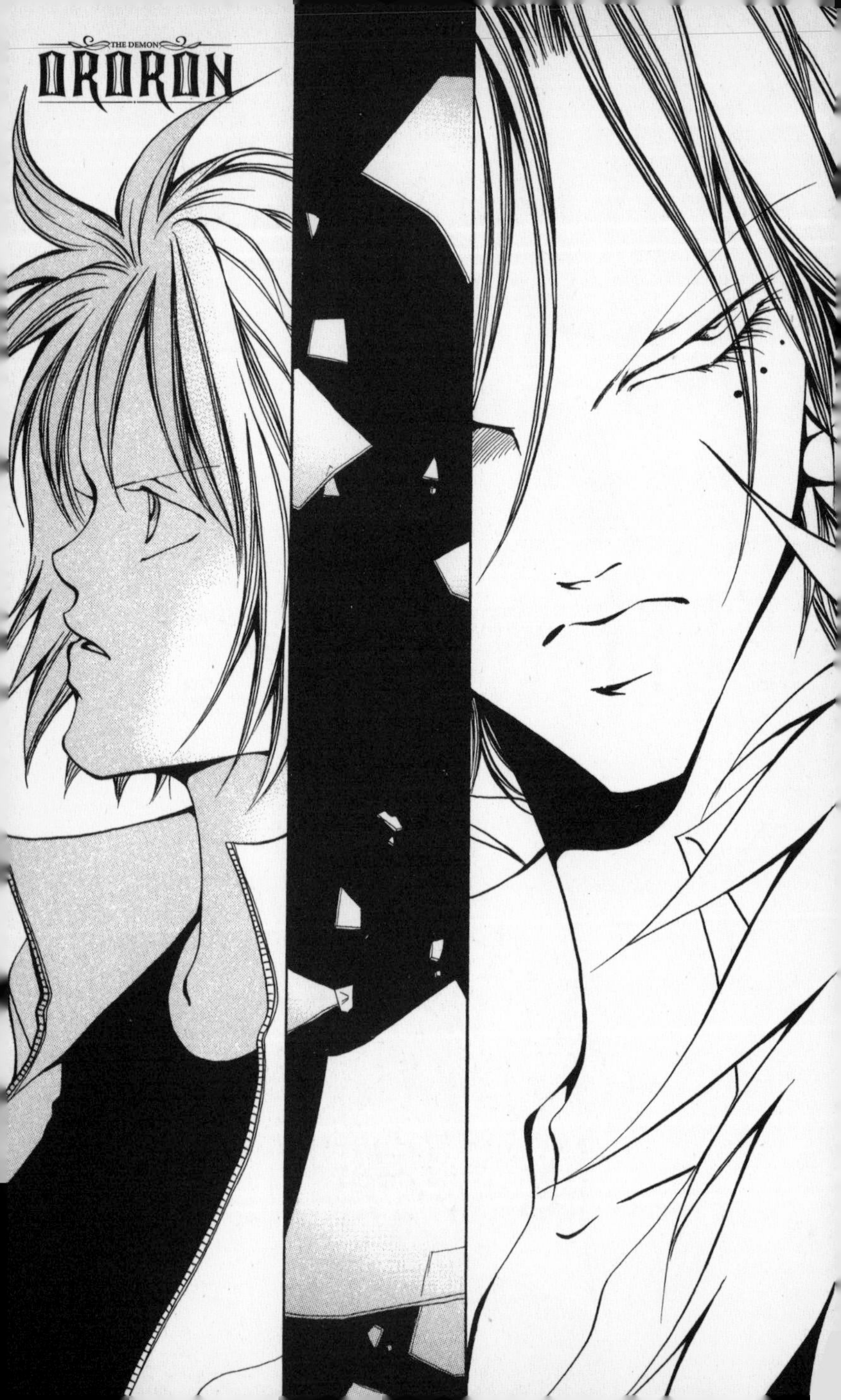
THE DEMON
ORORON

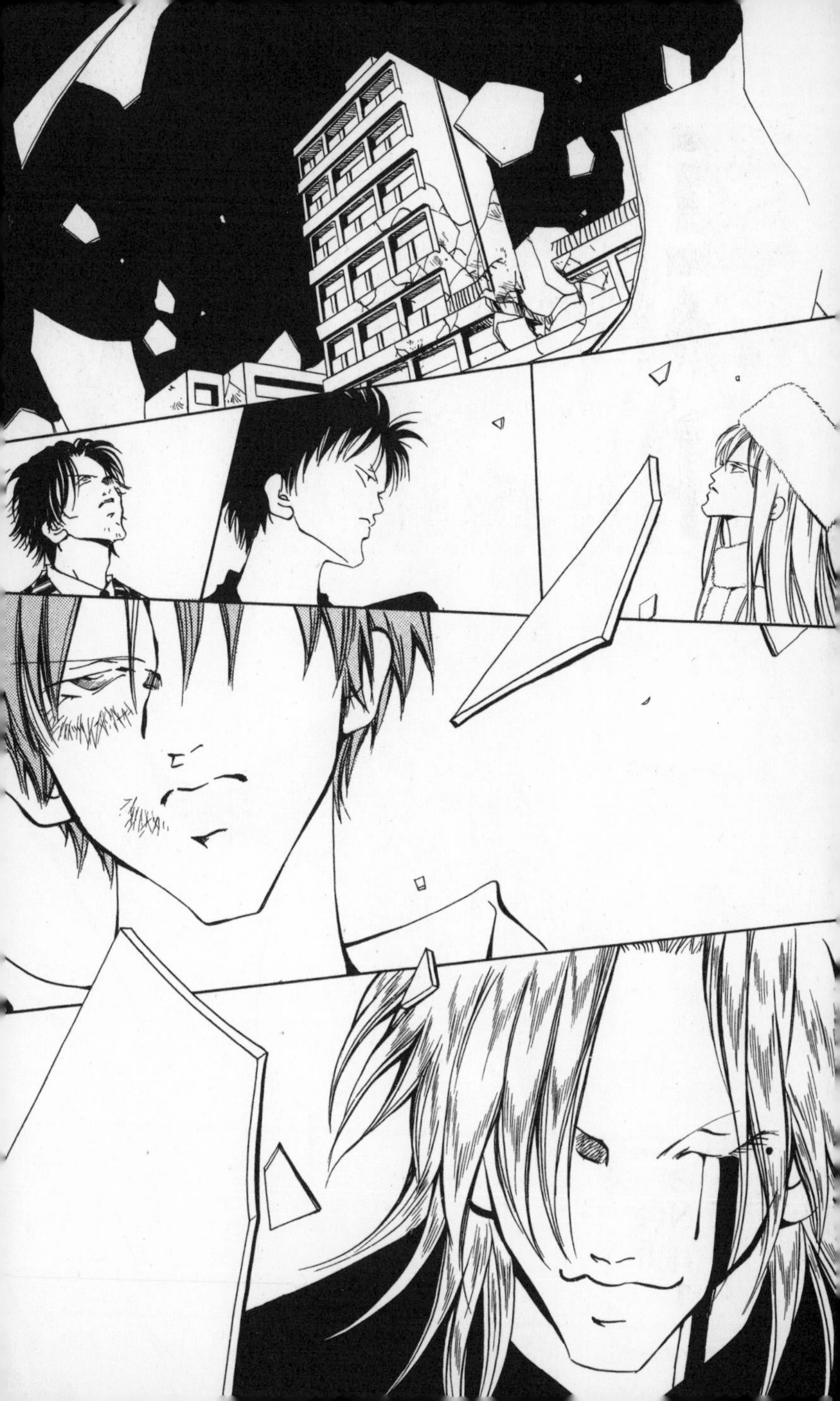

悪魔のオロロン

THE DEMON
ORORON

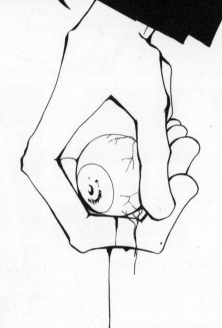

-16-
LONG
NIGHT
01

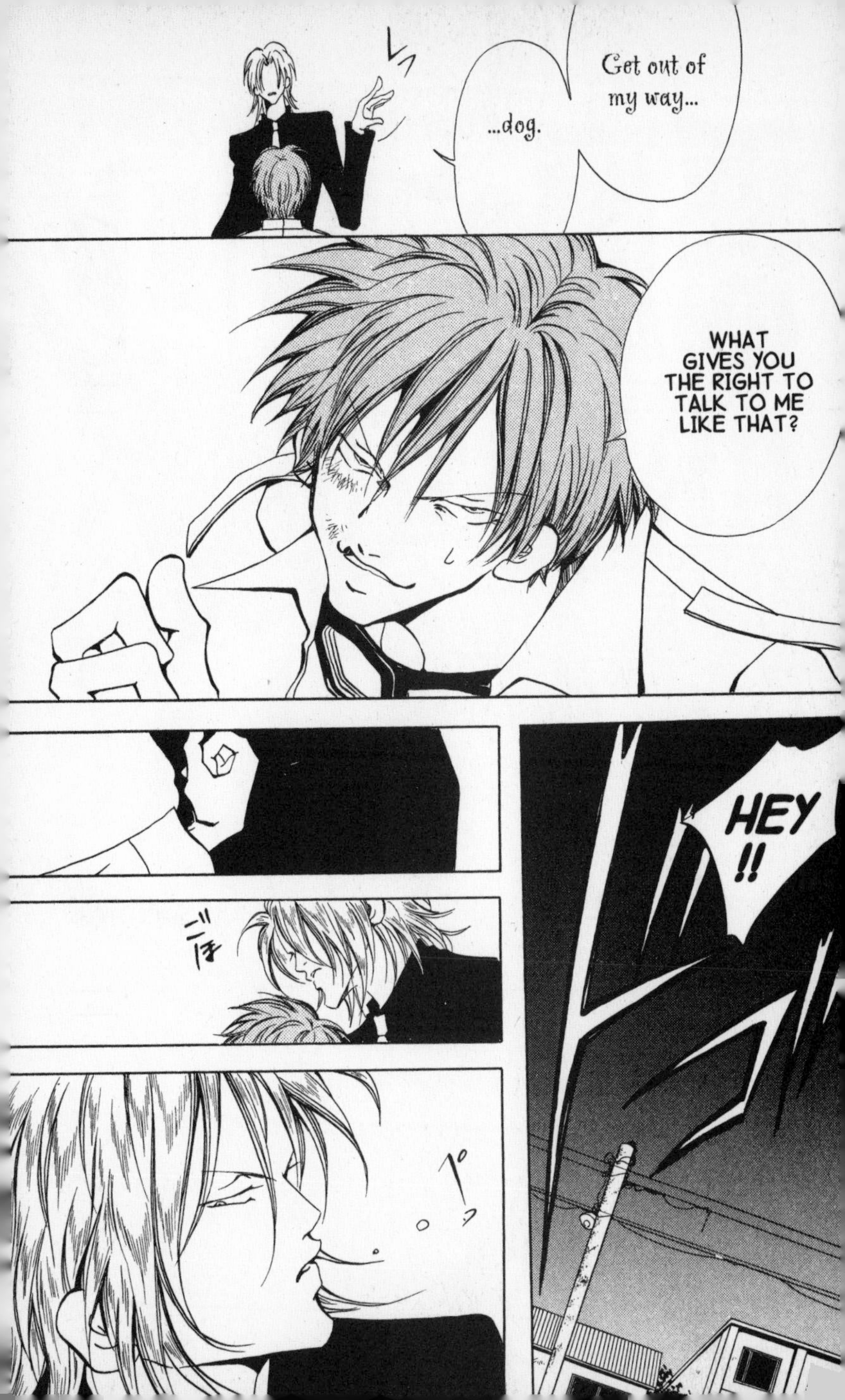
Get out of my way...
...dog.
WHAT GIVES YOU THE RIGHT TO TALK TO ME LIKE THAT?
HEY !!
ごほ

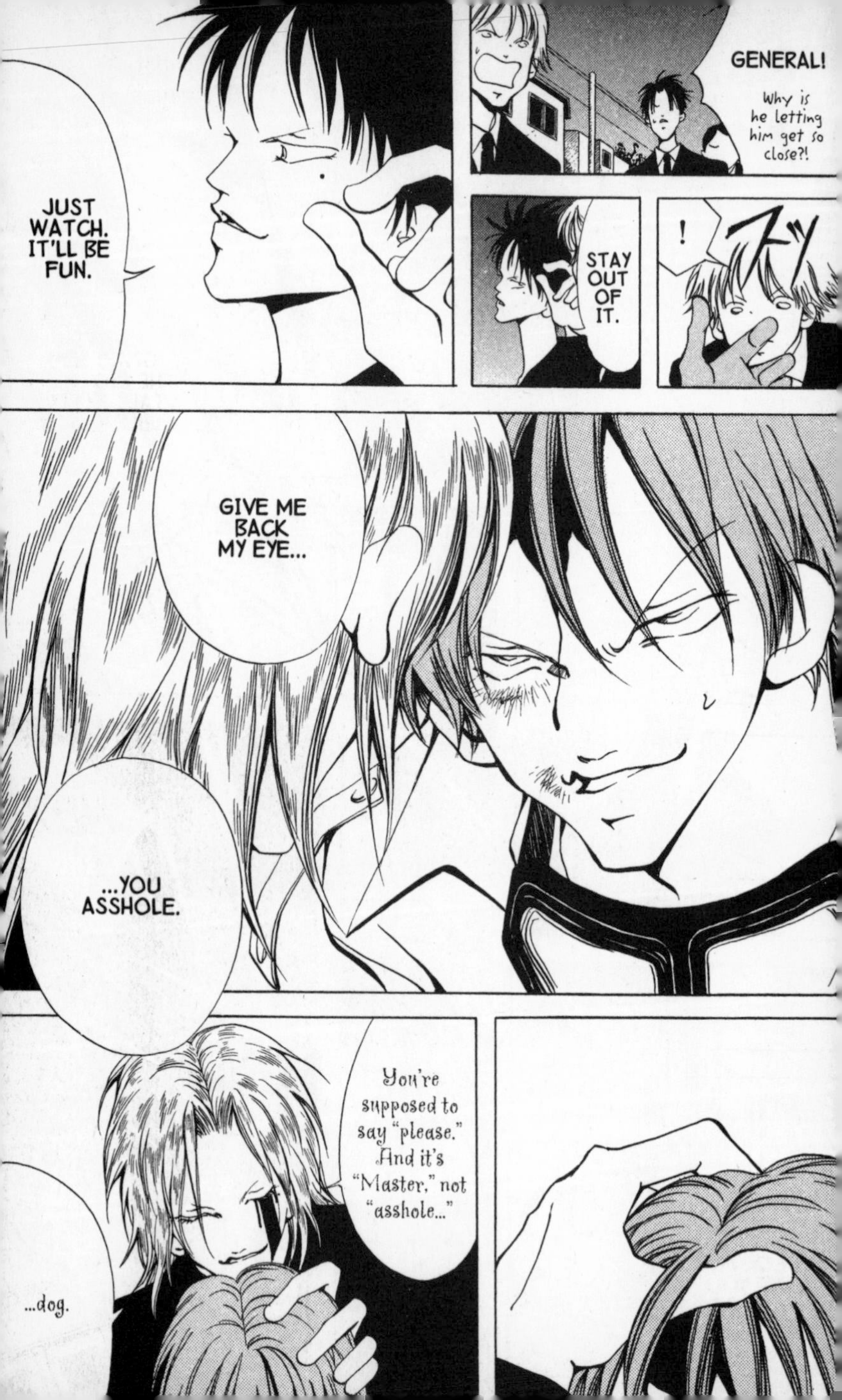
GENERAL!
Why is he letting him get so close?!
!
ズッ
STAY OUT OF IT.
JUST WATCH. IT'LL BE FUN.
GIVE ME BACK MY EYE...
...YOU ASSHOLE.
You're supposed to say "please." And it's "Master," not "asshole..."
...dog.

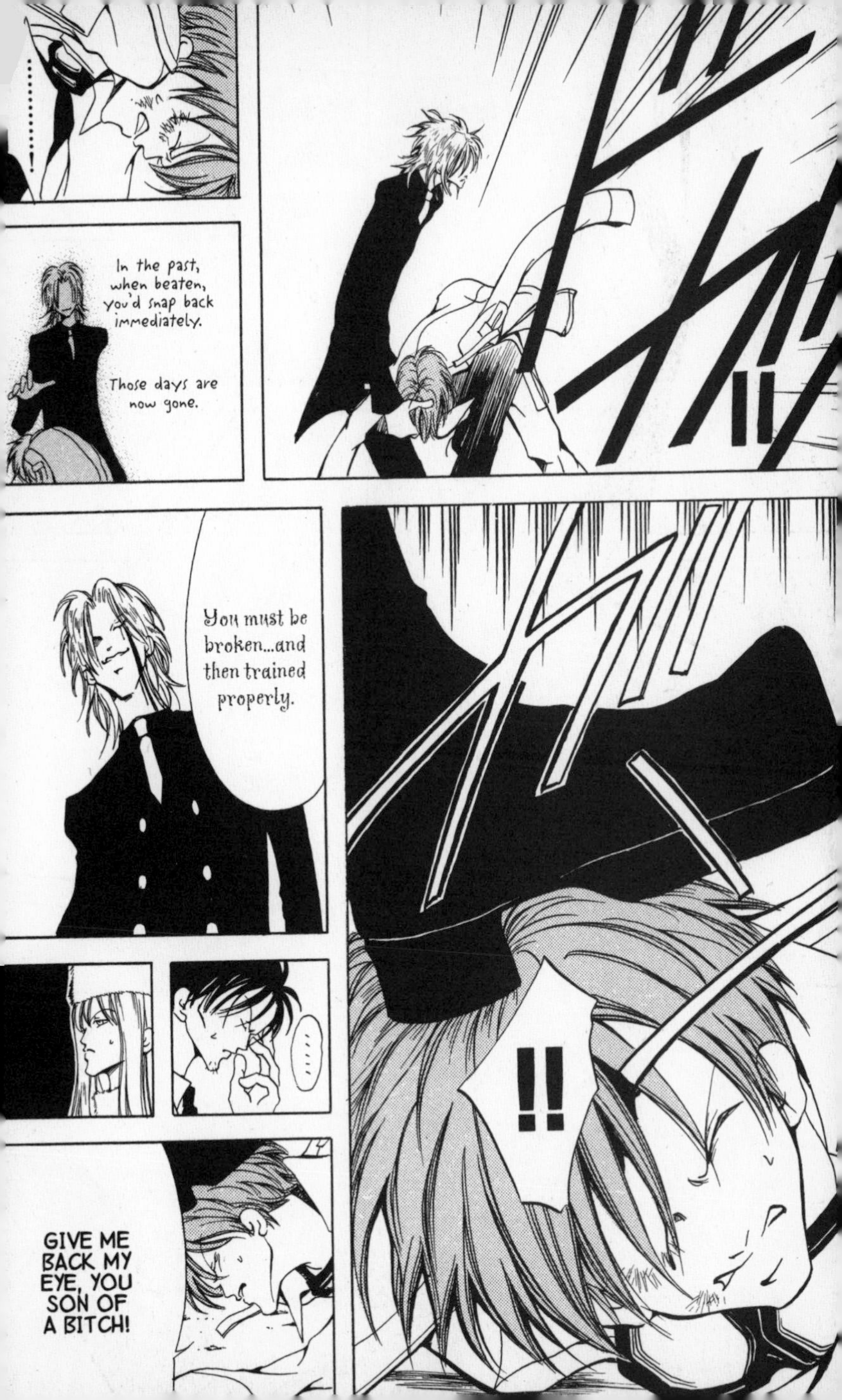

......!
In the past, when beaten, you'd snap back immediately.
Those days are now gone.
!!
You must be broken...and then trained properly.
......
GIVE ME BACK MY EYE, YOU SON OF A BITCH!

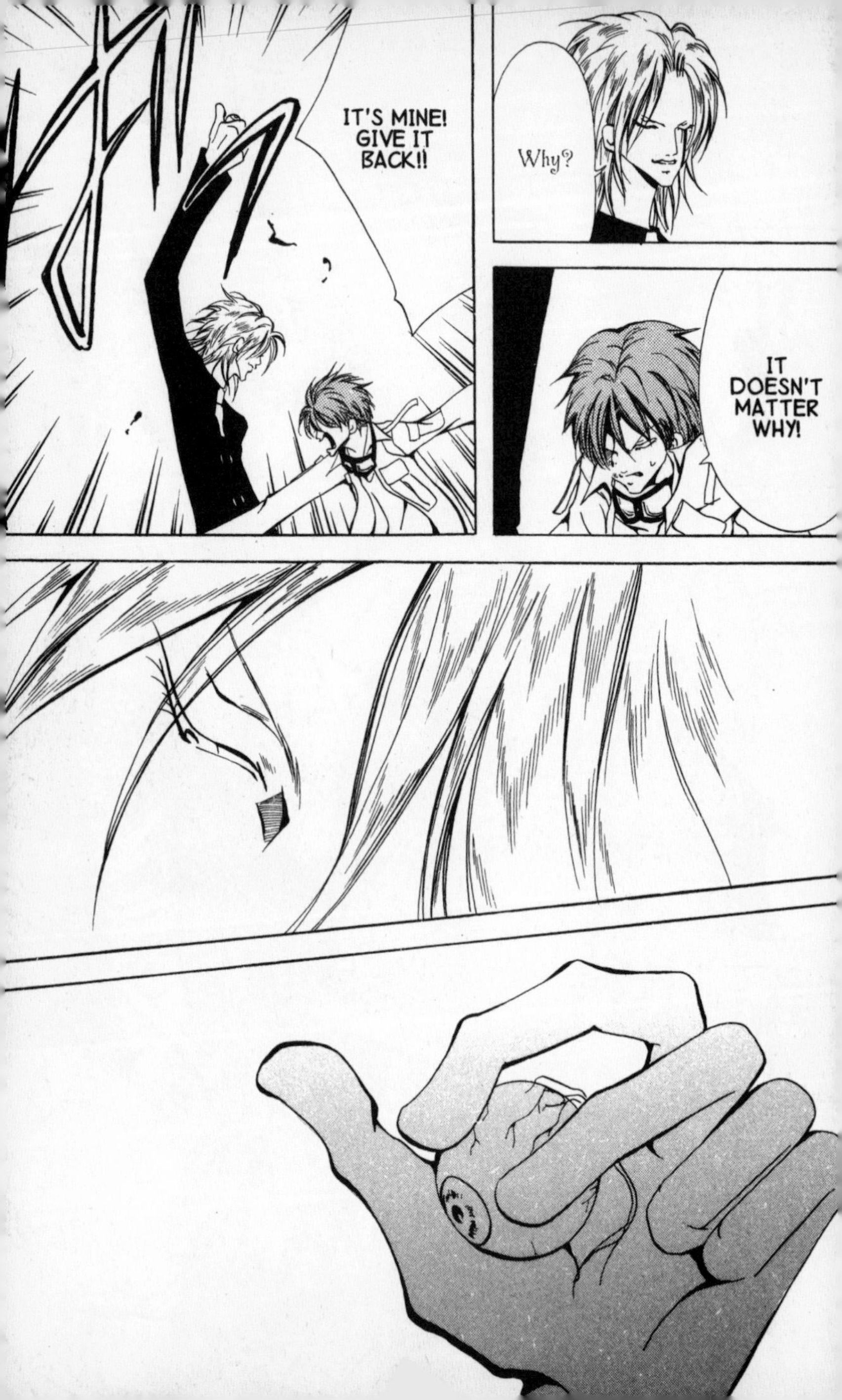
Why?
IT DOESN'T MATTER WHY!
IT'S MINE! GIVE IT BACK!!

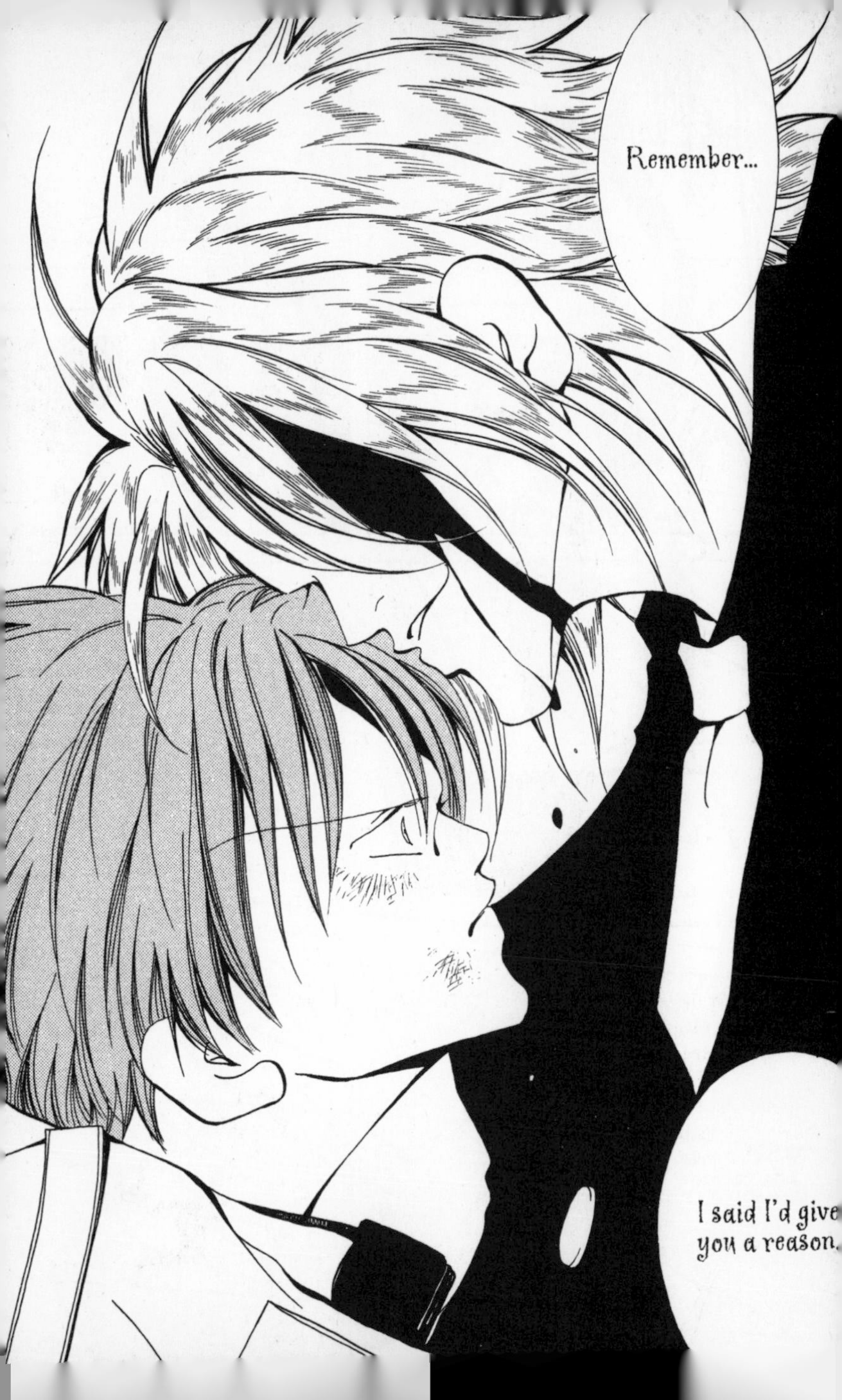
Remember...
I said I'd give you a reason.

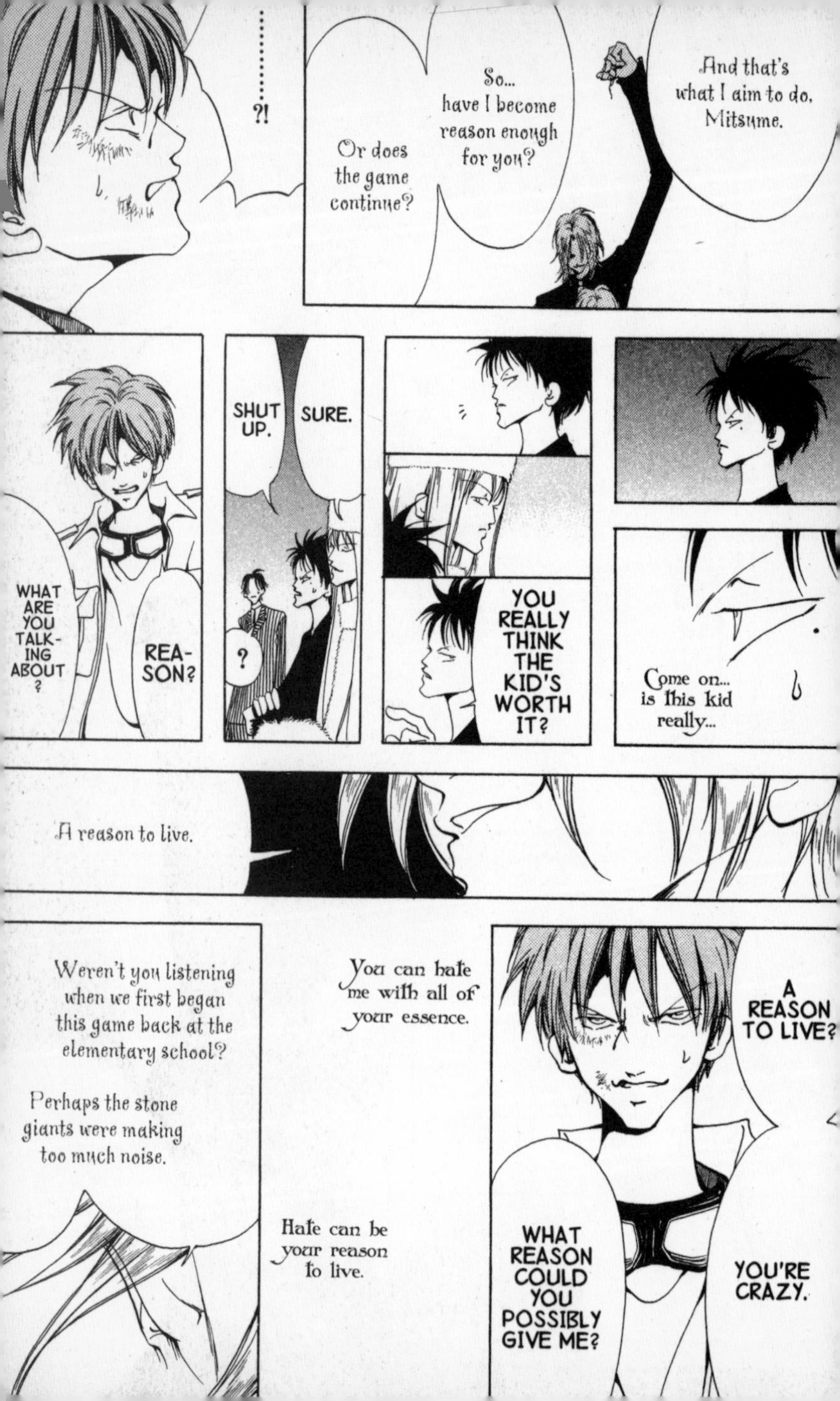
And that's what I aim to do, Mitsume.
So... have I become reason enough for you?
Or does the game continue?
......?!
Come on... is this kid really...
YOU REALLY THINK THE KID'S WORTH IT?
SURE.
SHUT UP.
?
REA-SON?
WHAT ARE YOU TALK-ING ABOUT?
A reason to live.
A REASON TO LIVE?
YOU'RE CRAZY.
WHAT REASON COULD YOU POSSIBLY GIVE ME?
You can hate me with all of your essence.
Hate can be your reason to live.
Weren't you listening when we first began this game back at the elementary school?
Perhaps the stone giants were making too much noise.

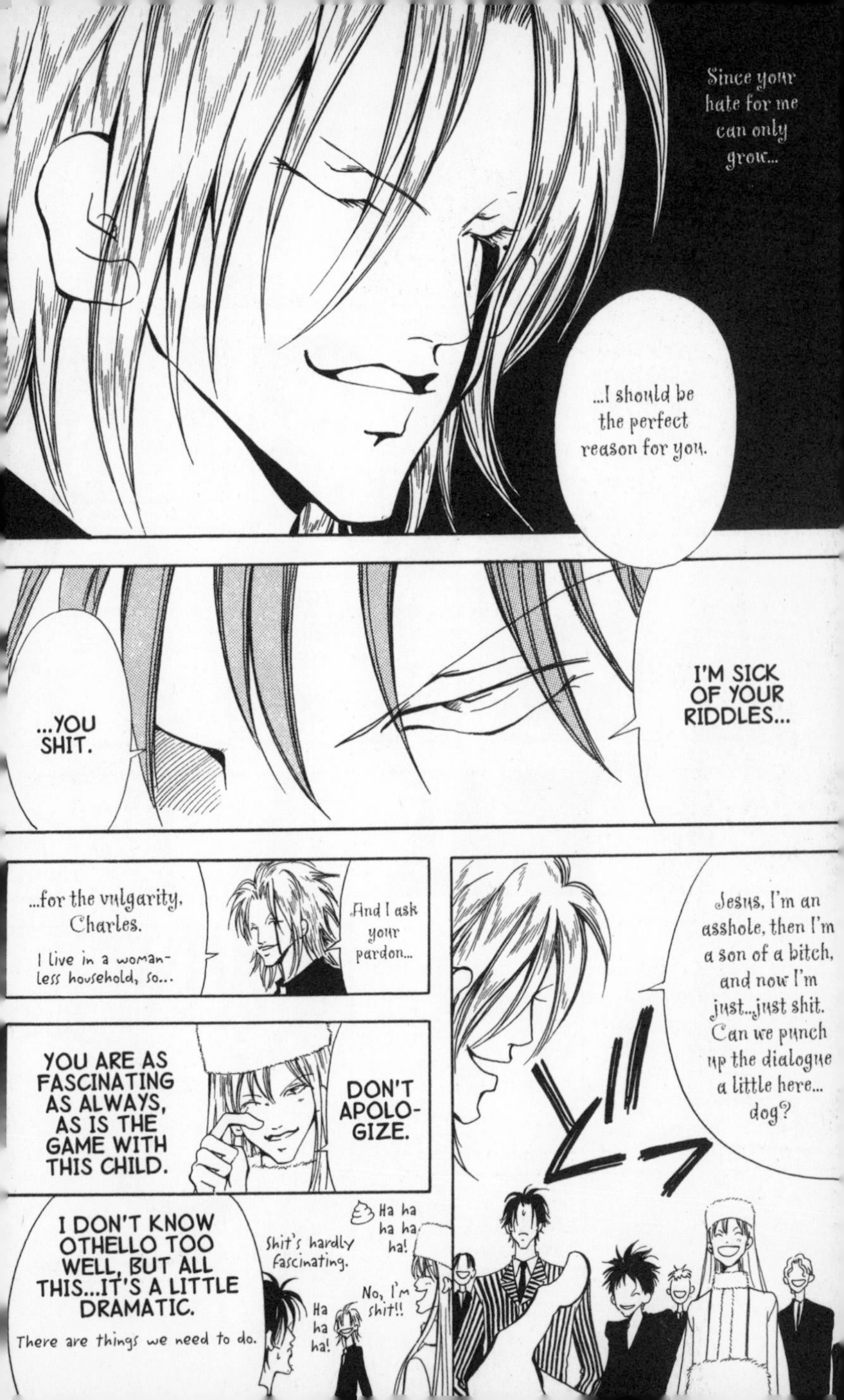

Since your hate for me can only grow...
...I should be the perfect reason for you.
I'M SICK OF YOUR RIDDLES...
...YOU SHIT.
Jesus, I'm an asshole, then I'm a son of a bitch, and now I'm just...just shit. Can we punch up the dialogue a little here... dog?
And I ask your pardon...
...for the vulgarity, Charles.
I live in a woman-less household, so...
DON'T APOLOGIZE.
YOU ARE AS FASCINATING AS ALWAYS, AS IS THE GAME WITH THIS CHILD.
Ha ha ha ha ha!
Shit's hardly fascinating.
No, I'm shit!!
Ha ha ha!
I DON'T KNOW OTHELLO TOO WELL, BUT ALL THIS...IT'S A LITTLE DRAMATIC.
There are things we need to do.

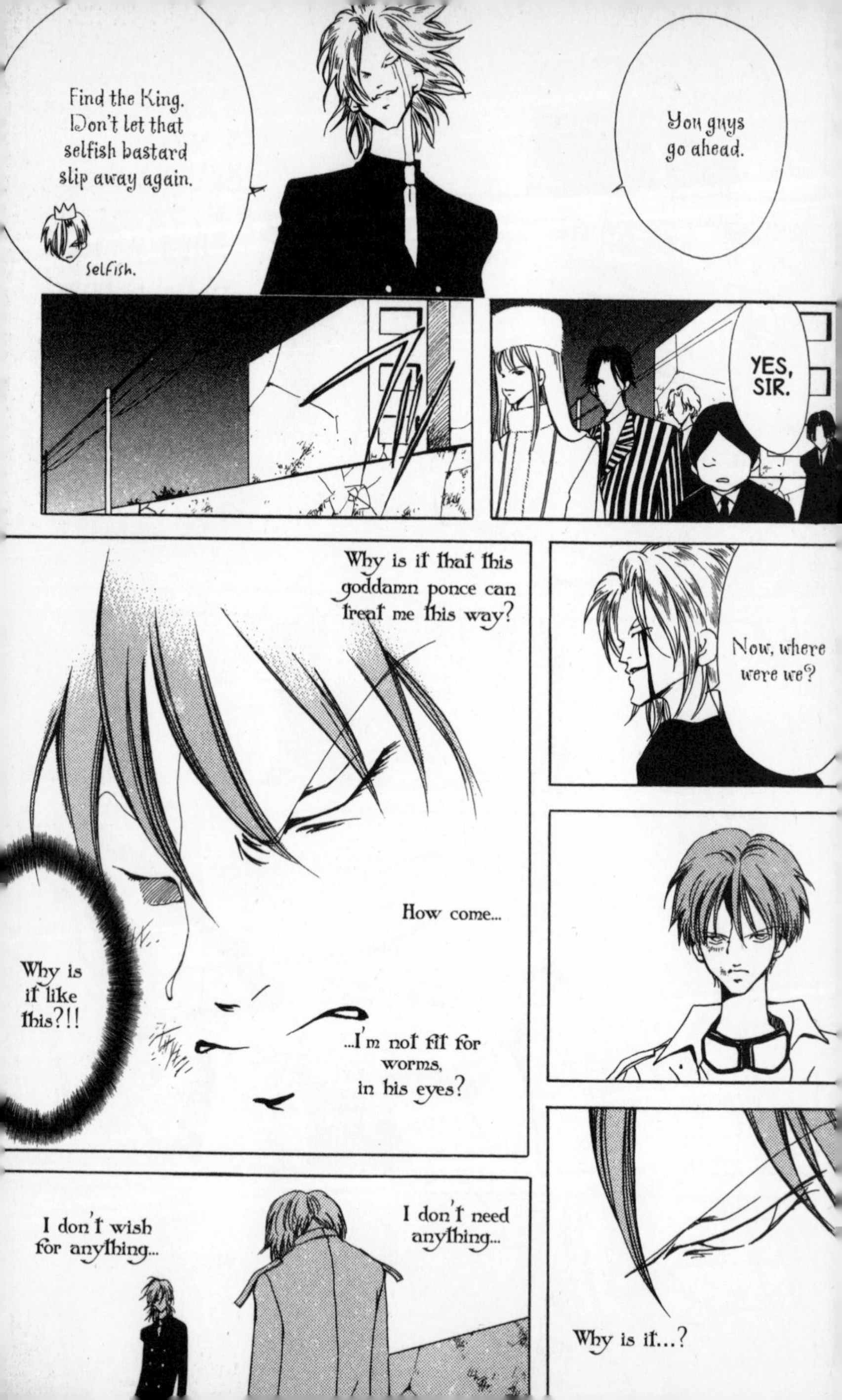
You guys go ahead.
Find the King. Don't let that selfish bastard slip away again.
Selfish.
YES, SIR.
Now, where were we?
Why is it...?
Why is it that this goddamn ponce can treat me this way?
How come...
...I'm not fit for worms, in his eyes?
Why is it like this?!!
I don't need anything...
I don't wish for anything...

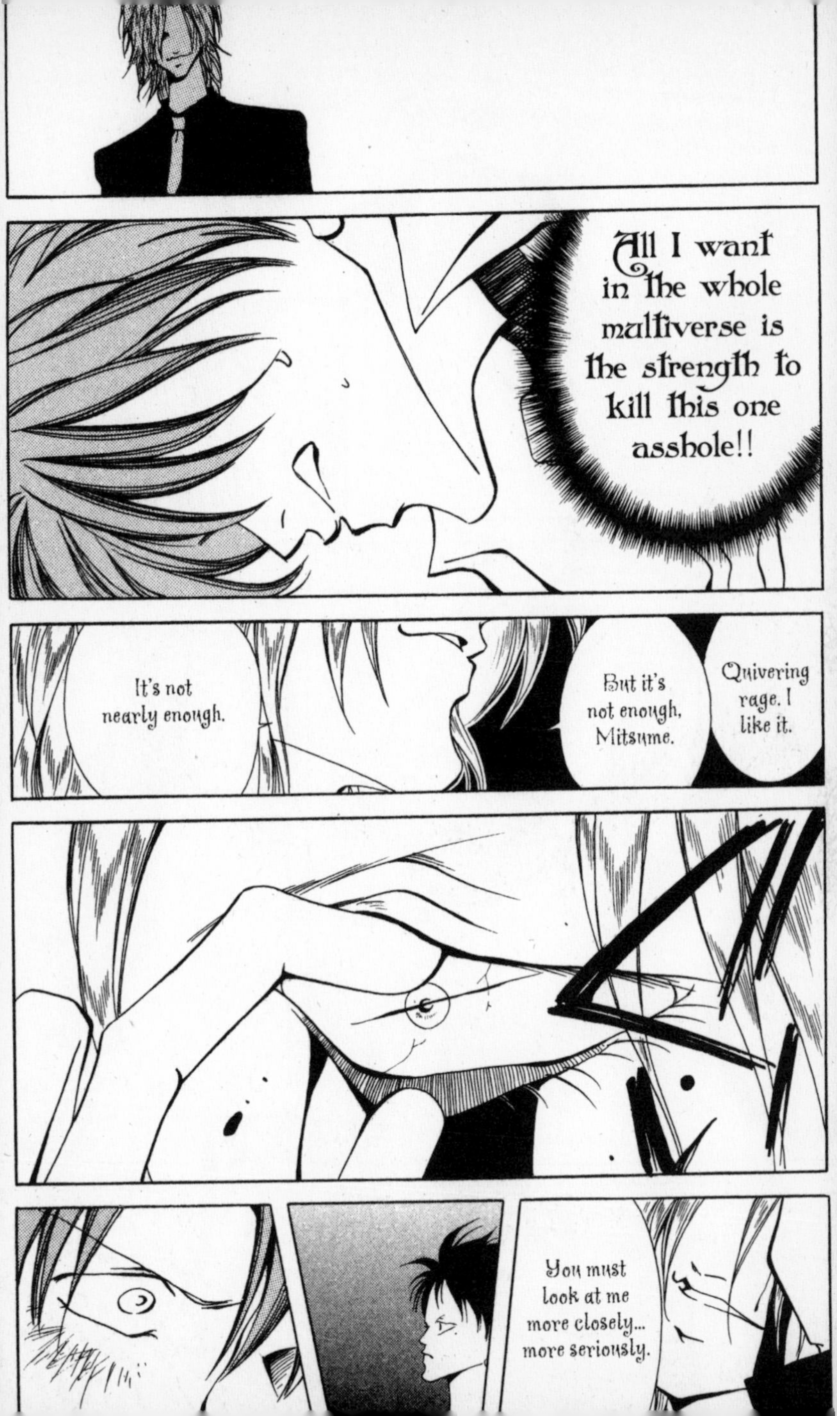
All I want in the whole multiverse is the strength to kill this one asshole!!
Quivering rage. I like it.
But it's not enough, Mitsume.
It's not nearly enough.
You must look at me more closely... more seriously.

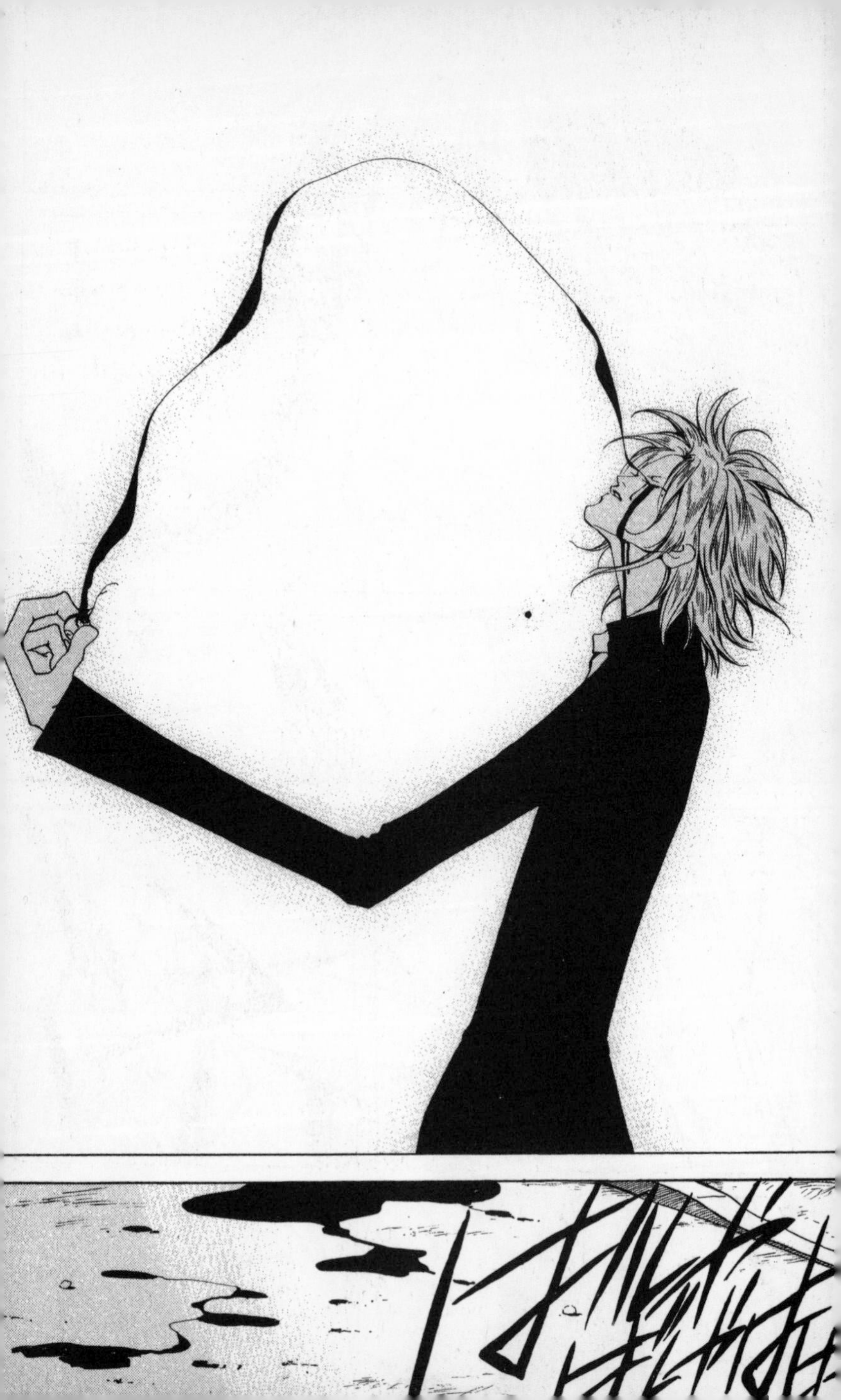

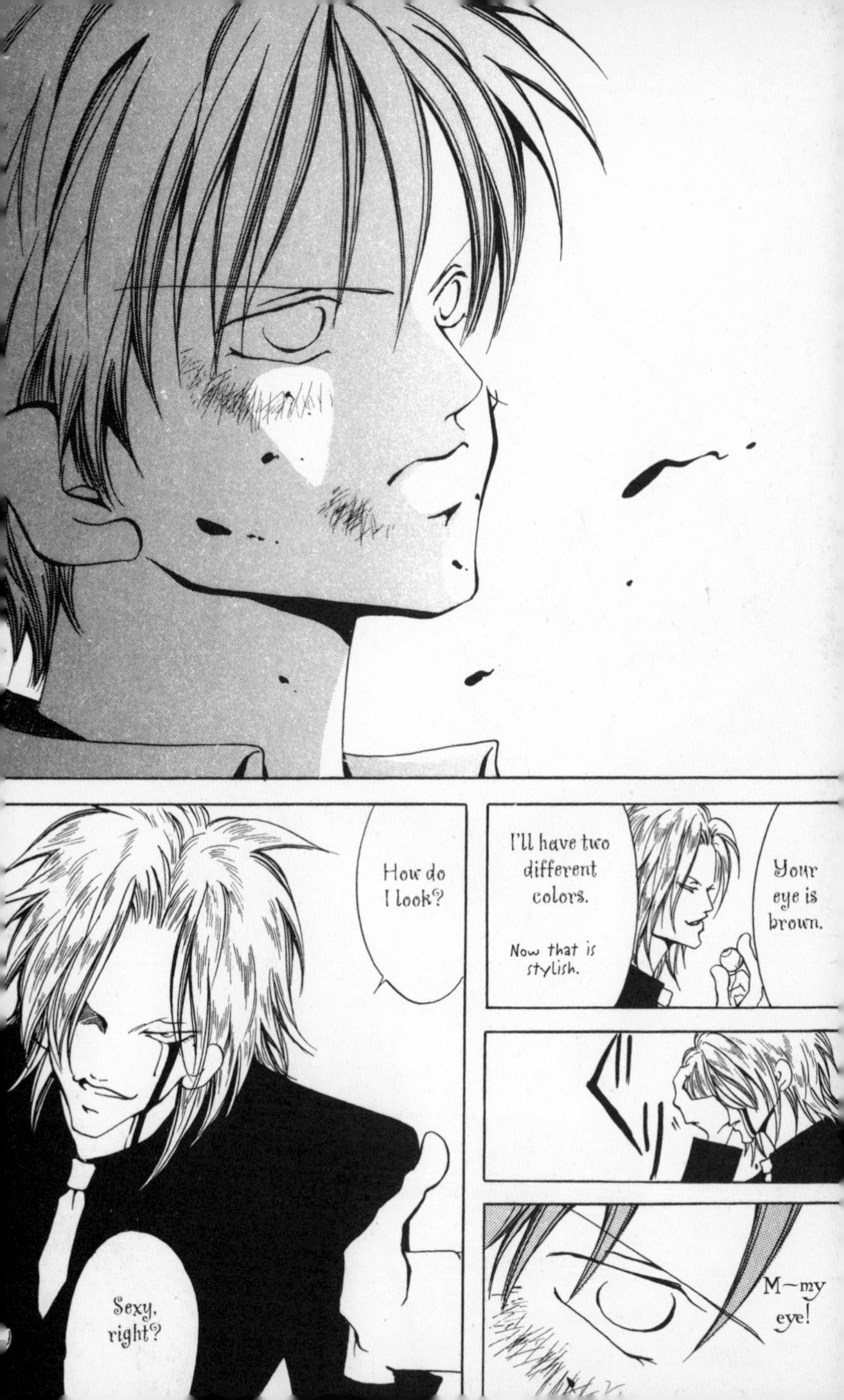
Your eye is brown.
I'll have two different colors.
Now that is stylish.
M~my eye!
How do I look?
Sexy, right?

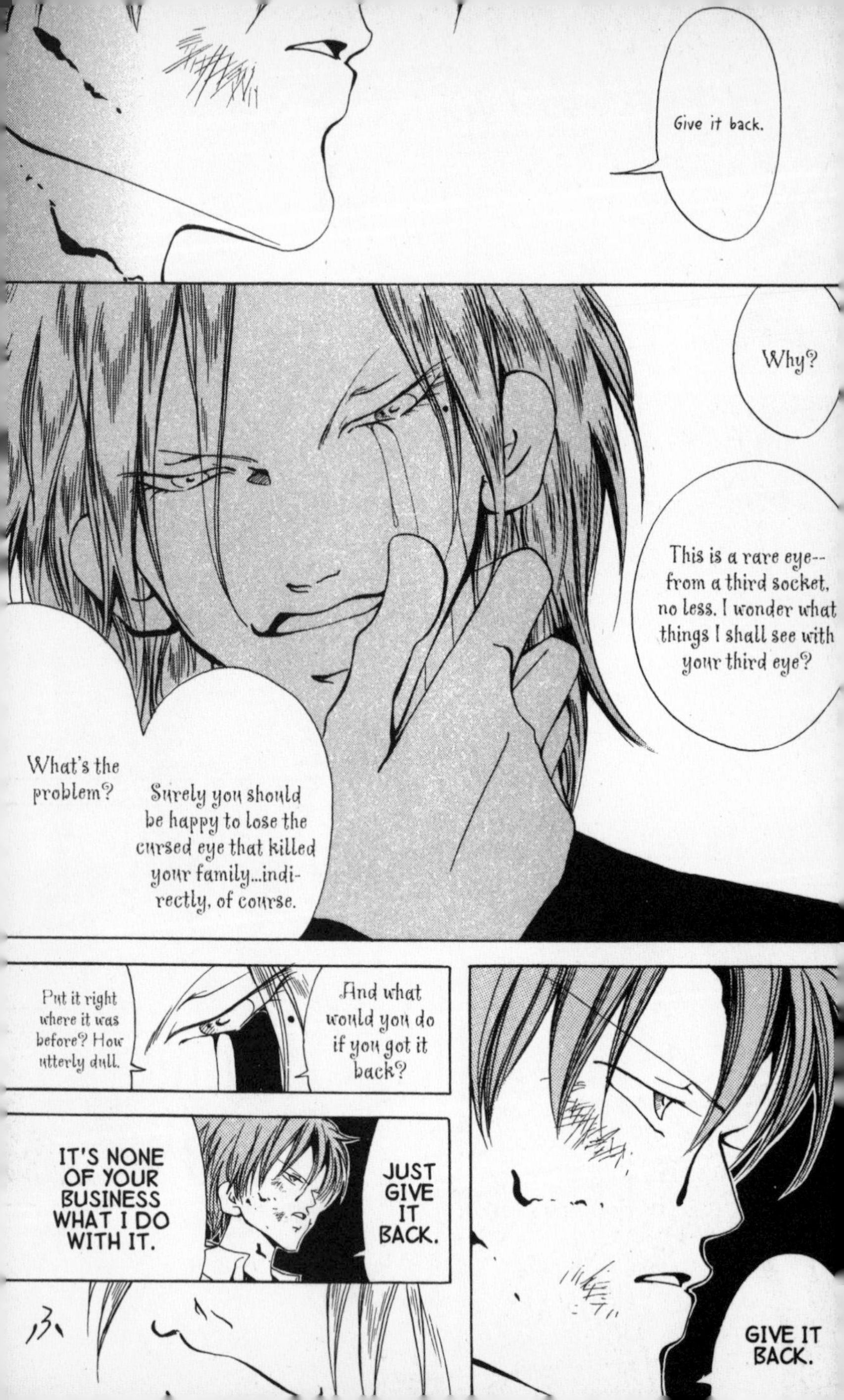
Give it back.
Why?
This is a rare eye--from a third socket, no less. I wonder what things I shall see with your third eye?
What's the problem?
Surely you should be happy to lose the cursed eye that killed your family...indirectly, of course.
GIVE IT BACK.
And what would you do if you got it back?
Put it right where it was before? How utterly dull.
JUST GIVE IT BACK.
IT'S NONE OF YOUR BUSINESS WHAT I DO WITH IT.
ふ

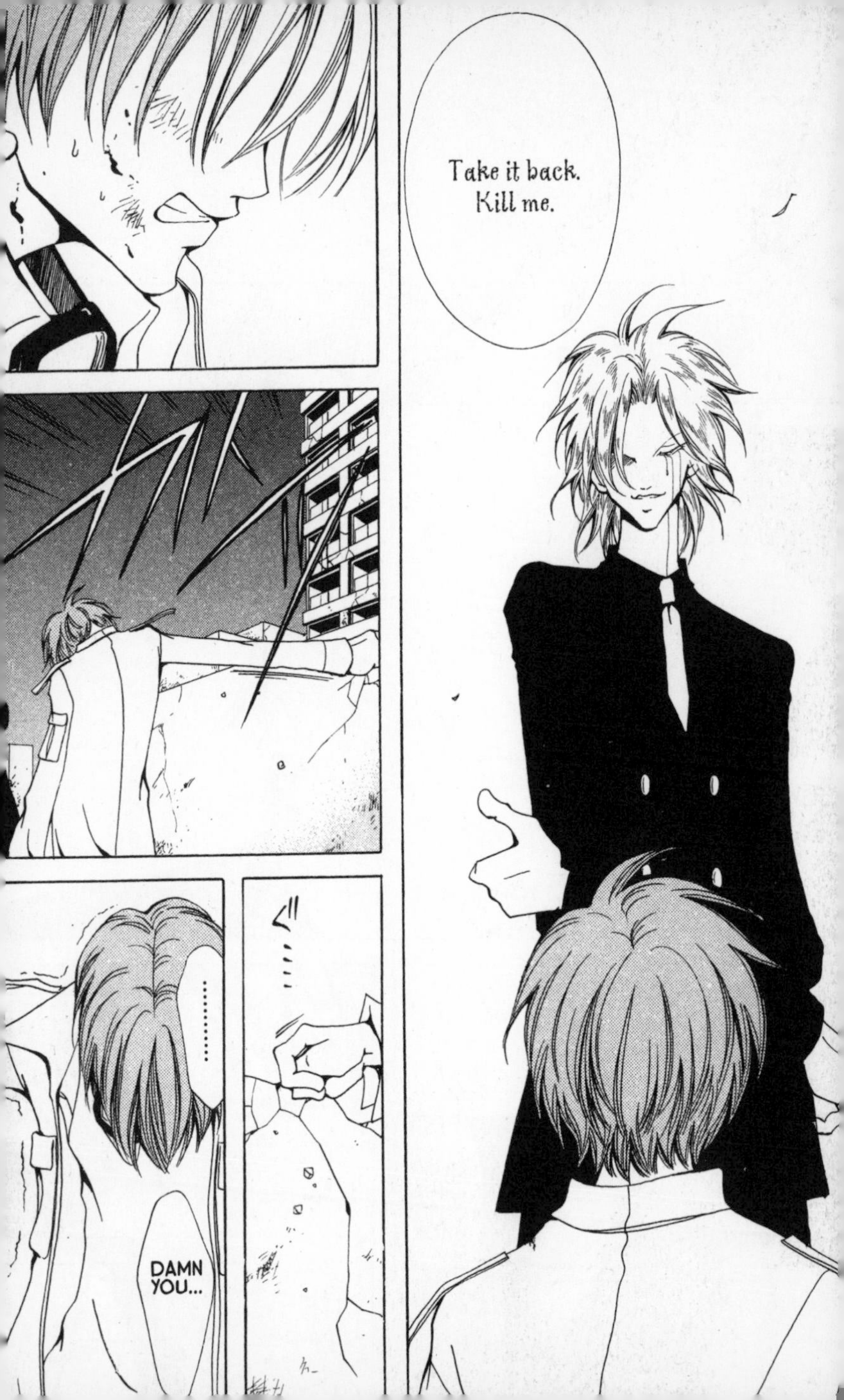
Take it back. Kill me.
DAMN YOU...

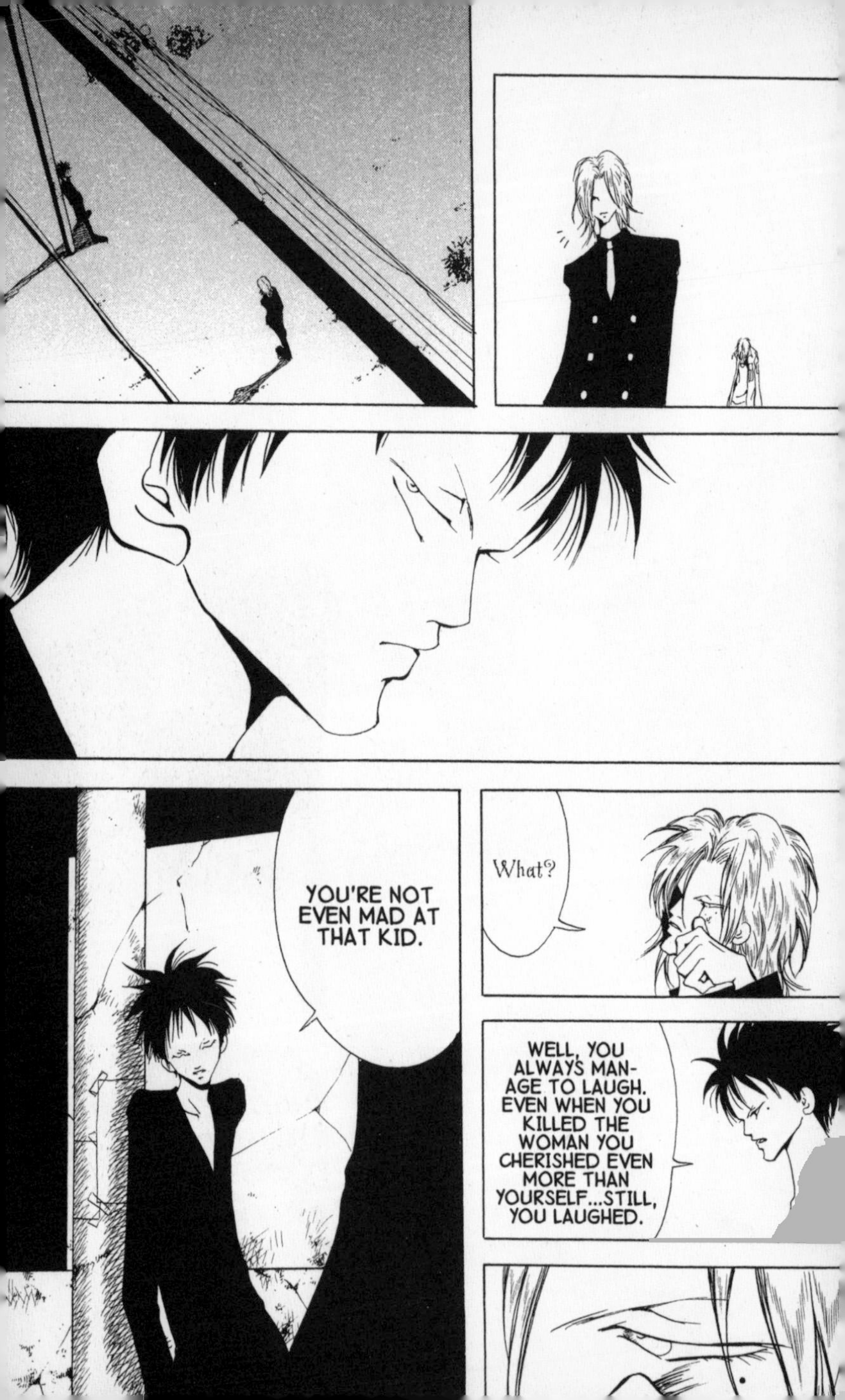
What?
YOU'RE NOT EVEN MAD AT THAT KID.
WELL, YOU ALWAYS MAN-AGE TO LAUGH. EVEN WHEN YOU KILLED THE WOMAN YOU CHERISHED EVEN MORE THAN YOURSELF...STILL, YOU LAUGHED.

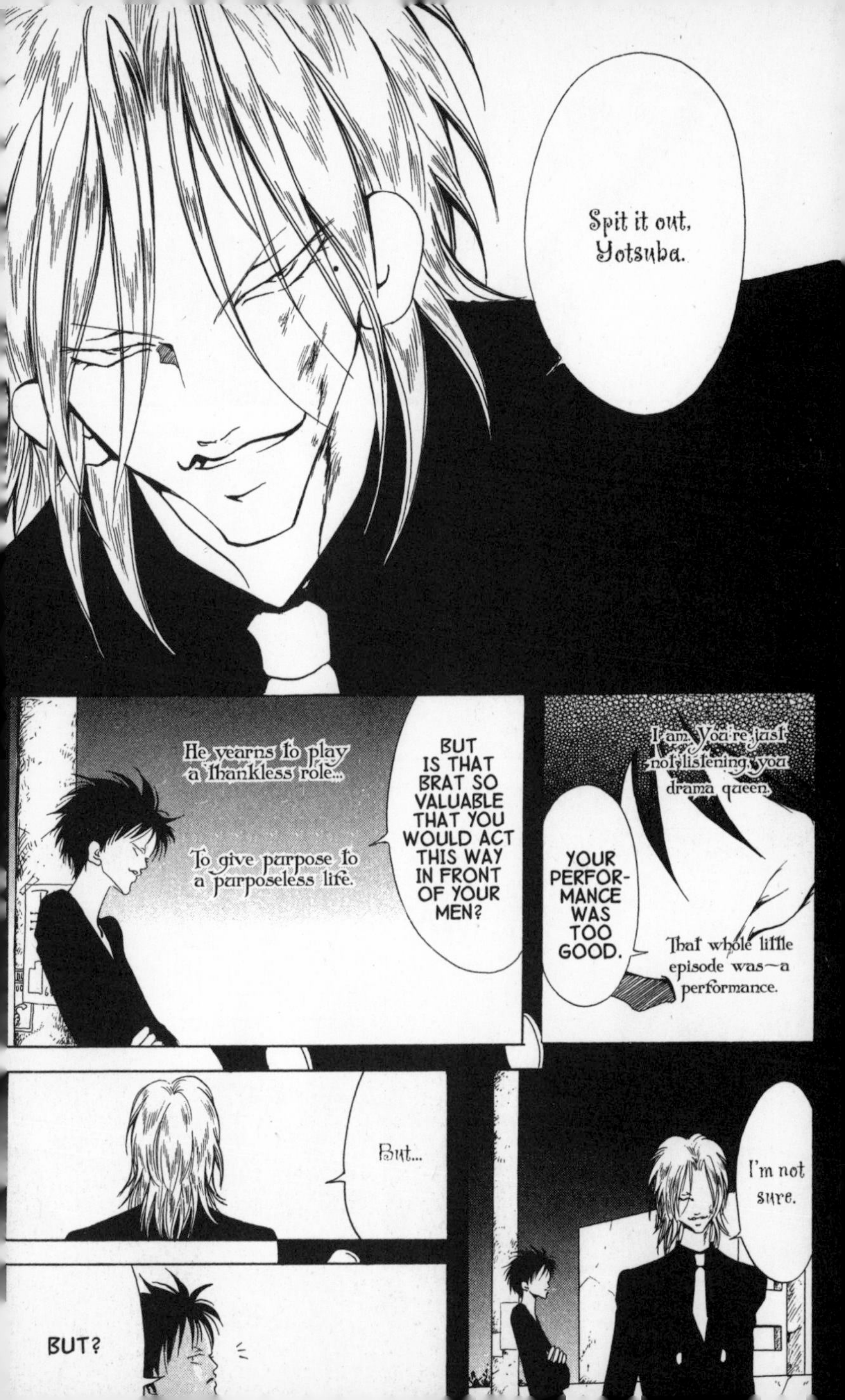

Spit it out, Yotsuba.
I am. You're just not listening, you drama queen.
That whole little episode was—a performance.
YOUR PERFORMANCE WAS TOO GOOD.
BUT IS THAT BRAT SO VALUABLE THAT YOU WOULD ACT THIS WAY IN FRONT OF YOUR MEN?
He yearns to play a thankless role...
To give purpose to a purposeless life.
I'm not sure.
But...
BUT?

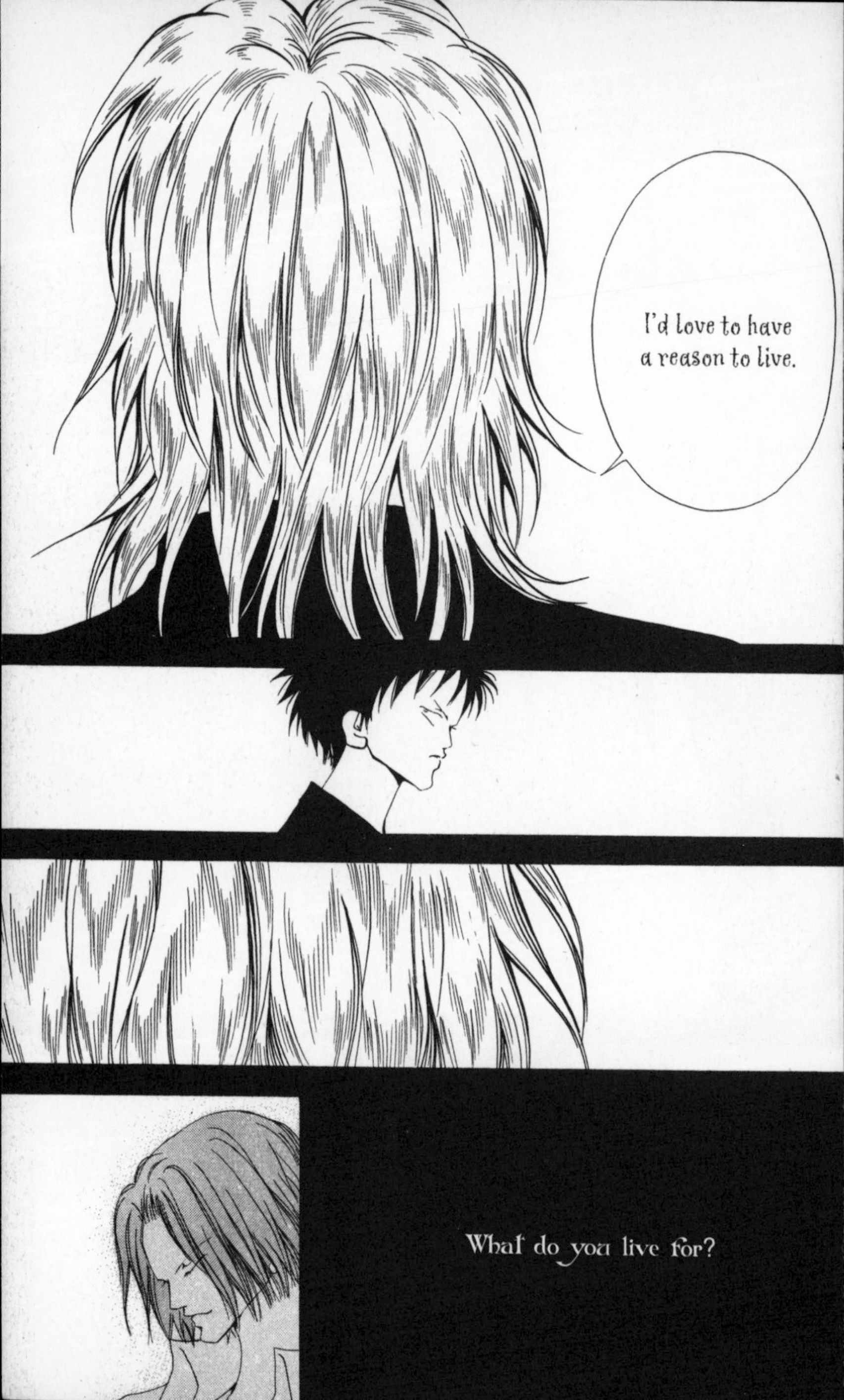
I'd love to have
a reason to live.
What do you live for?

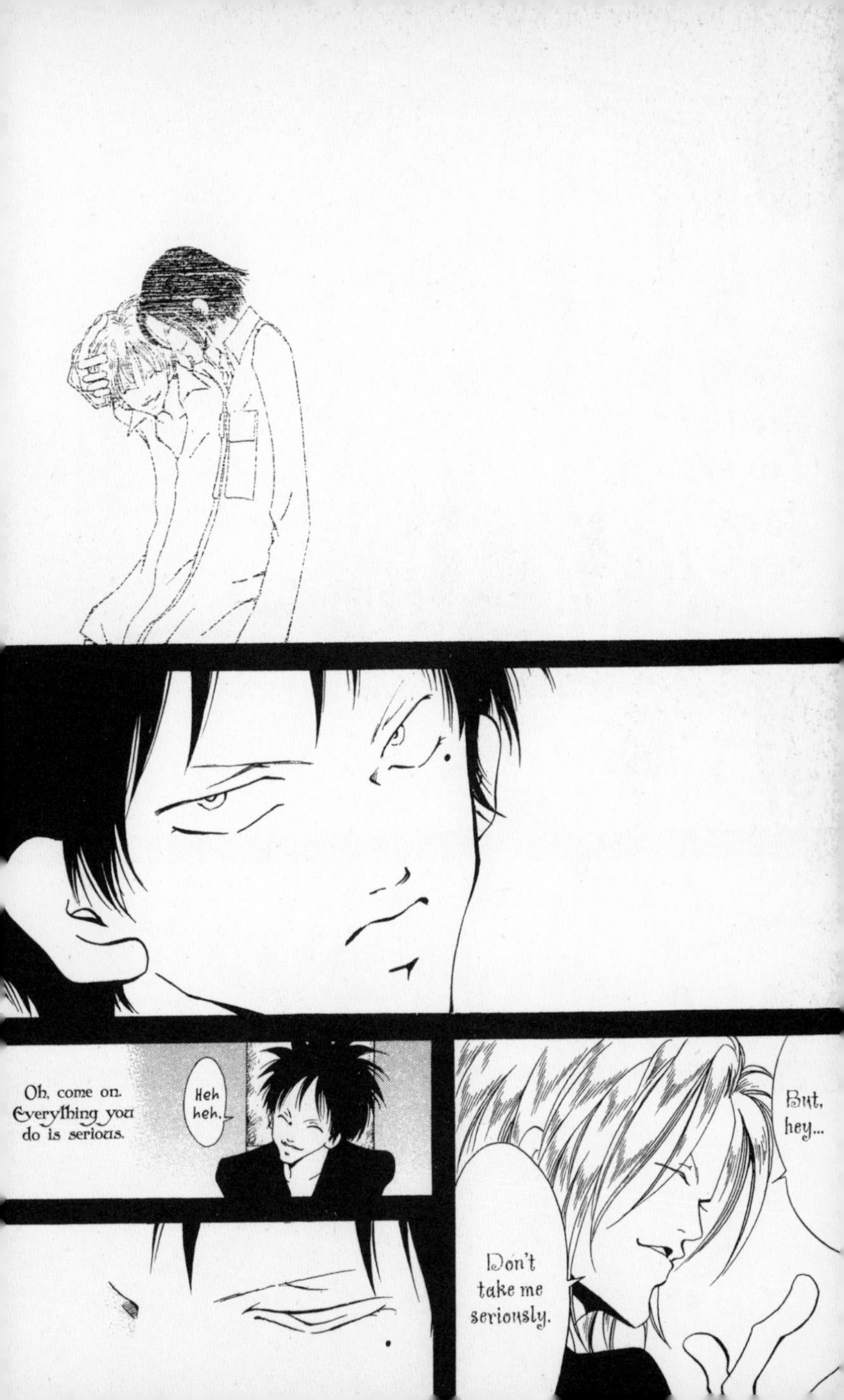
But, hey...
Don't take me seriously.
Heh heh.
Oh, come on. Everything you do is serious.

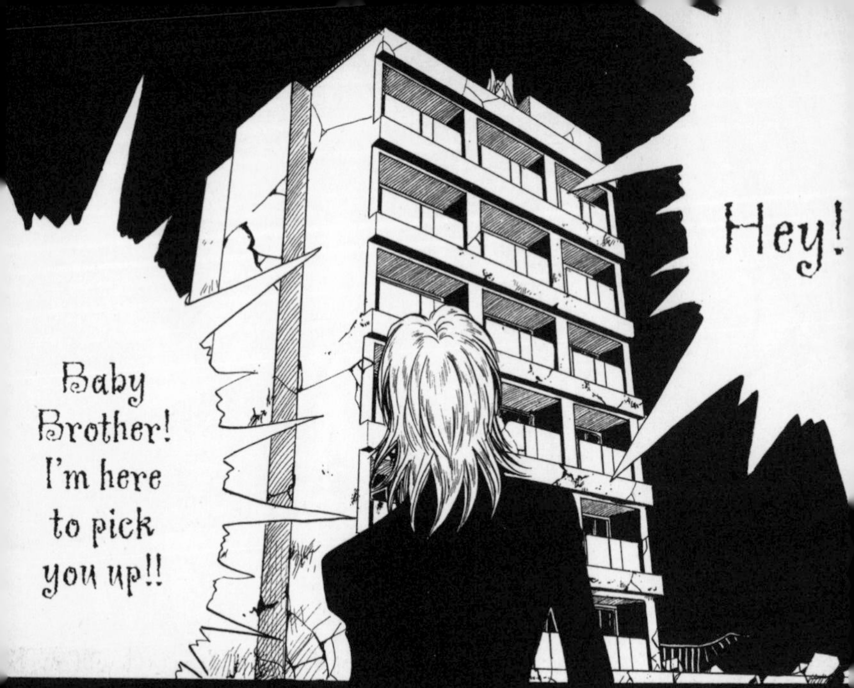
Hey!
Baby Brother! I'm here to pick you up!!
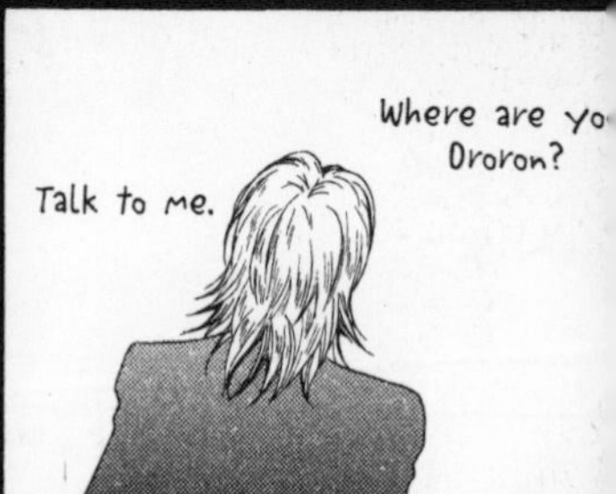
Where are yo Ororon?
Talk to me.
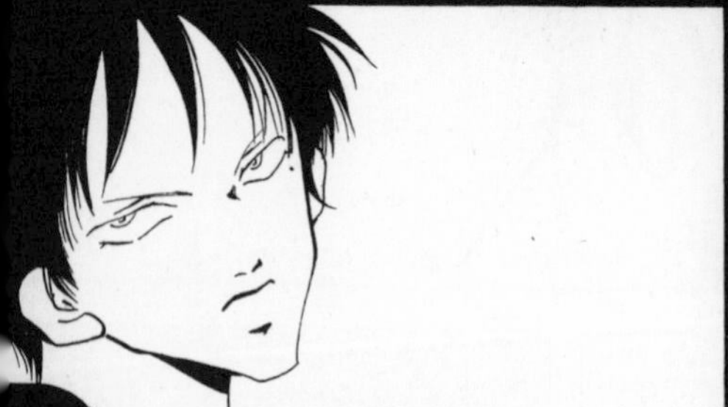

He's always serious...
that incessantly laughing man.

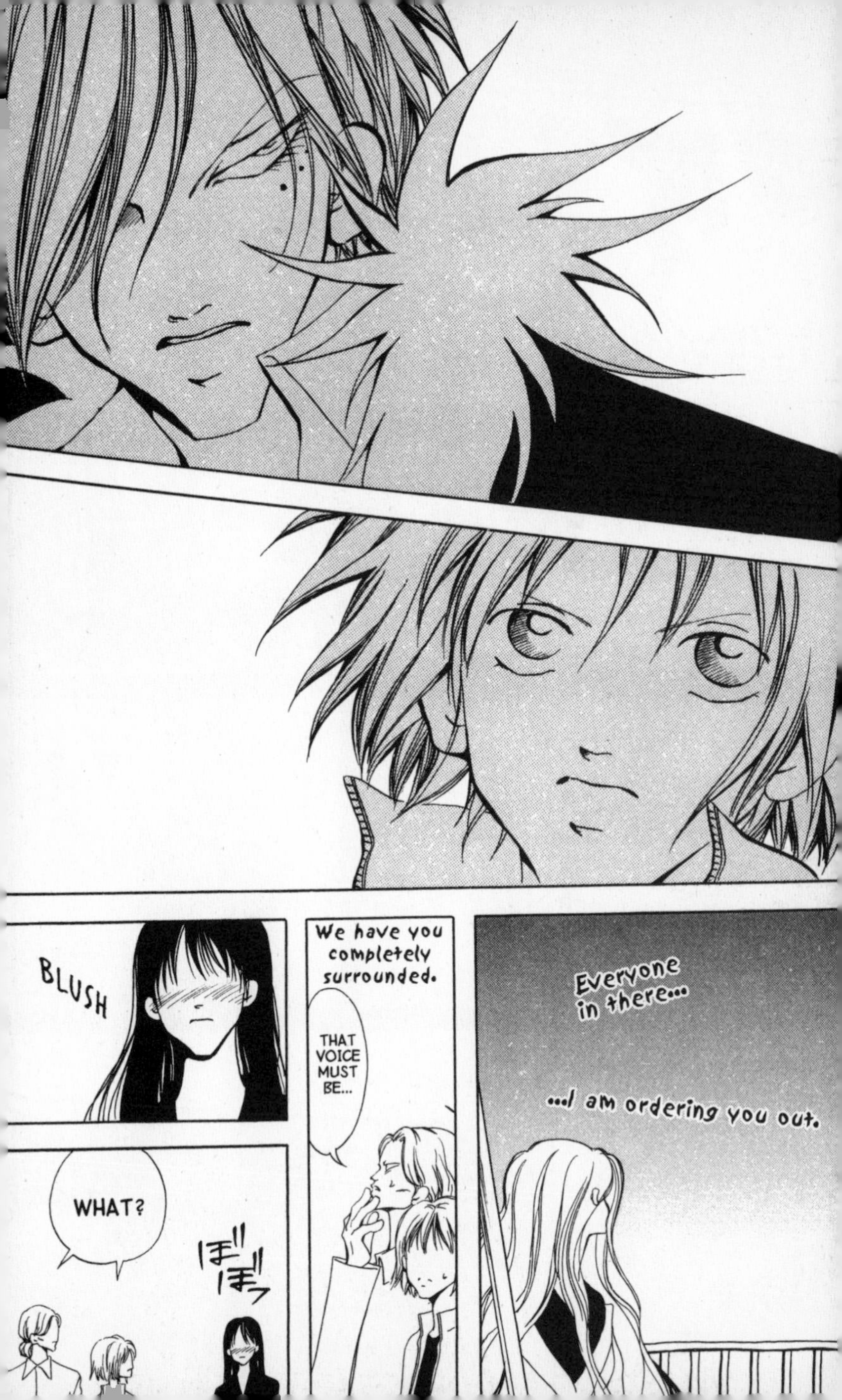
Everyone in there...
...I am ordering you out.
We have you completely surrounded.
THAT VOICE MUST BE...
BLUSH
WHAT?
ぼっぼっ

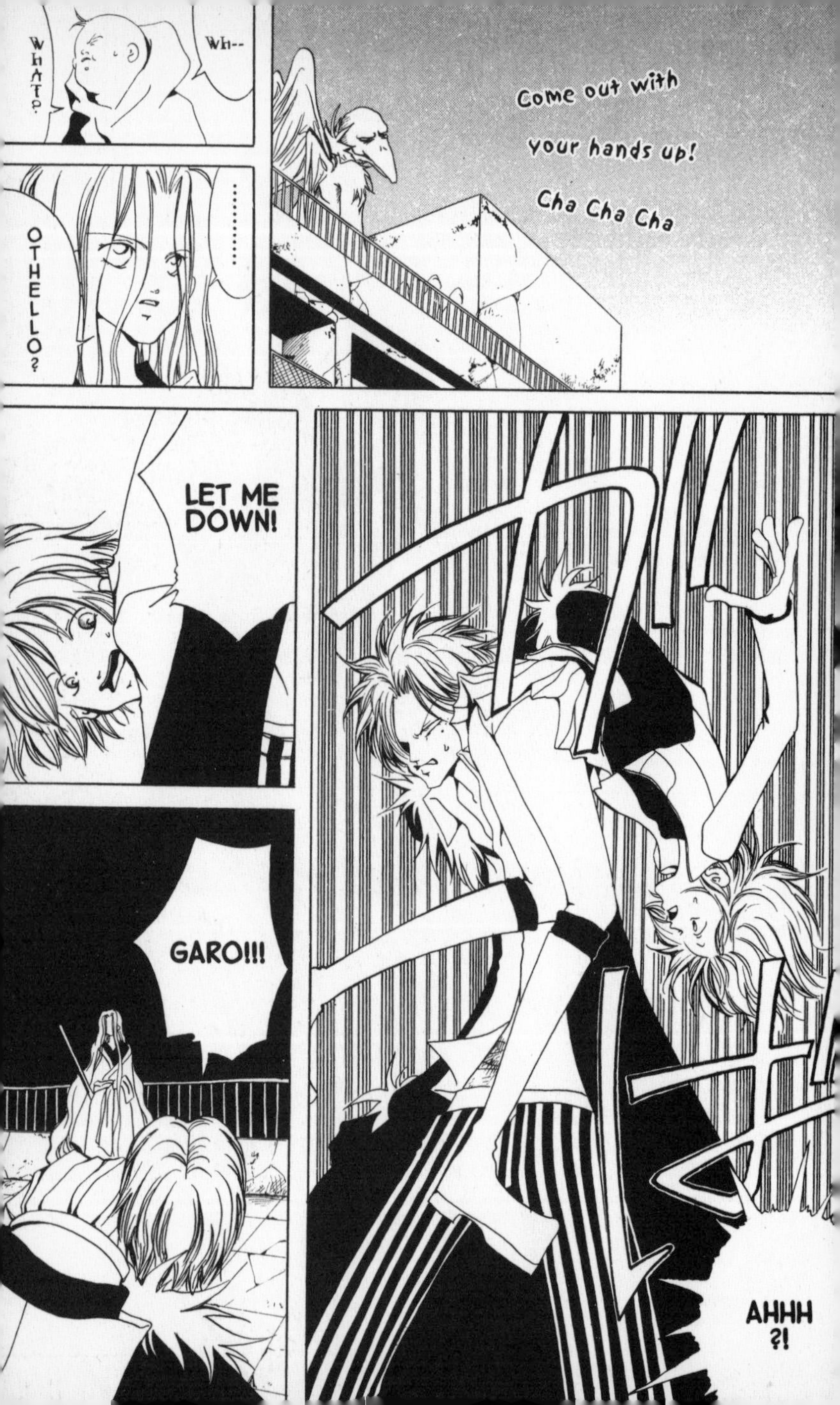
Come out with your hands up! Cha Cha Cha
Wh--
WHAT?
......
OTHELLO?
AHHH ?!
LET ME DOWN!
GARO!!!

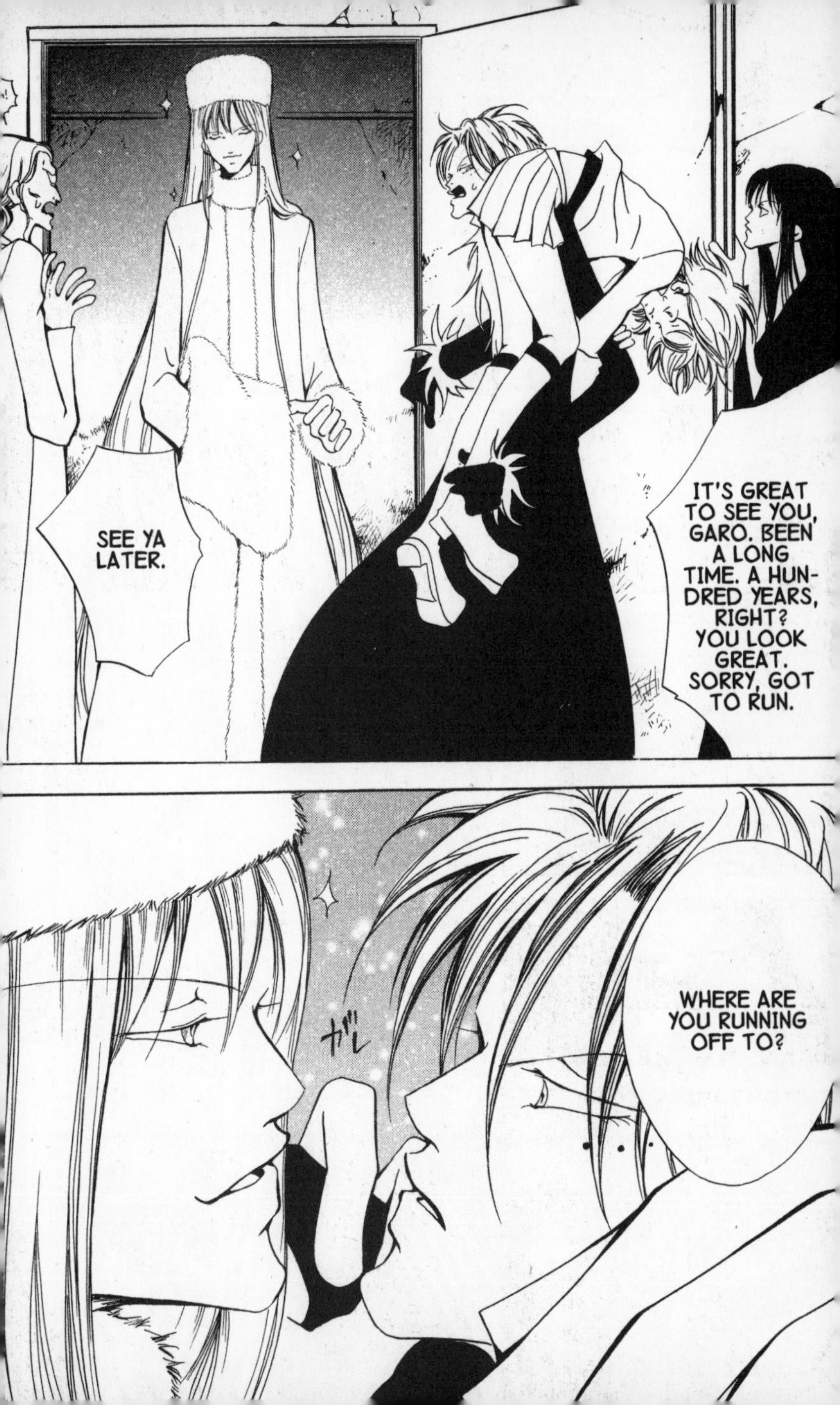
IT'S GREAT TO SEE YOU, GARO. BEEN A LONG TIME. A HUN-DRED YEARS, RIGHT? YOU LOOK GREAT. SORRY, GOT TO RUN.
SEE YA LATER.
WHERE ARE YOU RUNNING OFF TO?

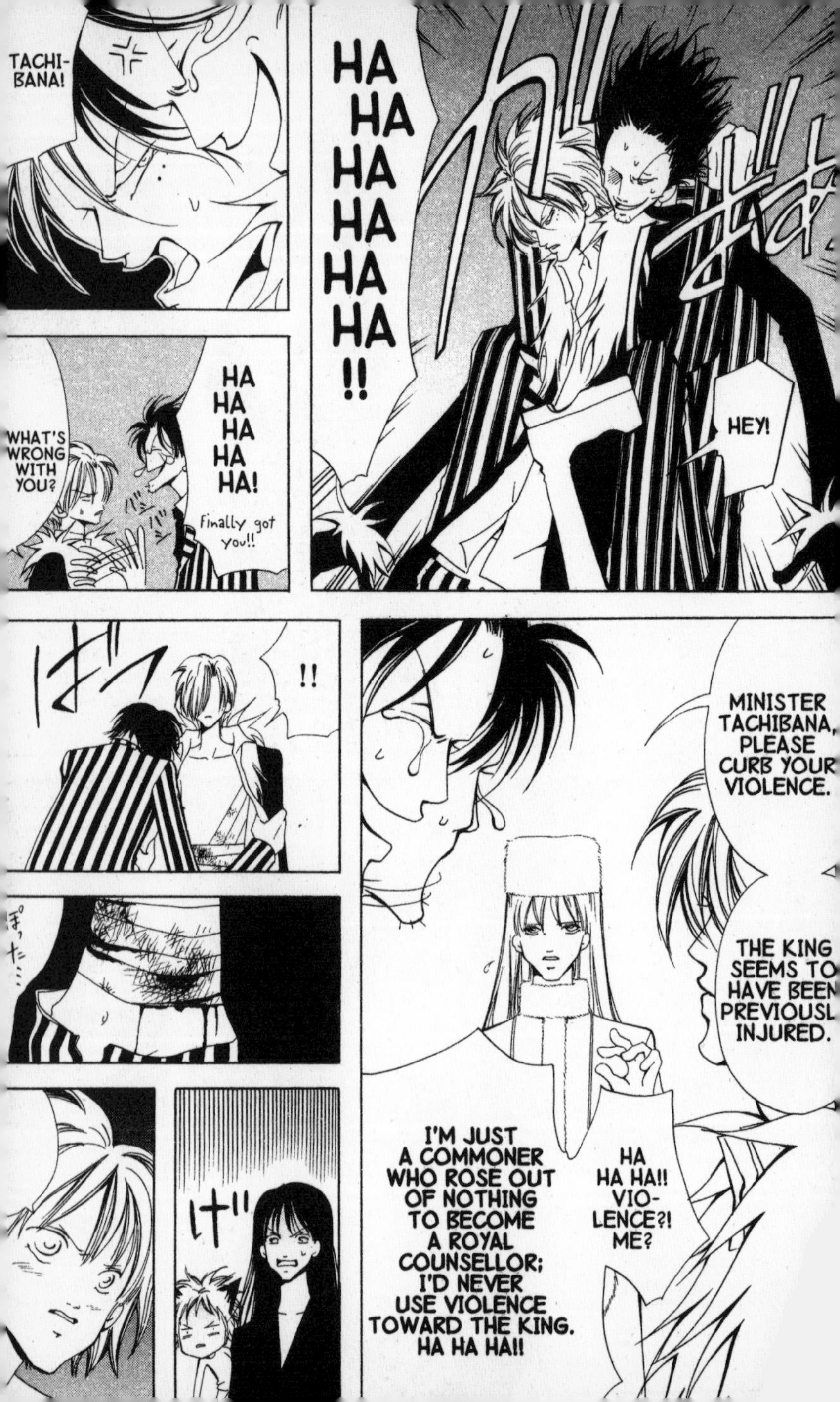
HA HA HA HA HA HA!!
HEY!
TACHIBANA!
HA HA HA HA HA HA!
finally got you!!
WHAT'S WRONG WITH YOU?
MINISTER TACHIBANA, PLEASE CURB YOUR VIOLENCE.
THE KING SEEMS TO HAVE BEEN PREVIOUSL INJURED.
HA HA HA!! VIOLENCE?! ME?
I'M JUST A COMMONER WHO ROSE OUT OF NOTHING TO BECOME A ROYAL COUNSELLOR; I'D NEVER USE VIOLENCE TOWARD THE KING. HA HA HA!!
!!

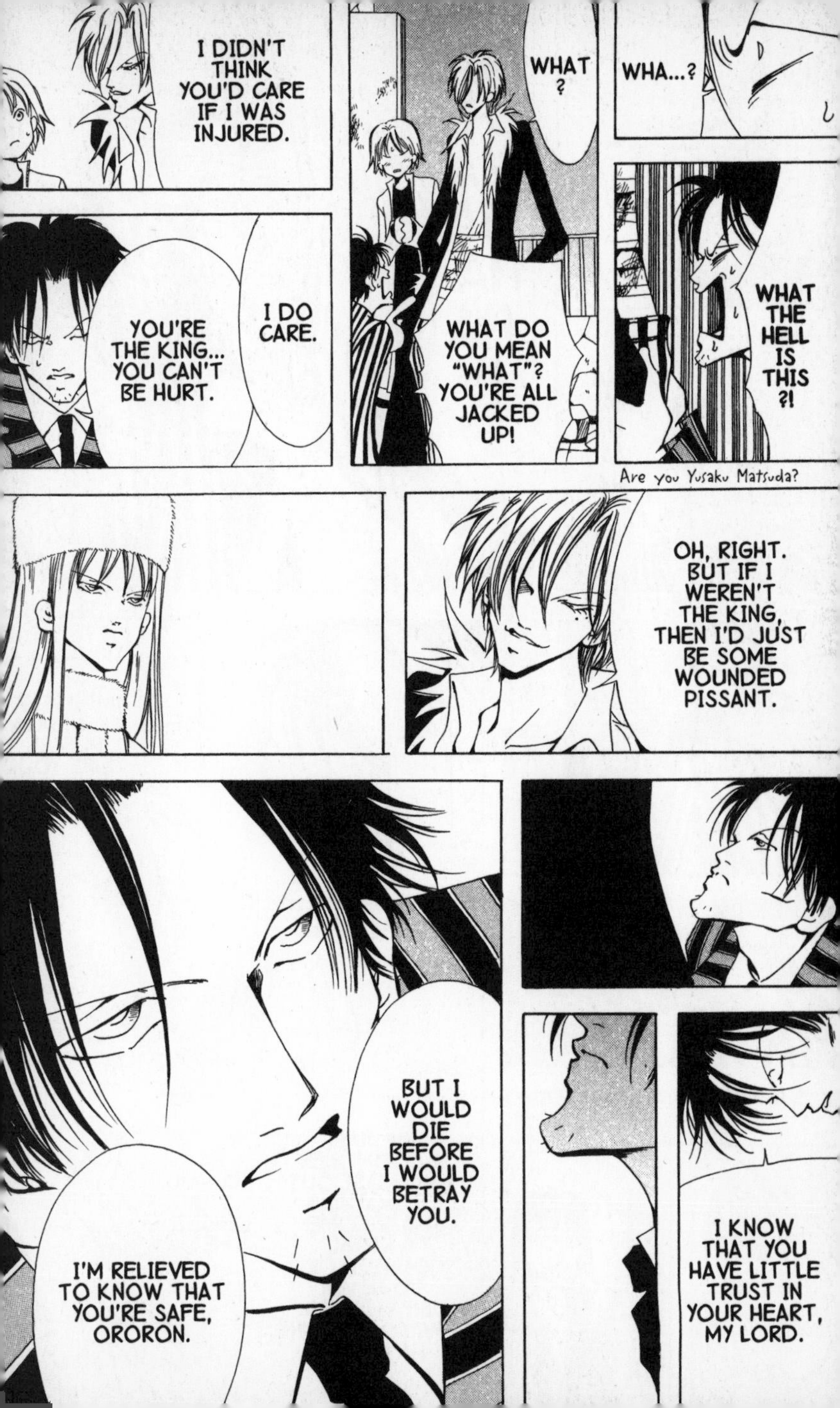

WHA...?
WHAT THE HELL IS THIS?!
Are you Yusaku Matsuda?
WHAT?
WHAT DO YOU MEAN "WHAT"? YOU'RE ALL JACKED UP!
I DIDN'T THINK YOU'D CARE IF I WAS INJURED.
I DO CARE.
YOU'RE THE KING... YOU CAN'T BE HURT.
OH, RIGHT. BUT IF I WEREN'T THE KING, THEN I'D JUST BE SOME WOUNDED PISSANT.
I KNOW THAT YOU HAVE LITTLE TRUST IN YOUR HEART, MY LORD.
BUT I WOULD DIE BEFORE I WOULD BETRAY YOU.
I'M RELIEVED TO KNOW THAT YOU'RE SAFE, ORORON.

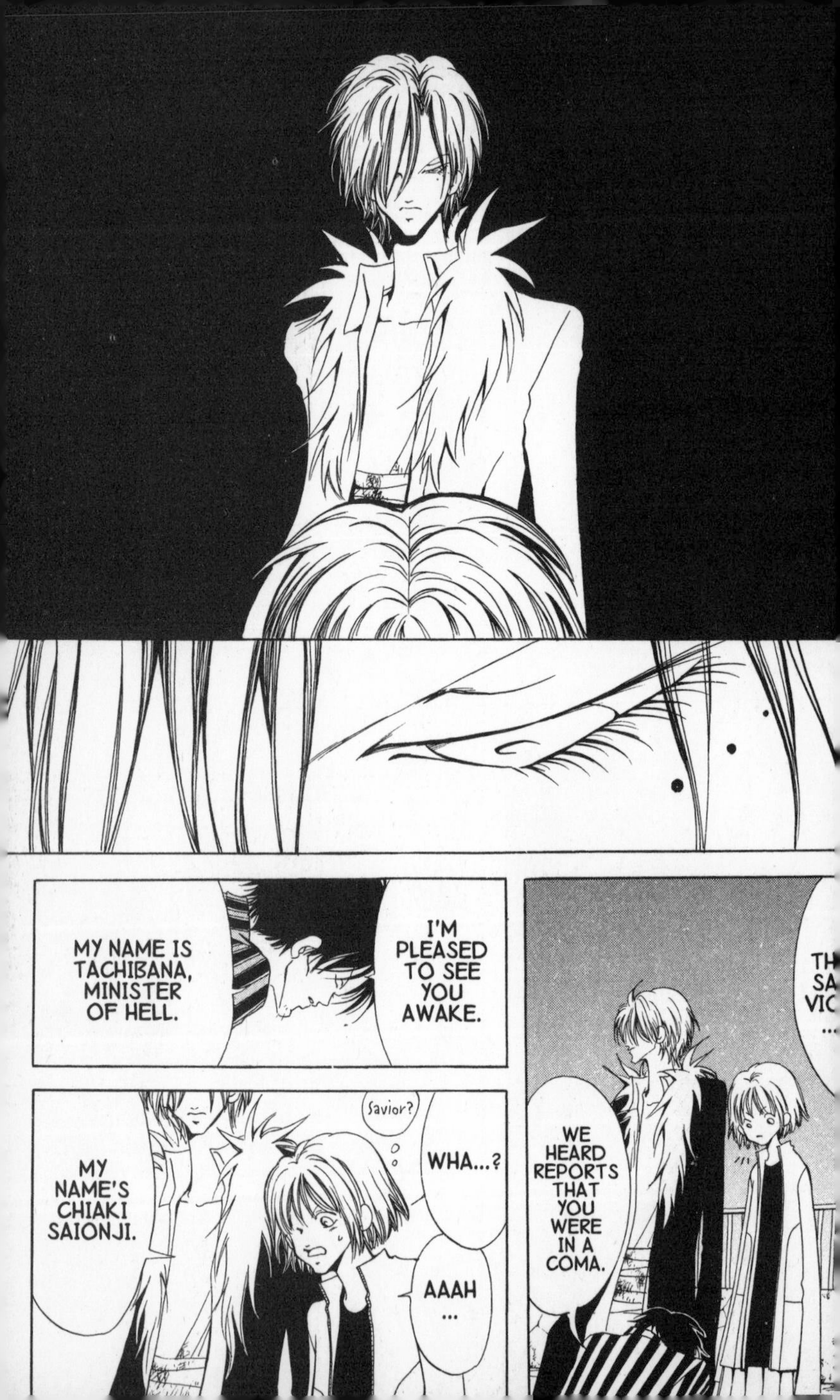
TH SA VIC ...
WE HEARD REPORTS THAT YOU WERE IN A COMA.
I'M PLEASED TO SEE YOU AWAKE.
MY NAME IS TACHIBANA, MINISTER OF HELL.
Savior?
WHA...?
AAAH ...
MY NAME'S CHIAKI SAIONJI.

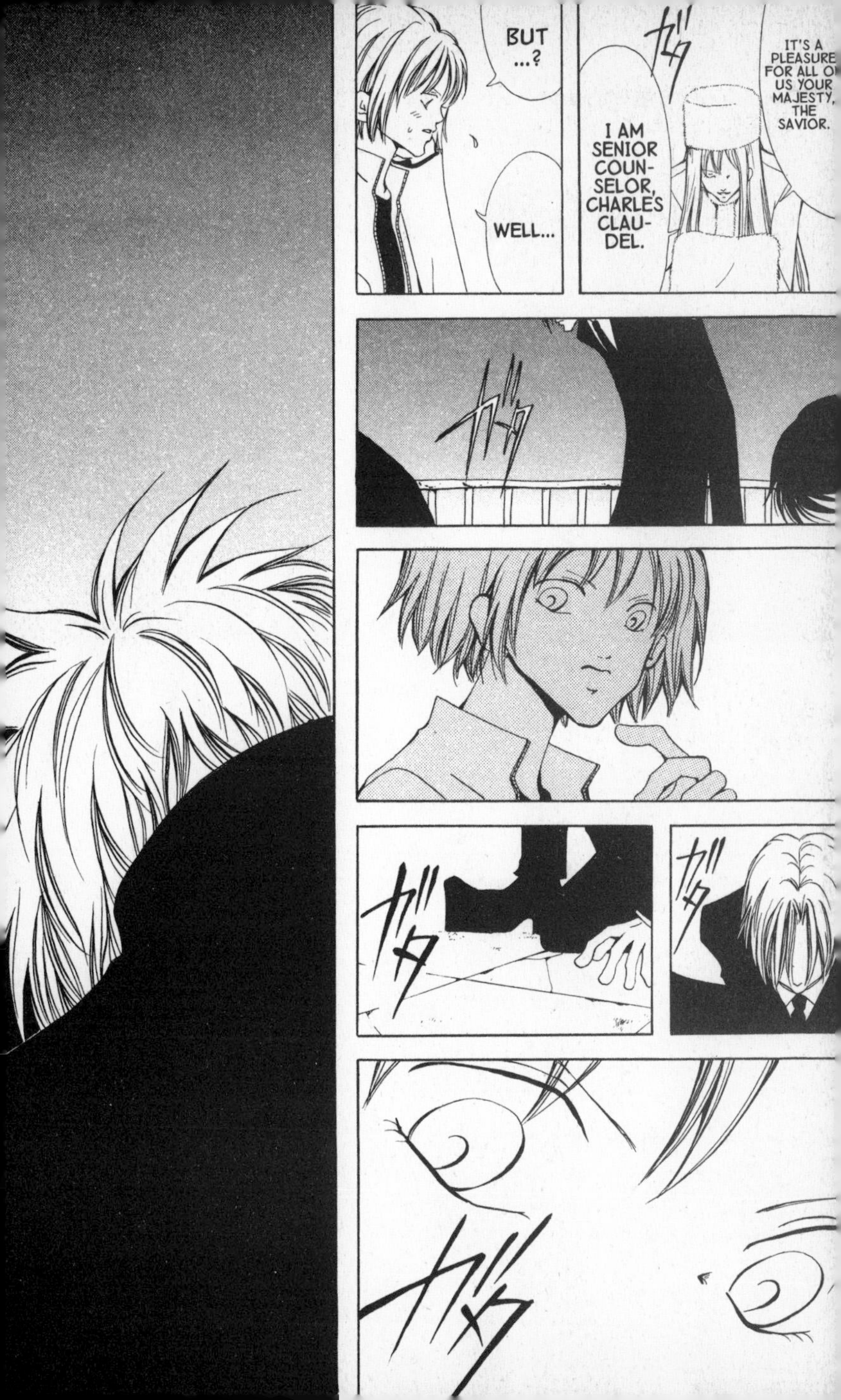
IT'S A PLEASURE FOR ALL O US YOUR MAJESTY, THE SAVIOR.
ガタ
I AM SENIOR COUN-SELOR, CHARLES CLAU-DEL.
BUT ...?
WELL...
ガタ
ガタ
ガタ
ガタ

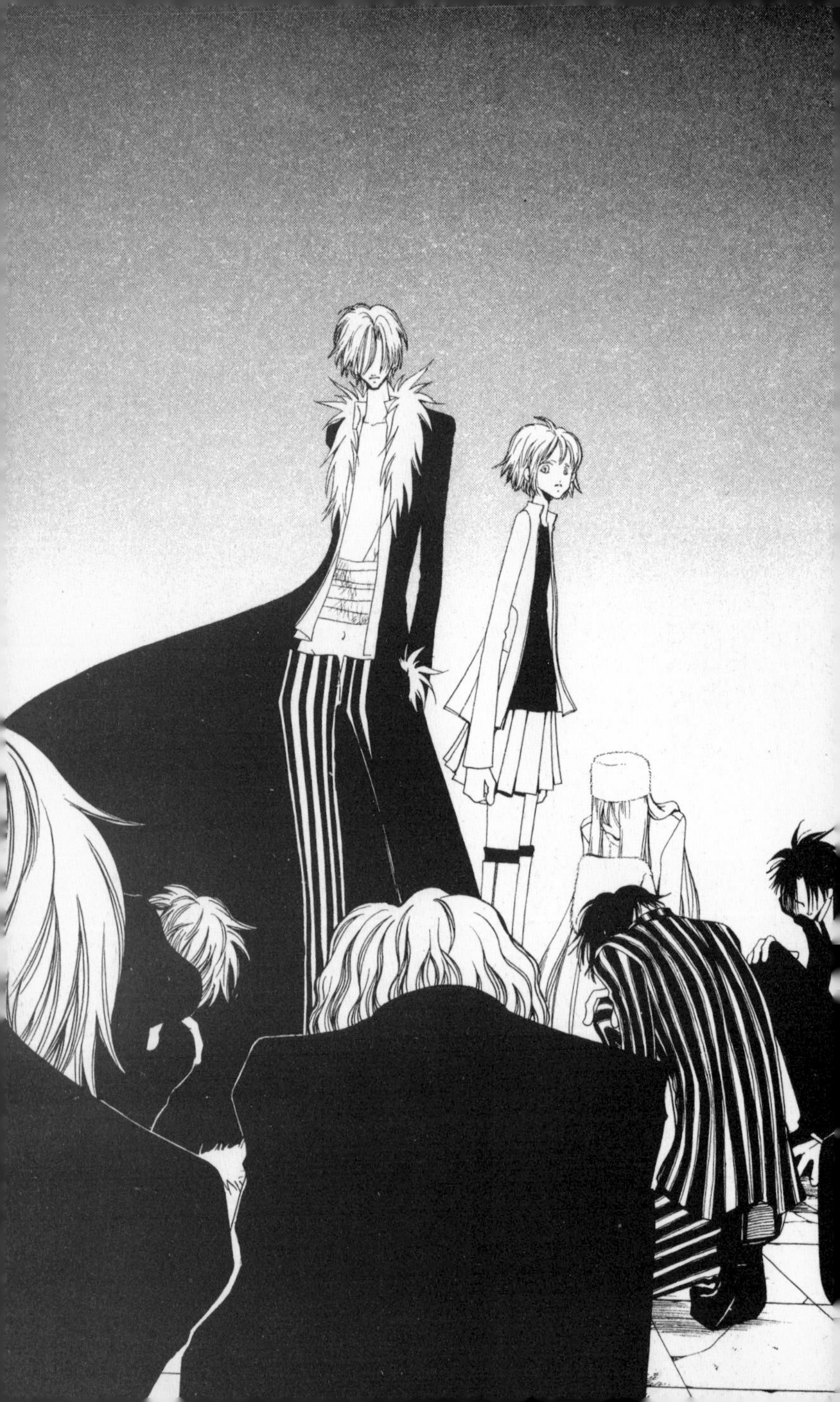

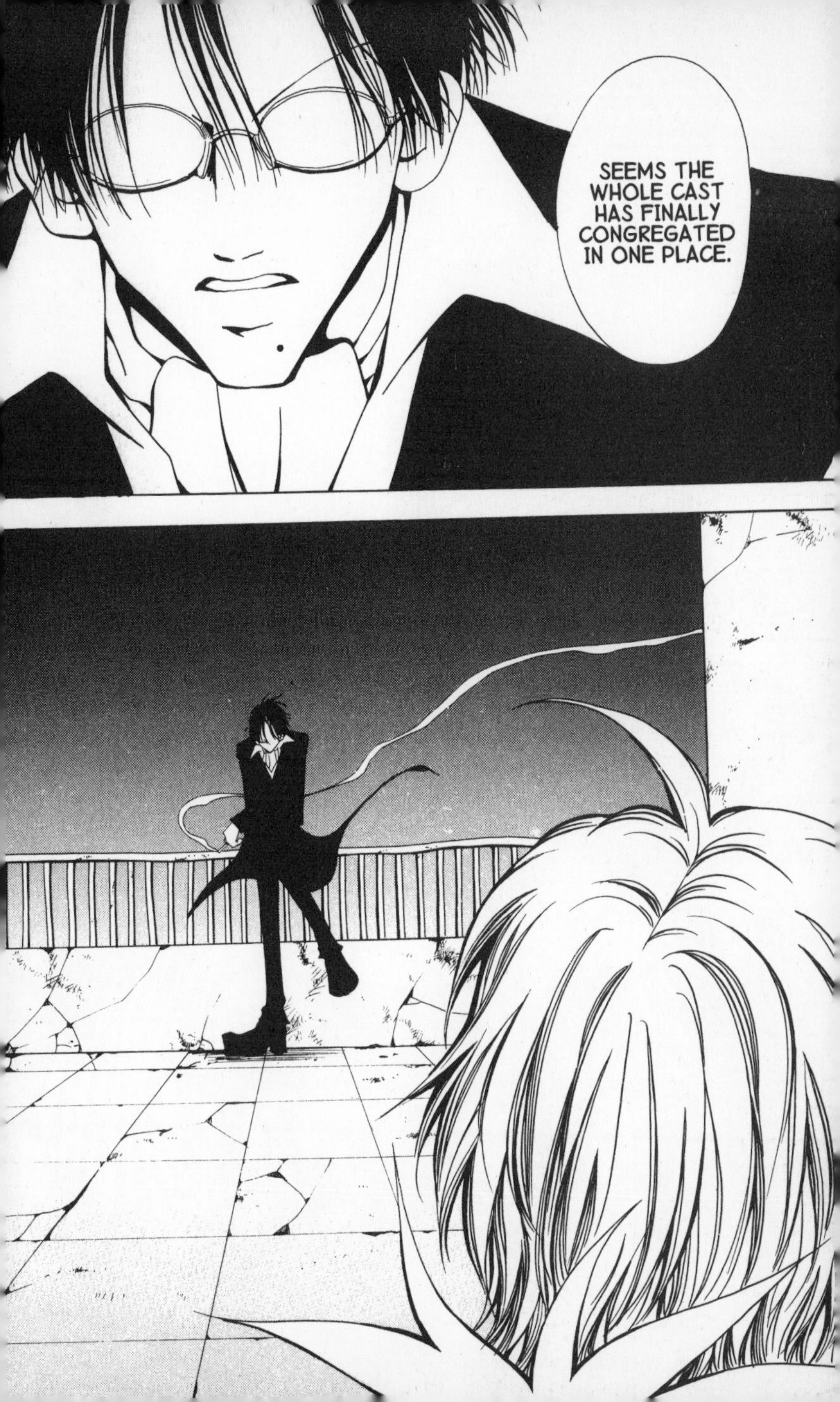
SEEMS THE WHOLE CAST HAS FINALLY CONGREGATED IN ONE PLACE.

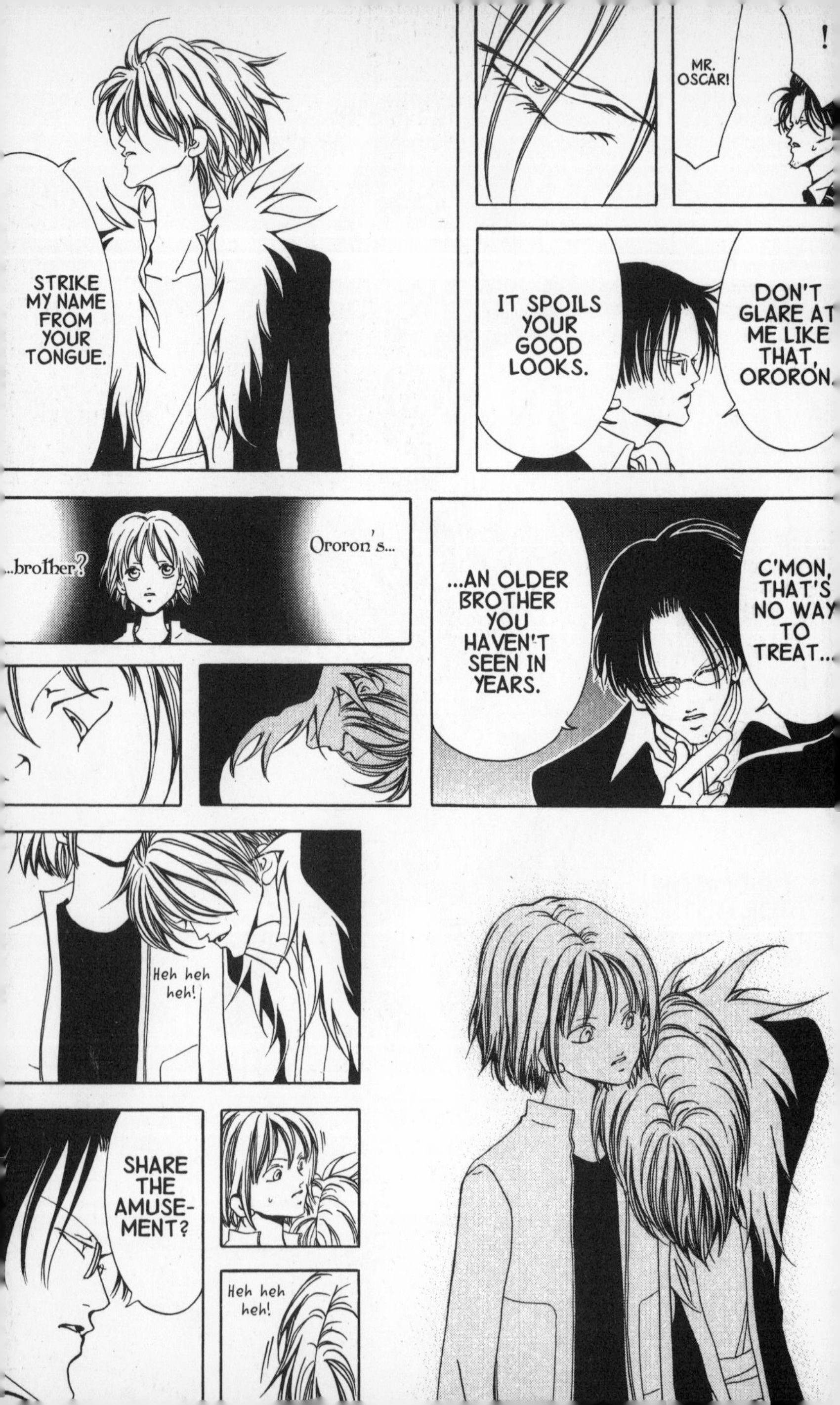
!
MR. OSCAR!
DON'T GLARE AT ME LIKE THAT, ORORON.
IT SPOILS YOUR GOOD LOOKS.
STRIKE MY NAME FROM YOUR TONGUE.
C'MON, THAT'S NO WAY TO TREAT...
...AN OLDER BROTHER YOU HAVEN'T SEEN IN YEARS.
Ororon's...
...brother?
Heh heh heh!
Heh heh heh!
SHARE THE AMUSEMENT?

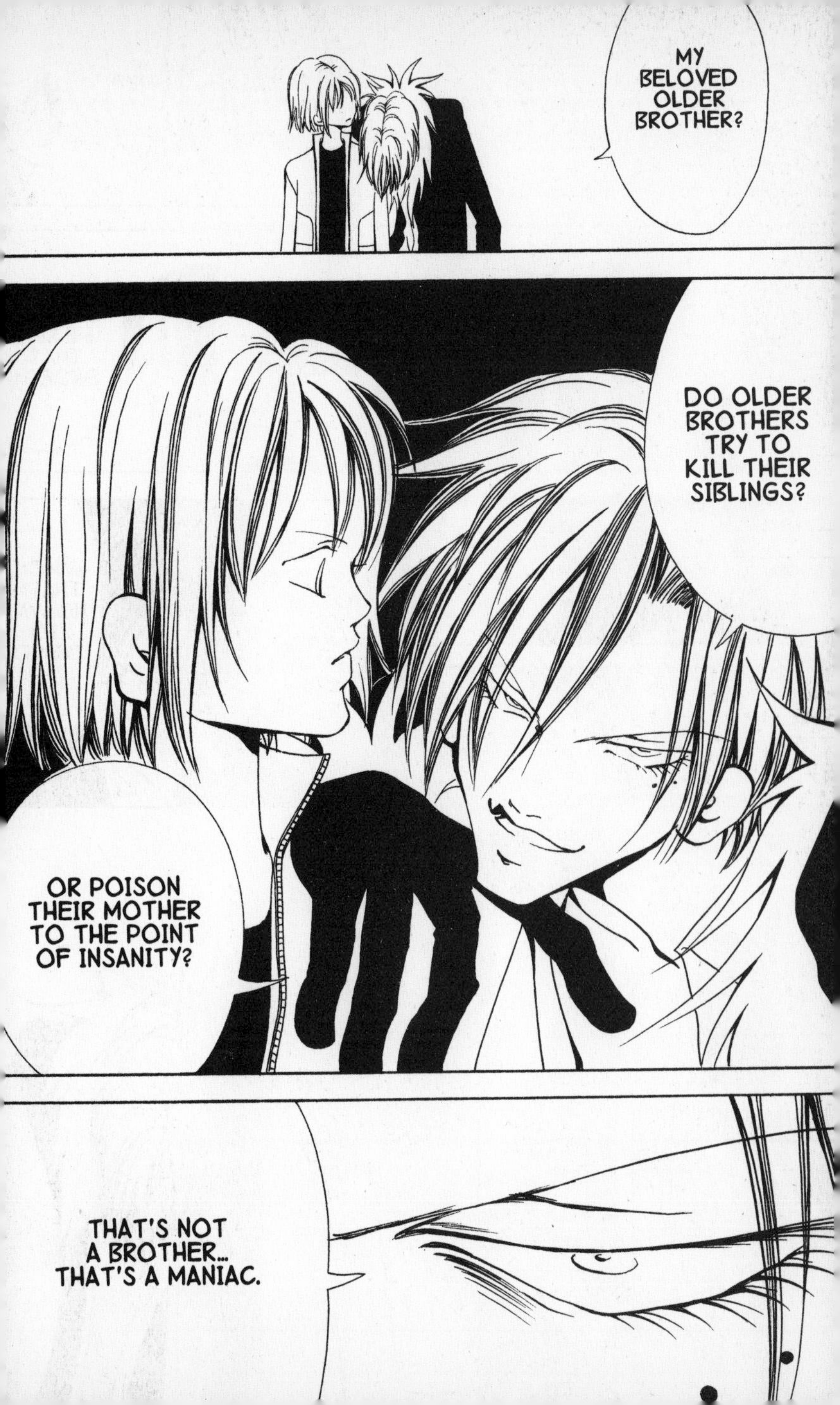
MY BELOVED OLDER BROTHER?
DO OLDER BROTHERS TRY TO KILL THEIR SIBLINGS?
OR POISON THEIR MOTHER TO THE POINT OF INSANITY?
THAT'S NOT A BROTHER... THAT'S A MANIAC.

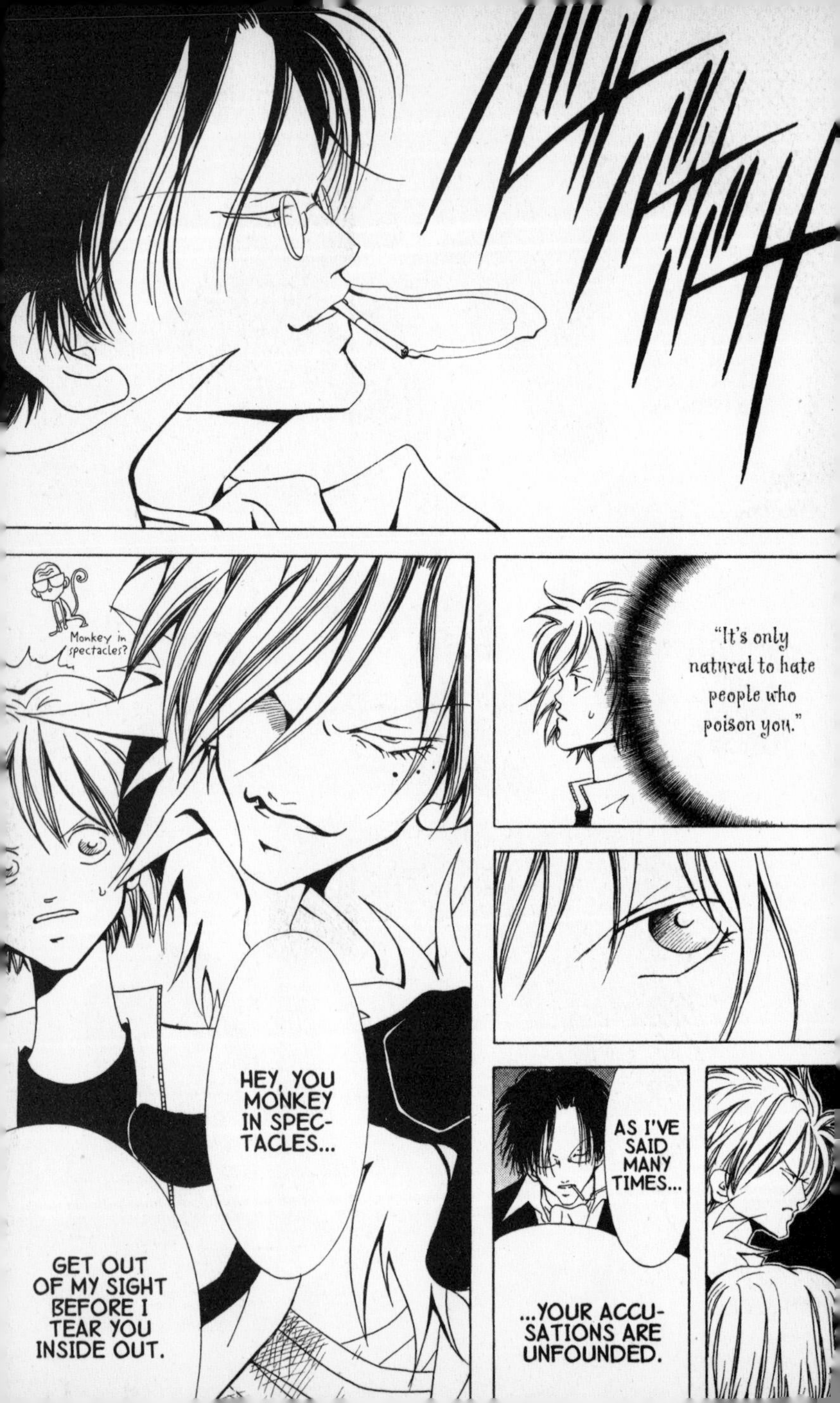
"It's only natural to hate people who poison you."
AS I'VE SAID MANY TIMES...
...YOUR ACCUSATIONS ARE UNFOUNDED.
HEY, YOU MONKEY IN SPEC-TACLES...
GET OUT OF MY SIGHT BEFORE I TEAR YOU INSIDE OUT.
Monkey in spectacles?

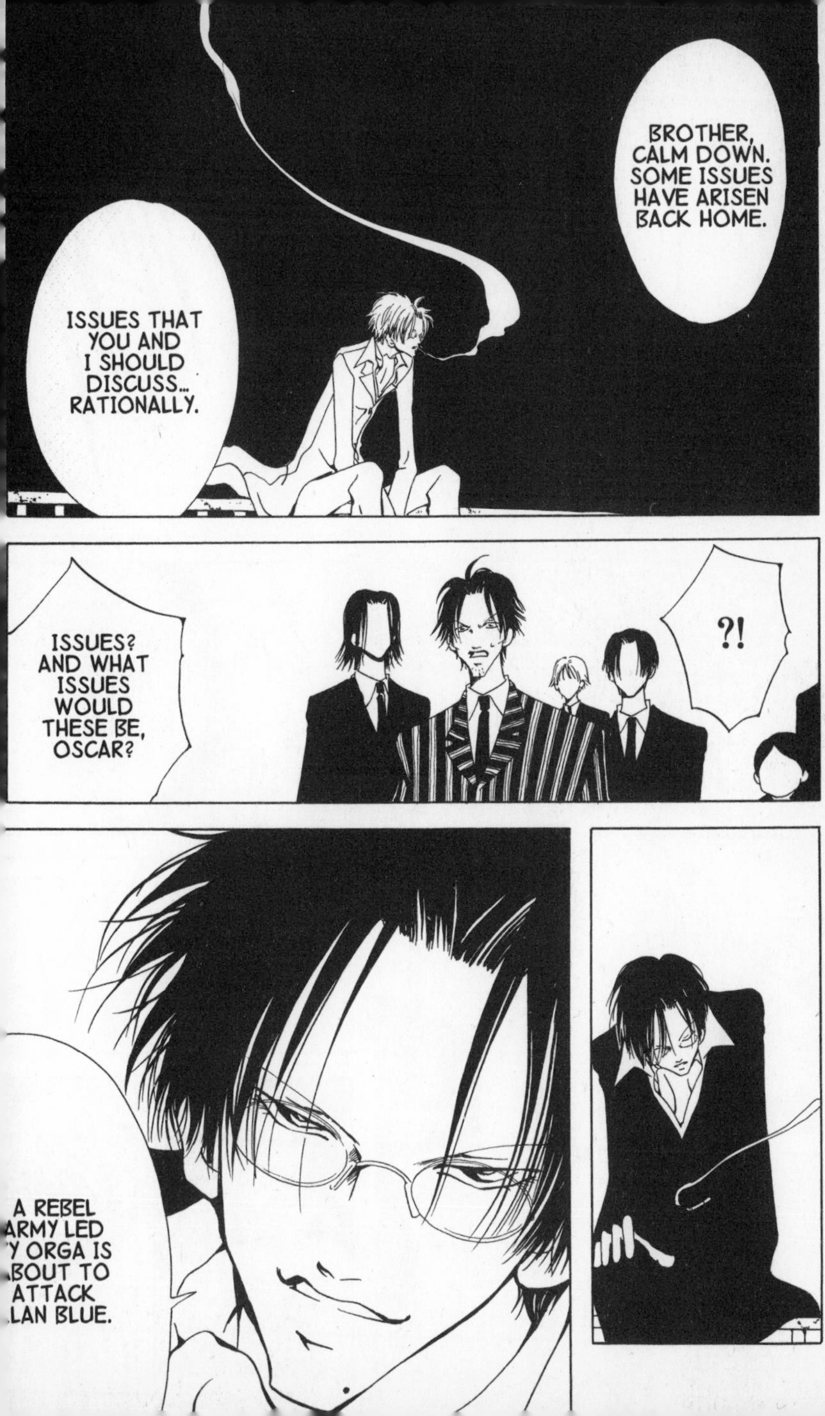
BROTHER, CALM DOWN. SOME ISSUES HAVE ARISEN BACK HOME.
ISSUES THAT YOU AND I SHOULD DISCUSS... RATIONALLY.
?!
ISSUES? AND WHAT ISSUES WOULD THESE BE, OSCAR?
A REBEL
ARMY LED
Y ORGA IS
BOUT TO
ATTACK
LAN BLUE.

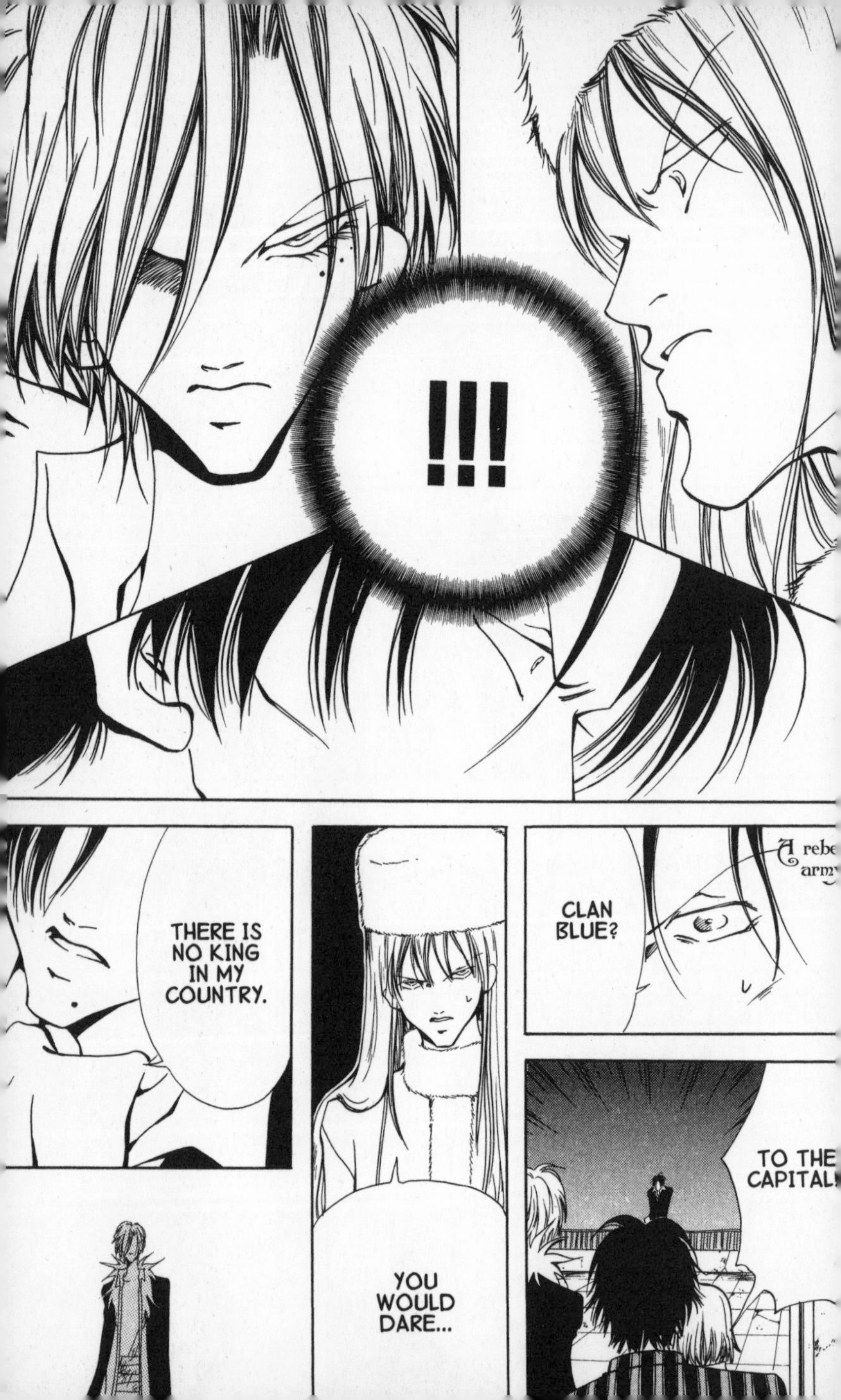
!!!
A rebe army
CLAN BLUE?
TO THE CAPITAL!
YOU WOULD DARE...
THERE IS NO KING IN MY COUNTRY.

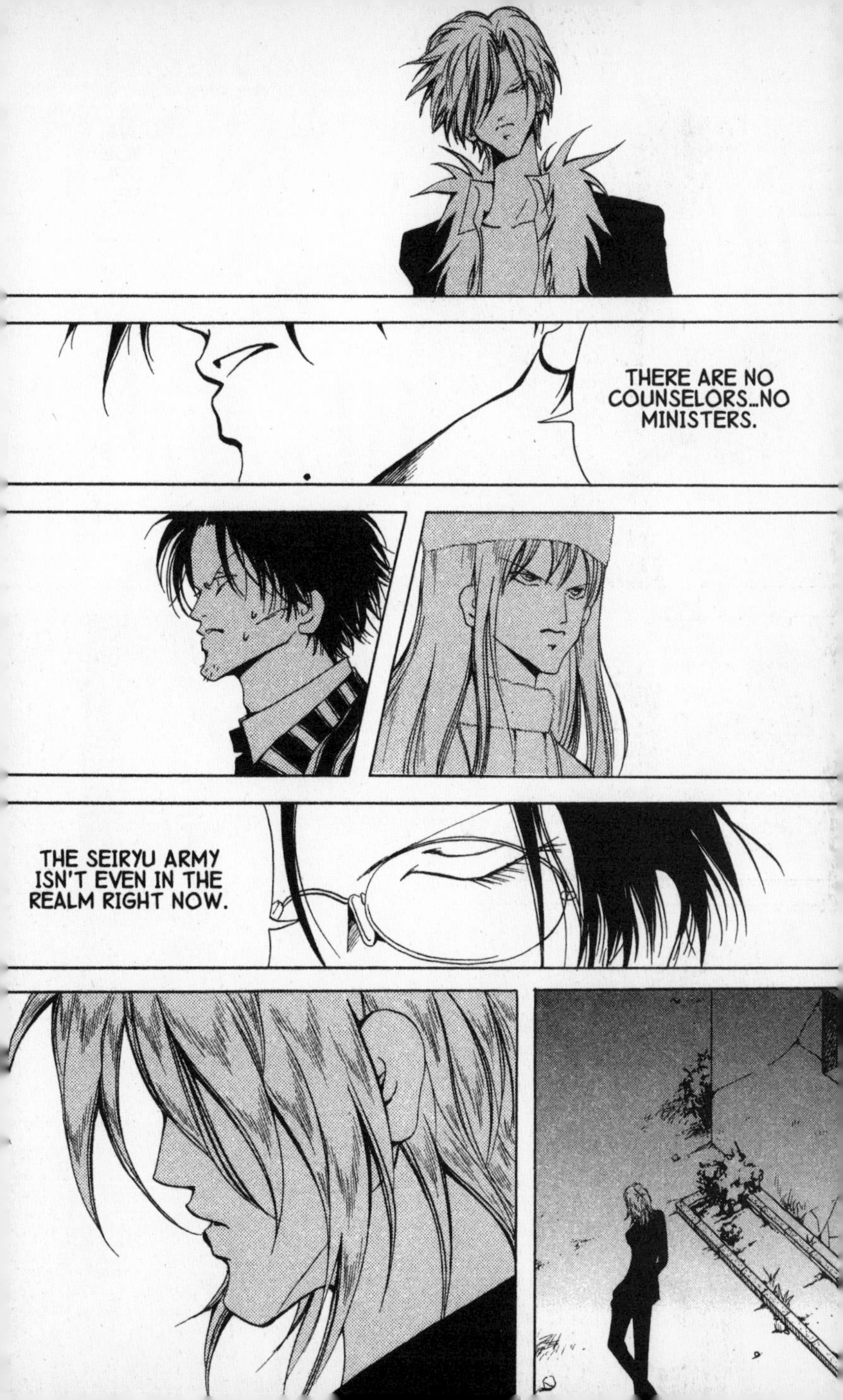
THERE ARE NO COUNSELORS...NO MINISTERS.
THE SEIRYU ARMY ISN'T EVEN IN THE REALM RIGHT NOW.

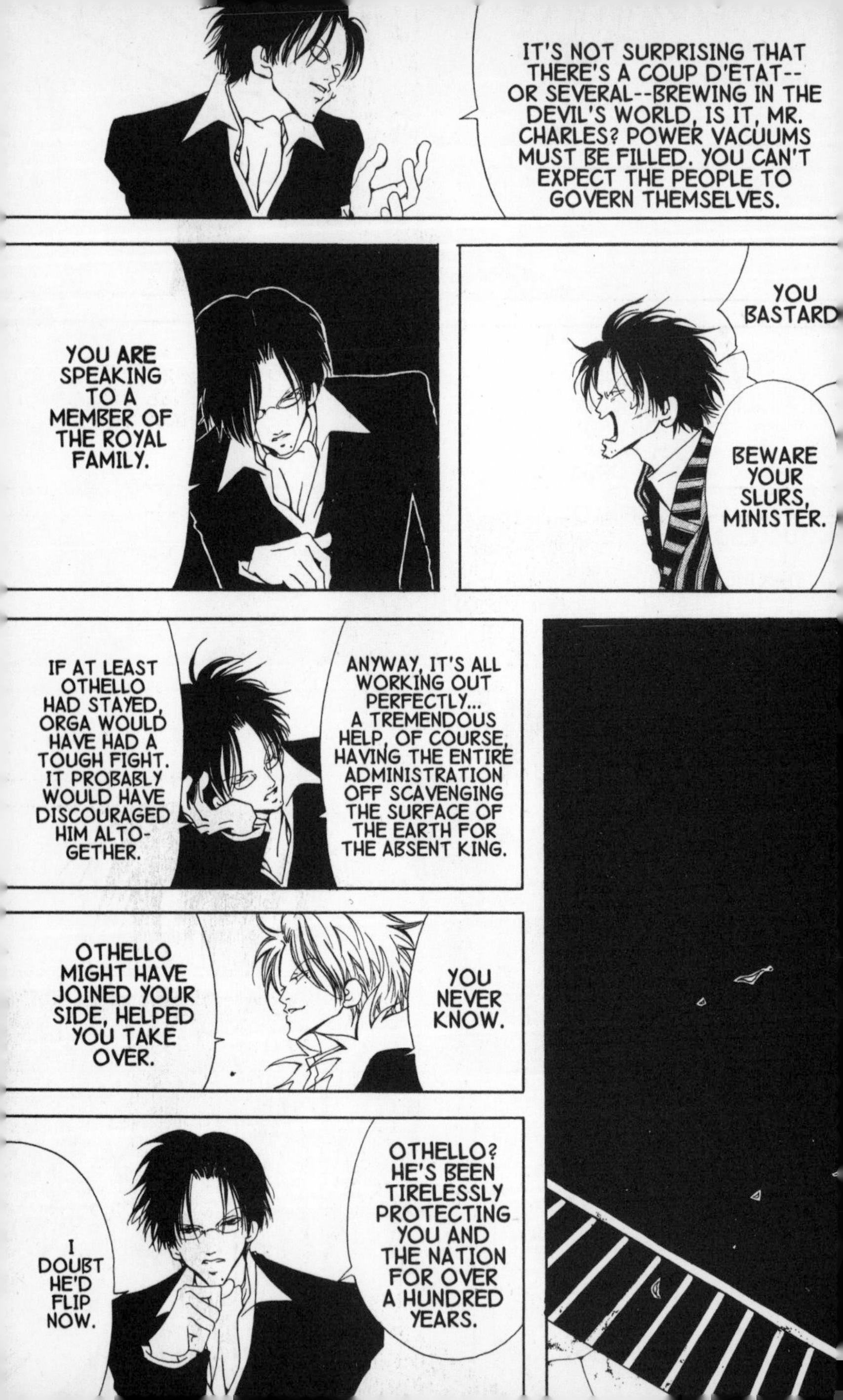
IT'S NOT SURPRISING THAT THERE'S A COUP D'ETAT--OR SEVERAL--BREWING IN THE DEVIL'S WORLD, IS IT, MR. CHARLES? POWER VACUUMS MUST BE FILLED. YOU CAN'T EXPECT THE PEOPLE TO GOVERN THEMSELVES.
YOU BASTARD
BEWARE YOUR SLURS, MINISTER.
YOU ARE SPEAKING TO A MEMBER OF THE ROYAL FAMILY.
ANYWAY, IT'S ALL WORKING OUT PERFECTLY... A TREMENDOUS HELP, OF COURSE, HAVING THE ENTIRE ADMINISTRATION OFF SCAVENGING THE SURFACE OF THE EARTH FOR THE ABSENT KING.
IF AT LEAST OTHELLO HAD STAYED, ORGA WOULD HAVE HAD A TOUGH FIGHT. IT PROBABLY WOULD HAVE DISCOURAGED HIM ALTO-GETHER.
YOU NEVER KNOW.
OTHELLO MIGHT HAVE JOINED YOUR SIDE, HELPED YOU TAKE OVER.
OTHELLO? HE'S BEEN TIRELESSLY PROTECTING YOU AND THE NATION FOR OVER A HUNDRED YEARS.
I DOUBT HE'D FLIP NOW.

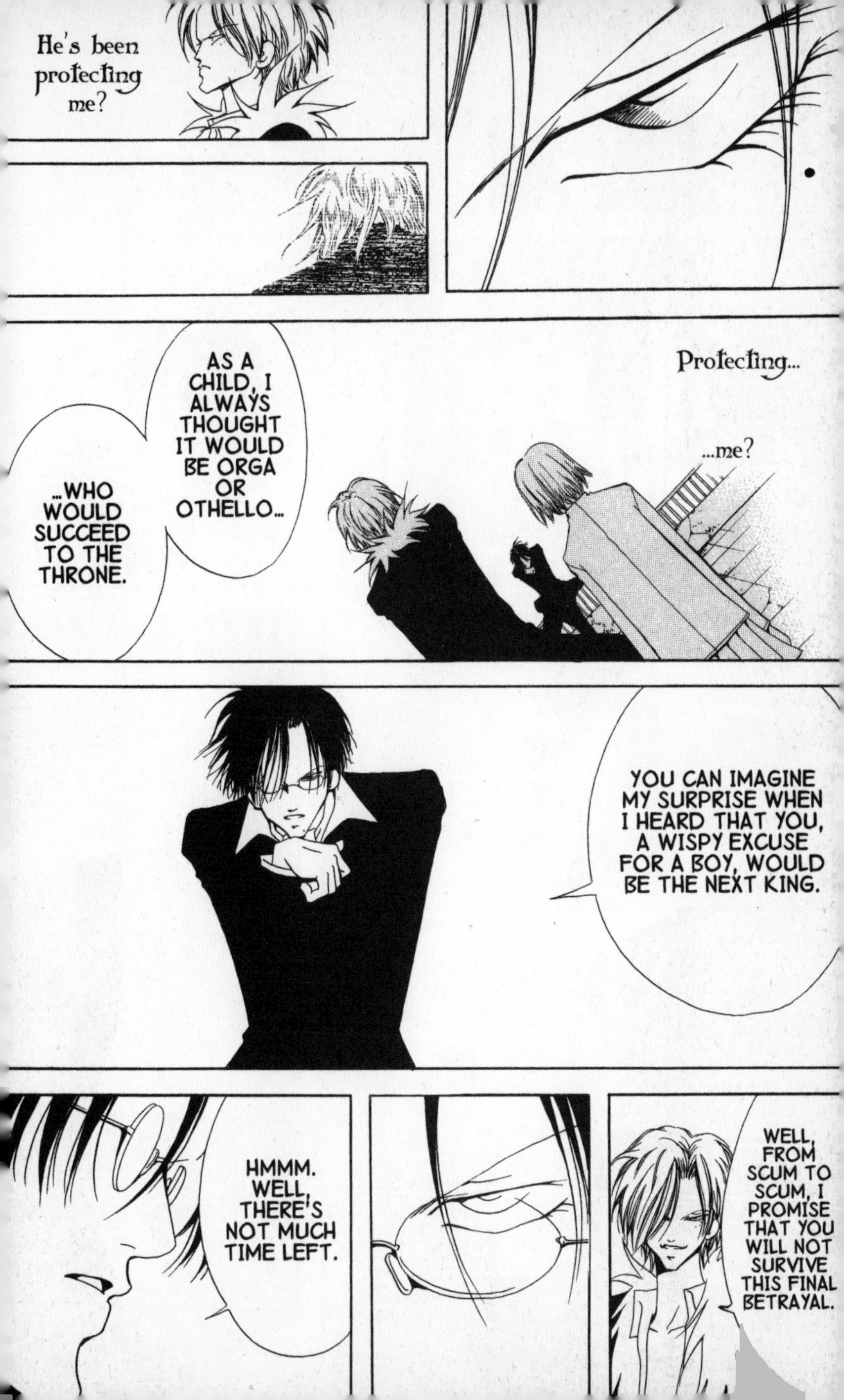
He's been protecting me?
Protecting...
...me?
AS A CHILD, I ALWAYS THOUGHT IT WOULD BE ORGA OR OTHELLO...
...WHO WOULD SUCCEED TO THE THRONE.
YOU CAN IMAGINE MY SURPRISE WHEN I HEARD THAT YOU, A WISPY EXCUSE FOR A BOY, WOULD BE THE NEXT KING.
WELL, FROM SCUM TO SCUM, I PROMISE THAT YOU WILL NOT SURVIVE THIS FINAL BETRAYAL.
HMMM. WELL, THERE'S NOT MUCH TIME LEFT.

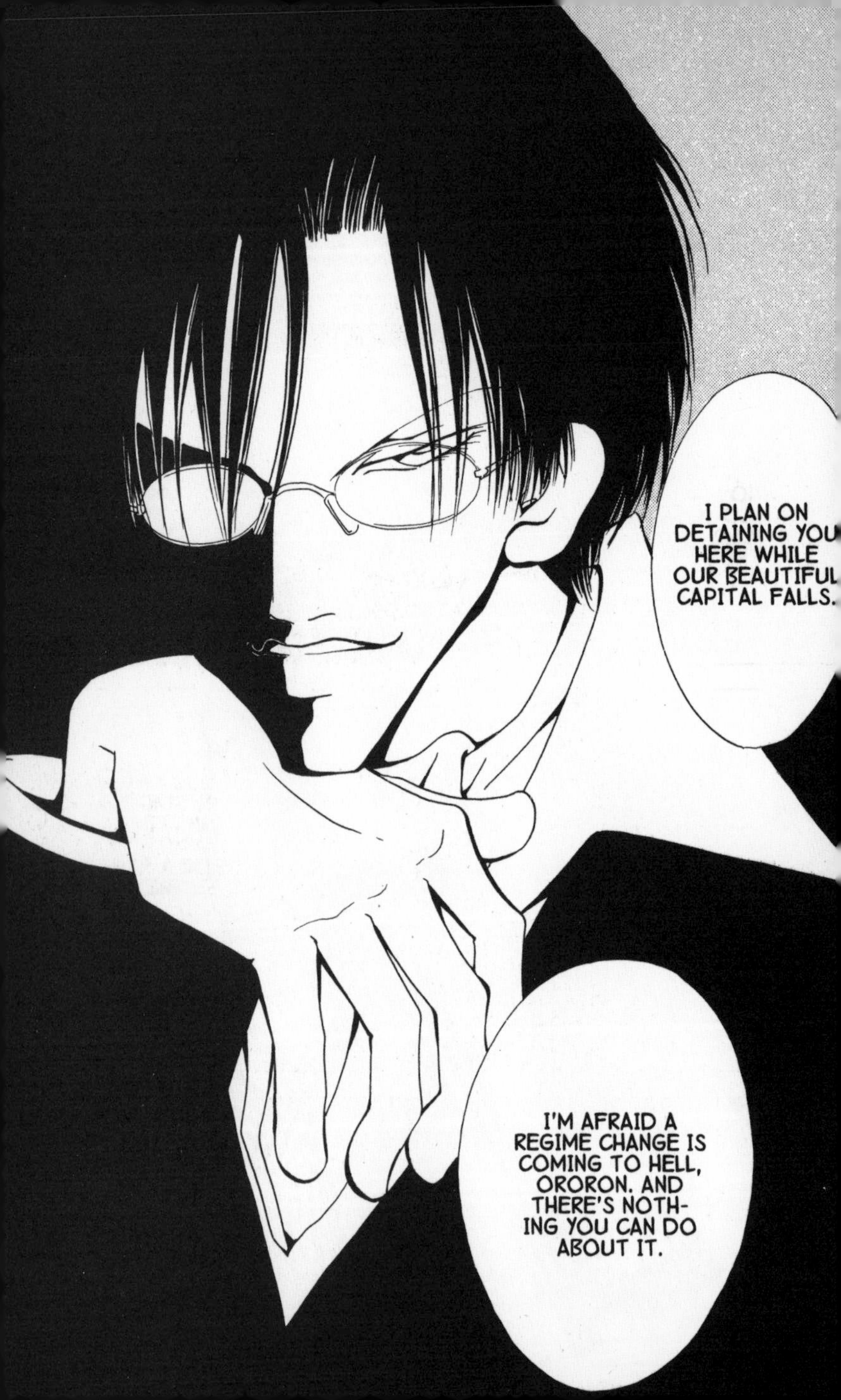
I PLAN ON DETAINING YOU HERE WHILE OUR BEAUTIFUL CAPITAL FALLS.
I'M AFRAID A REGIME CHANGE IS COMING TO HELL, ORORON. AND THERE'S NOTHING YOU CAN DO ABOUT IT.

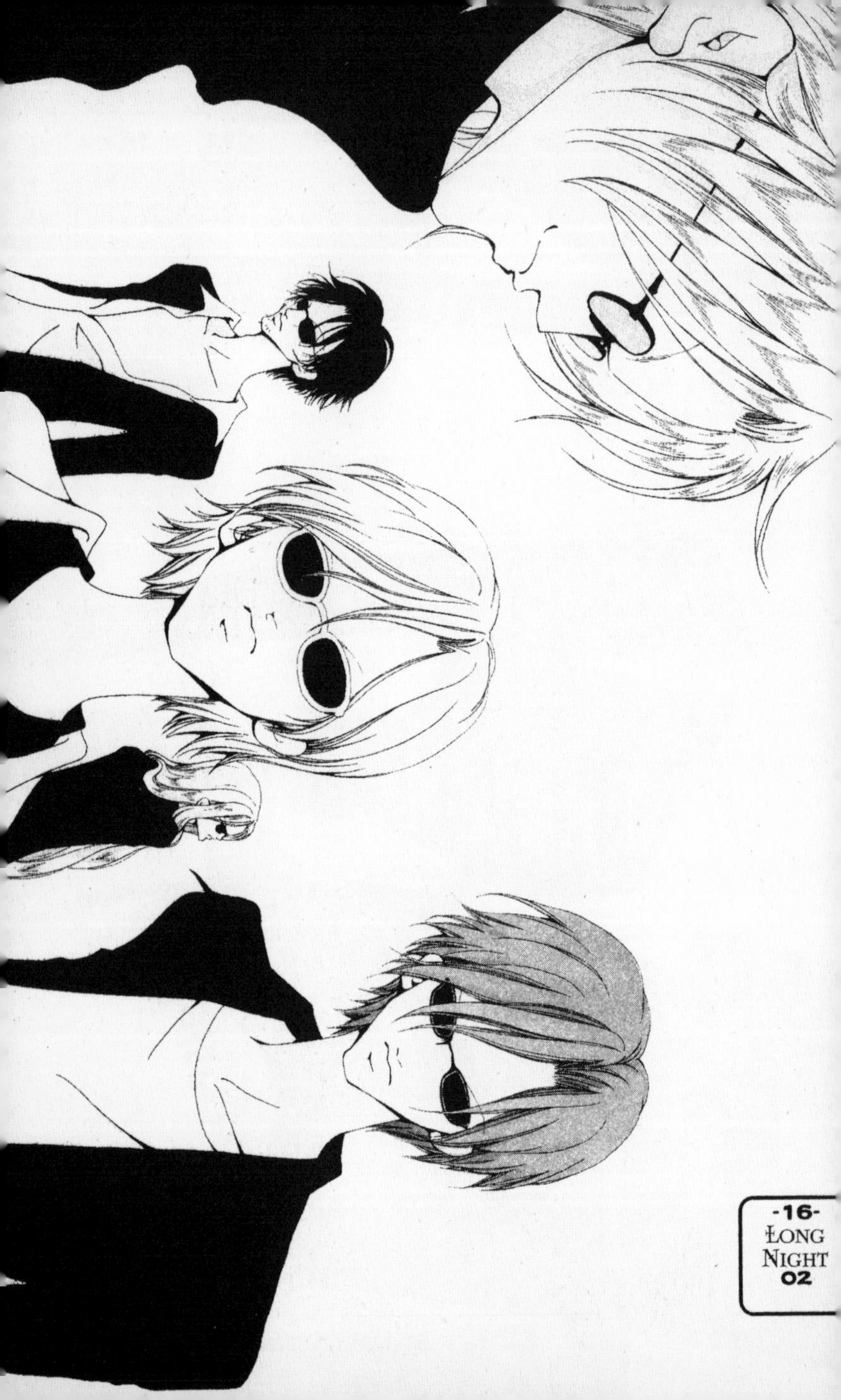
-16-
LONG
NIGHT
02

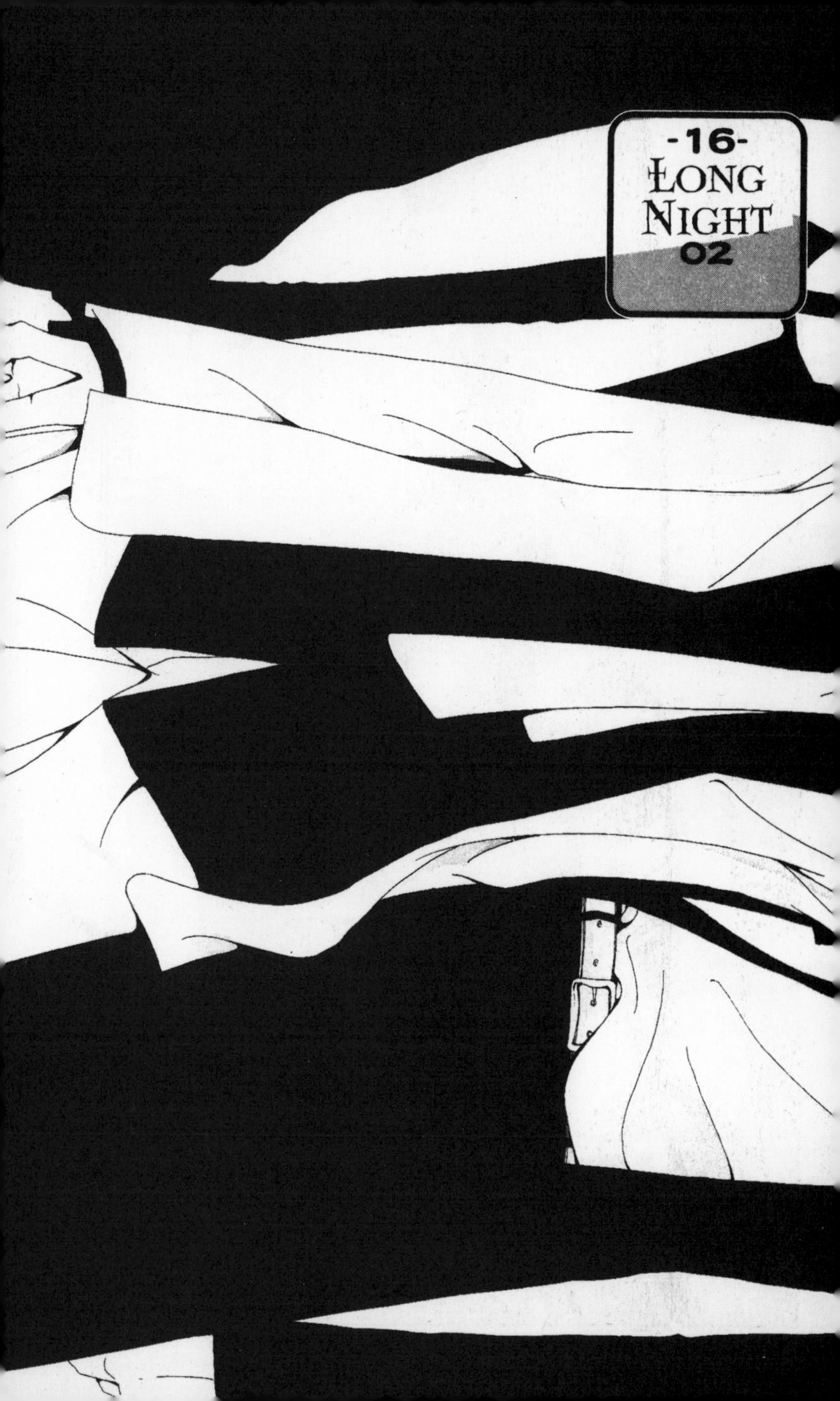
-16-
LONG
NIGHT
02

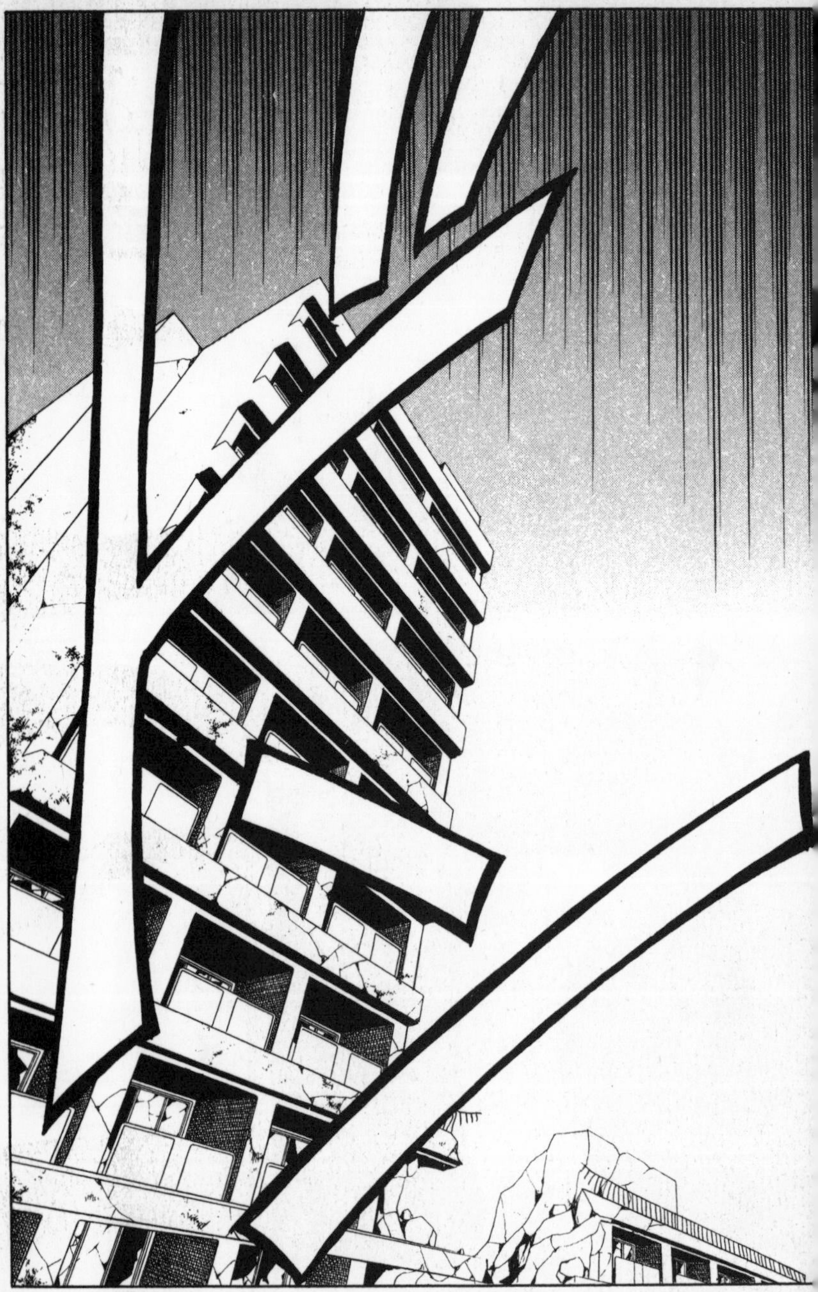

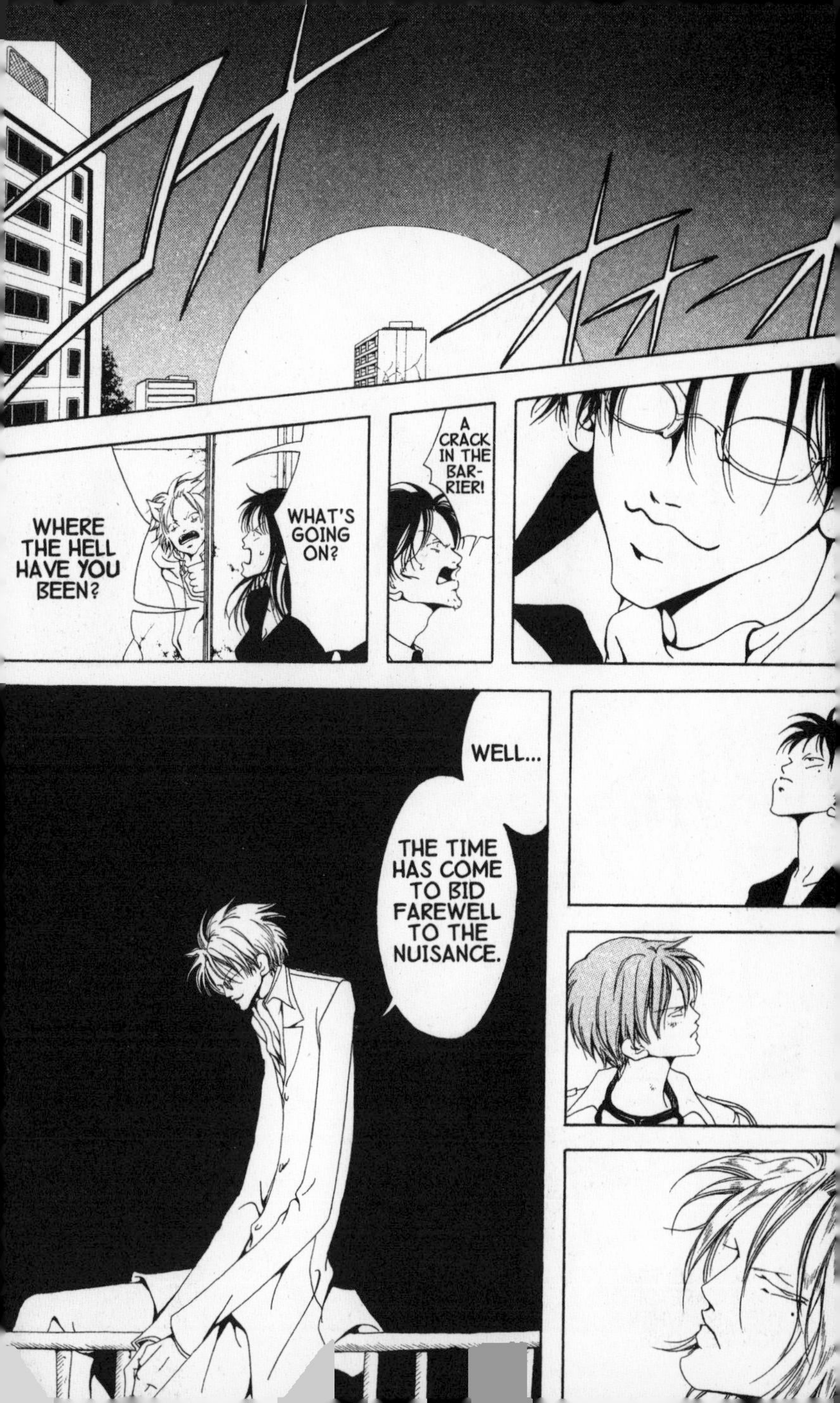
A CRACK IN THE BARRIER!
WHAT'S GOING ON?
WHERE THE HELL HAVE YOU BEEN?
WELL...
THE TIME HAS COME TO BID FAREWELL TO THE NUISANCE.

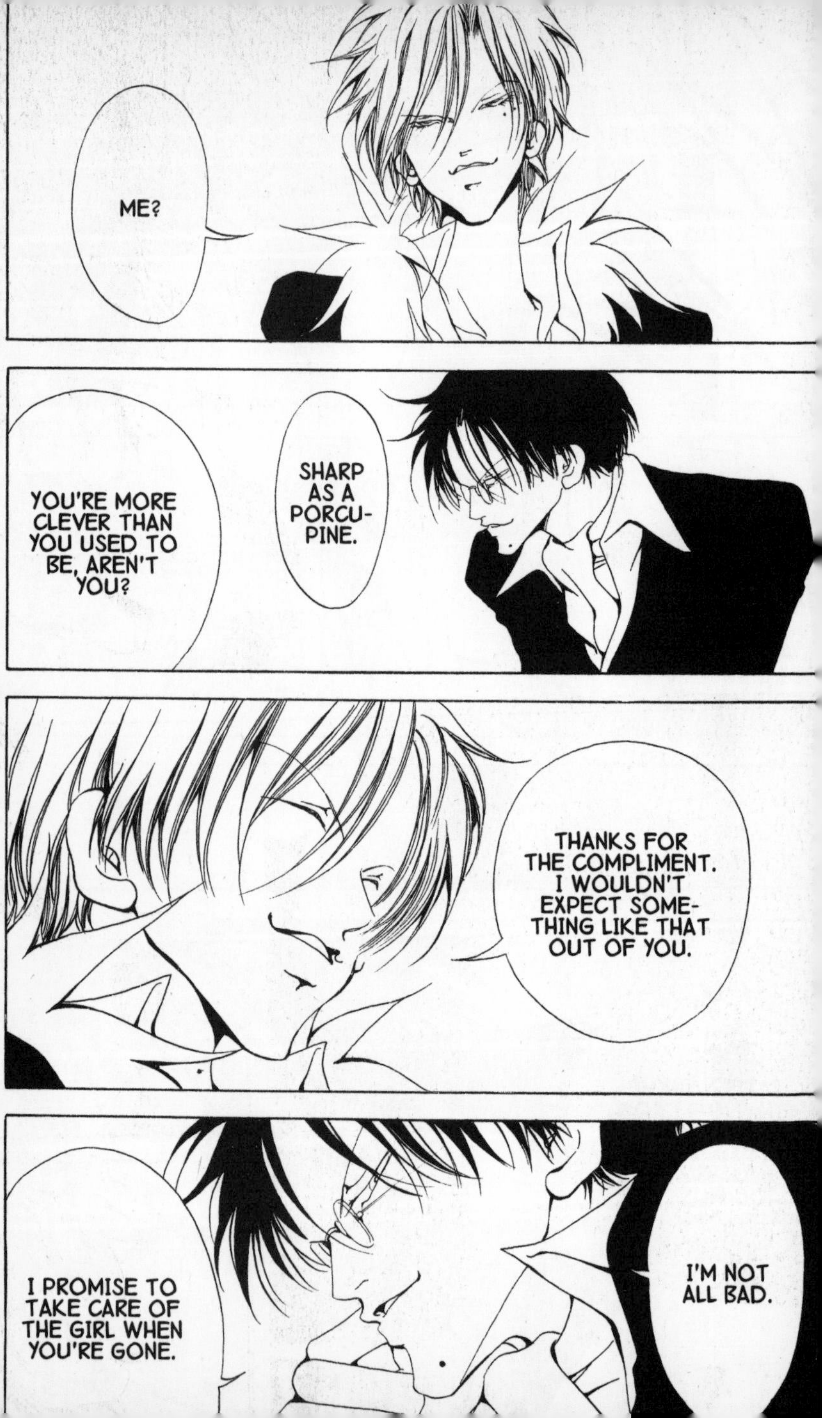
ME?
SHARP AS A PORCUPINE.
YOU'RE MORE CLEVER THAN YOU USED TO BE, AREN'T YOU?
THANKS FOR THE COMPLIMENT. I WOULDN'T EXPECT SOMETHING LIKE THAT OUT OF YOU.
I'M NOT ALL BAD.
I PROMISE TO TAKE CARE OF THE GIRL WHEN YOU'RE GONE.

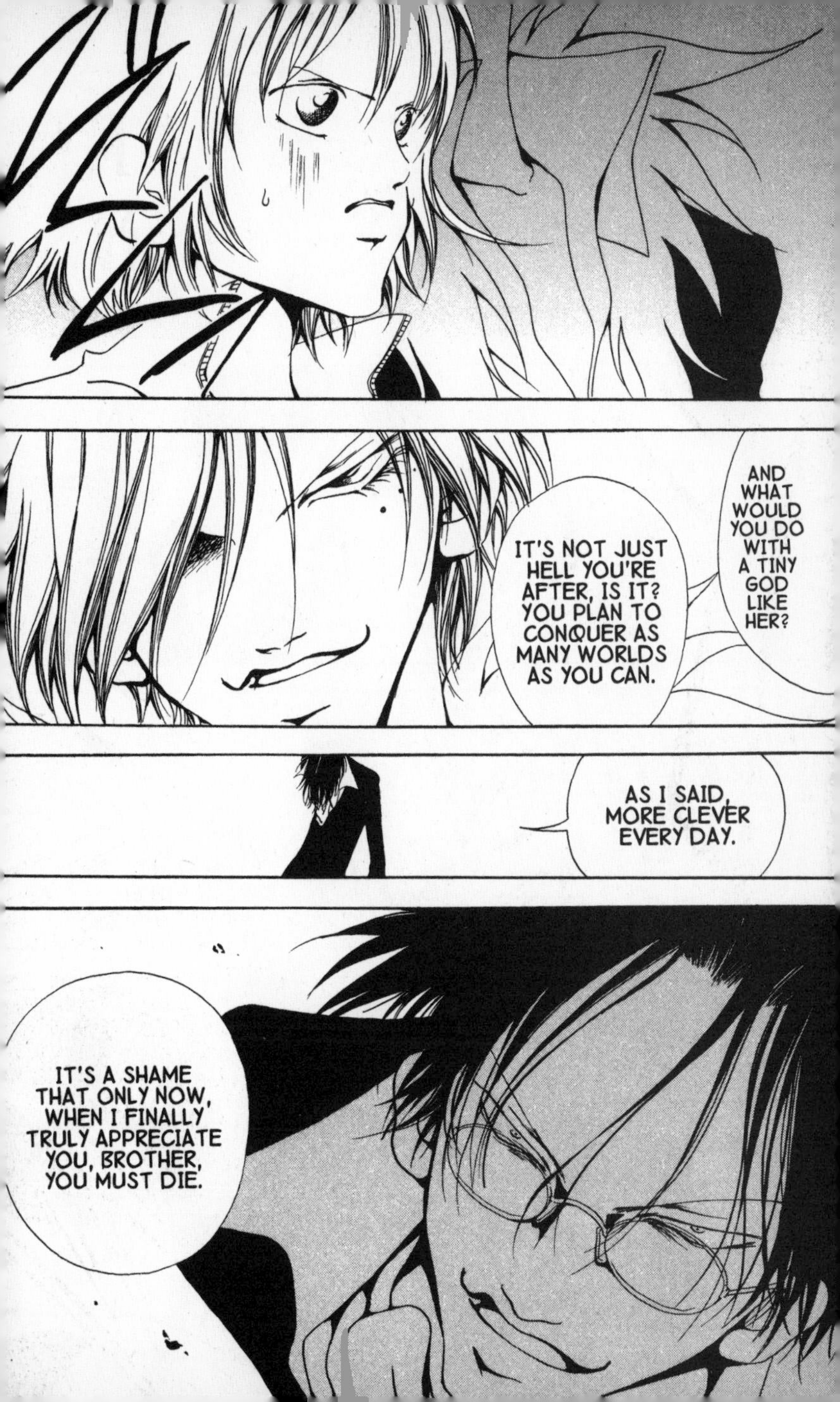
AND WHAT WOULD YOU DO WITH A TINY GOD LIKE HER?
IT'S NOT JUST HELL YOU'RE AFTER, IS IT? YOU PLAN TO CONQUER AS MANY WORLDS AS YOU CAN.
AS I SAID, MORE CLEVER EVERY DAY.
IT'S A SHAME THAT ONLY NOW, WHEN I FINALLY TRULY APPRECIATE YOU, BROTHER, YOU MUST DIE.

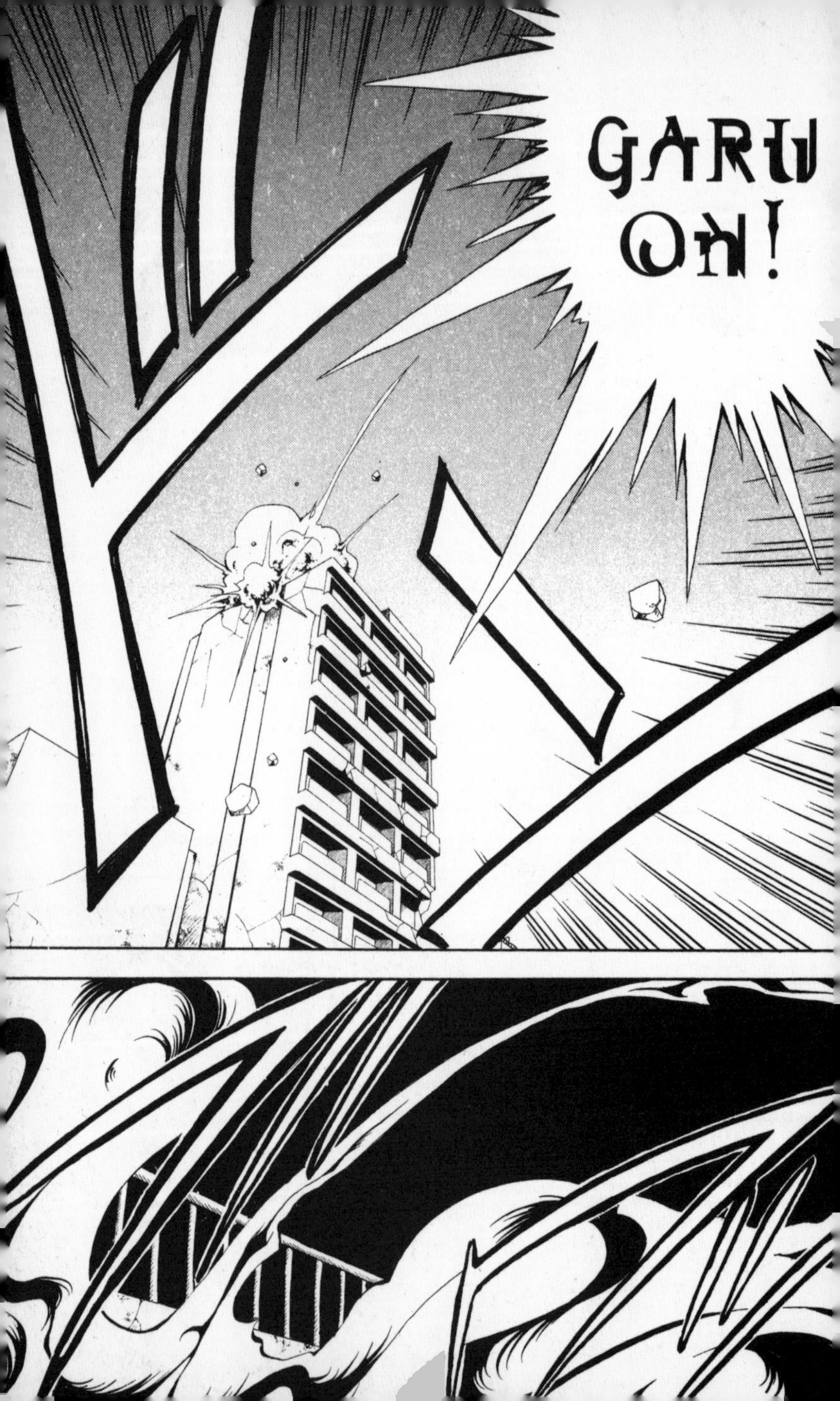
GARU ON!

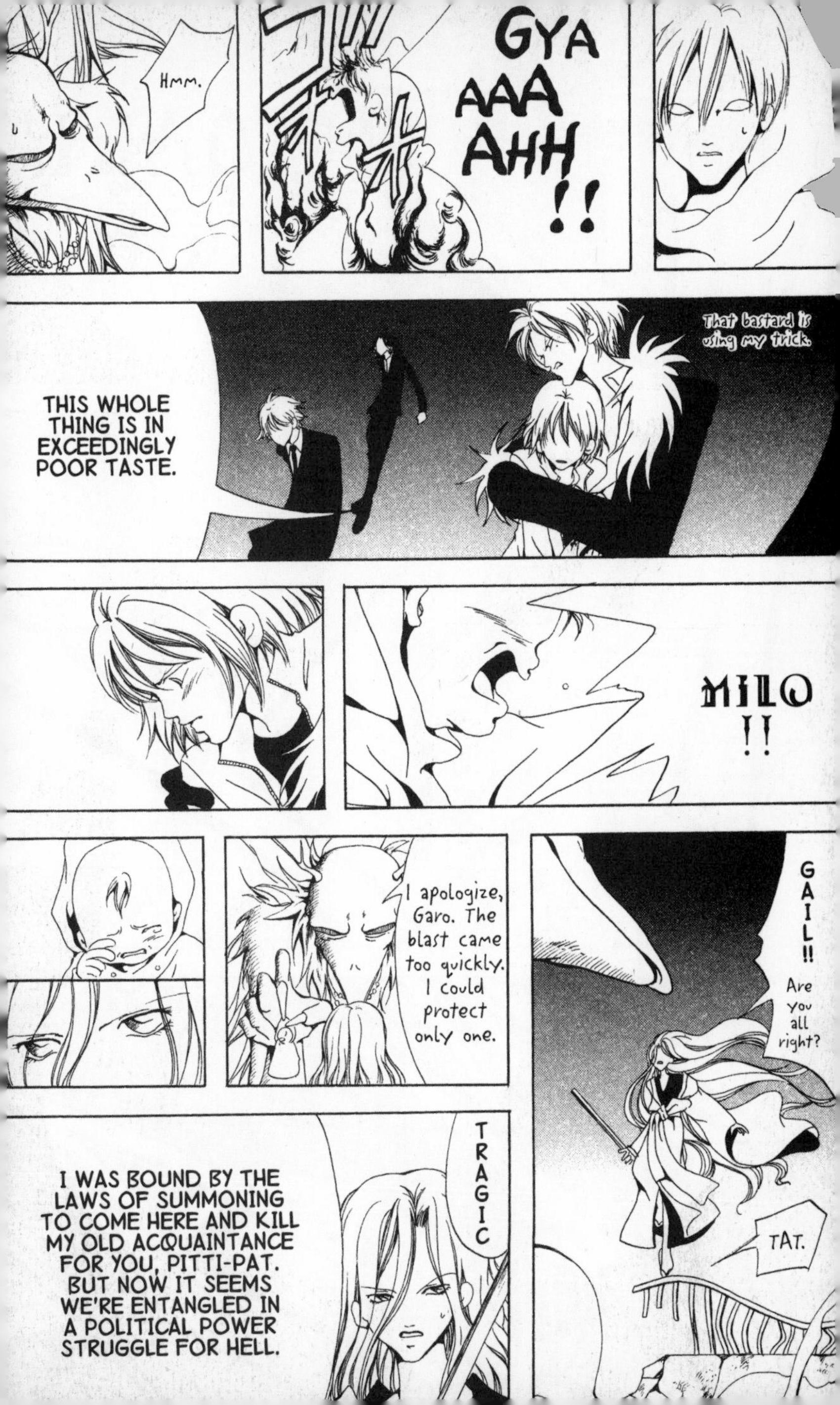
GYA AAA AHH !!
Hmm.
That bastard is using my trick.
THIS WHOLE THING IS IN EXCEEDINGLY POOR TASTE.
MILO !!
GAIL!!
Are you all right?
TAT.
I apologize, Garo. The blast came too quickly. I could protect only one.
TRAGIC
I WAS BOUND BY THE LAWS OF SUMMONING TO COME HERE AND KILL MY OLD ACQUAINTANCE FOR YOU, PITTI-PAT. BUT NOW IT SEEMS WE'RE ENTANGLED IN A POLITICAL POWER STRUGGLE FOR HELL.

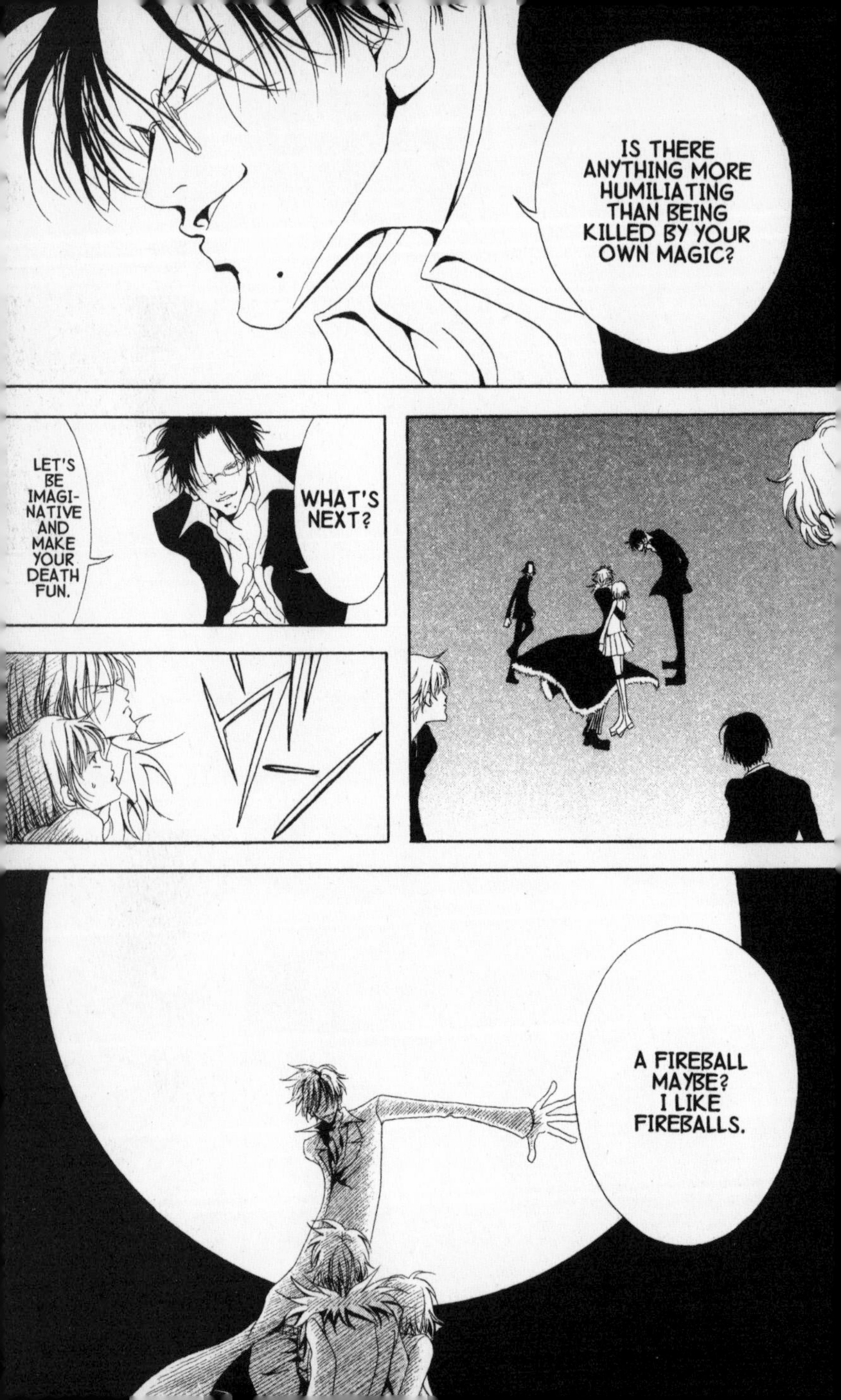
IS THERE ANYTHING MORE HUMILIATING THAN BEING KILLED BY YOUR OWN MAGIC?
WHAT'S NEXT?
LET'S BE IMAGI-NATIVE AND MAKE YOUR DEATH FUN.
A FIREBALL MAYBE? I LIKE FIREBALLS.

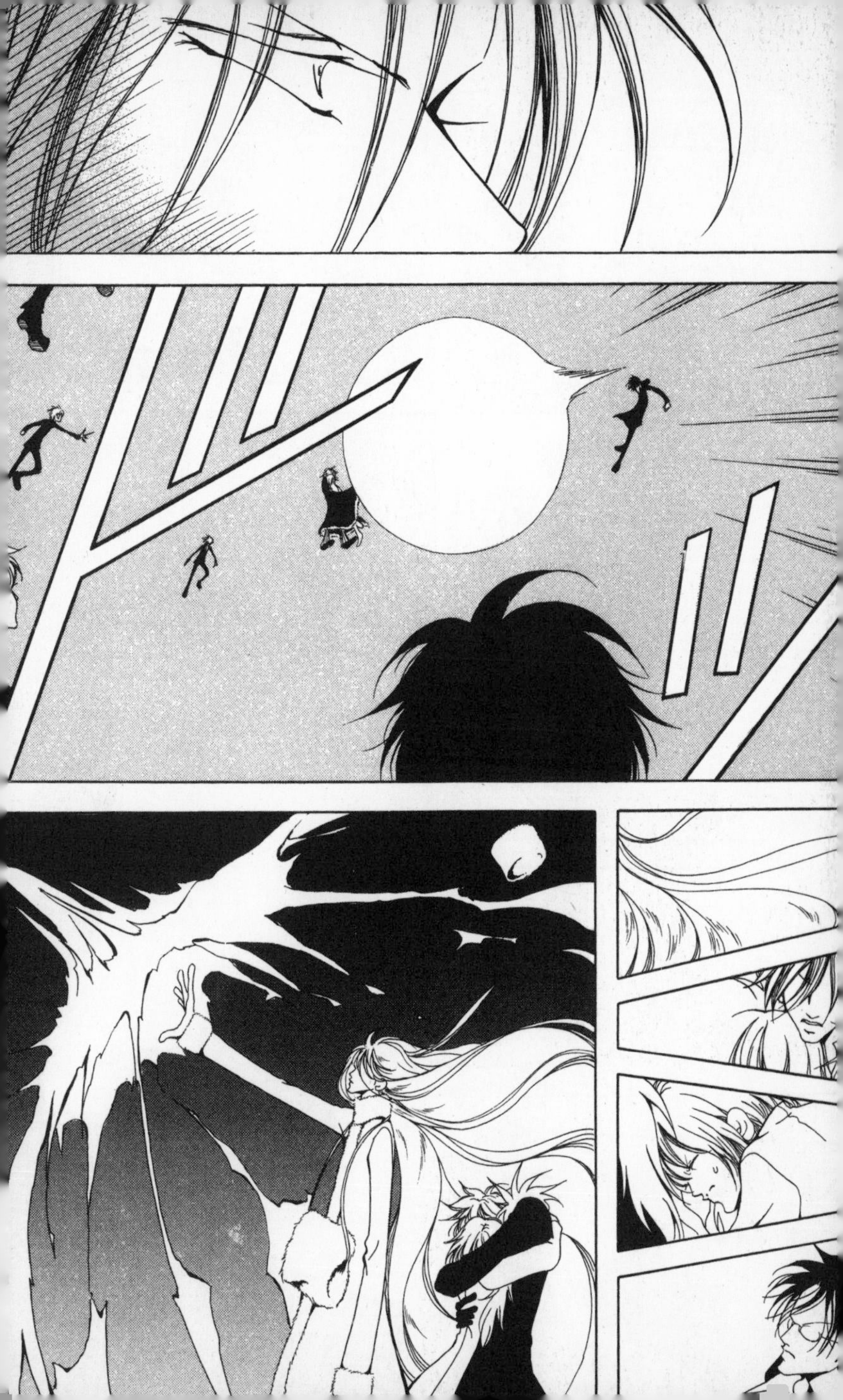

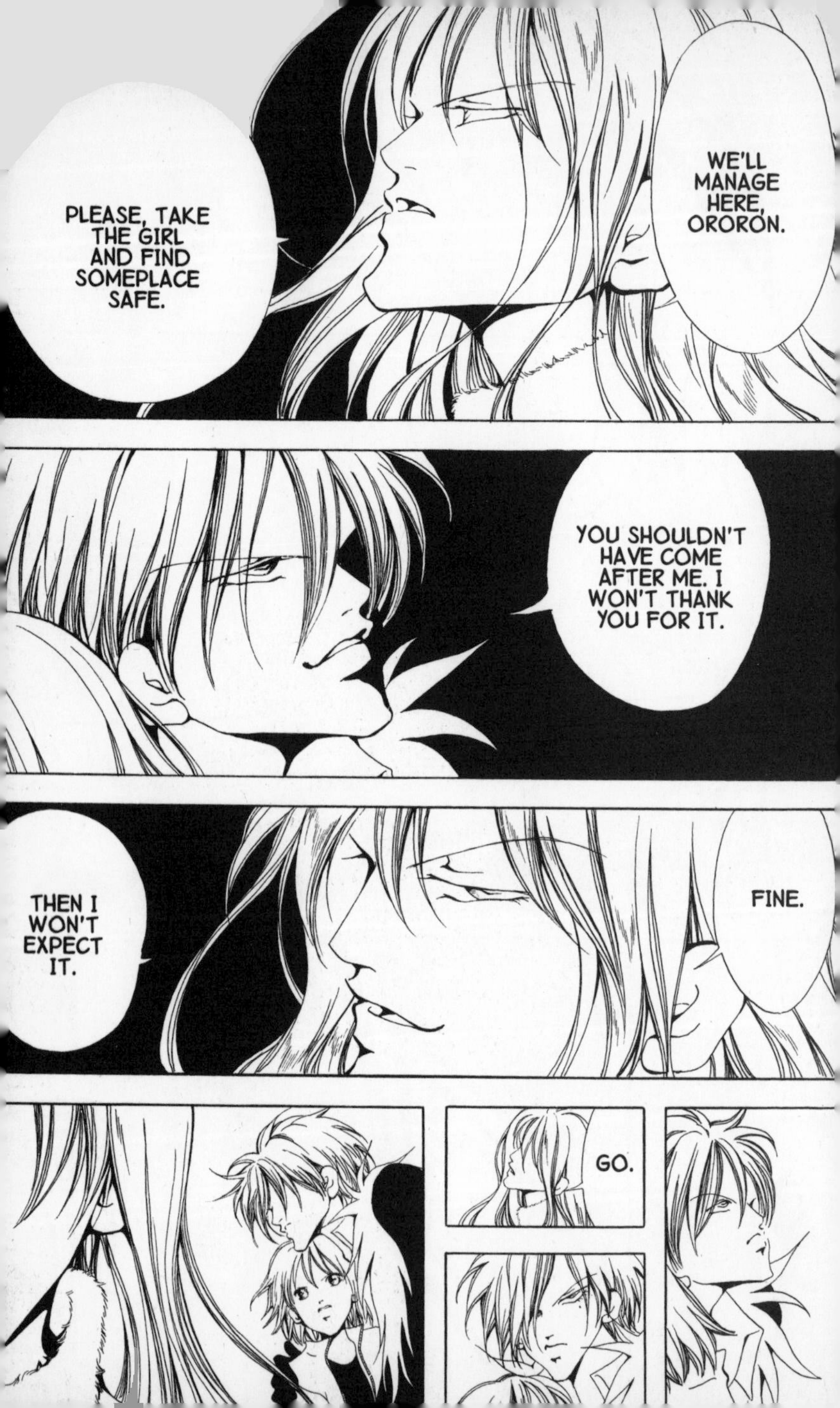
WE'LL MANAGE HERE, ORORON.
PLEASE, TAKE THE GIRL AND FIND SOMEPLACE SAFE.
YOU SHOULDN'T HAVE COME AFTER ME. I WON'T THANK YOU FOR IT.
FINE.
THEN I WON'T EXPECT IT.
GO.

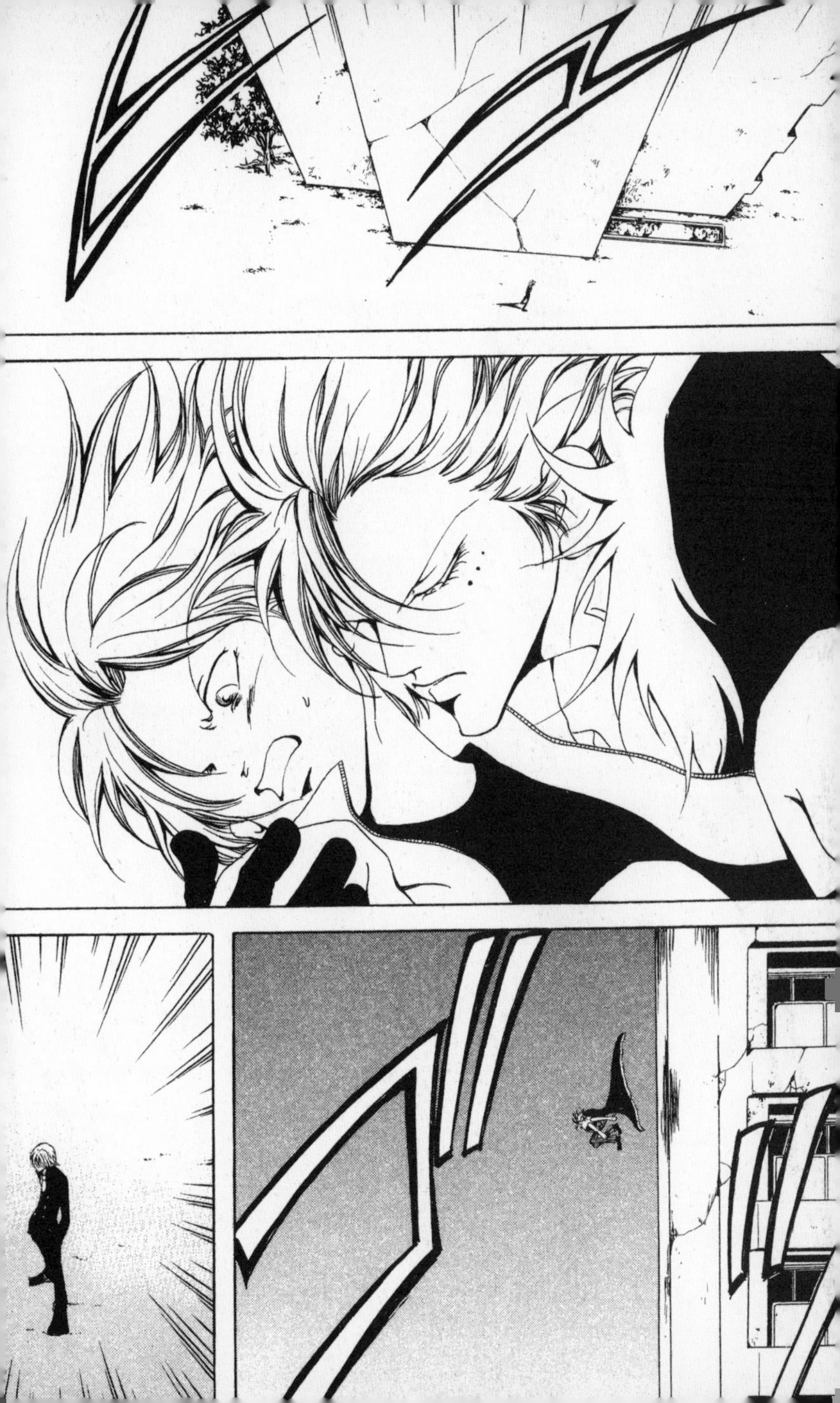

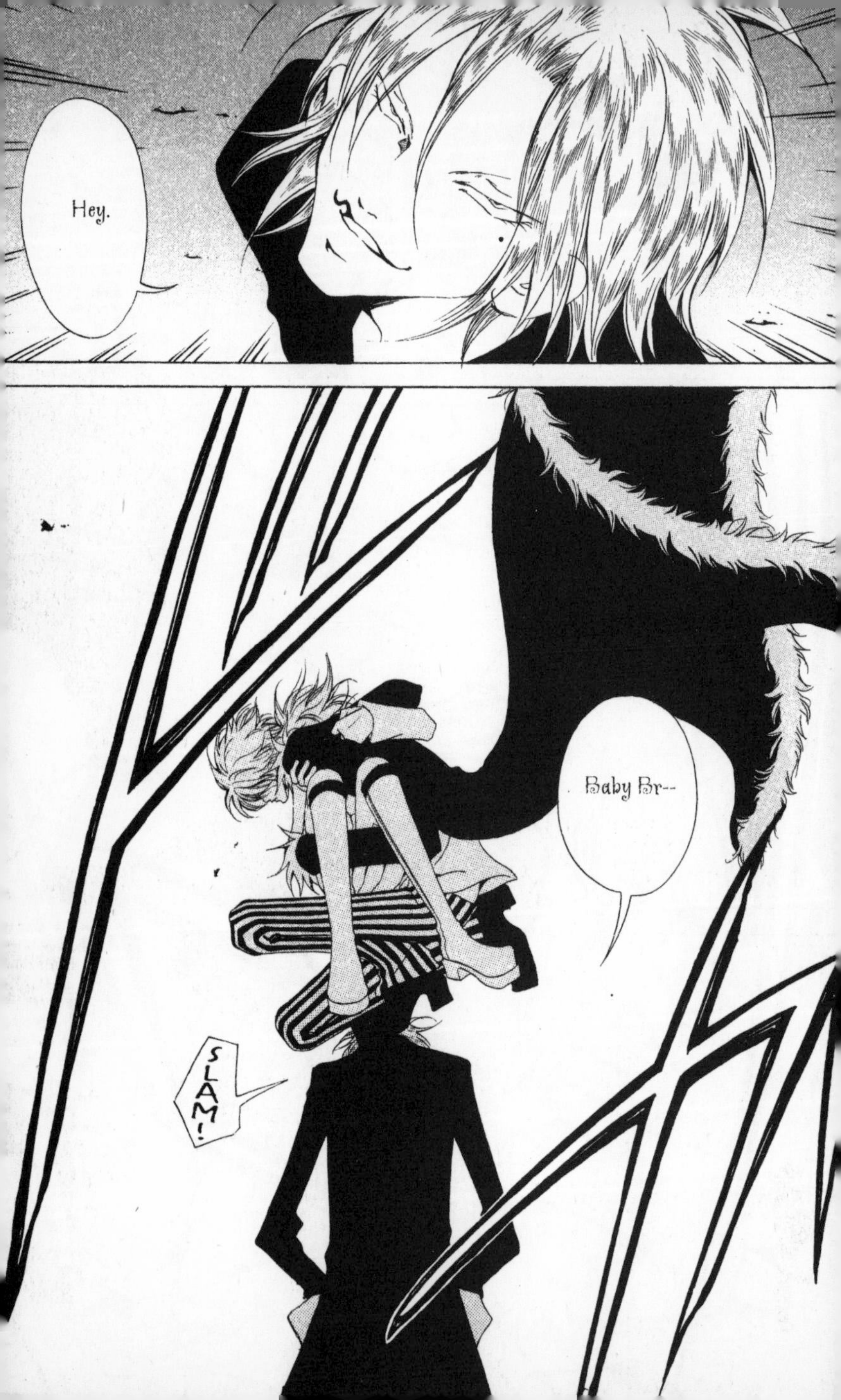
Hey.
Baby Br--
SLAM!

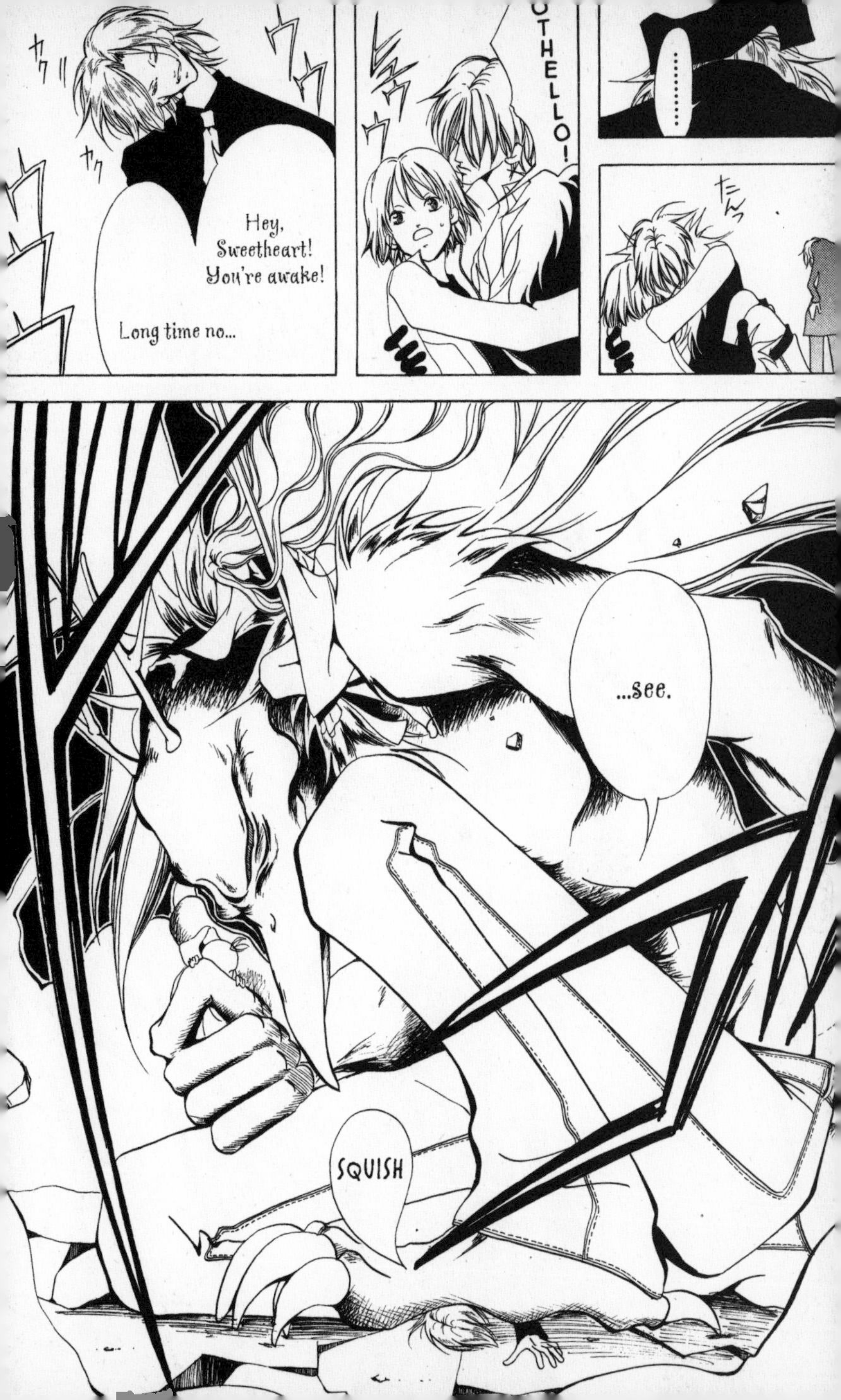
....
たんっ
OTHELLO!
Hey, Sweetheart! You're awake!
Long time no...
...see.
SQUISH

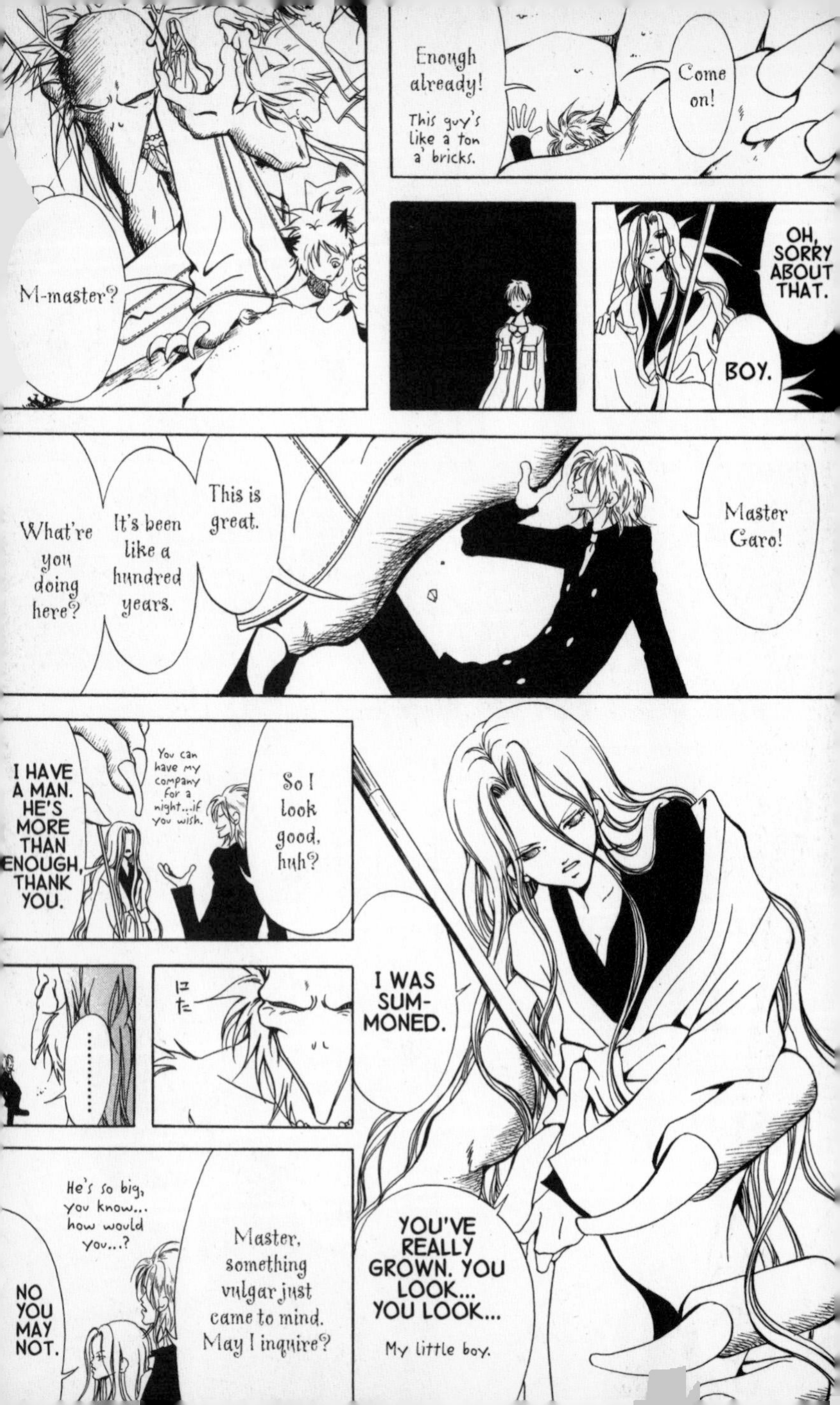
Come on!
Enough already!
This guy's like a ton a' bricks.
OH, SORRY ABOUT THAT.
BOY.
M-master?
Master Garo!
This is great.
It's been like a hundred years.
What're you doing here?
I WAS SUM-MONED.
YOU'VE REALLY GROWN. YOU LOOK... YOU LOOK...
My little boy.
So I look good, huh?
You can have my company for a night...if you wish.
I HAVE A MAN. HE'S MORE THAN ENOUGH, THANK YOU.
にた
......
Master, something vulgar just came to mind. May I inquire?
He's so big, you know... how would you...?
NO YOU MAY NOT.

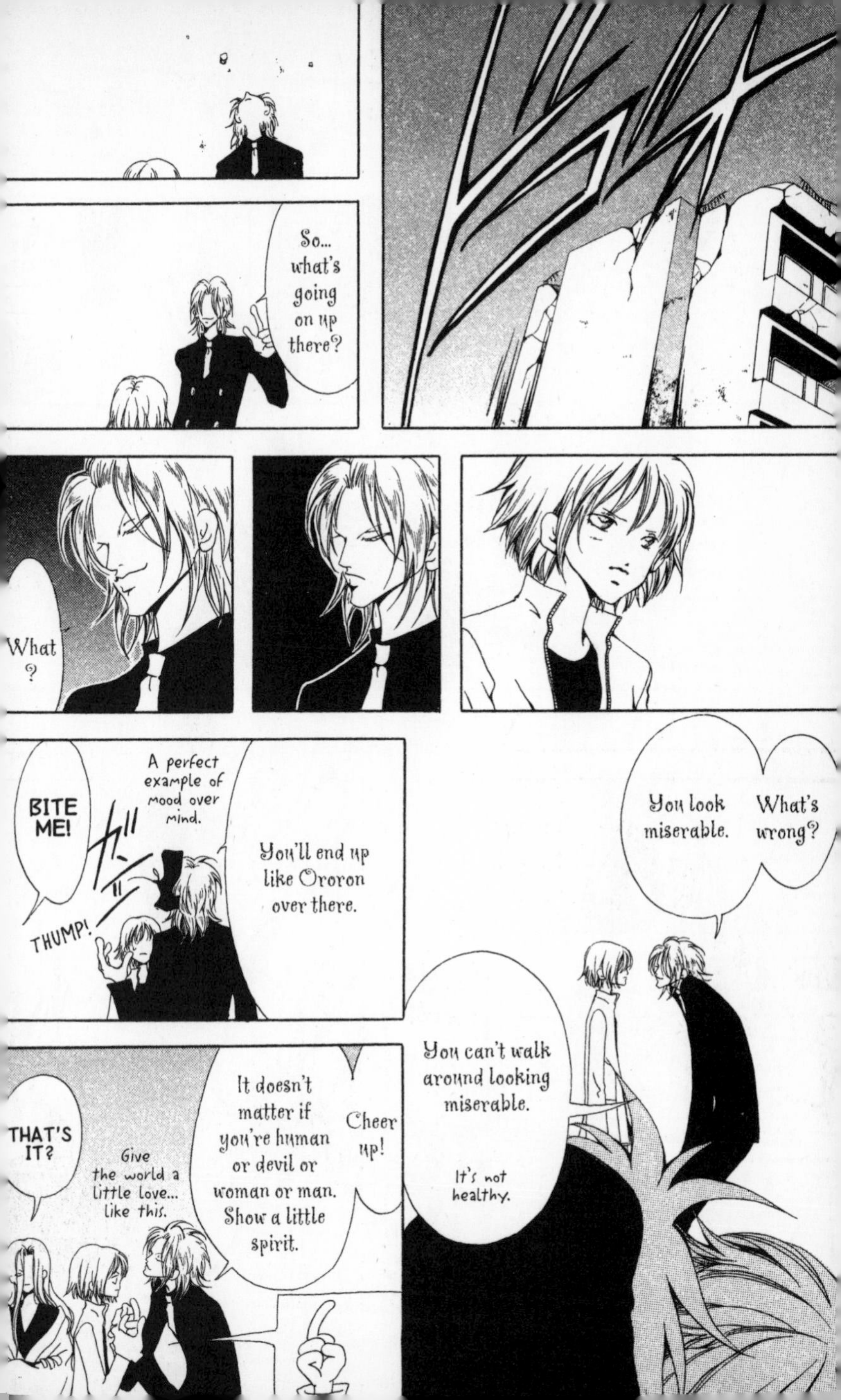
So... what's going on up there?
What?
What's wrong?
You look miserable.
You can't walk around looking miserable.
It's not healthy.
You'll end up like Ororon over there.
A perfect example of mood over mind.
BITE ME!
THUMP!
Cheer up!
It doesn't matter if you're human or devil or woman or man. Show a little spirit.
Give the world a little love... like this.
THAT'S IT?

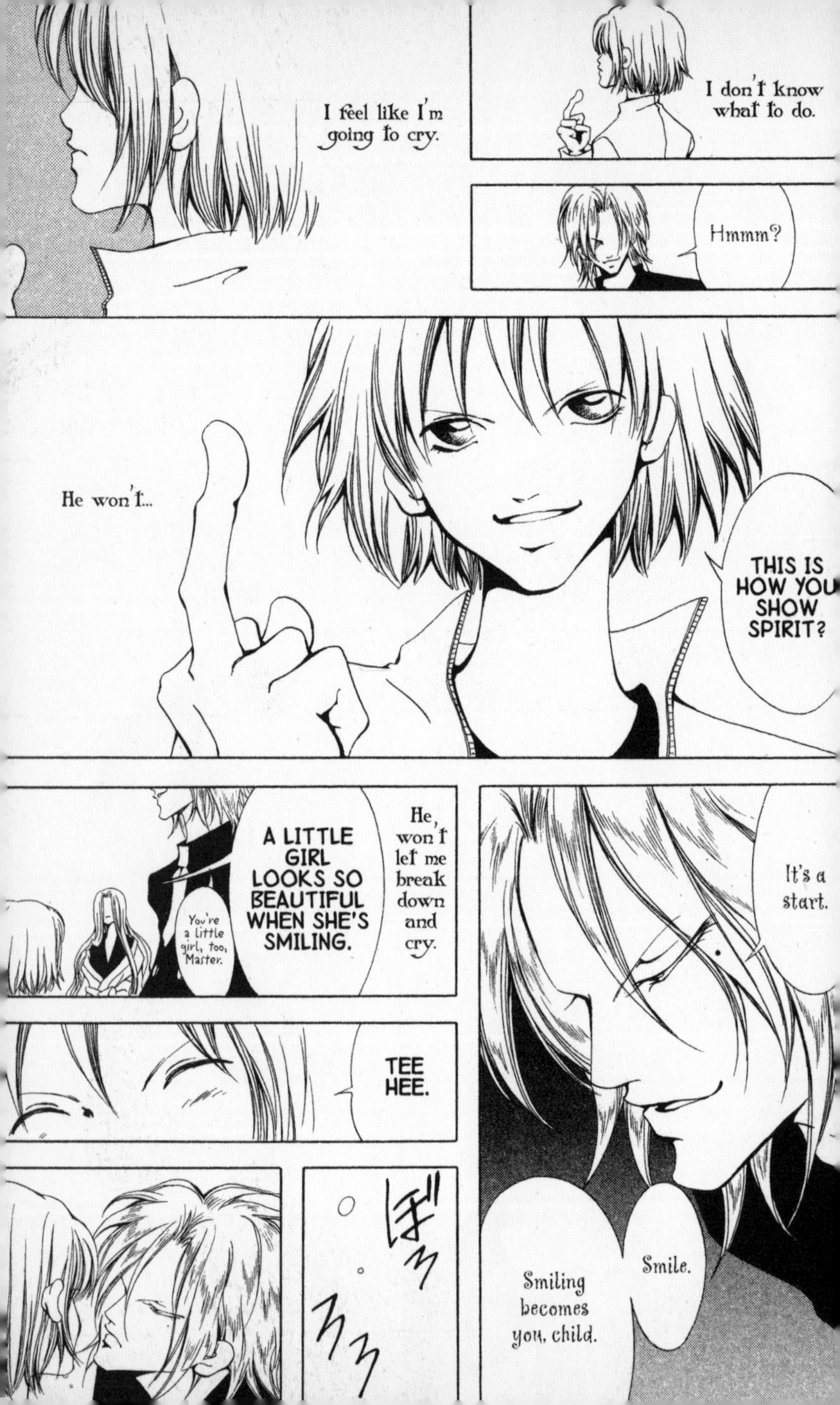

I don't know what to do.
Hmmm?
I feel like I'm going to cry.
THIS IS HOW YOU SHOW SPIRIT?
He won't...
It's a start.
Smile.
Smiling becomes you, child.
He, won't let me break down and cry.
A LITTLE GIRL LOOKS SO BEAUTIFUL WHEN SHE'S SMILING.
You're a little girl, too, Master.
TEE HEE.

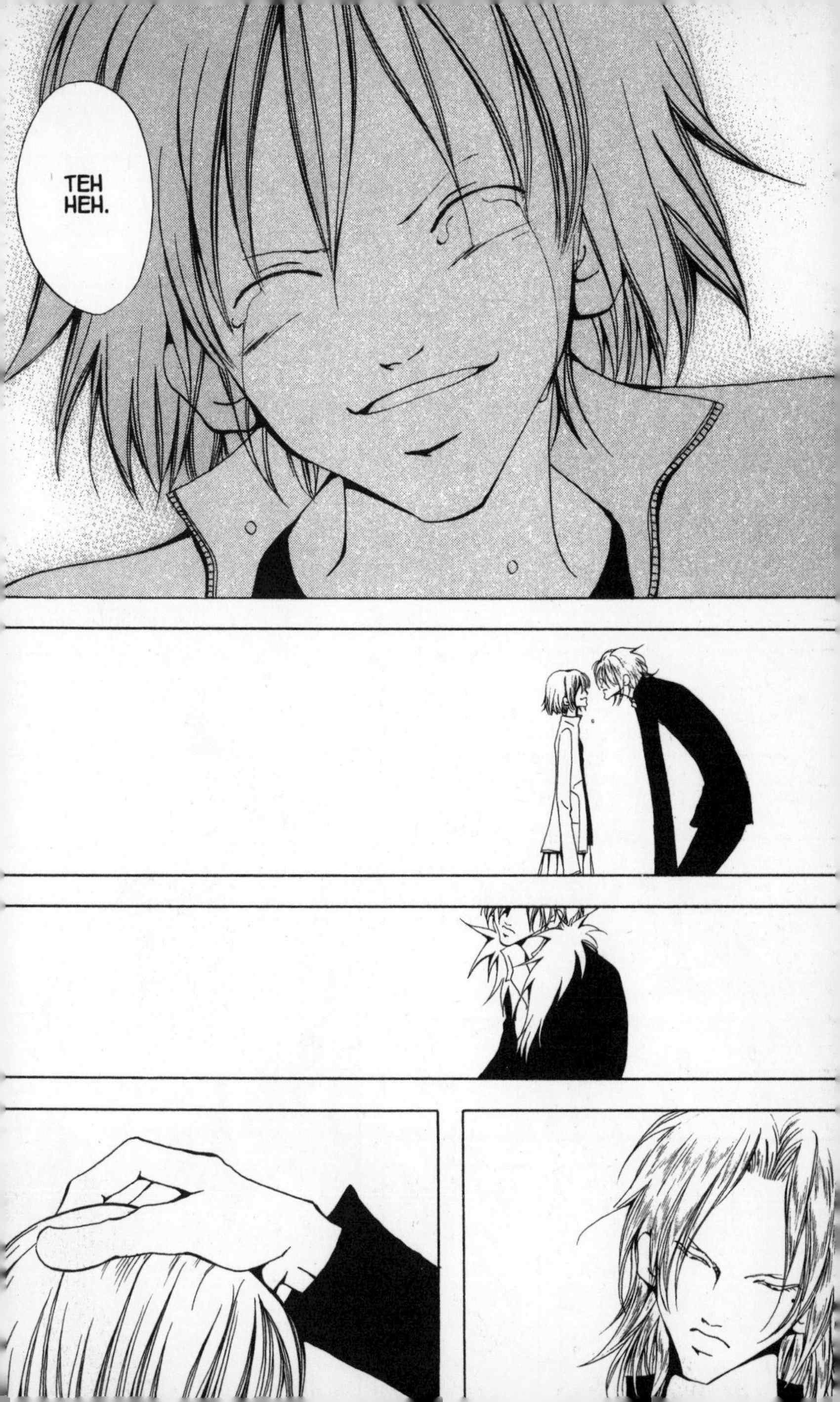
TEH HEH.

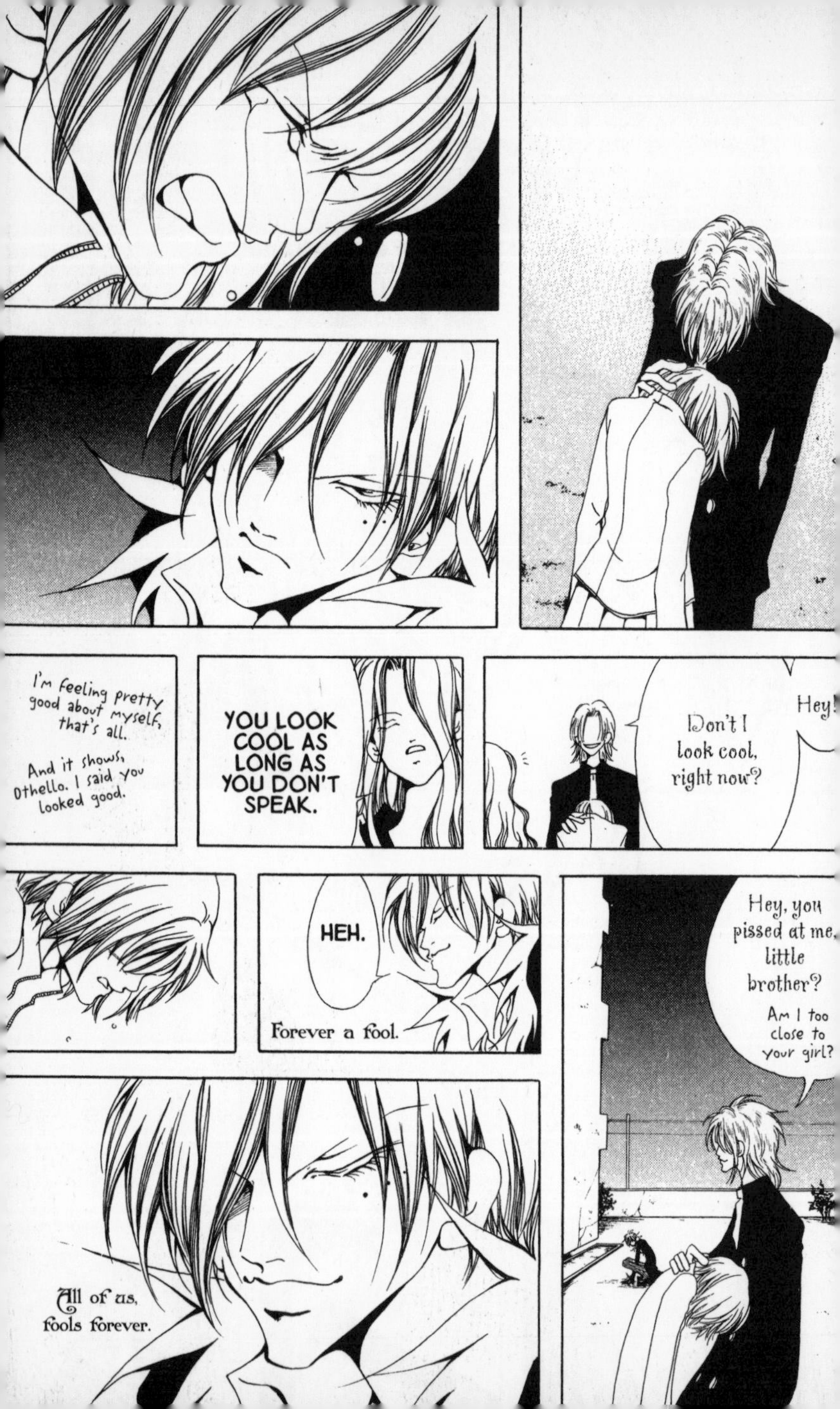
Hey!
Don't I look cool, right now?
YOU LOOK COOL AS LONG AS YOU DON'T SPEAK.
I'm feeling pretty good about myself, that's all.
And it shows, Othello. I said you looked good.
Hey, you pissed at me, little brother?
Am I too close to your girl?
HEH.
Forever a fool.
All of us, fools forever.

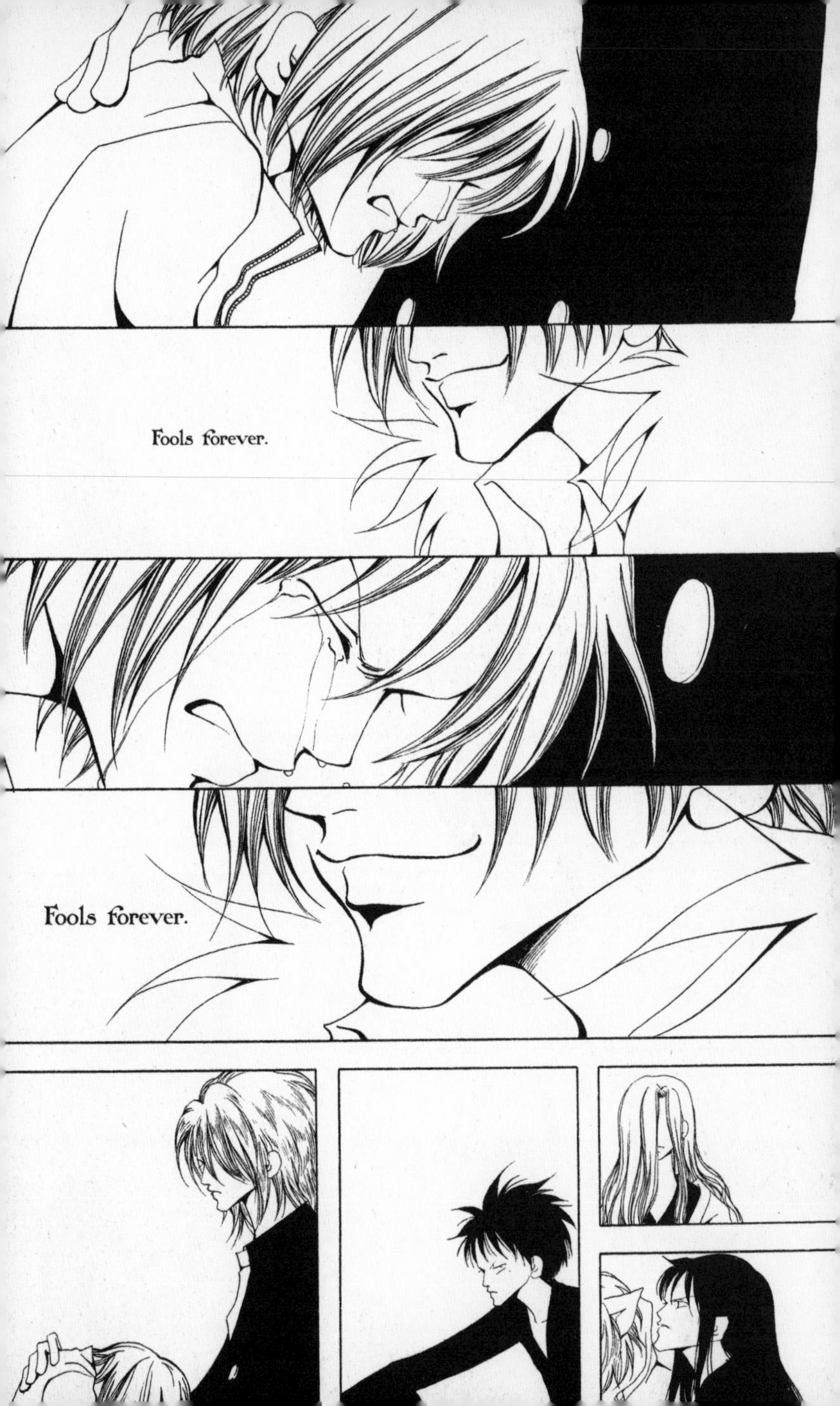
Fools forever.
Fools forever.

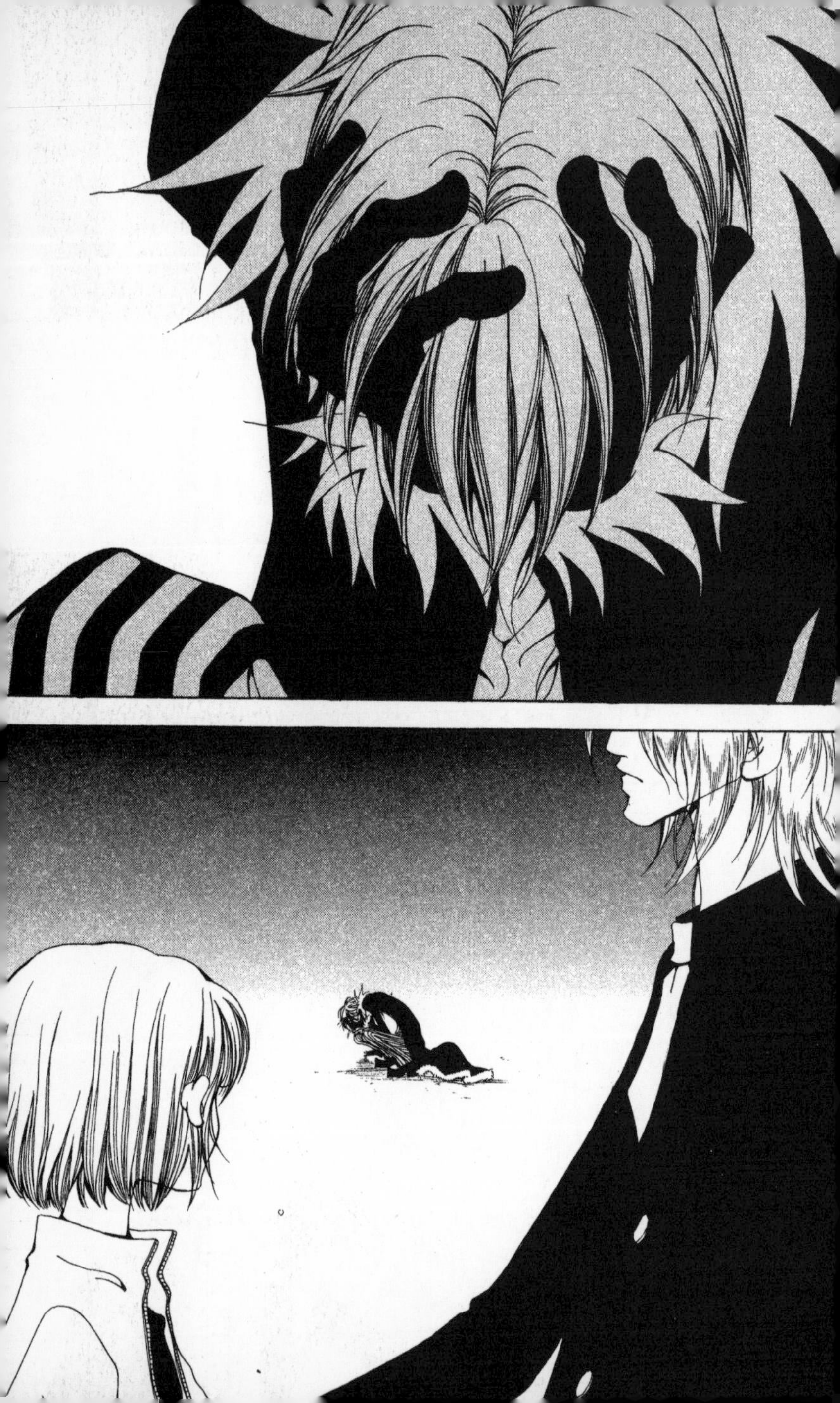

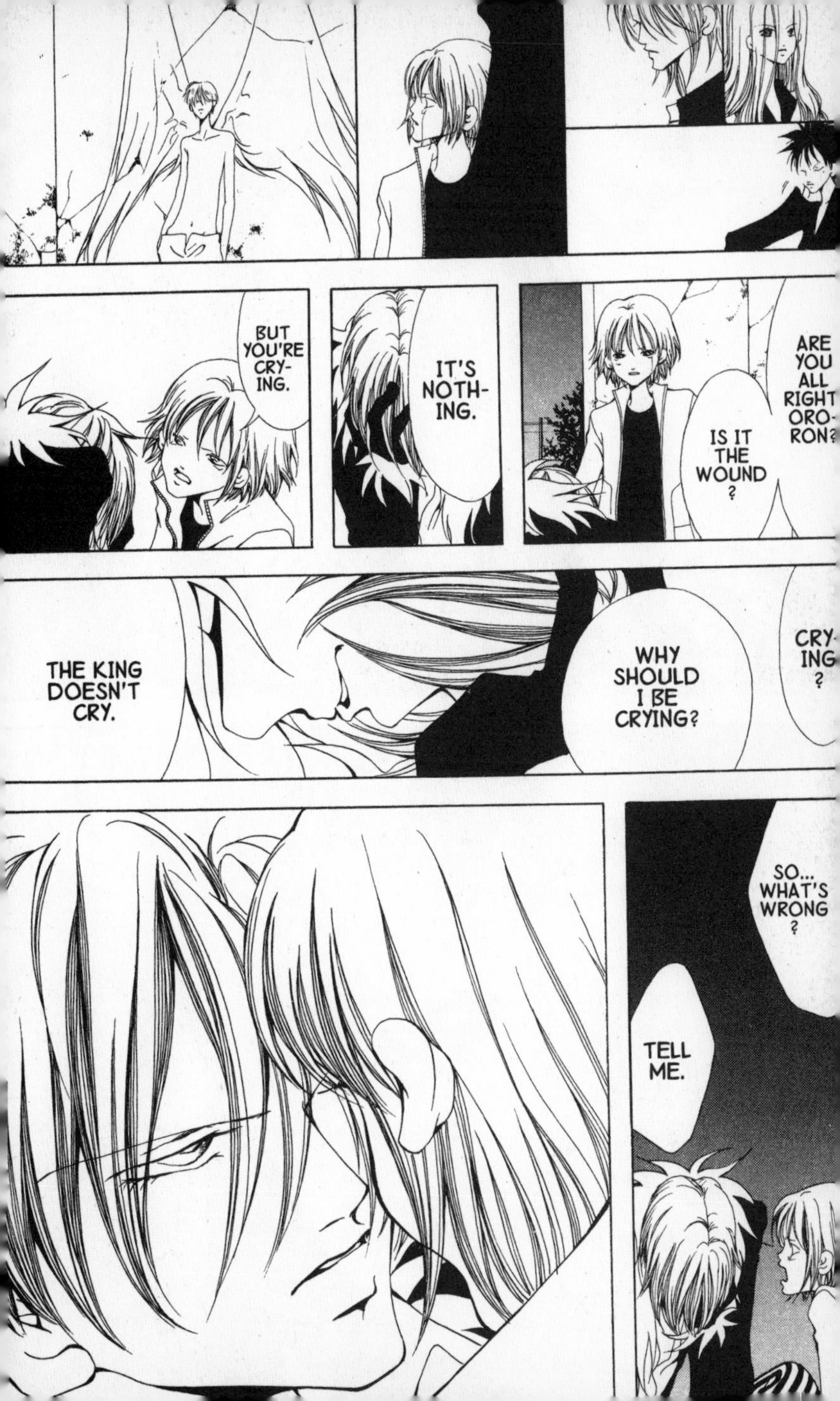
ARE YOU ALL RIGHT ORORON?
IS IT THE WOUND?
IT'S NOTHING.
BUT YOU'RE CRYING.
CRYING?
WHY SHOULD I BE CRYING?
THE KING DOESN'T CRY.
SO... WHAT'S WRONG?
TELL ME.

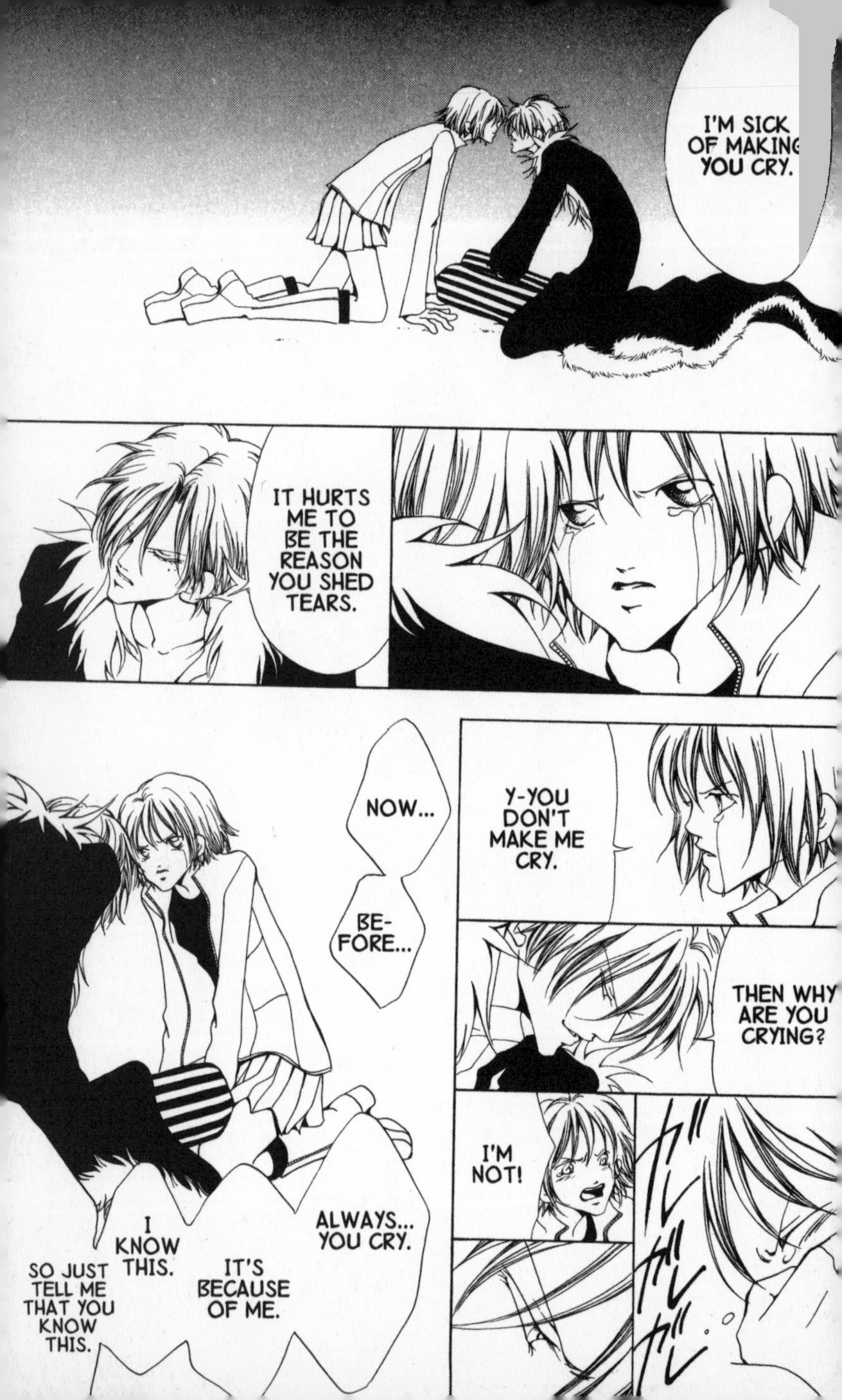
I'M SICK OF MAKING YOU CRY.
IT HURTS ME TO BE THE REASON YOU SHED TEARS.
Y-YOU DON'T MAKE ME CRY.
THEN WHY ARE YOU CRYING?
I'M NOT!
NOW...
BE-FORE...
ALWAYS... YOU CRY.
IT'S BECAUSE OF ME.
I KNOW THIS.
SO JUST TELL ME THAT YOU KNOW THIS.

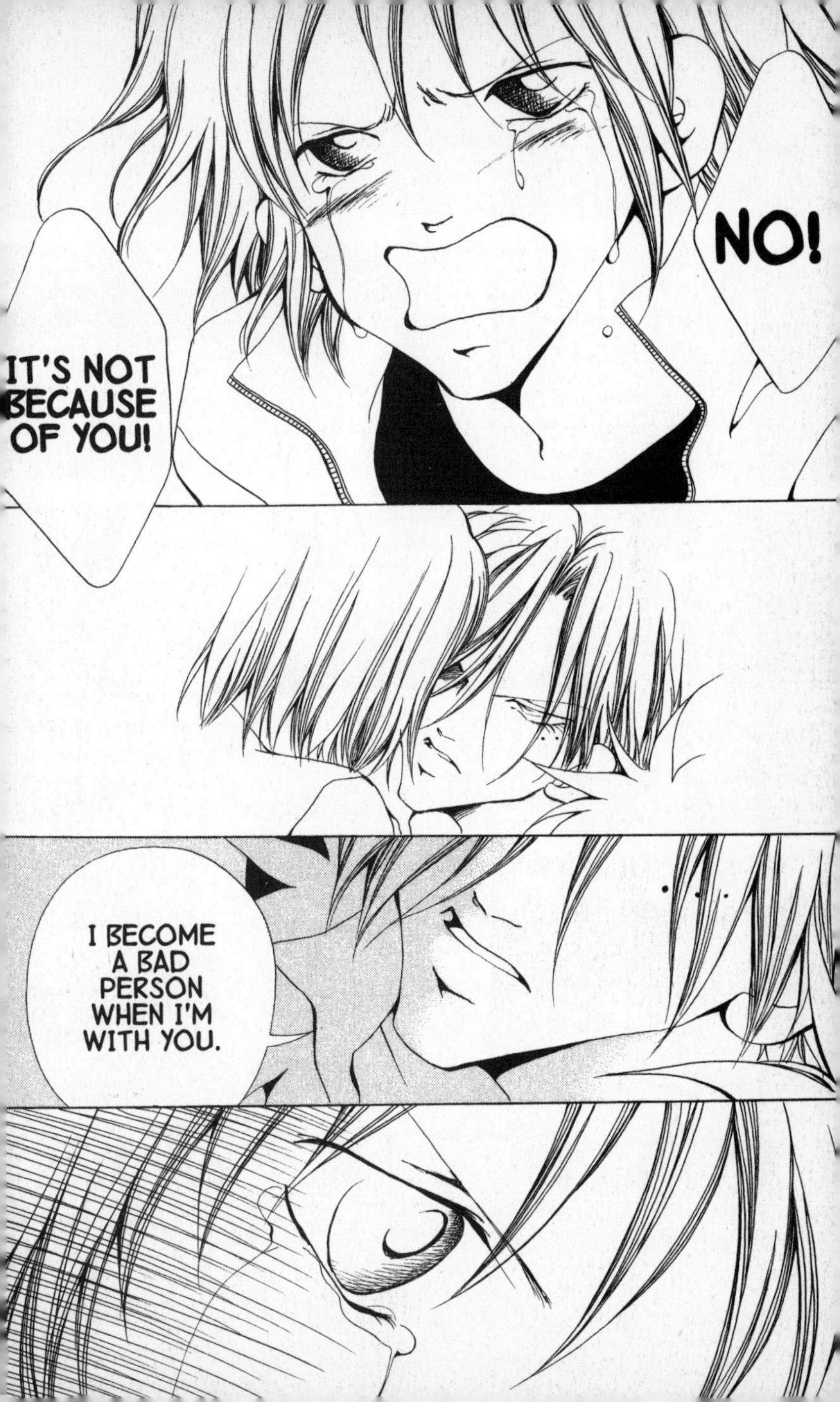
NO!
IT'S NOT BECAUSE OF YOU!
I BECOME A BAD PERSON WHEN I'M WITH YOU.

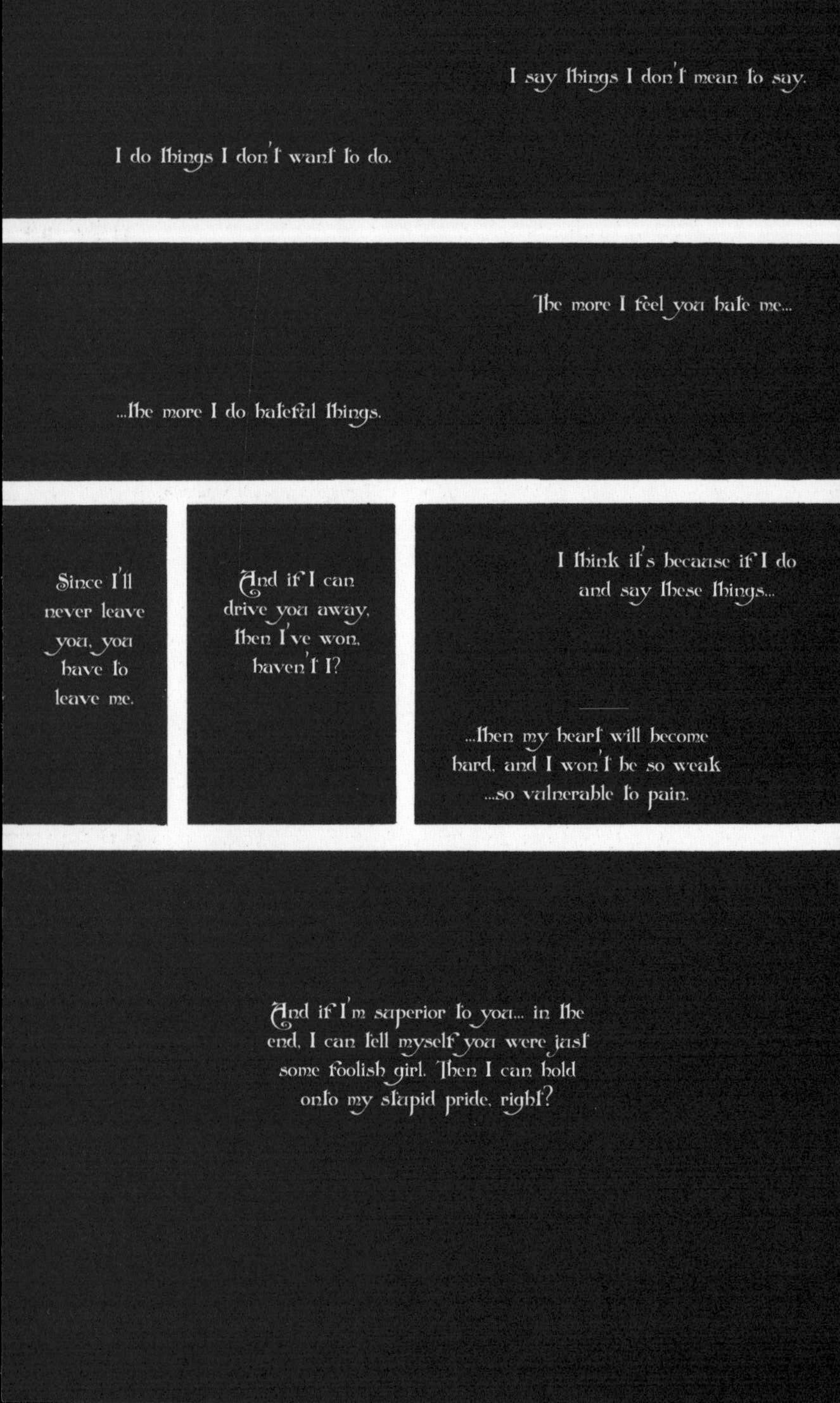
I say things I don't mean to say.
I do things I don't want to do.
The more I feel you hate me...
...the more I do hateful things.
I think it's because if I do and say these things...
...then my heart will become hard, and I won't be so weak ...so vulnerable to pain.
And if I can drive you away, then I've won, haven't I?
Since I'll never leave you, you have to leave me.
And if I'm superior to you... in the end, I can tell myself you were just some foolish girl. Then I can hold onto my stupid pride, right?

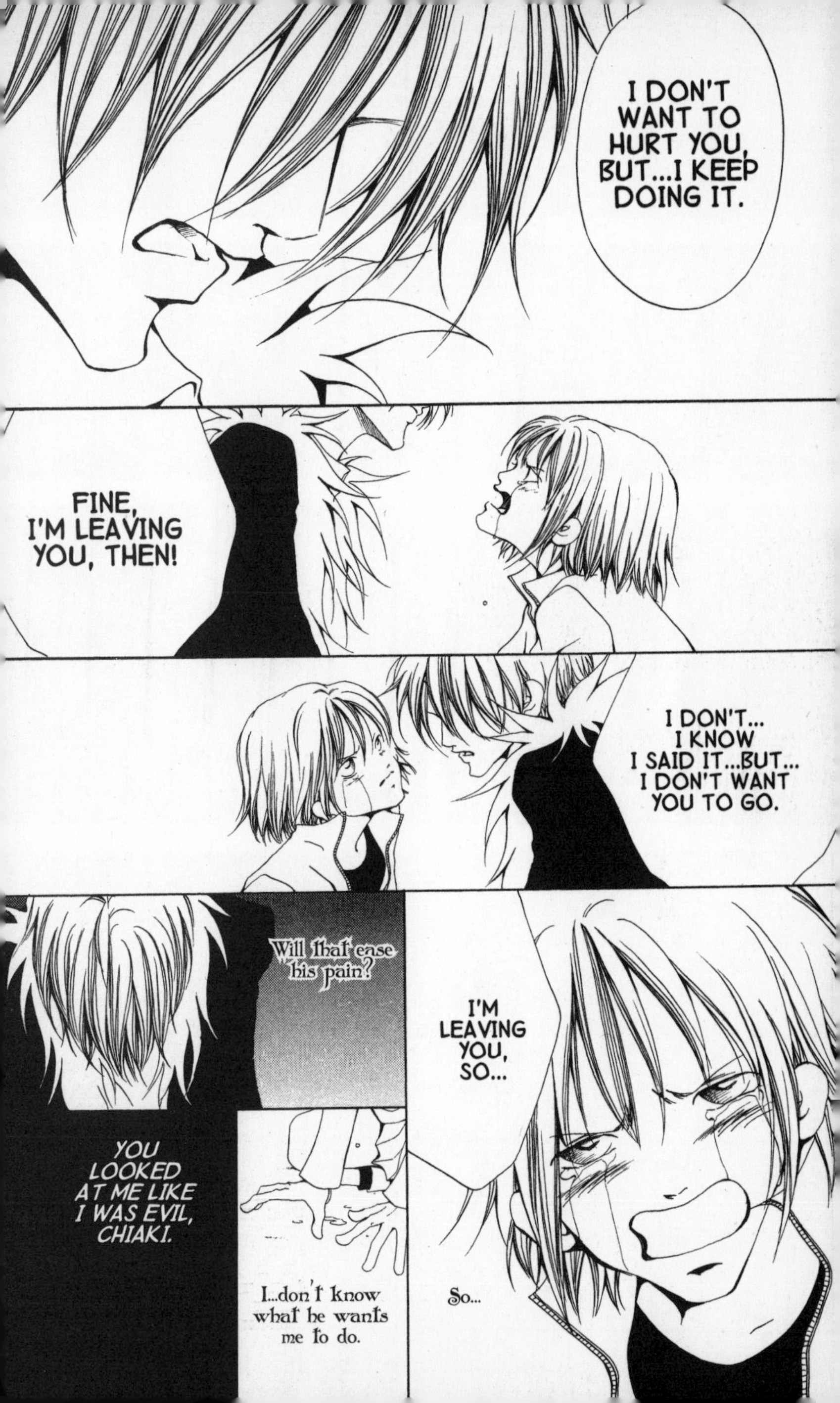
I DON'T WANT TO HURT YOU, BUT...I KEEP DOING IT.
FINE, I'M LEAVING YOU, THEN!
I DON'T... I KNOW I SAID IT...BUT... I DON'T WANT YOU TO GO.
I'M LEAVING YOU, SO...
So...
Will that ease his pain?
I...don't know what he wants me to do.
YOU LOOKED AT ME LIKE I WAS EVIL, CHIAKI.

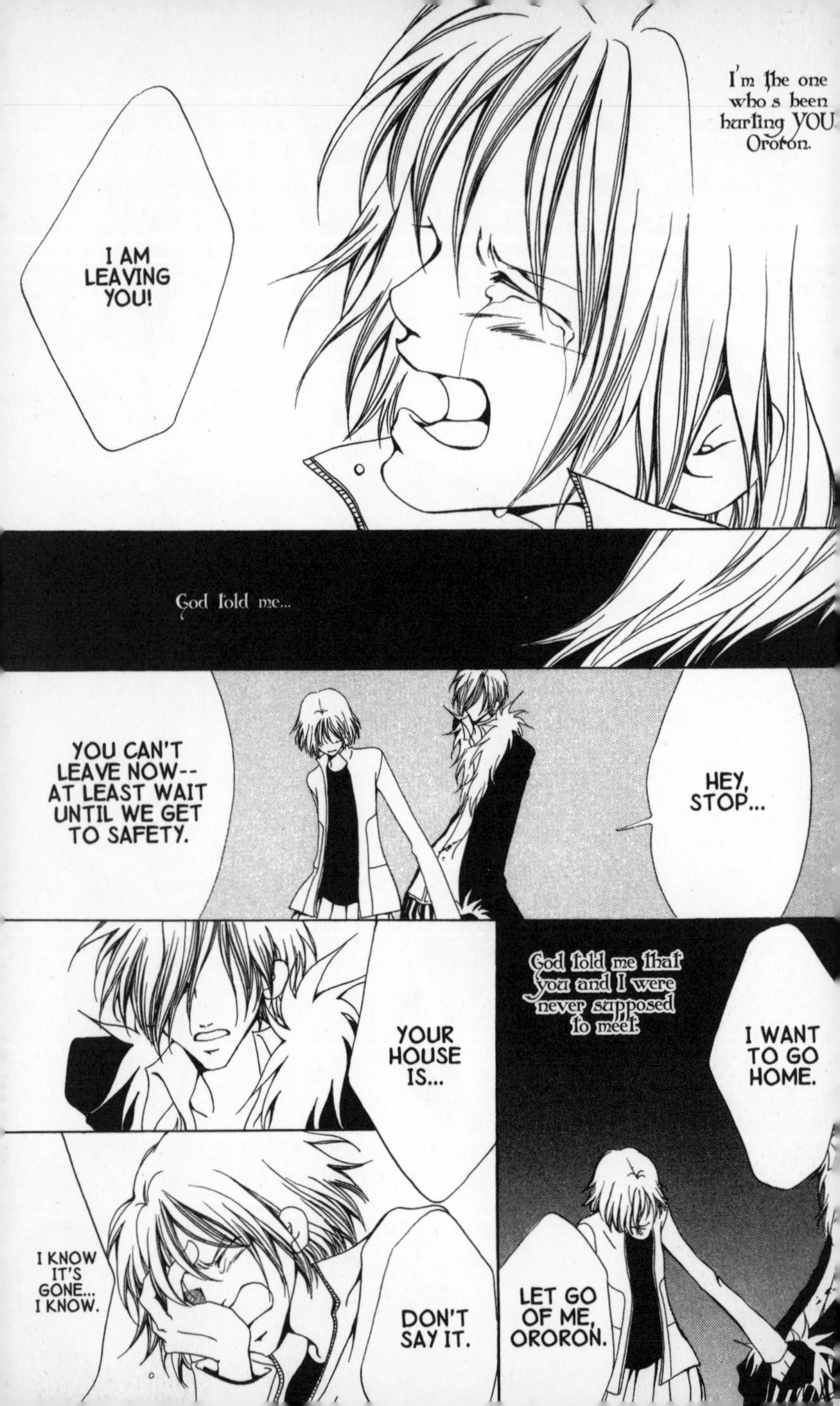
I'm the one who's been hurting YOU, Ororon.
I AM LEAVING YOU!
God told me...
HEY, STOP...
YOU CAN'T LEAVE NOW-- AT LEAST WAIT UNTIL WE GET TO SAFETY.
I WANT TO GO HOME.
God told me that you and I were never supposed to meet.
LET GO OF ME, ORORON.
YOUR HOUSE IS...
DON'T SAY IT.
I KNOW IT'S GONE... I KNOW.

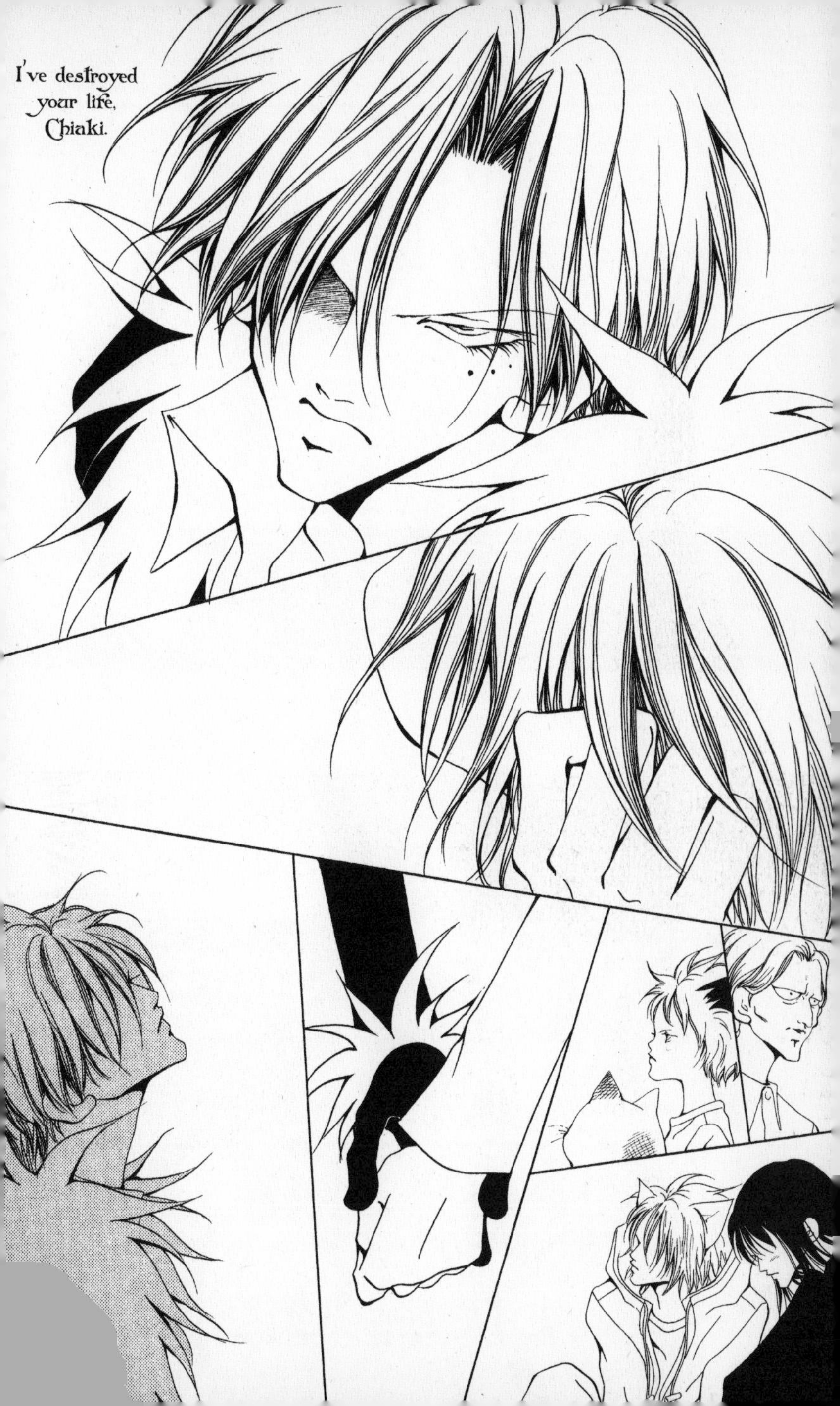
I've destroyed your life, Chiaki.

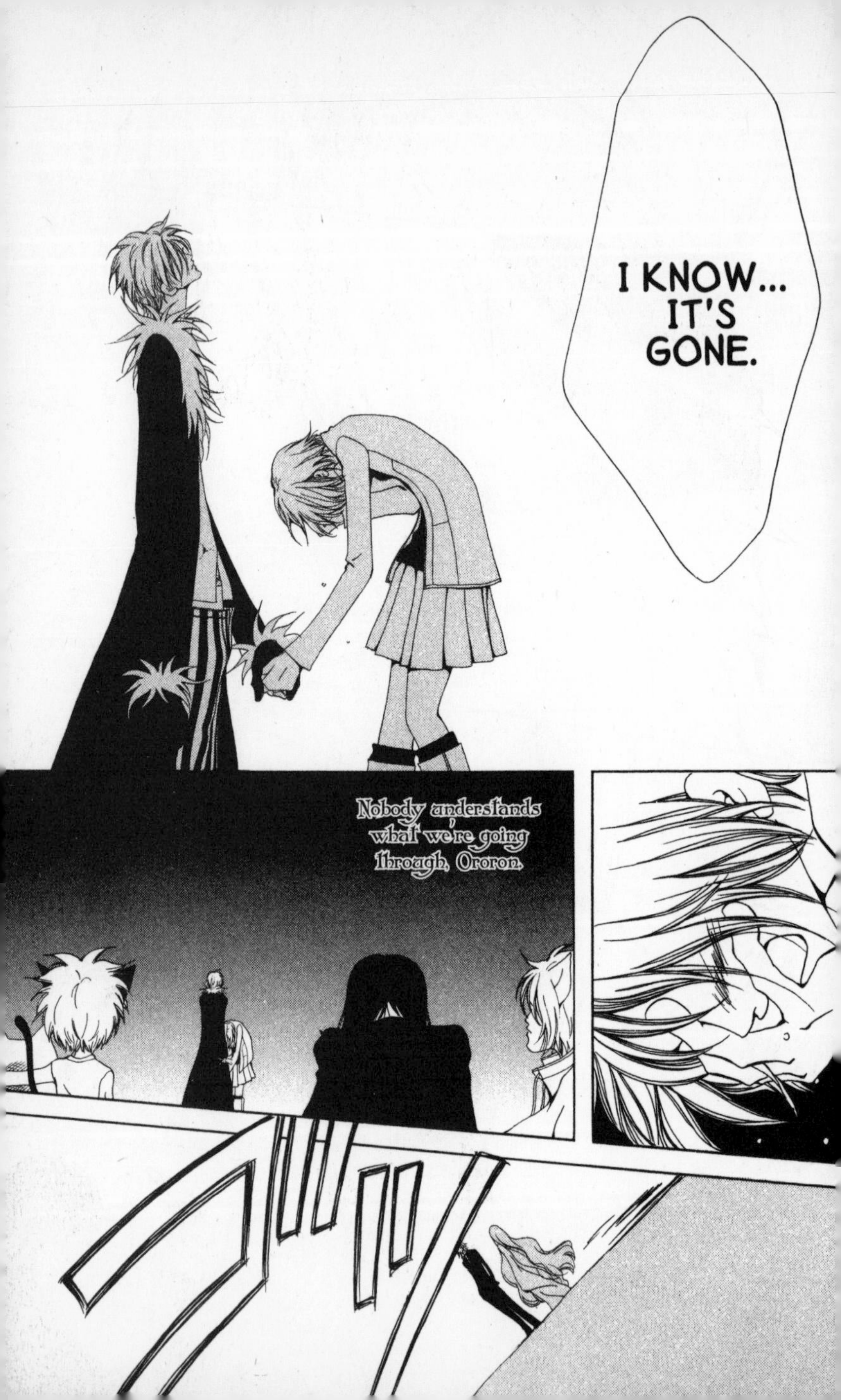
I KNOW... IT'S GONE.
Nobody understands what we're going through, Ororon.

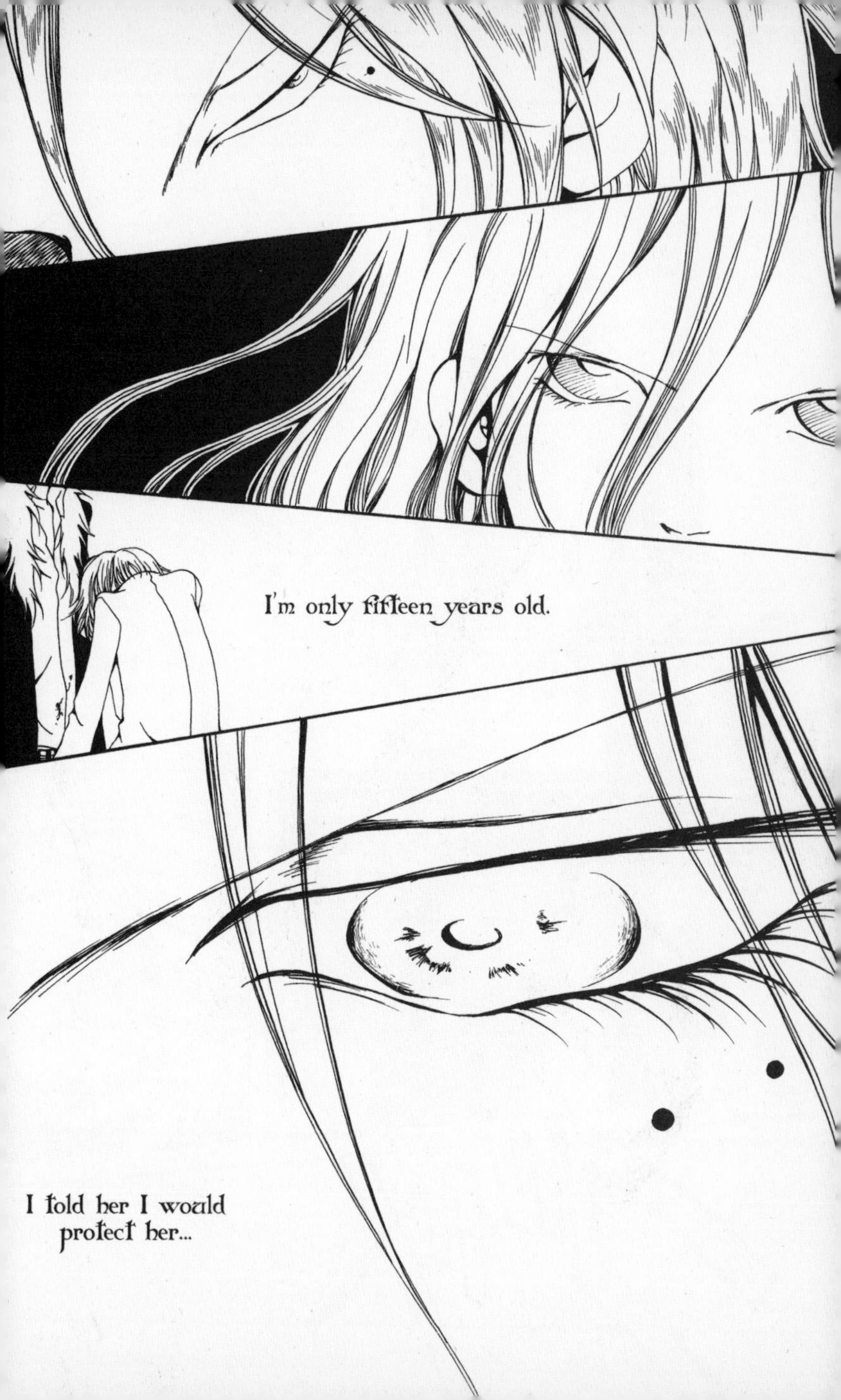
I'm only fifteen years old.
I told her I would protect her...

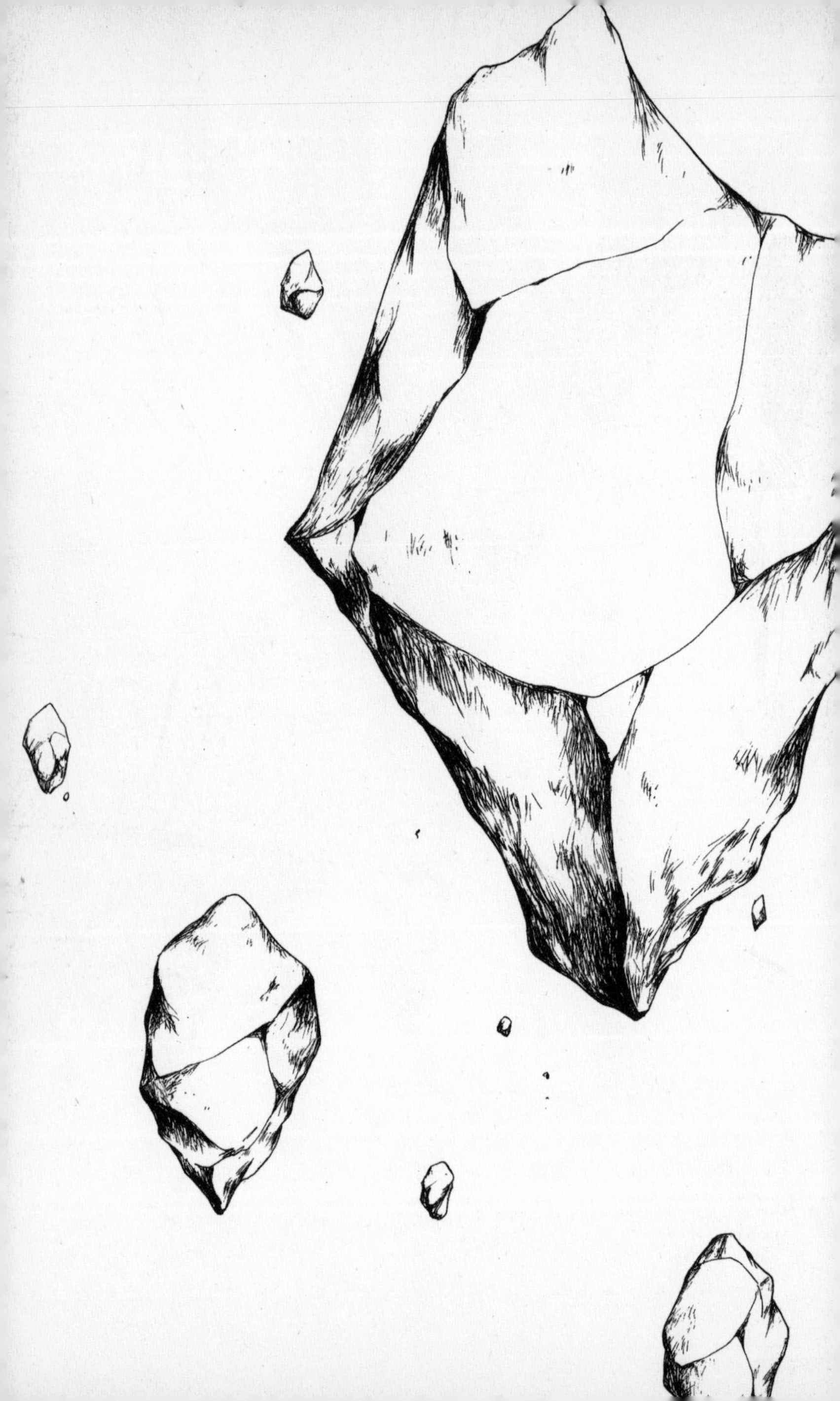

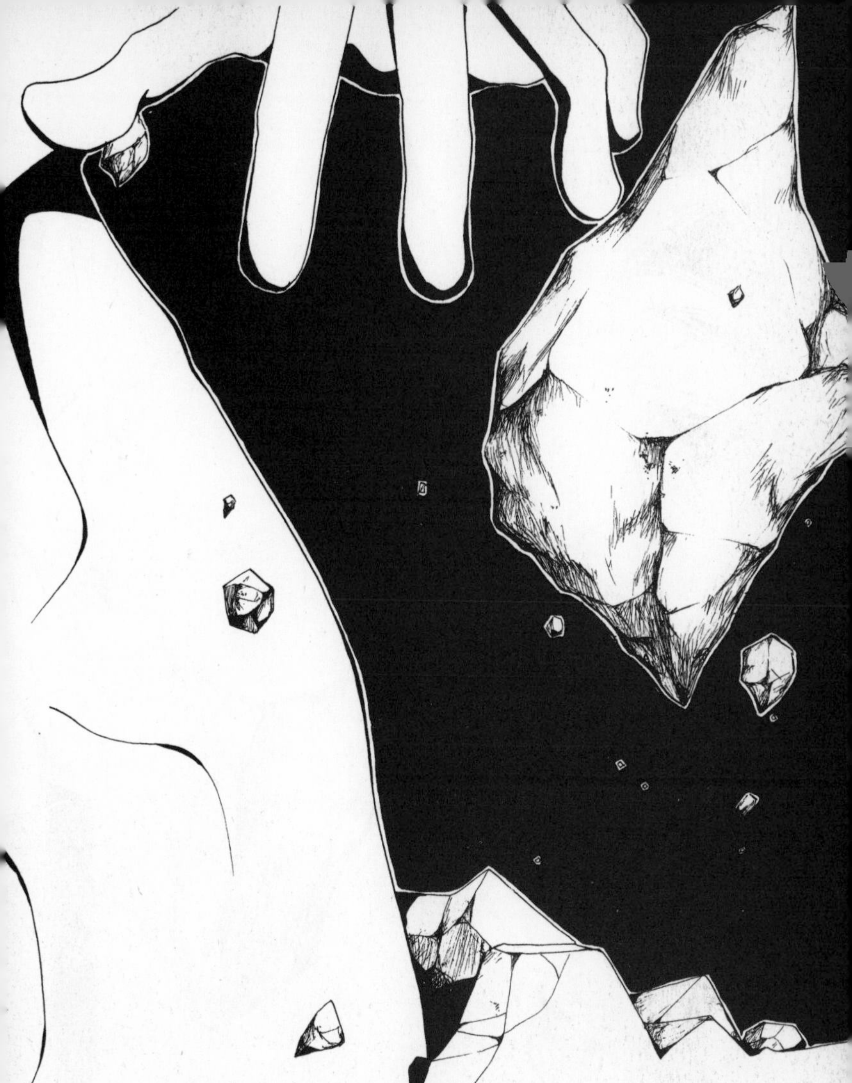

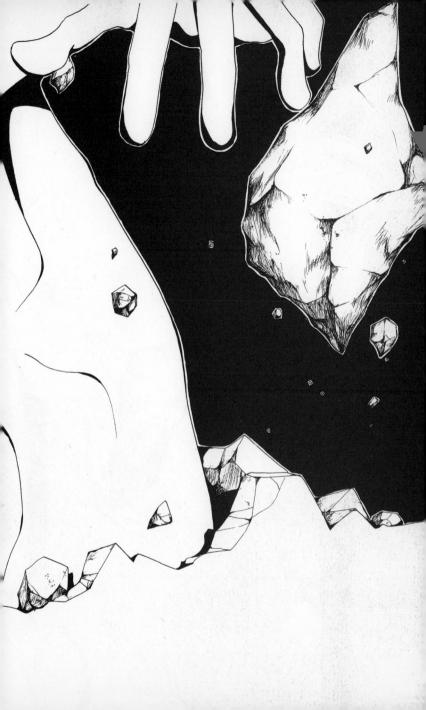

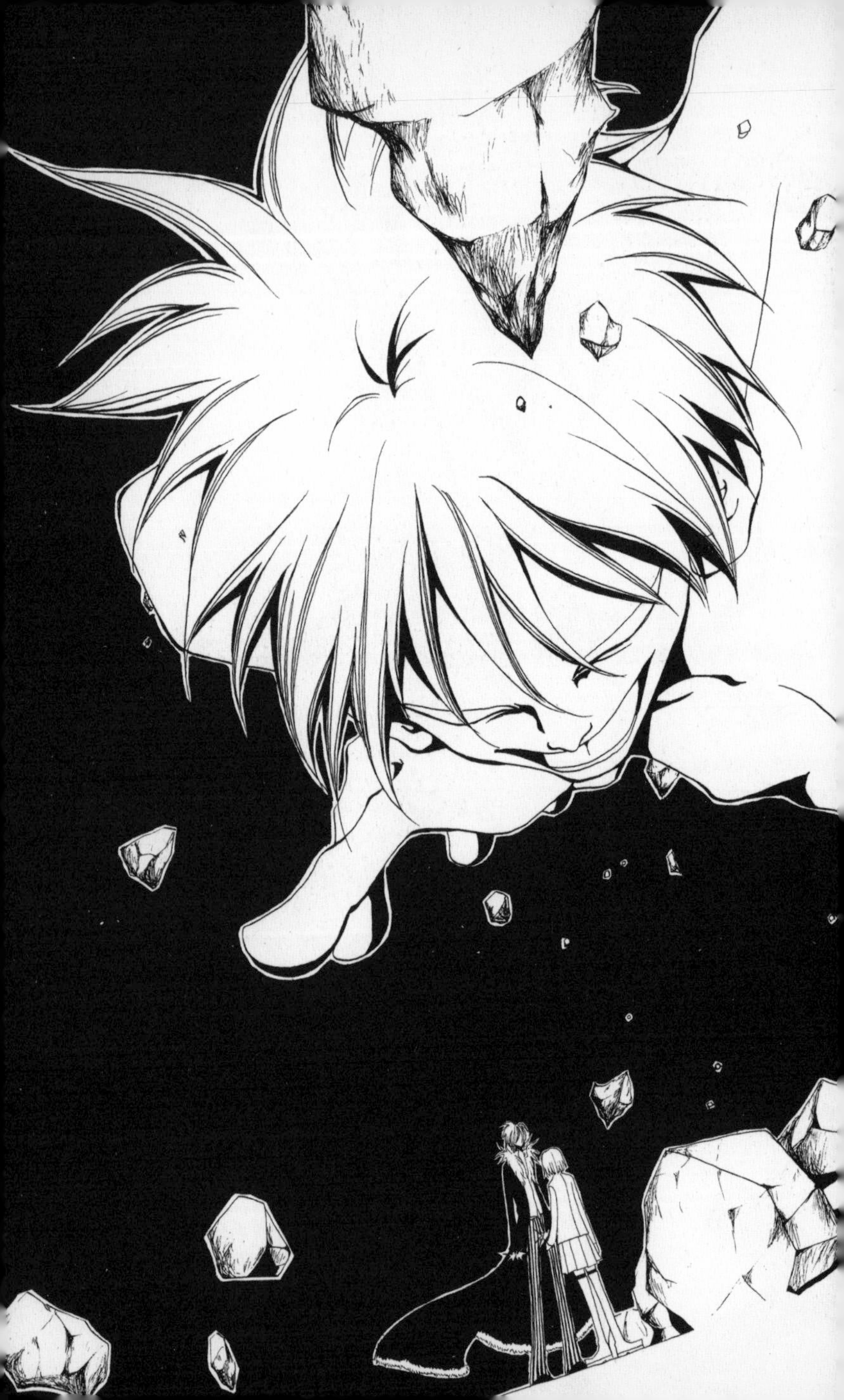

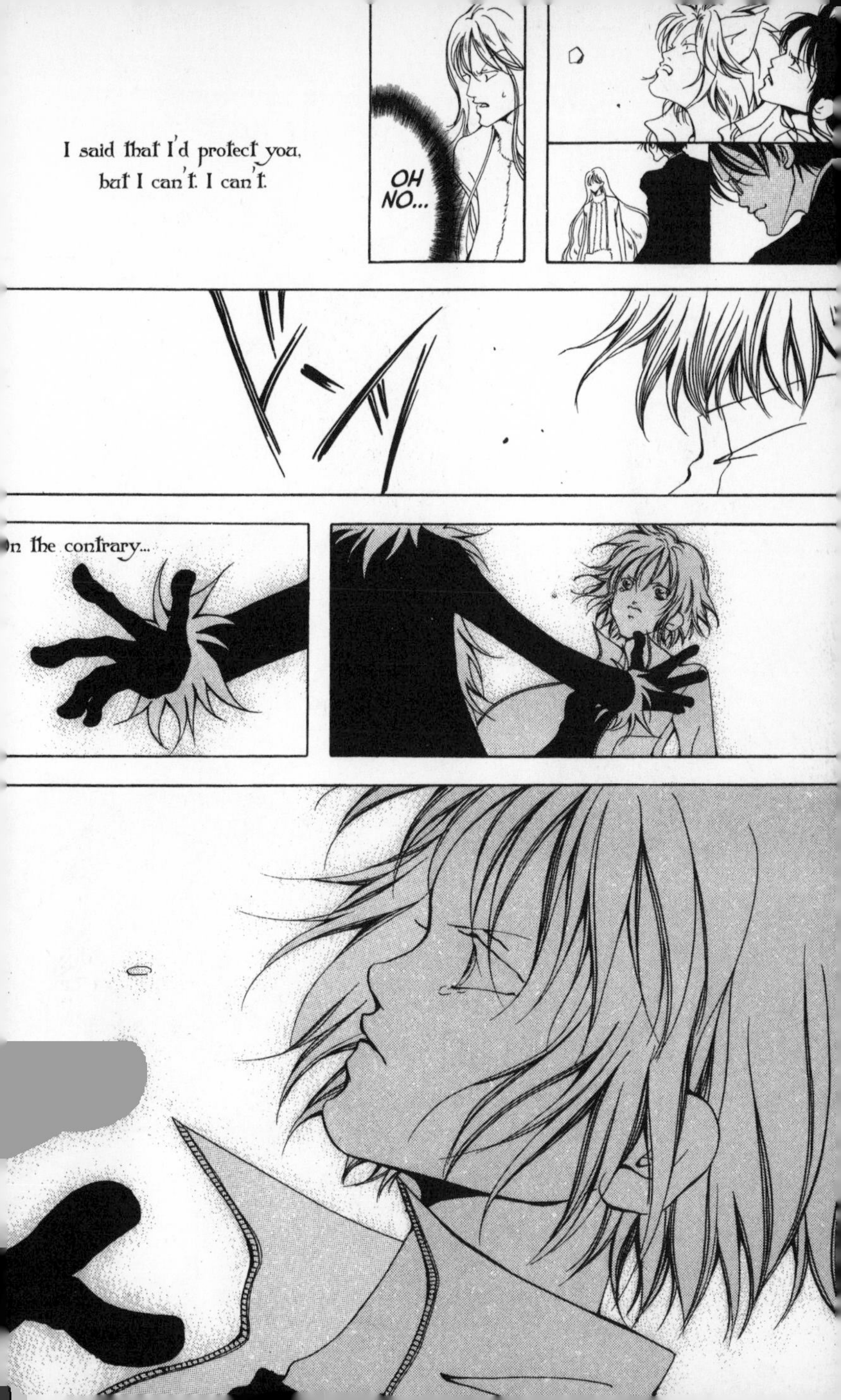
OH NO...
I said that I'd protect you,
but I can't. I can't.
n the contrary...

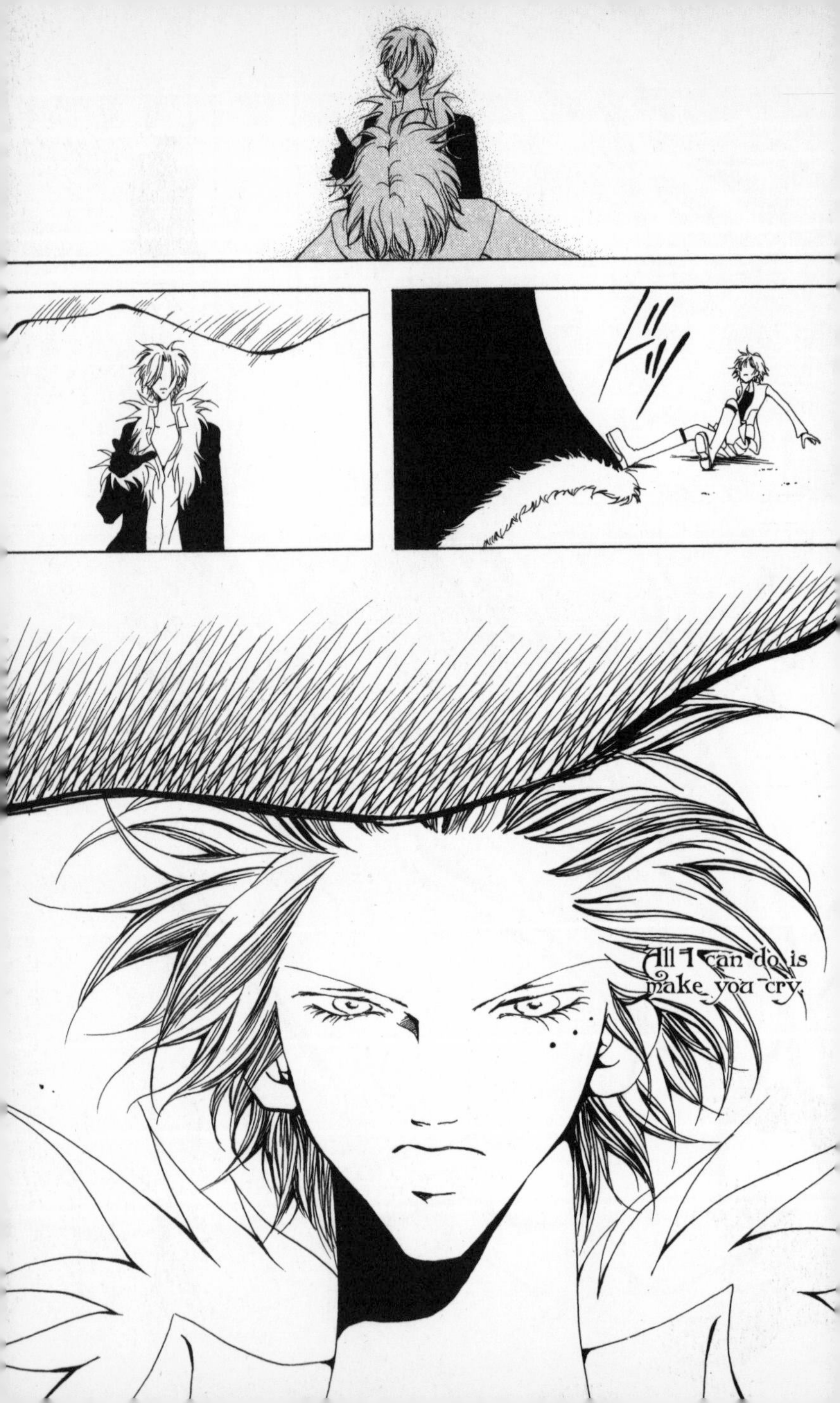
All I can do is make you cry.

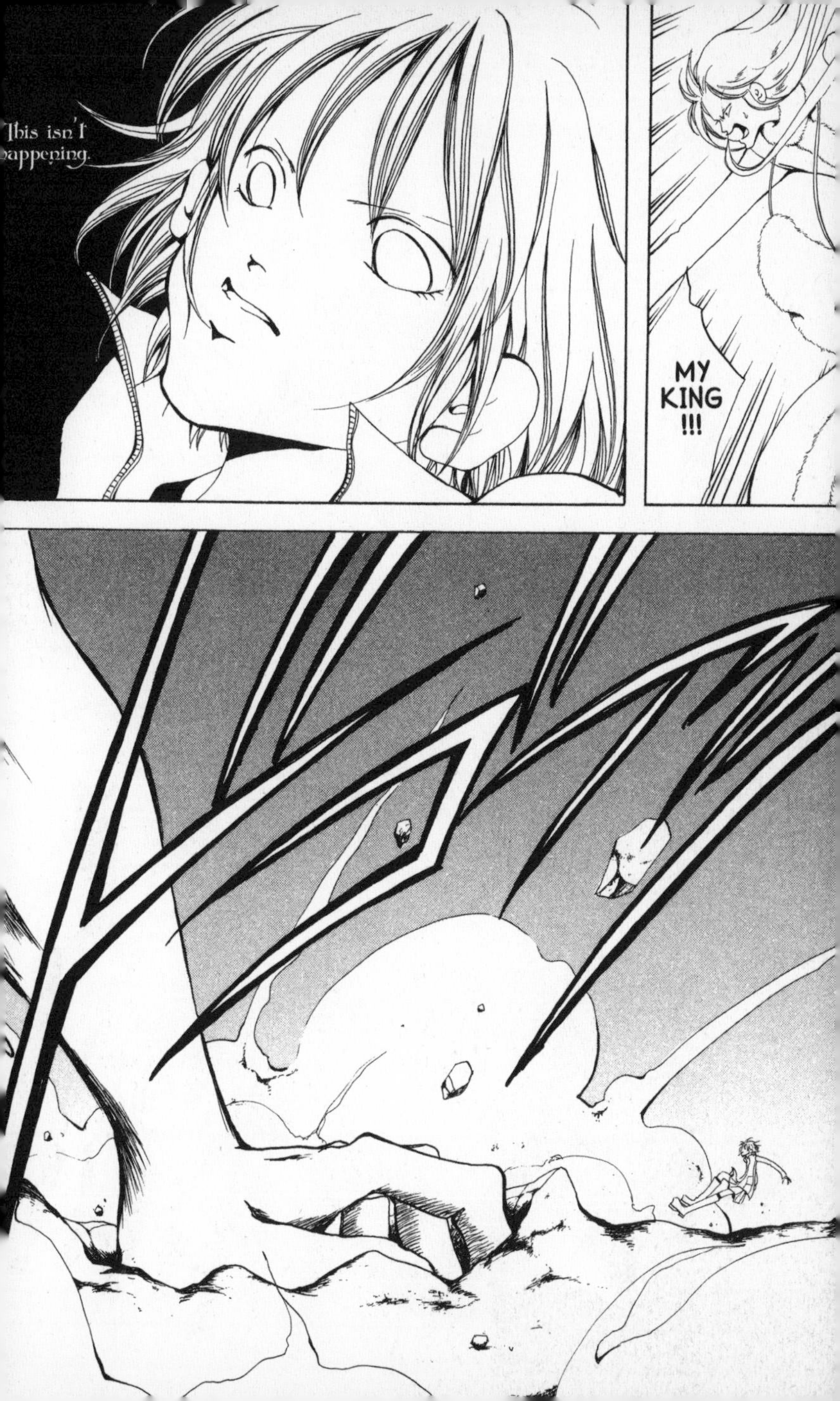
MY KING !!!
This isn't appening.

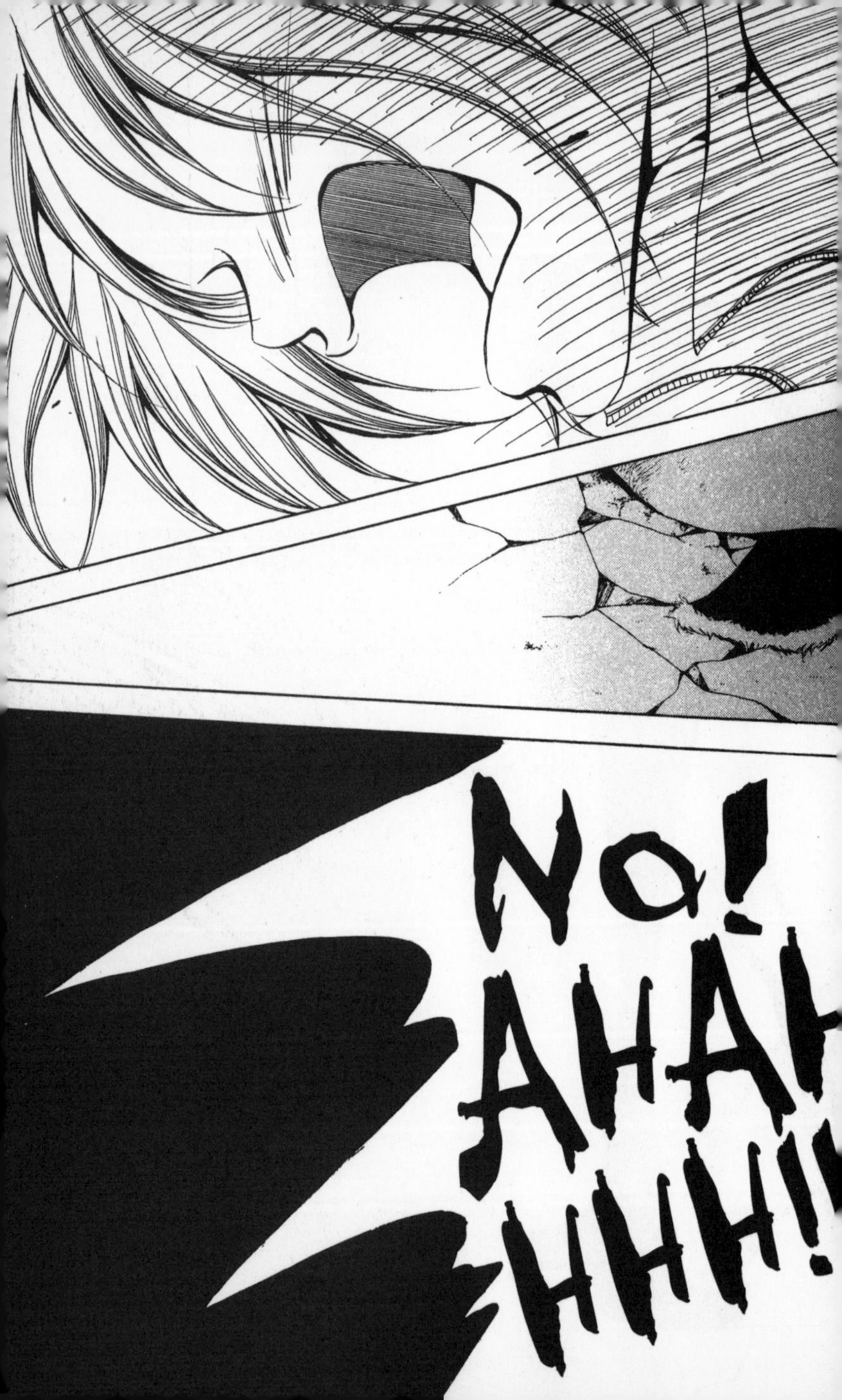
No! AHAHHH!!

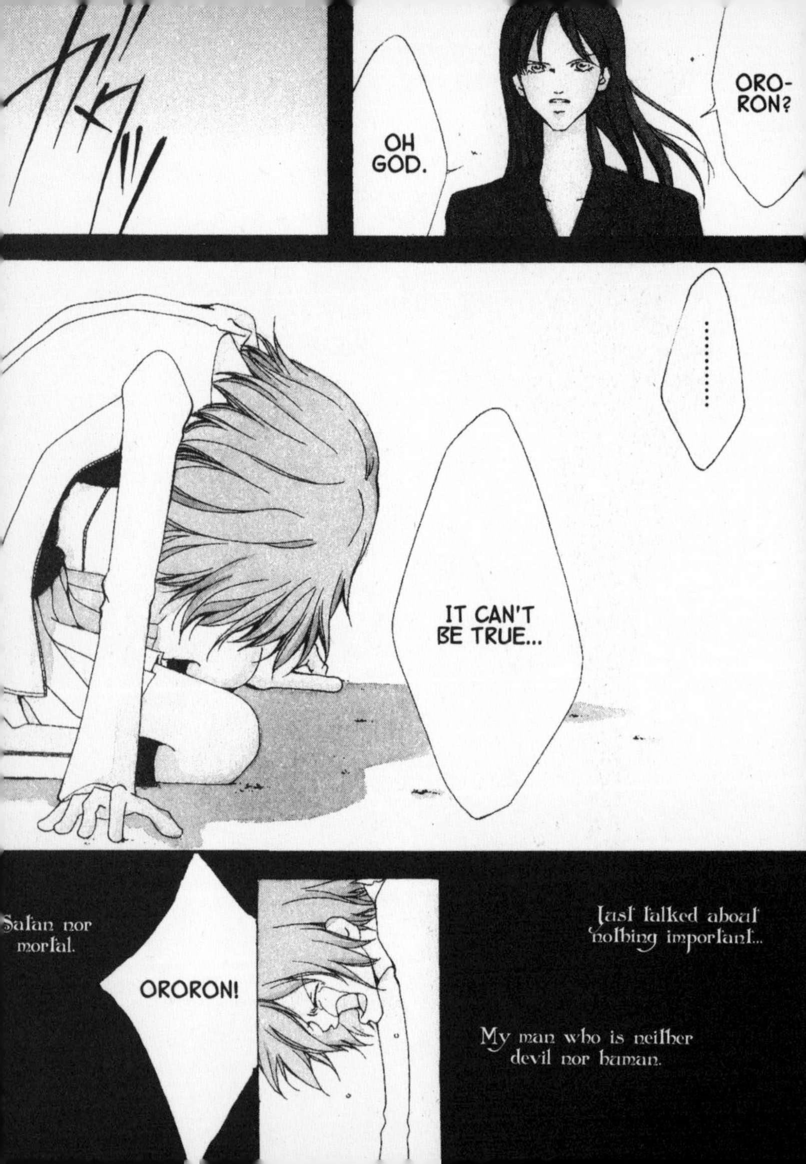
ORO-RON?
OH GOD.
......
IT CAN'T BE TRUE...
Just talked about nothing important...
My man who is neither devil nor human.
ORORON!
Satan nor mortal.

-16- Long Night 03

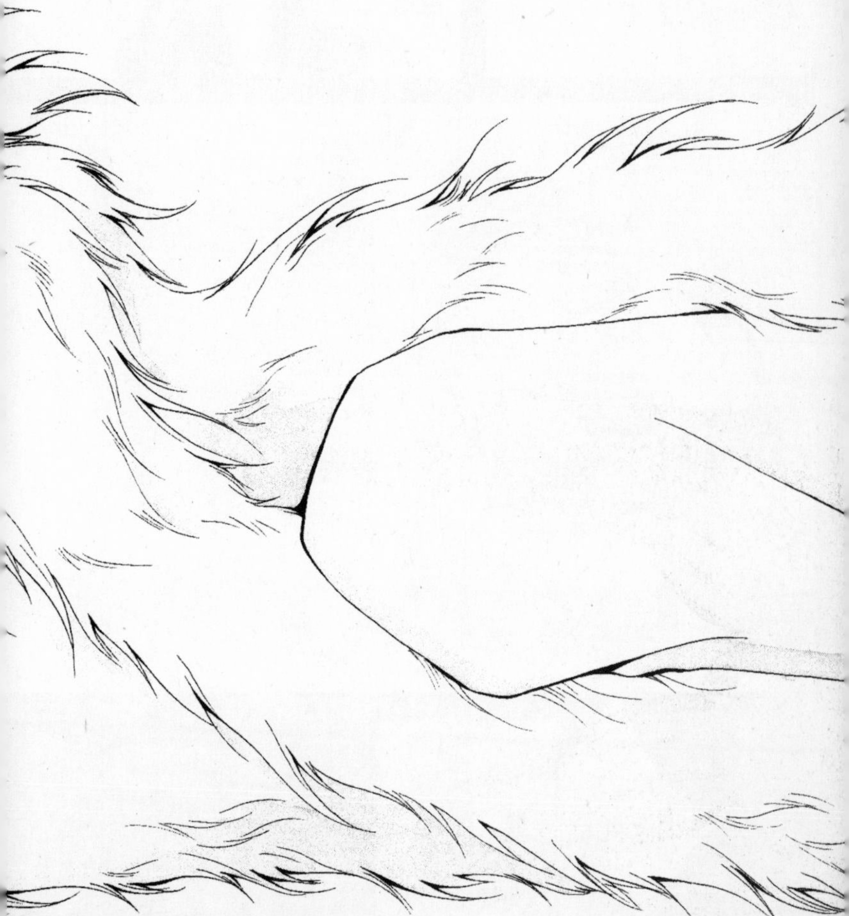

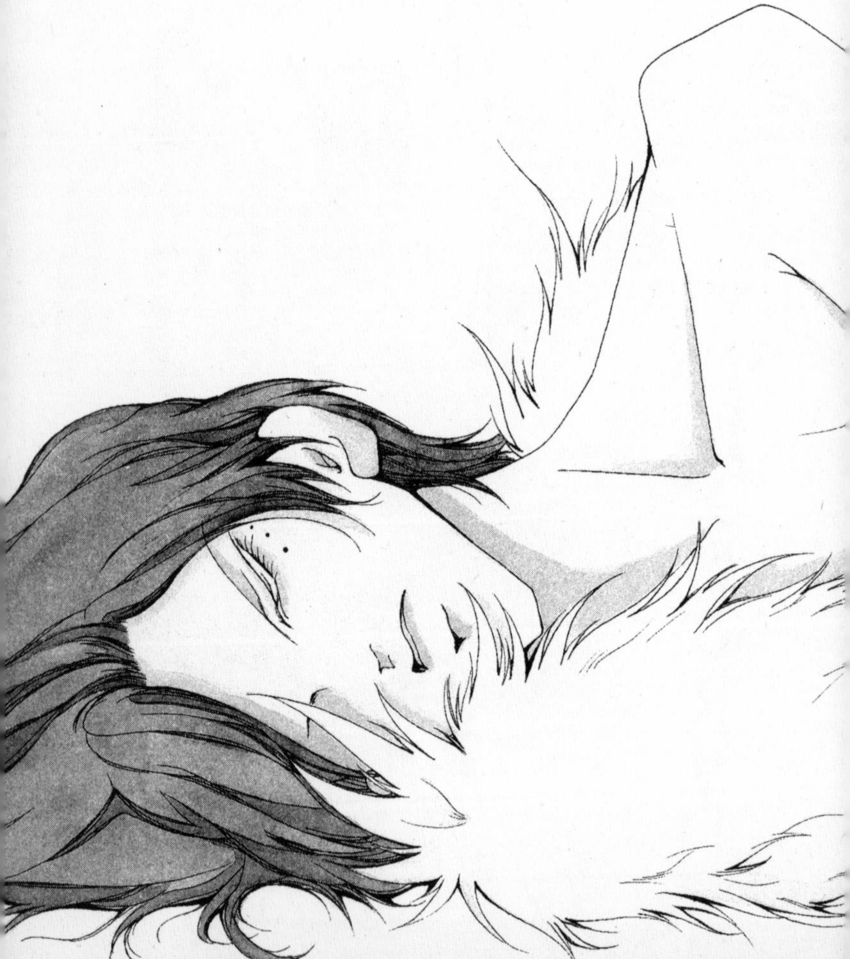

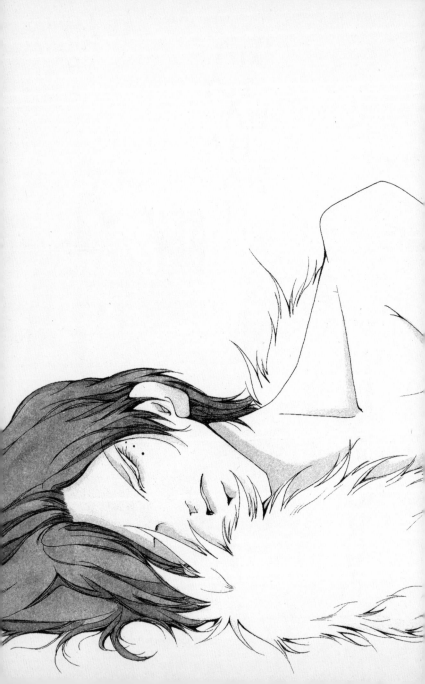

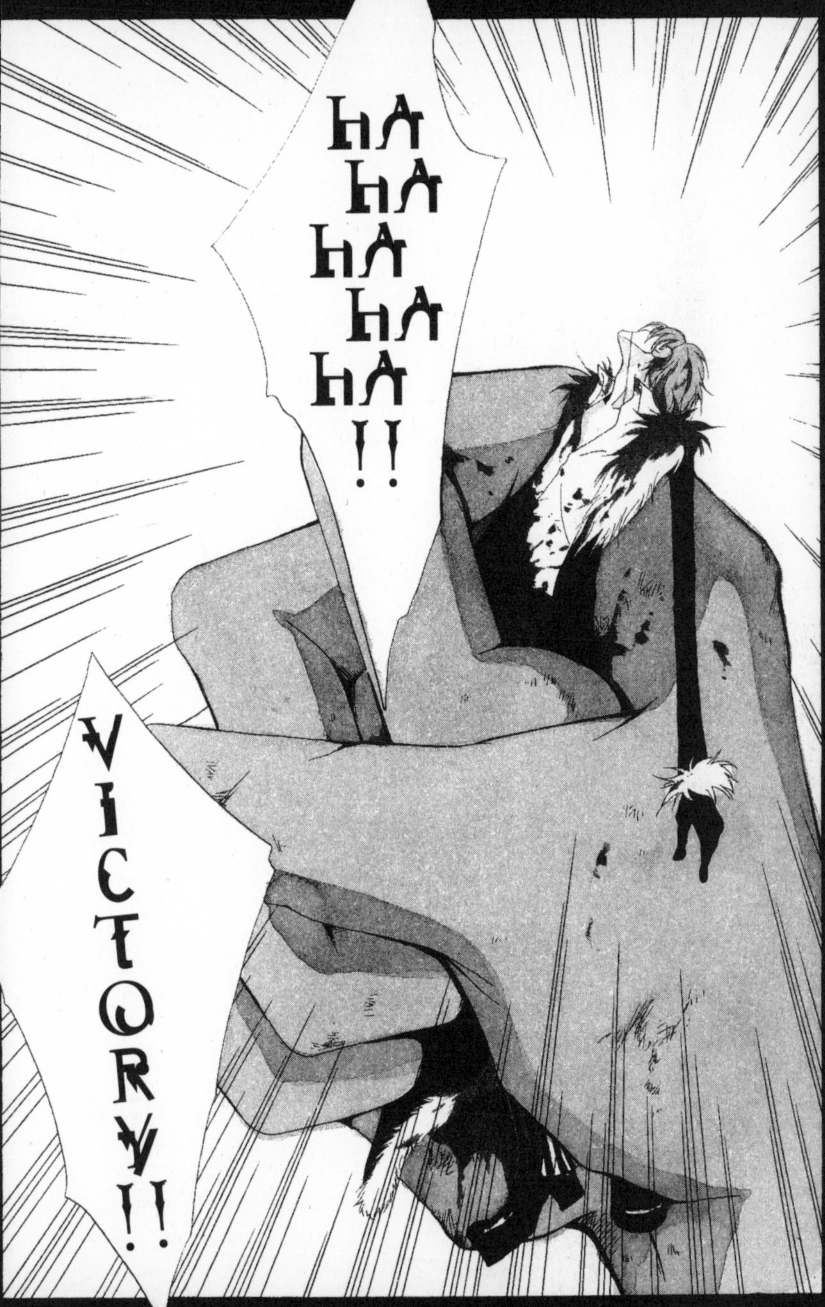
HA HA HA HA HA!!
VICTORY!!

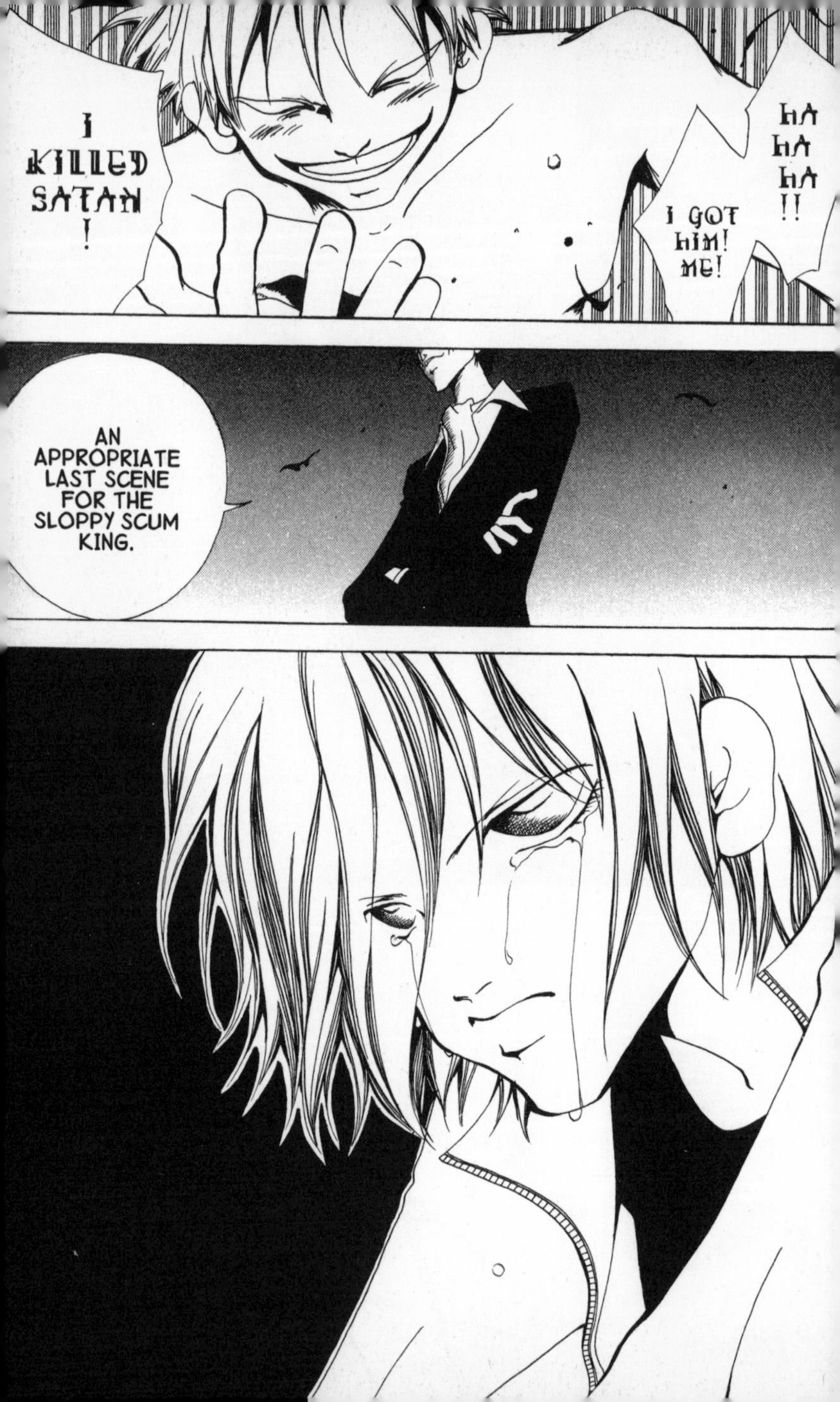
HA HA HA!!
I GOT HIM! ME!
I KILLED SATAN!
AN APPROPRIATE LAST SCENE FOR THE SLOPPY SCUM KING.

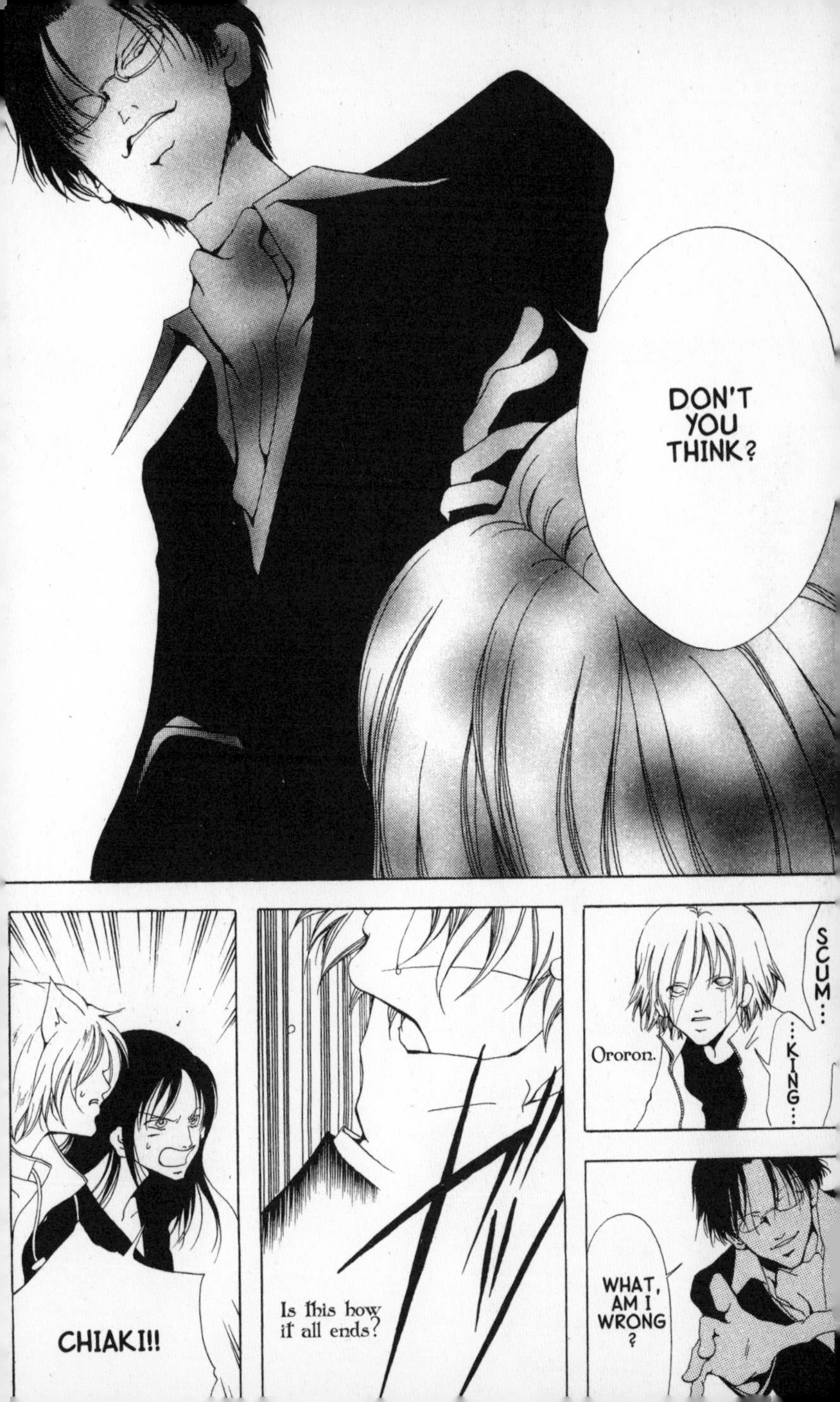
DON'T YOU THINK?
SCUM...
...KING...
Ororon.
WHAT, AM I WRONG?
Is this how it all ends?
CHIAKI!!

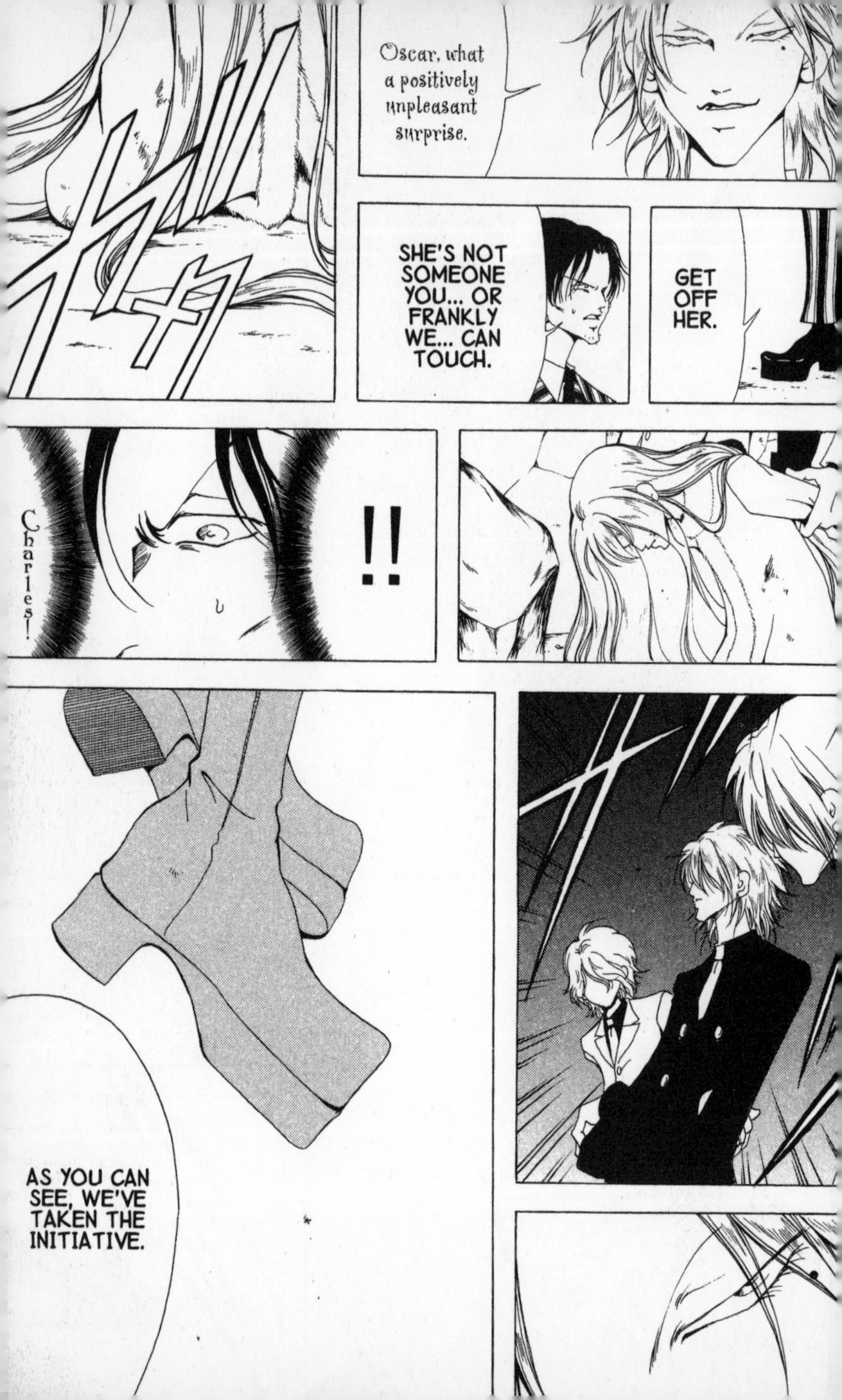
Oscar, what a positively unpleasant surprise.
GET OFF HER.
SHE'S NOT SOMEONE YOU... OR FRANKLY WE... CAN TOUCH.
!!
Charles!
AS YOU CAN SEE, WE'VE TAKEN THE INITIATIVE.

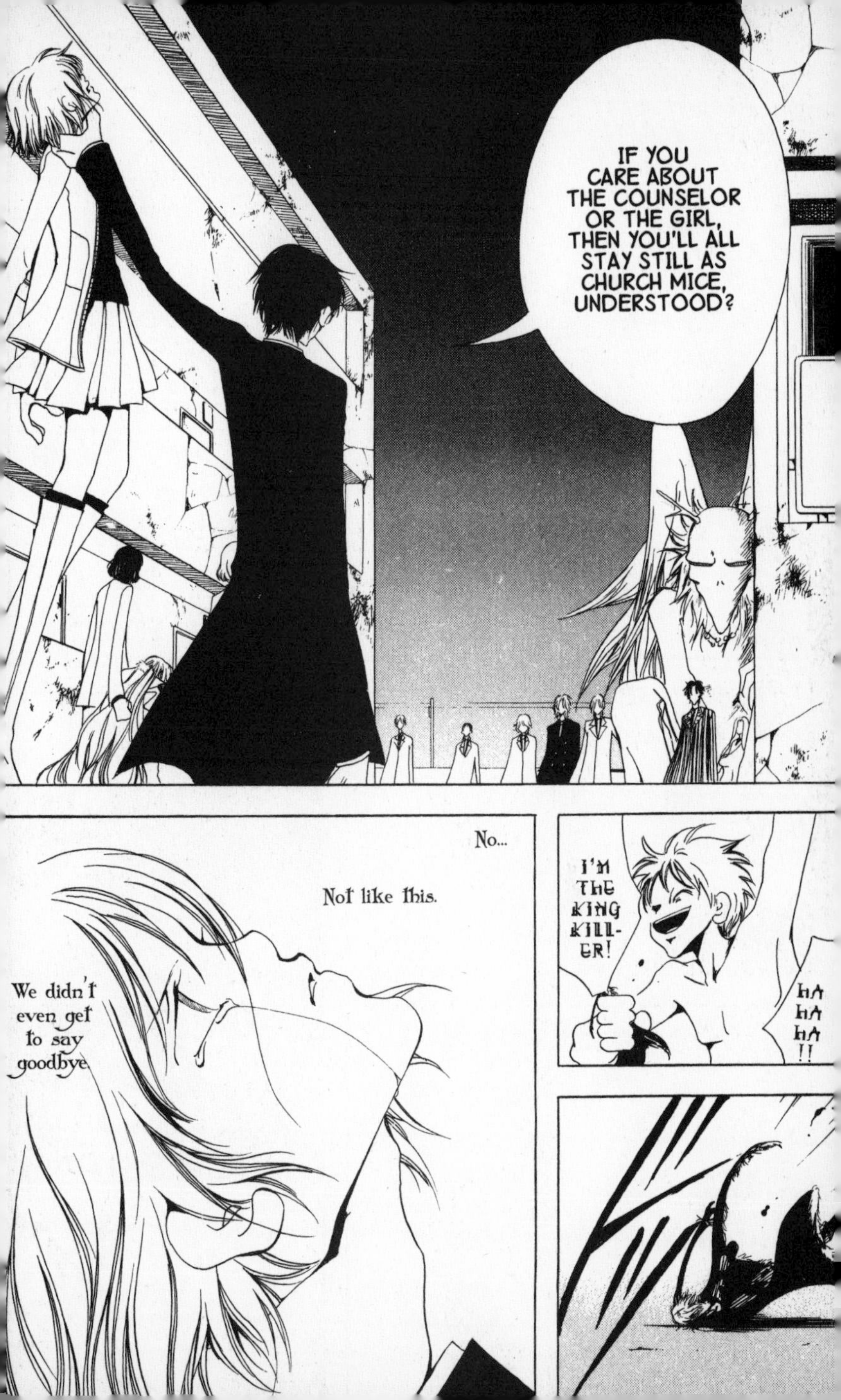
IF YOU CARE ABOUT THE COUNSELOR OR THE GIRL, THEN YOU'LL ALL STAY STILL AS CHURCH MICE, UNDERSTOOD?
I'M THE KING KILL-ER!
HA HA HA!!
No...
Not like this.
We didn't even get to say goodbye.

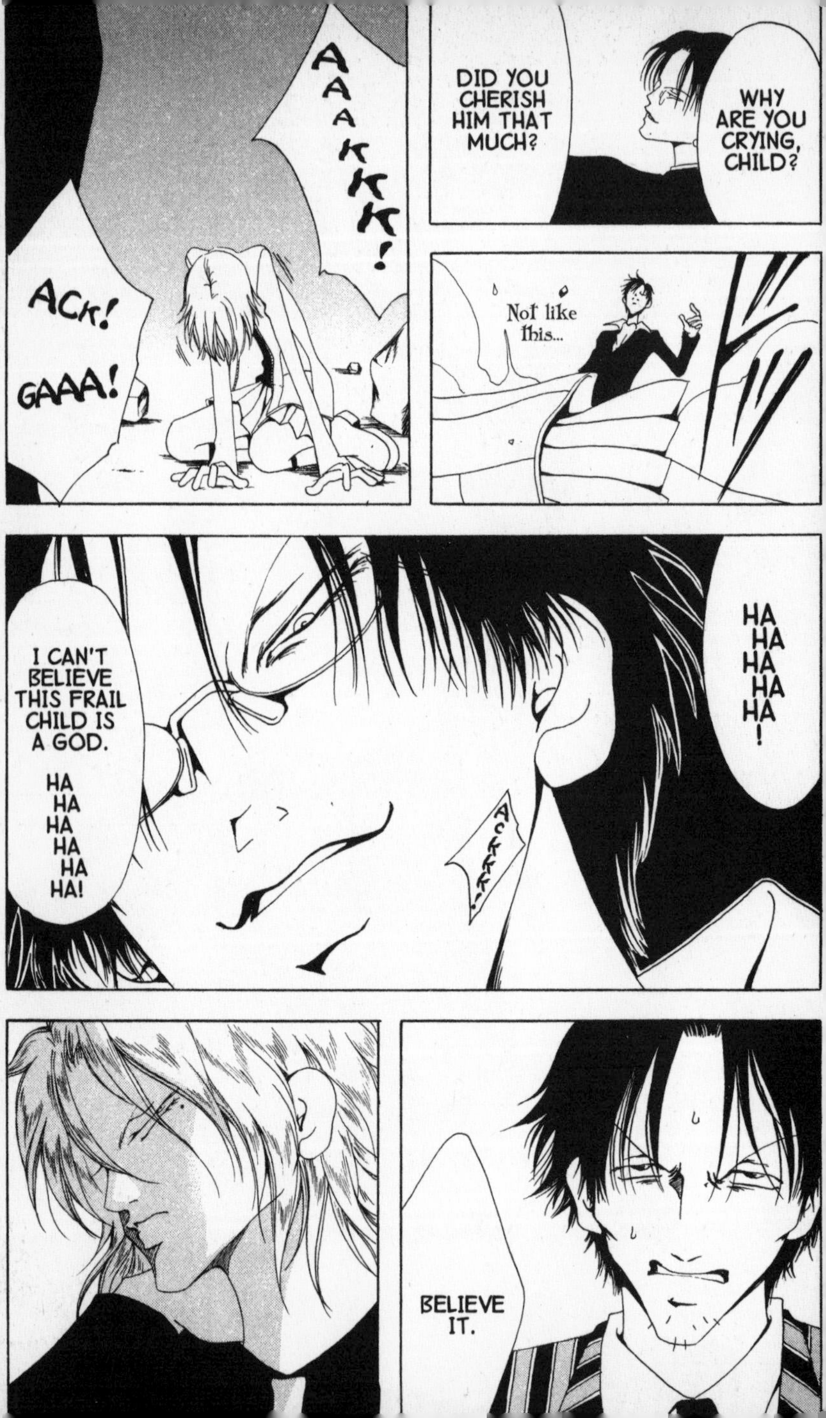
WHY ARE YOU CRYING, CHILD?
DID YOU CHERISH HIM THAT MUCH?
Not like this...
AAAKKKK!
ACK!
GAAA!
HA HA HA HA HA!
ACKKK!
I CAN'T BELIEVE THIS FRAIL CHILD IS A GOD.
HA HA HA HA HA HA!
BELIEVE IT.

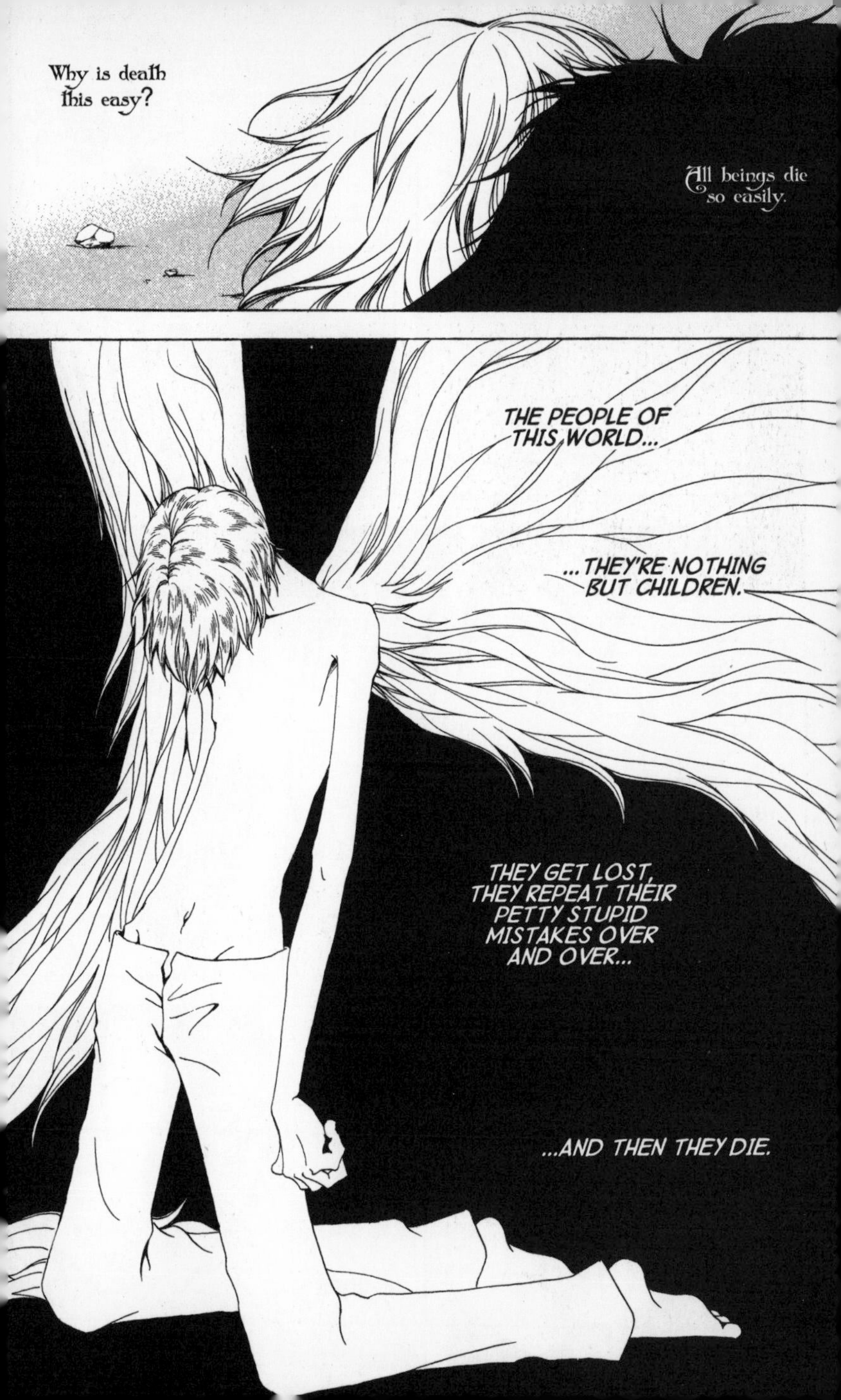
Why is death this easy?
All beings die so easily.
THE PEOPLE OF THIS WORLD...
...THEY'RE NOTHING BUT CHILDREN.
THEY GET LOST, THEY REPEAT THEIR PETTY STUPID MISTAKES OVER AND OVER...
...AND THEN THEY DIE.

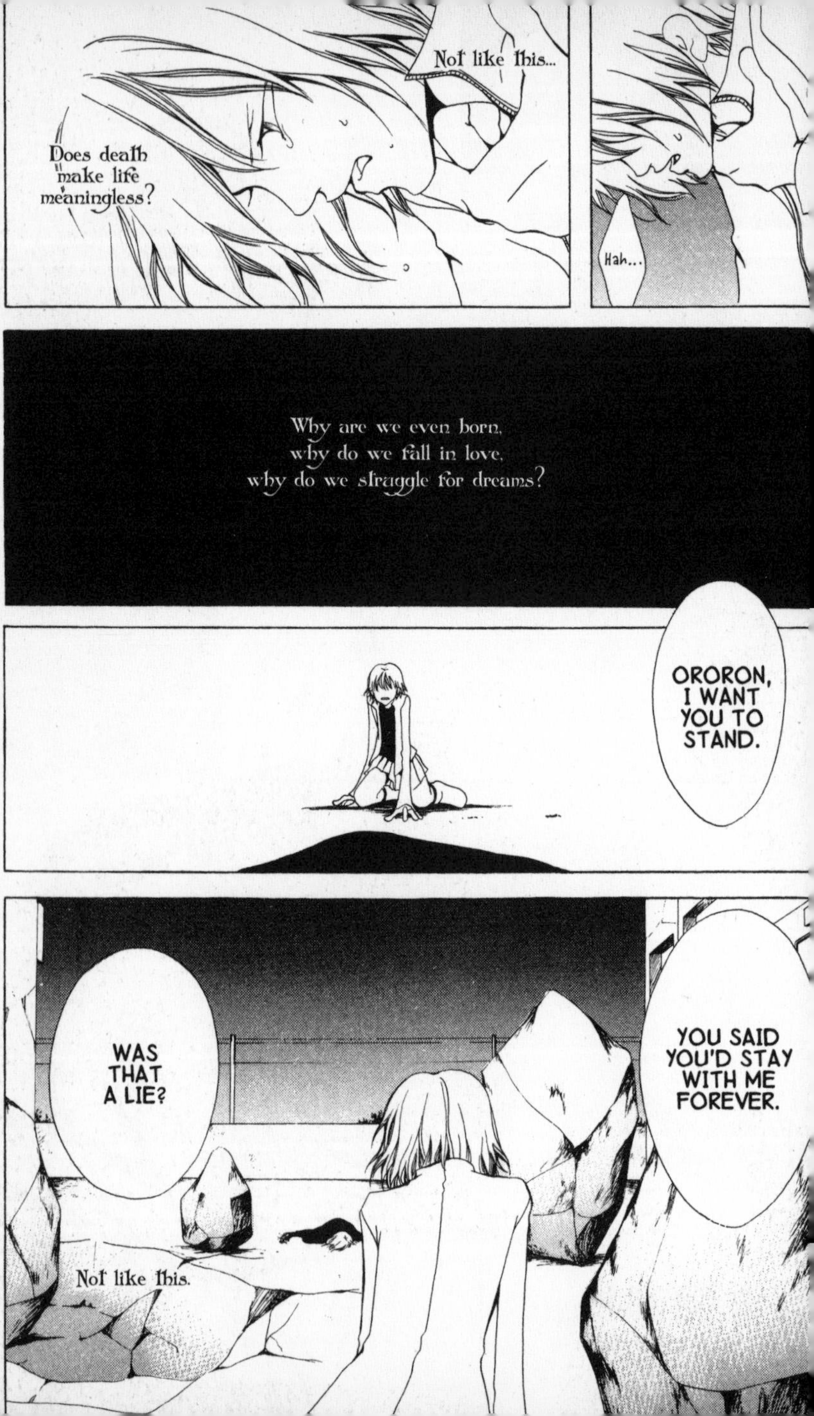
Hah...
Not like this...
Does death make life meaningless?
Why are we even born, why do we fall in love, why do we struggle for dreams?
ORORON, I WANT YOU TO STAND.
YOU SAID YOU'D STAY WITH ME FOREVER.
WAS THAT A LIE?
Not like this.

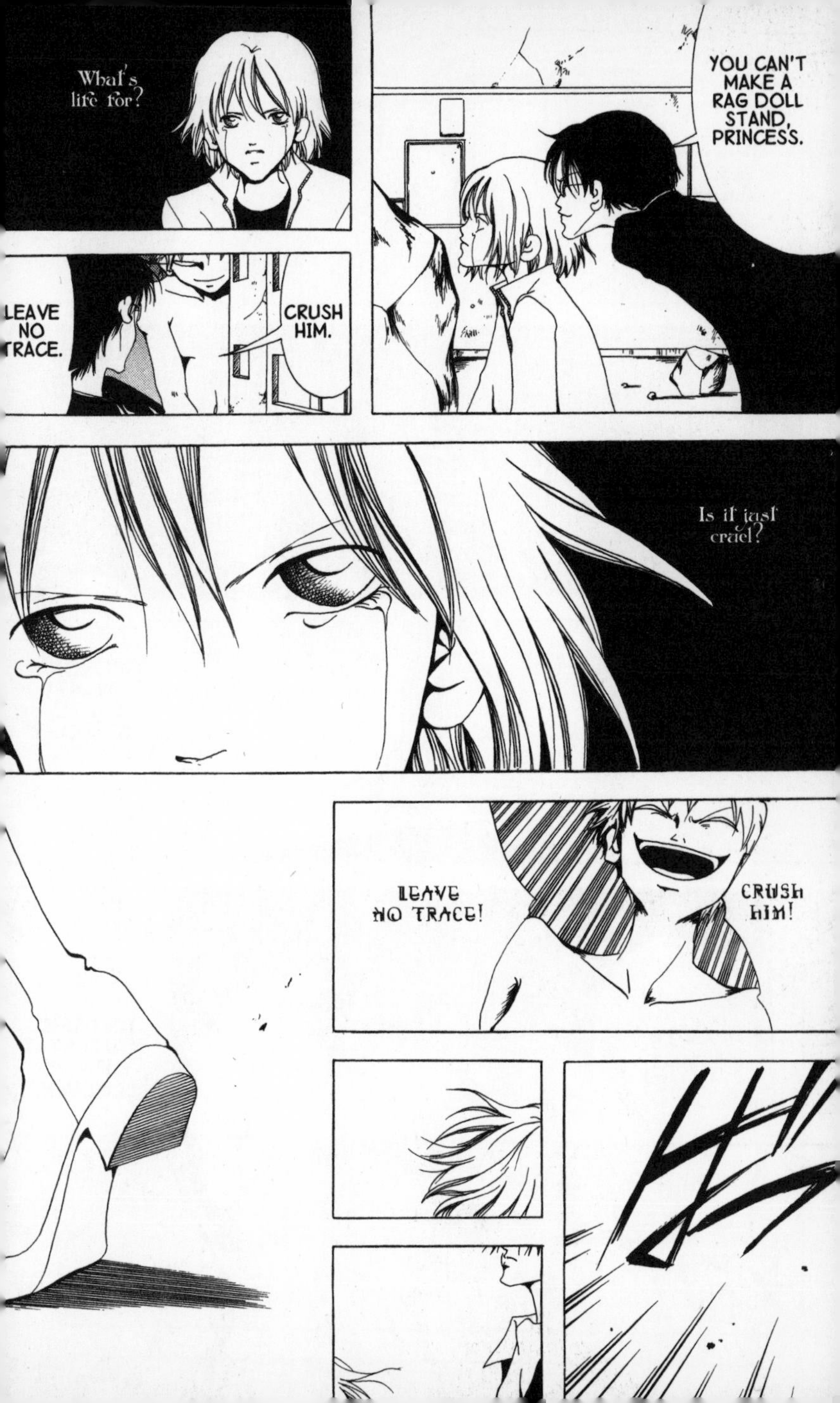
YOU CAN'T MAKE A RAG DOLL STAND, PRINCESS.
What's life for?
CRUSH HIM.
LEAVE NO TRACE.
Is it just cruel?
CRUSH HIM!
LEAVE NO TRACE!

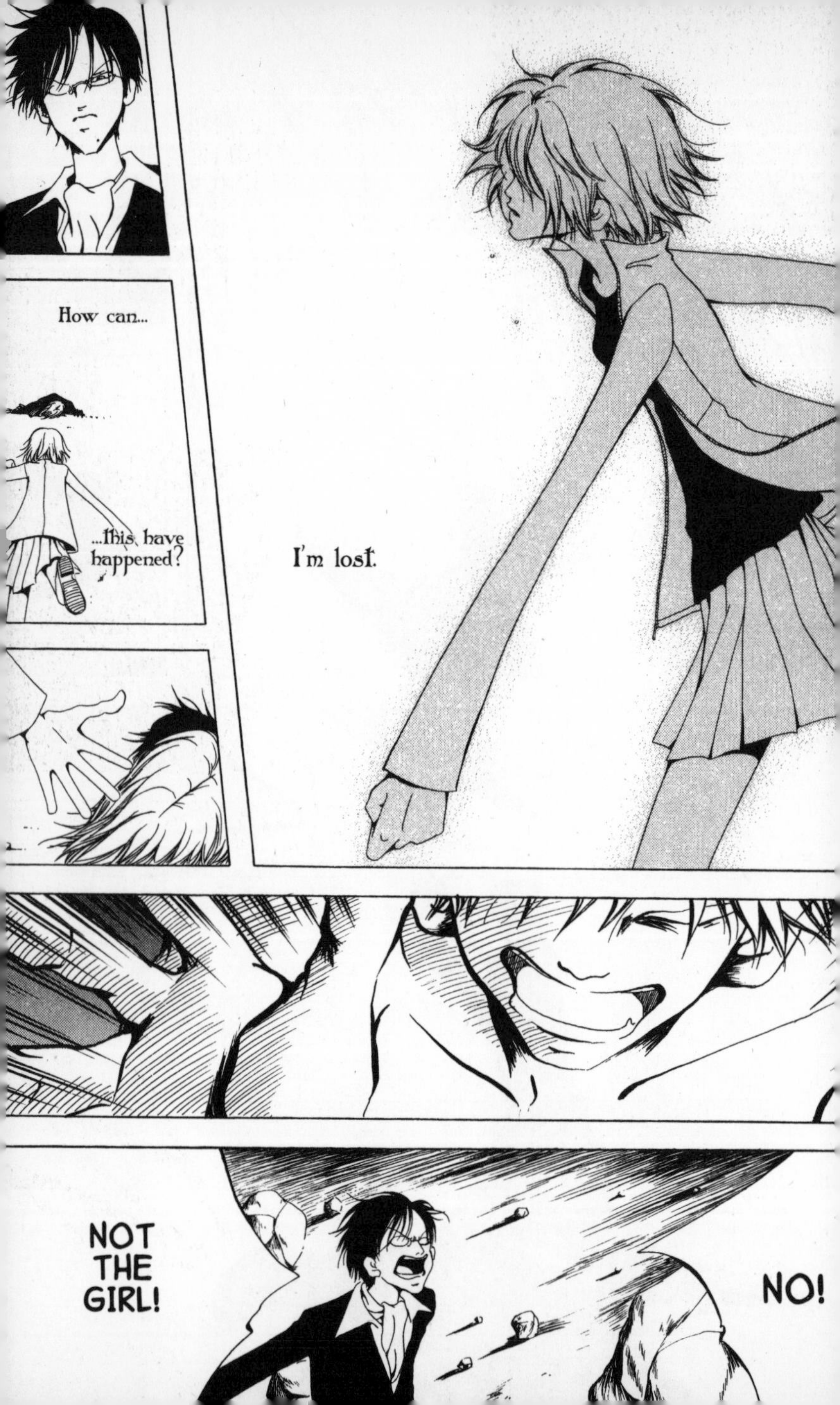
I'm lost.
How can...
...this have happened?
NO!
NOT THE GIRL!

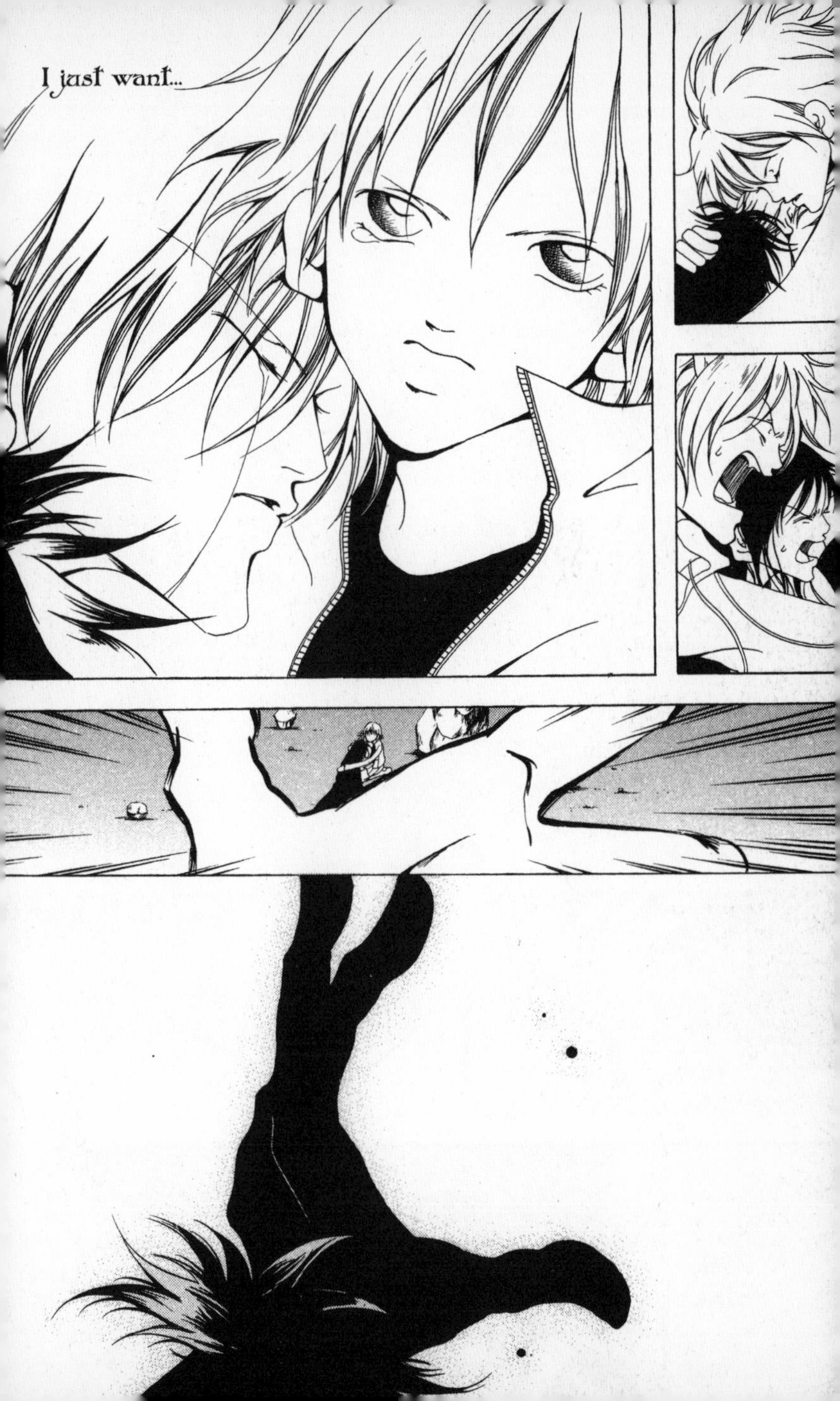
I just want...

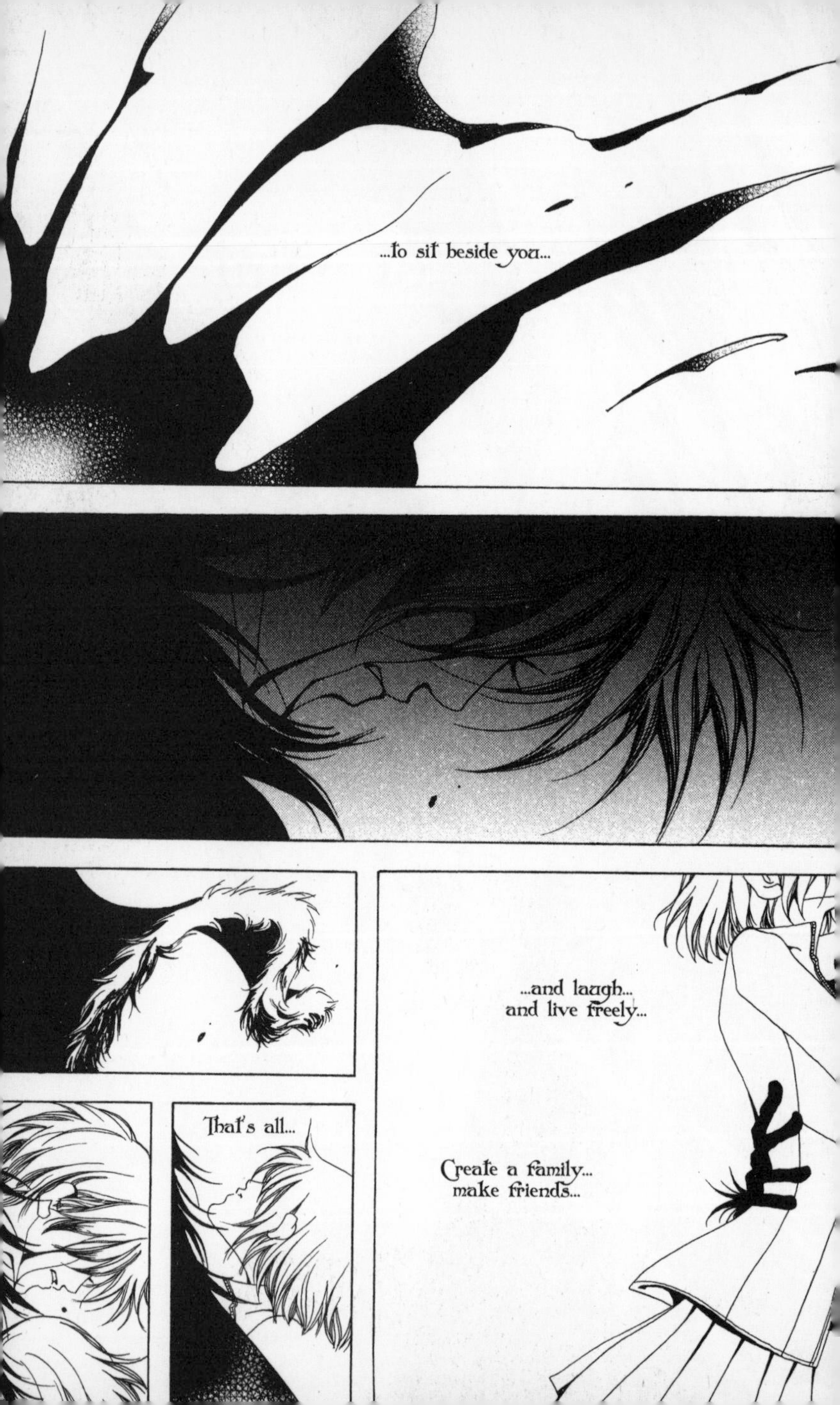
...to sit beside you...
...and laugh... and live freely...
Create a family... make friends...
That's all...

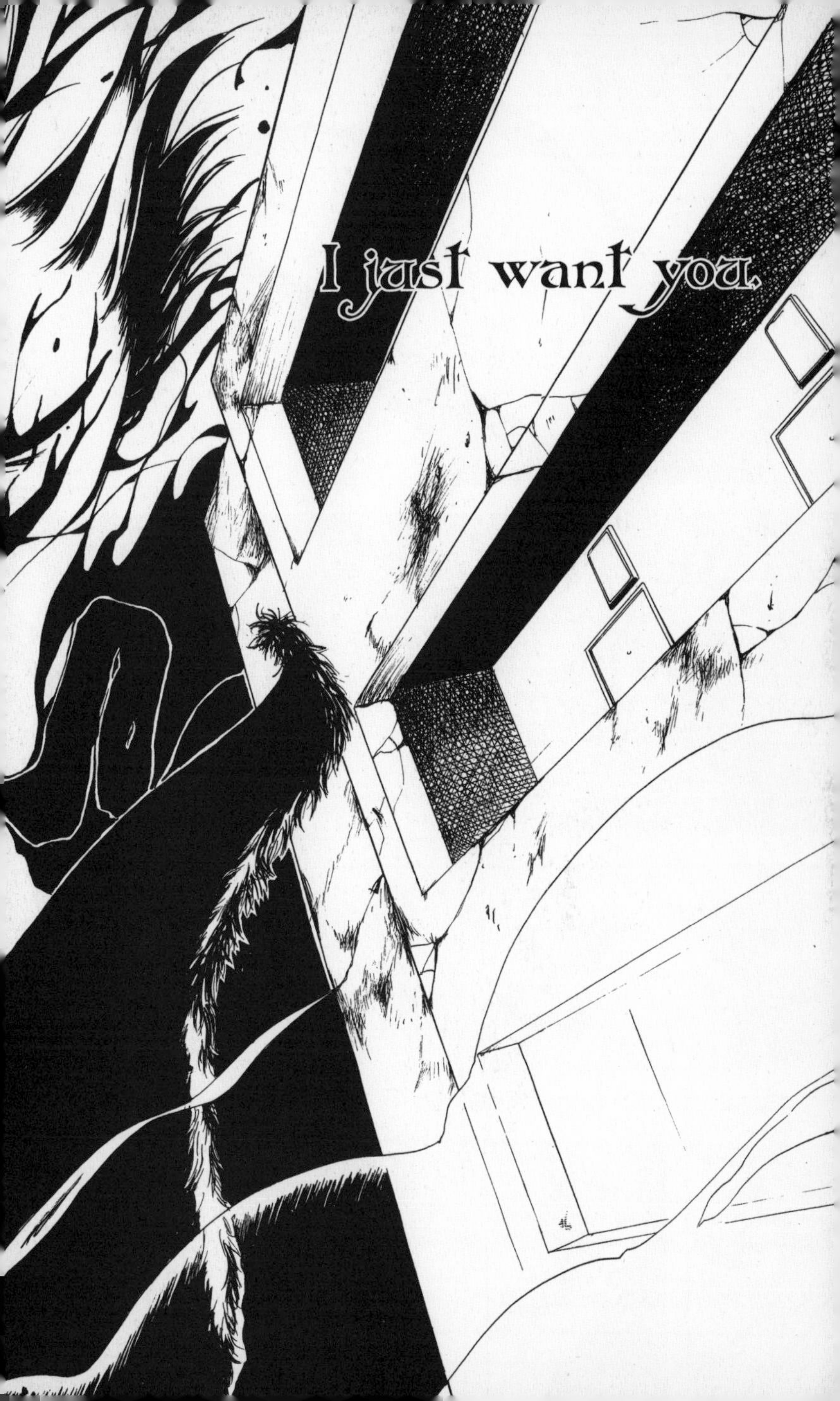
I just want you.

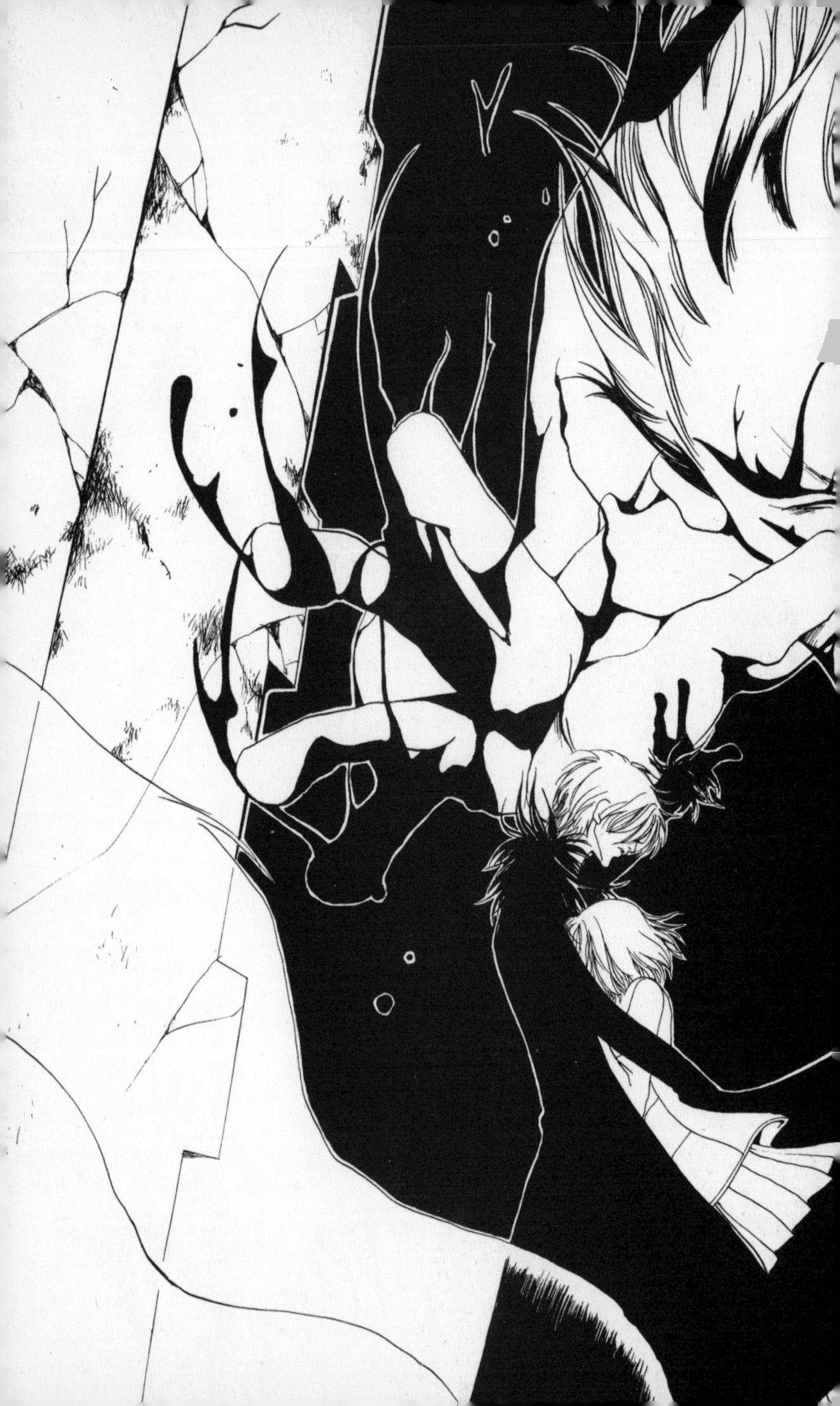

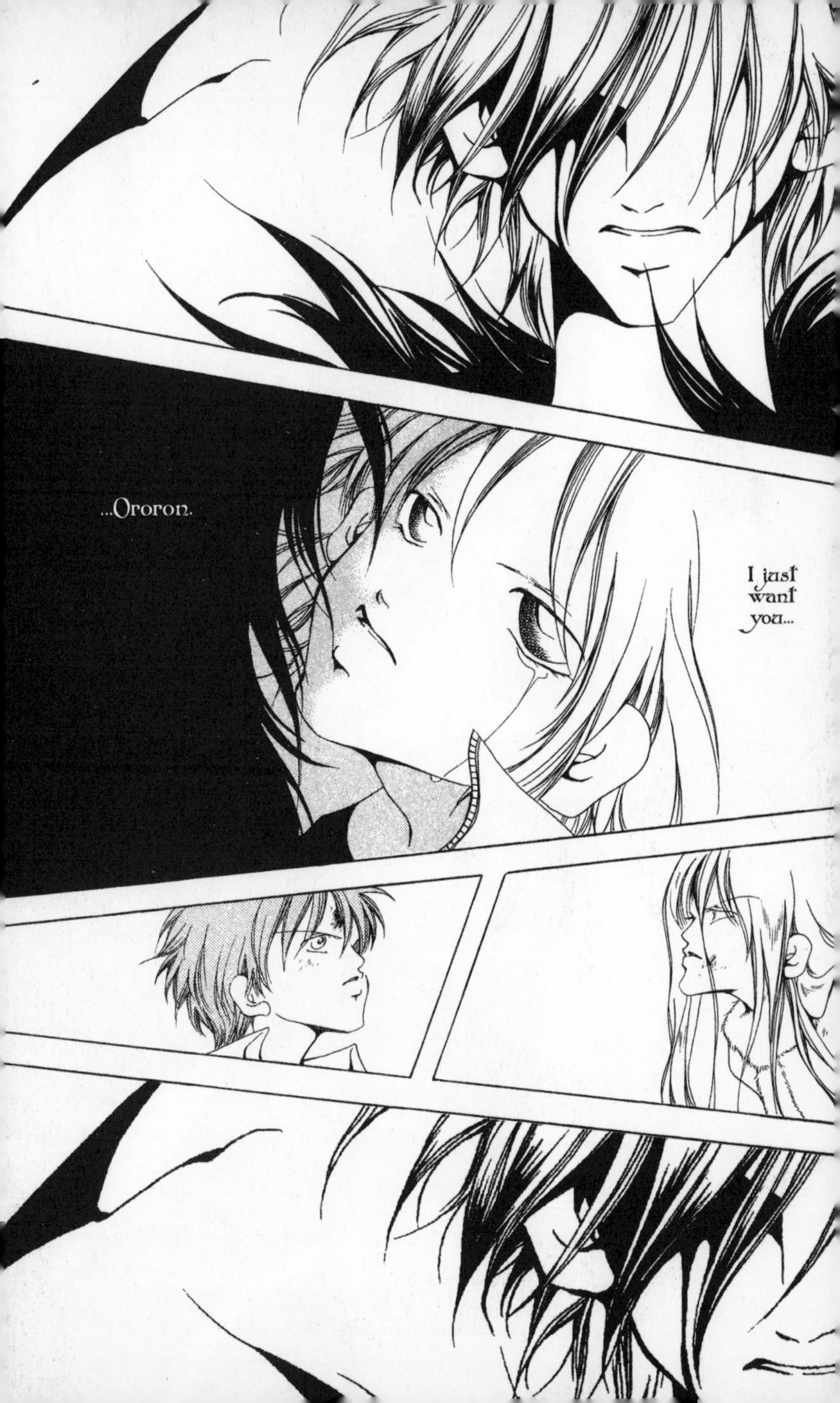
I just want you...
...Ororon.

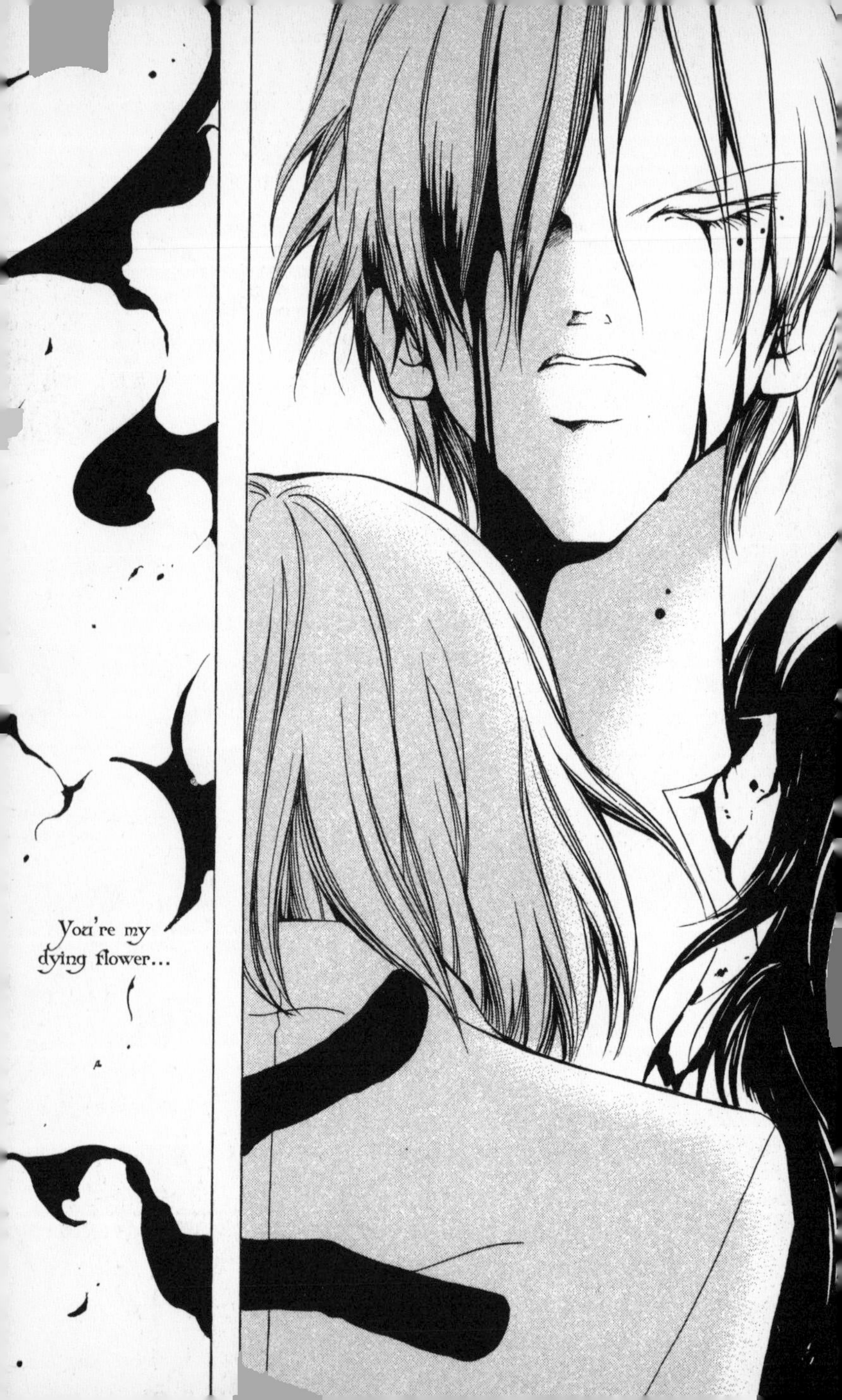
You're my dying flower...

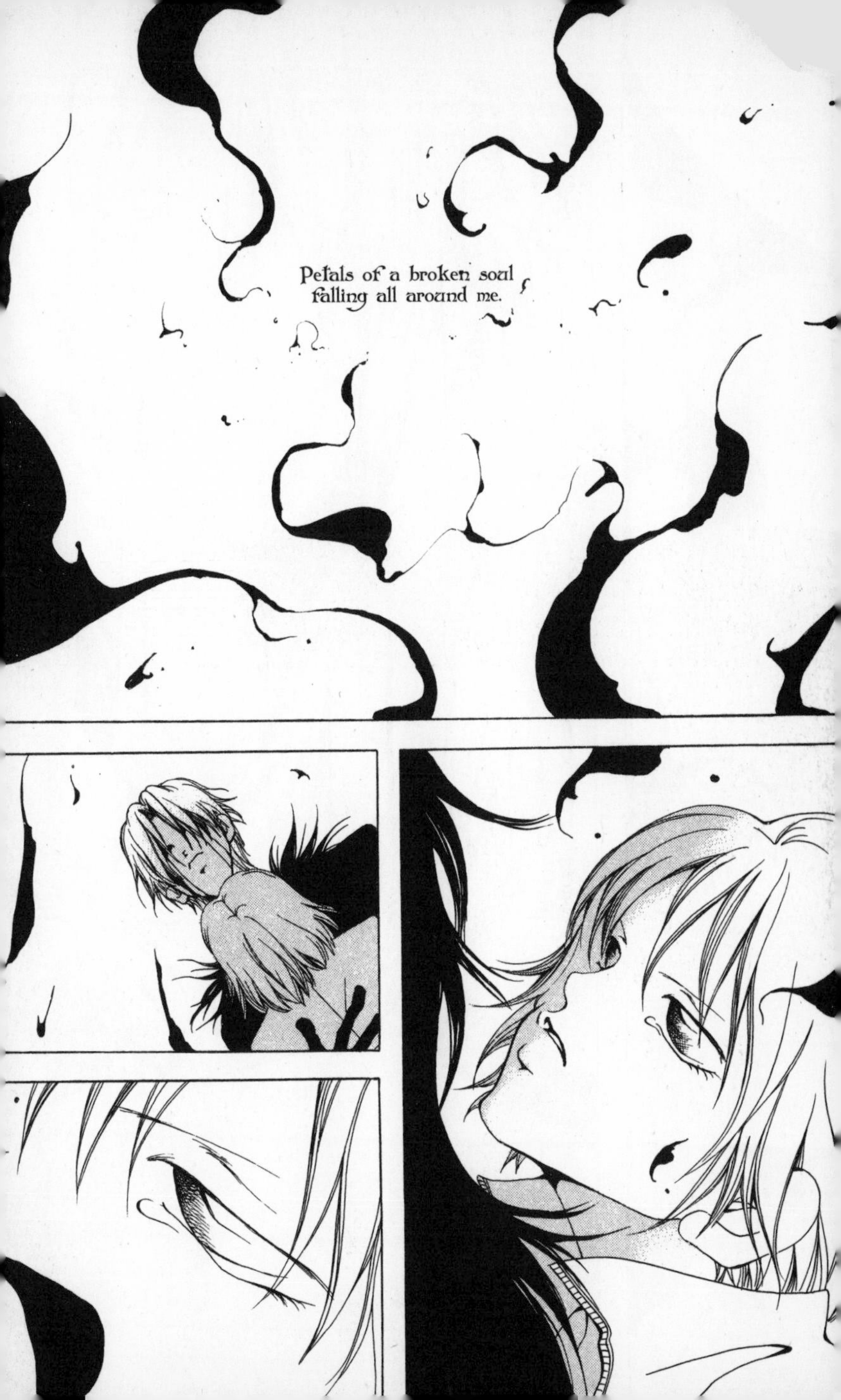
Petals of a broken soul falling all around me.

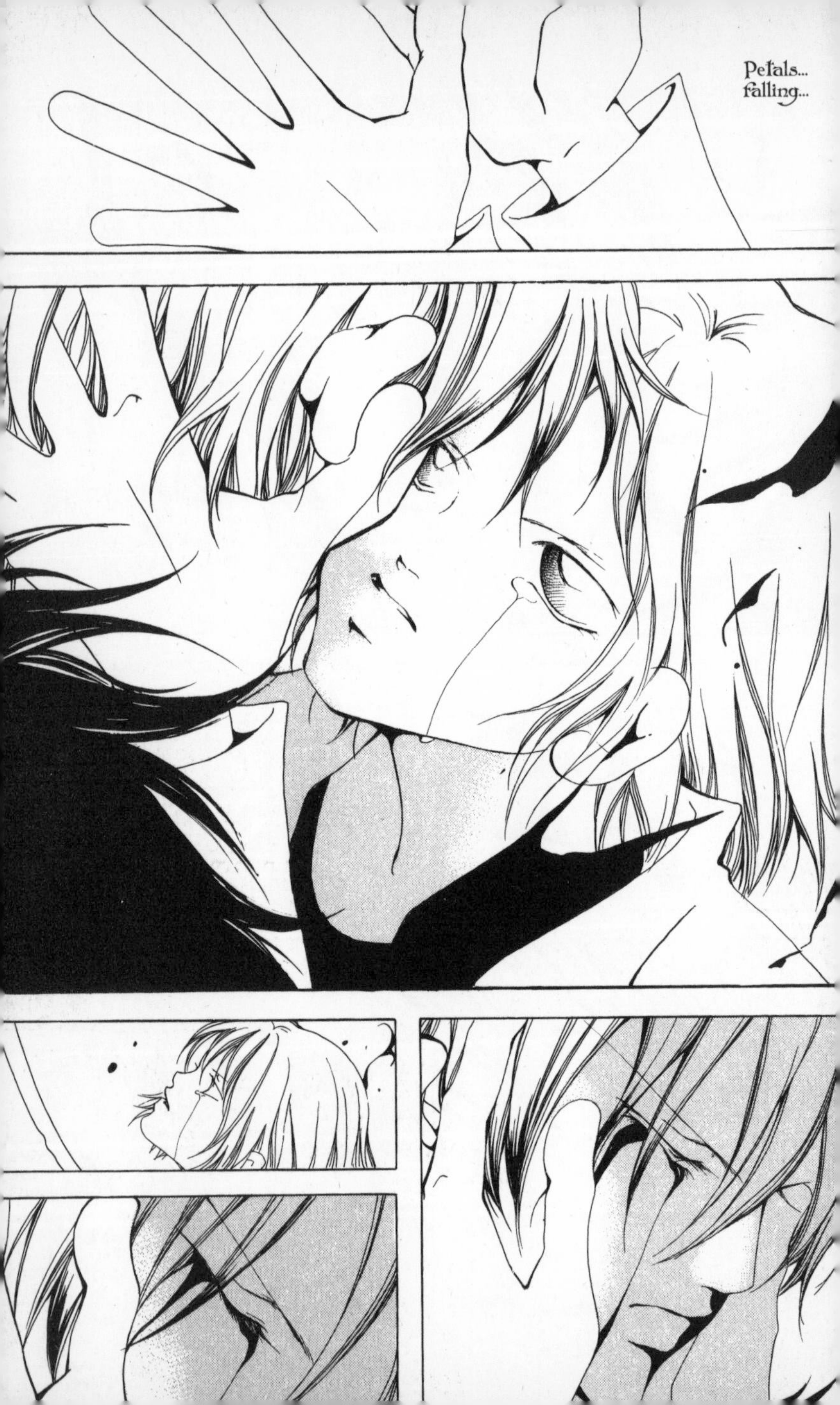
Petals... falling...

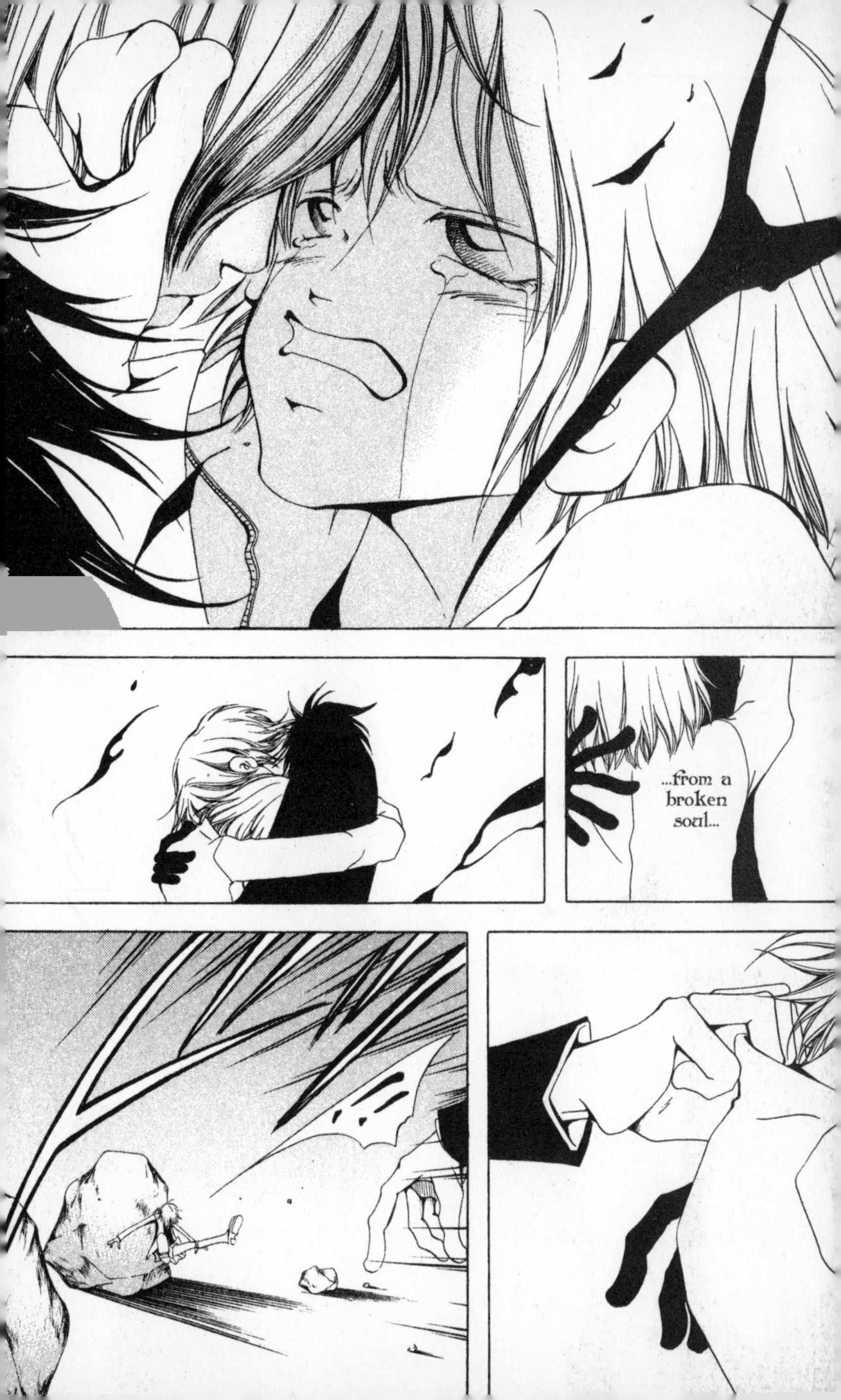
...from a broken soul...

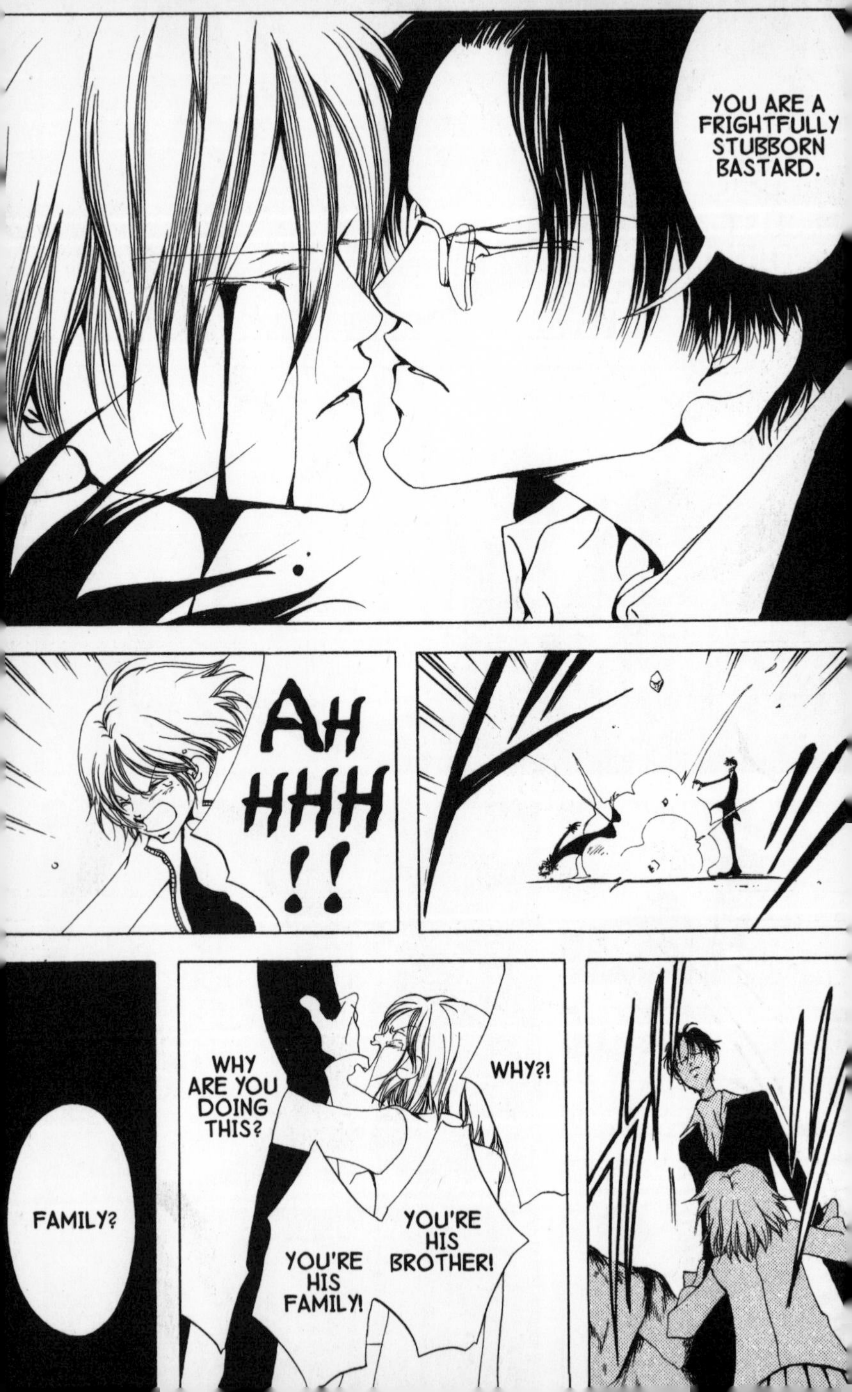
YOU ARE A FRIGHTFULLY STUBBORN BASTARD.
AH HHH!!
WHY?!
WHY ARE YOU DOING THIS?
YOU'RE HIS BROTHER!
YOU'RE HIS FAMILY!
FAMILY?

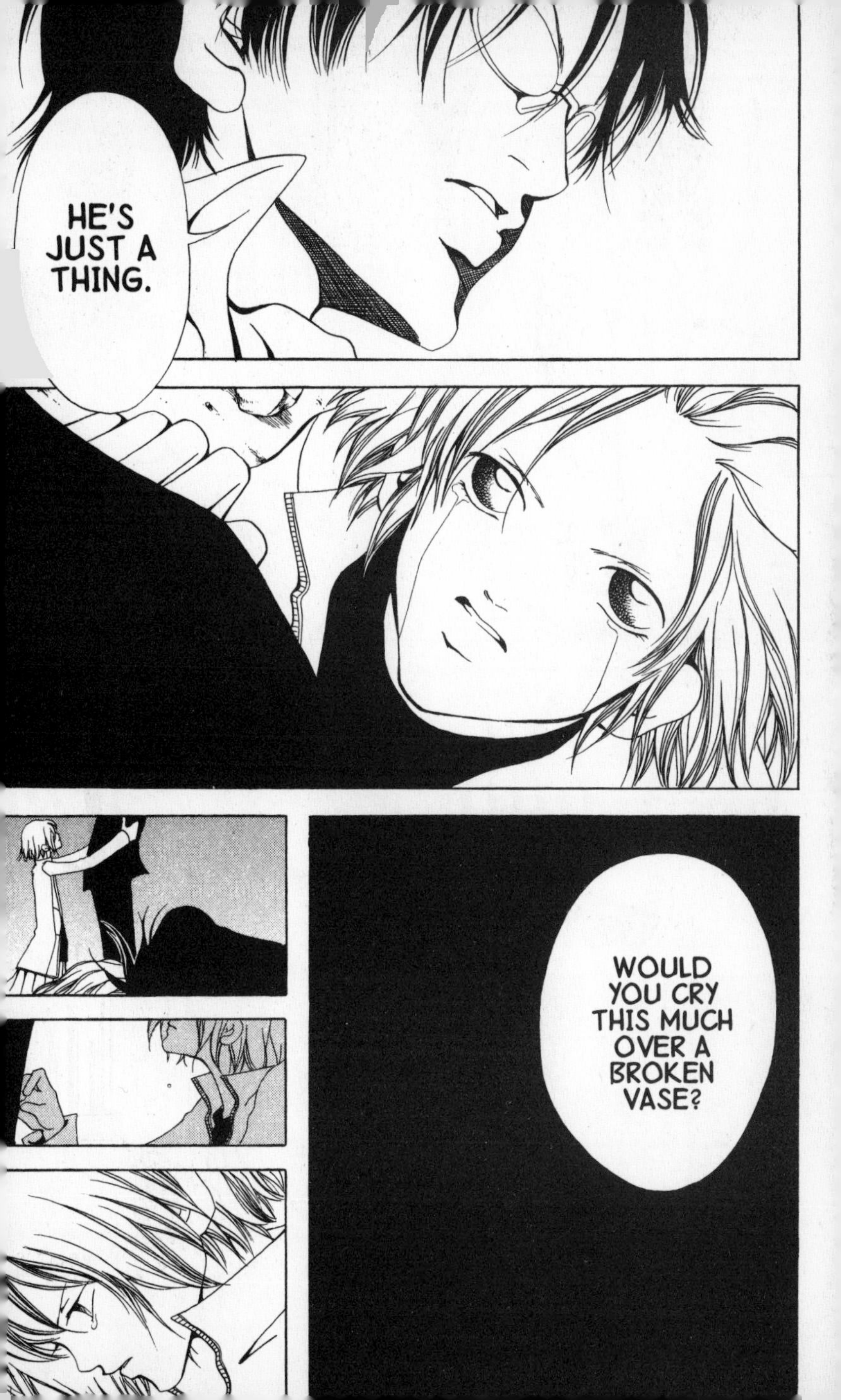
HE'S JUST A THING.
WOULD YOU CRY THIS MUCH OVER A BROKEN VASE?

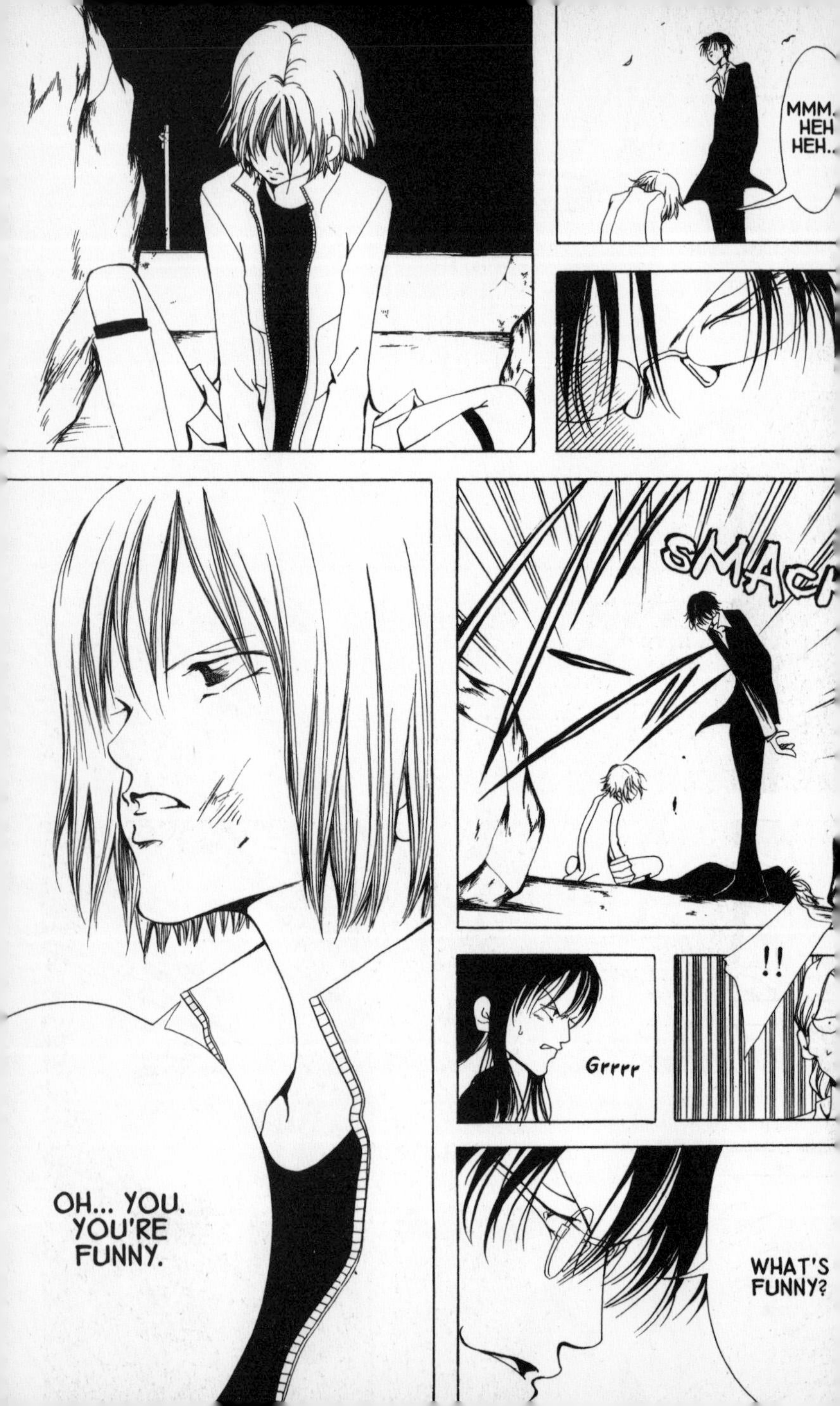
MMM. HEH HEH..
SMAC
!!
Grrr
WHAT'S FUNNY?
OH... YOU. YOU'RE FUNNY.

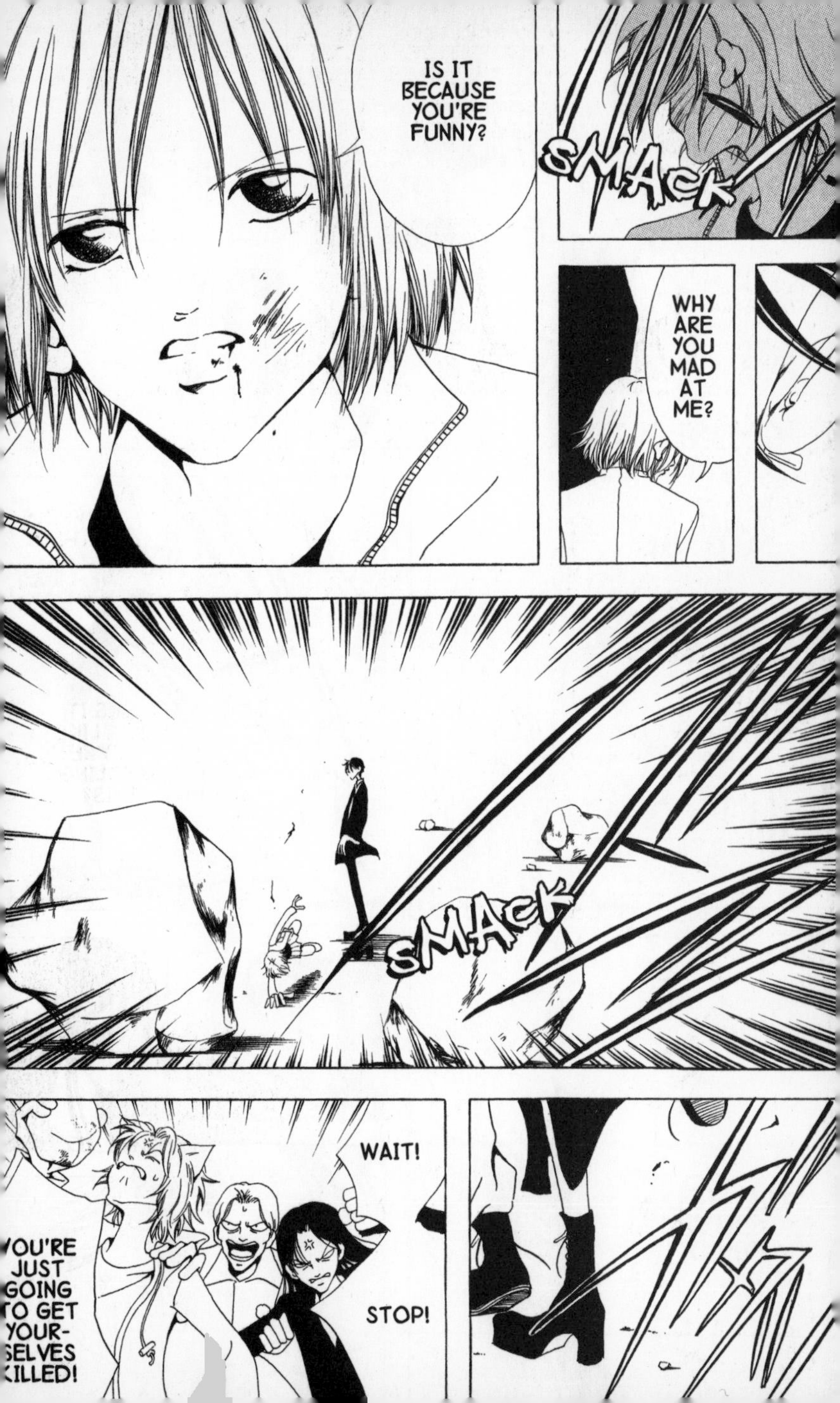

SMACK
WHY ARE YOU MAD AT ME?
IS IT BECAUSE YOU'RE FUNNY?
SMACK
WAIT!
YOU'RE JUST GOING TO GET YOUR-SELVES KILLED!
STOP!

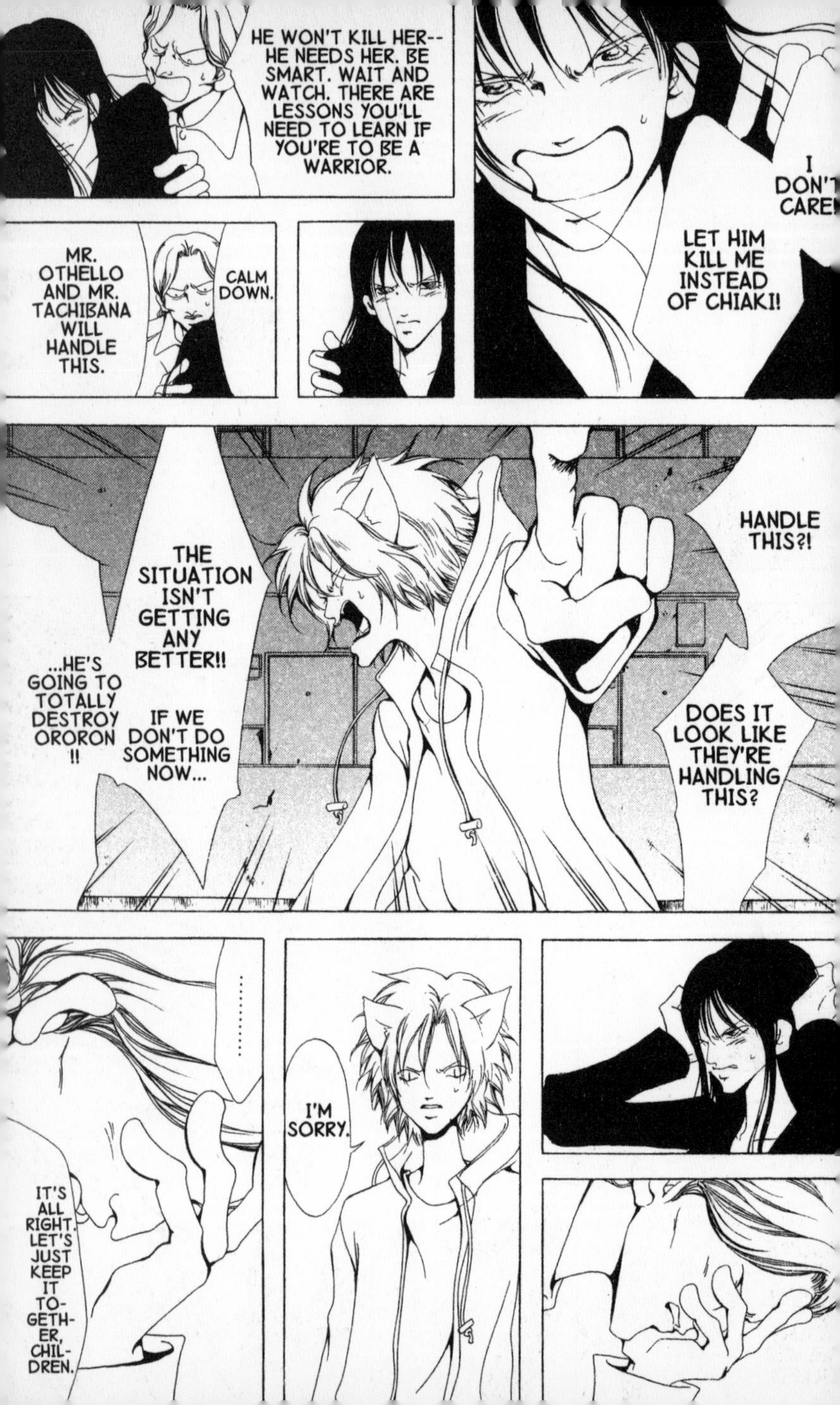
I DON'T CARE!
LET HIM KILL ME INSTEAD OF CHIAKI!
HE WON'T KILL HER--HE NEEDS HER. BE SMART. WAIT AND WATCH. THERE ARE LESSONS YOU'LL NEED TO LEARN IF YOU'RE TO BE A WARRIOR.
CALM DOWN.
MR. OTHELLO AND MR. TACHIBANA WILL HANDLE THIS.
HANDLE THIS?!
DOES IT LOOK LIKE THEY'RE HANDLING THIS?
THE SITUATION ISN'T GETTING ANY BETTER!!
IF WE DON'T DO SOMETHING NOW...
...HE'S GOING TO TOTALLY DESTROY ORORON!!
I'M SORRY.
......
IT'S ALL RIGHT. LET'S JUST KEEP IT TO-GETH-ER, CHIL-DREN.

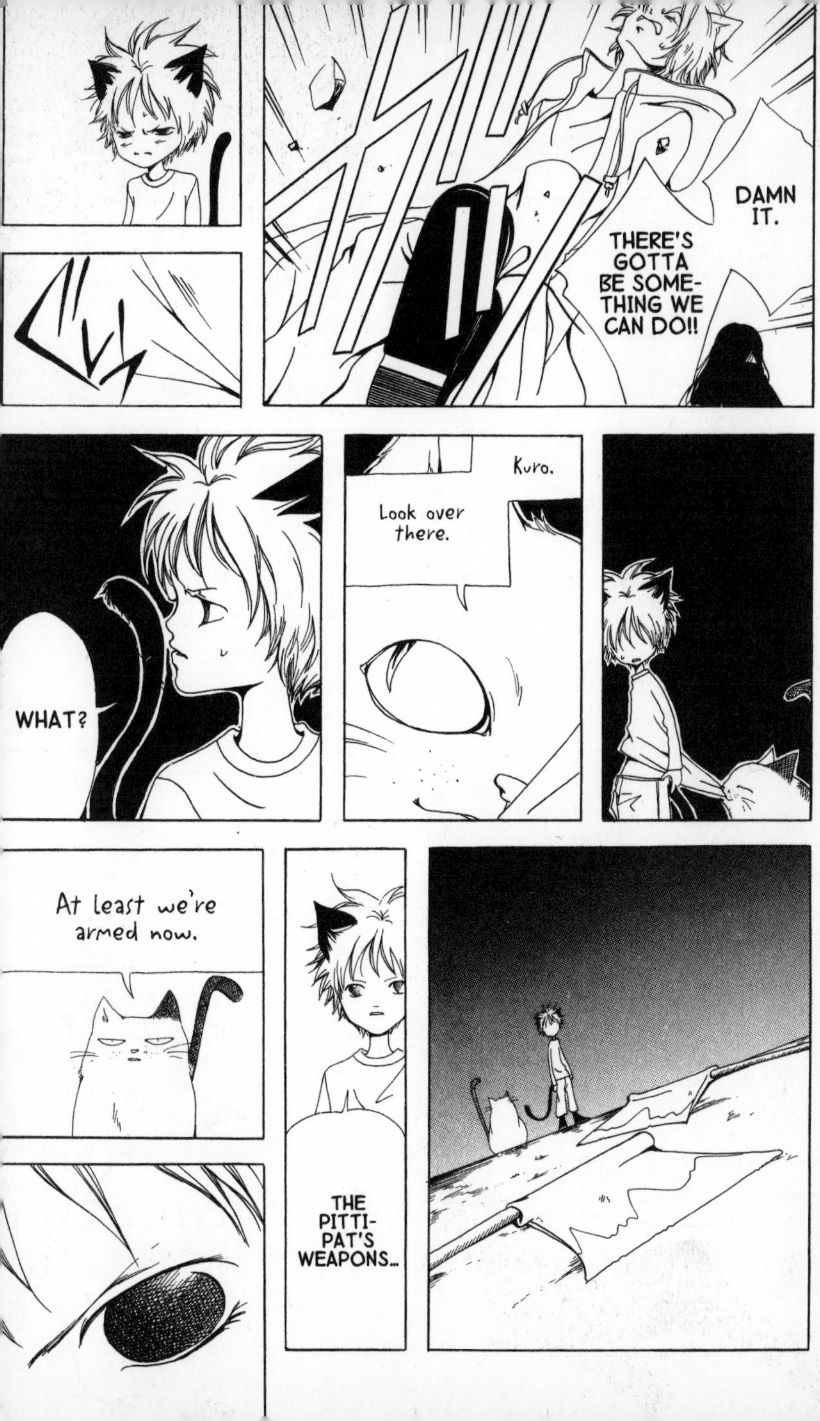
DAMN IT.
THERE'S GOTTA BE SOME-THING WE CAN DO!!
Kuro.
Look over there.
WHAT?
THE PITTI-PAT'S WEAPONS...
At least we're armed now.

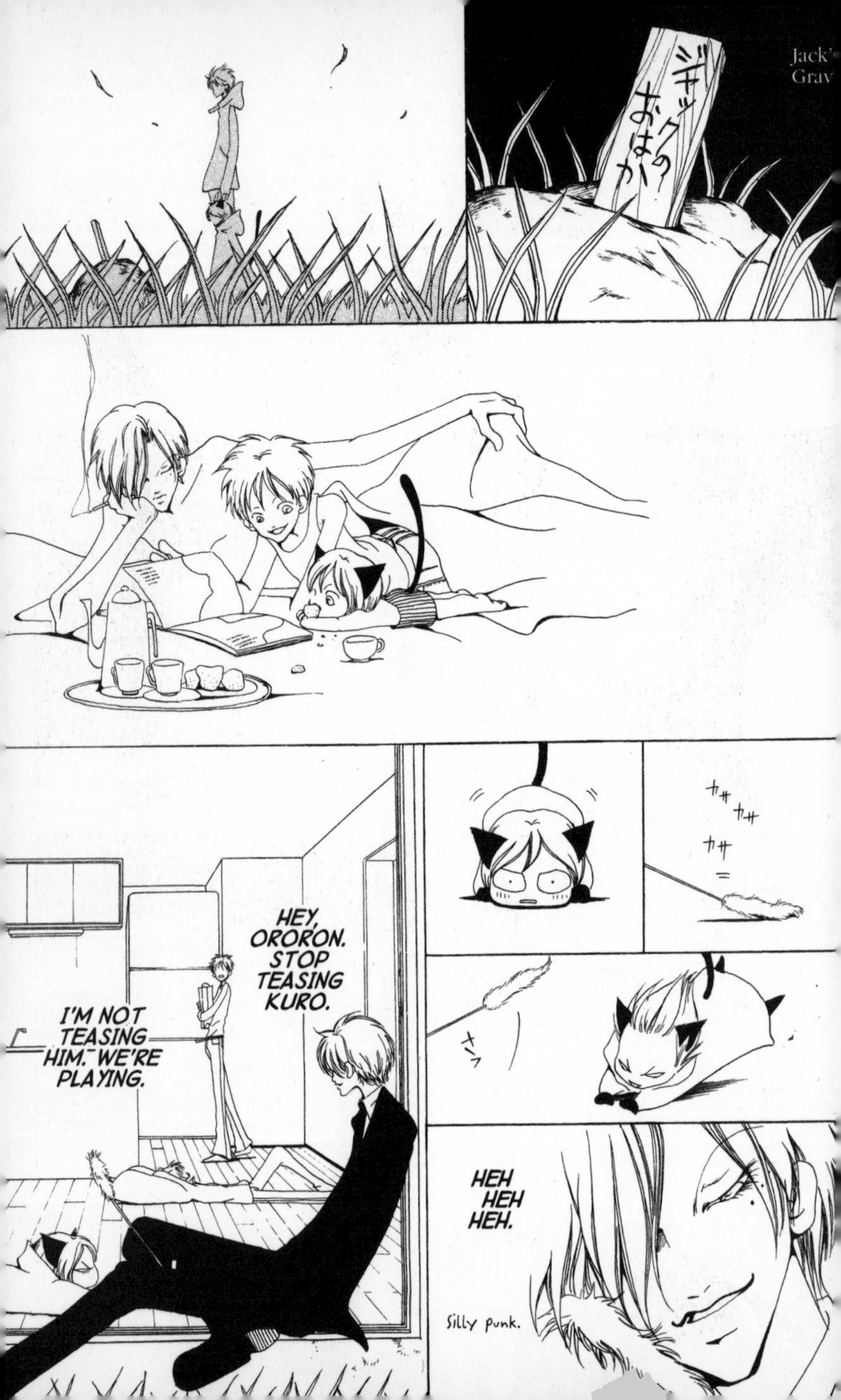
ジャックのおはか
Jack's Grav
カサ カサ
カサ
HEH HEH HEH.
Silly punk.
HEY, ORORON. STOP TEASING KURO.
I'M NOT TEASING HIM. WE'RE PLAYING.

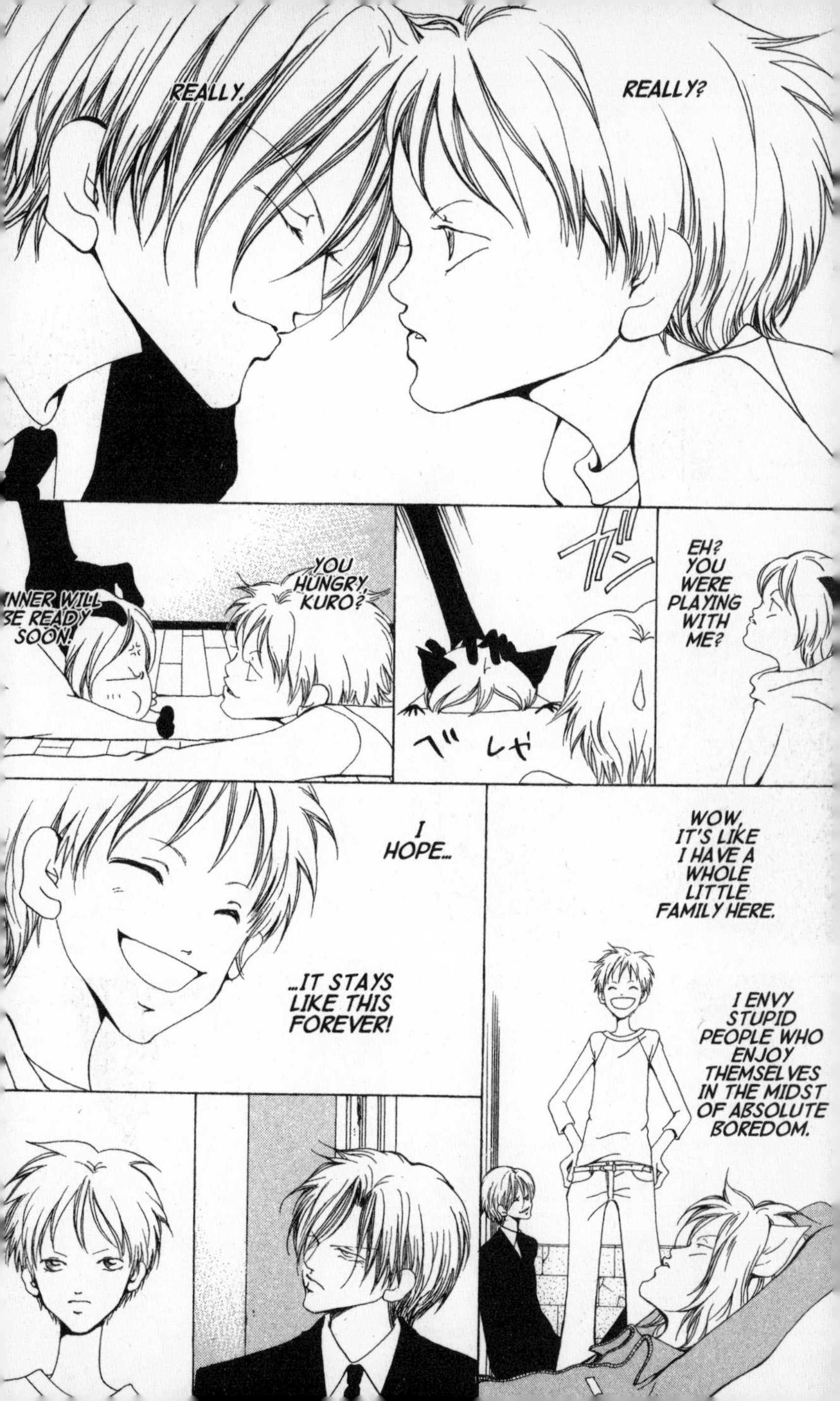
REALLY?
REALLY.
EH? YOU WERE PLAYING WITH ME?
YOU HUNGRY, KURO?
INNER WILL BE READY SOON!
WOW, IT'S LIKE I HAVE A WHOLE LITTLE FAMILY HERE.
I ENVY STUPID PEOPLE WHO ENJOY THEMSELVES IN THE MIDST OF ABSOLUTE BOREDOM.
I HOPE...
...IT STAYS LIKE THIS FOREVER!

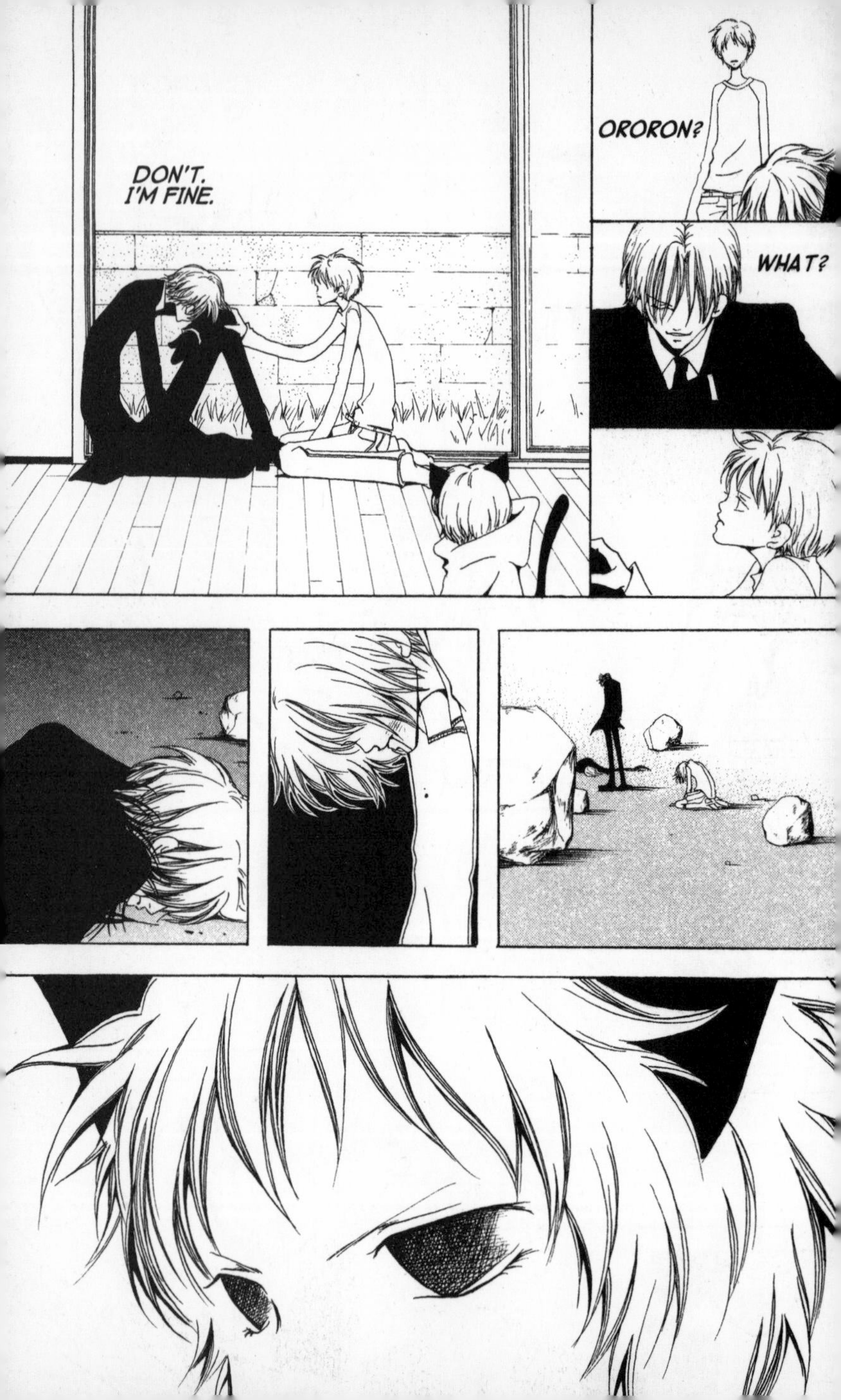
ORORON?
WHAT?
DON'T.
I'M FINE.

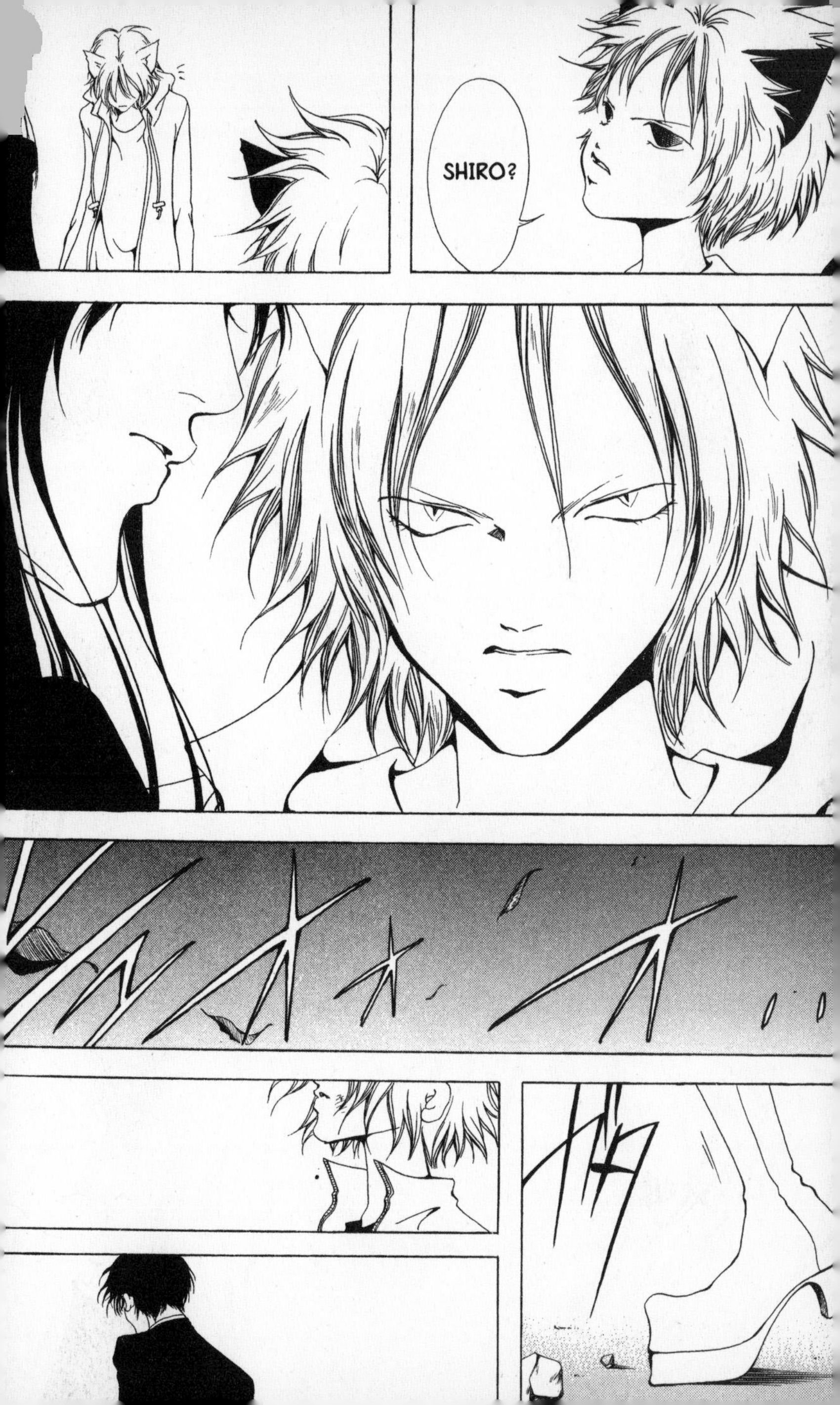
SHIRO?

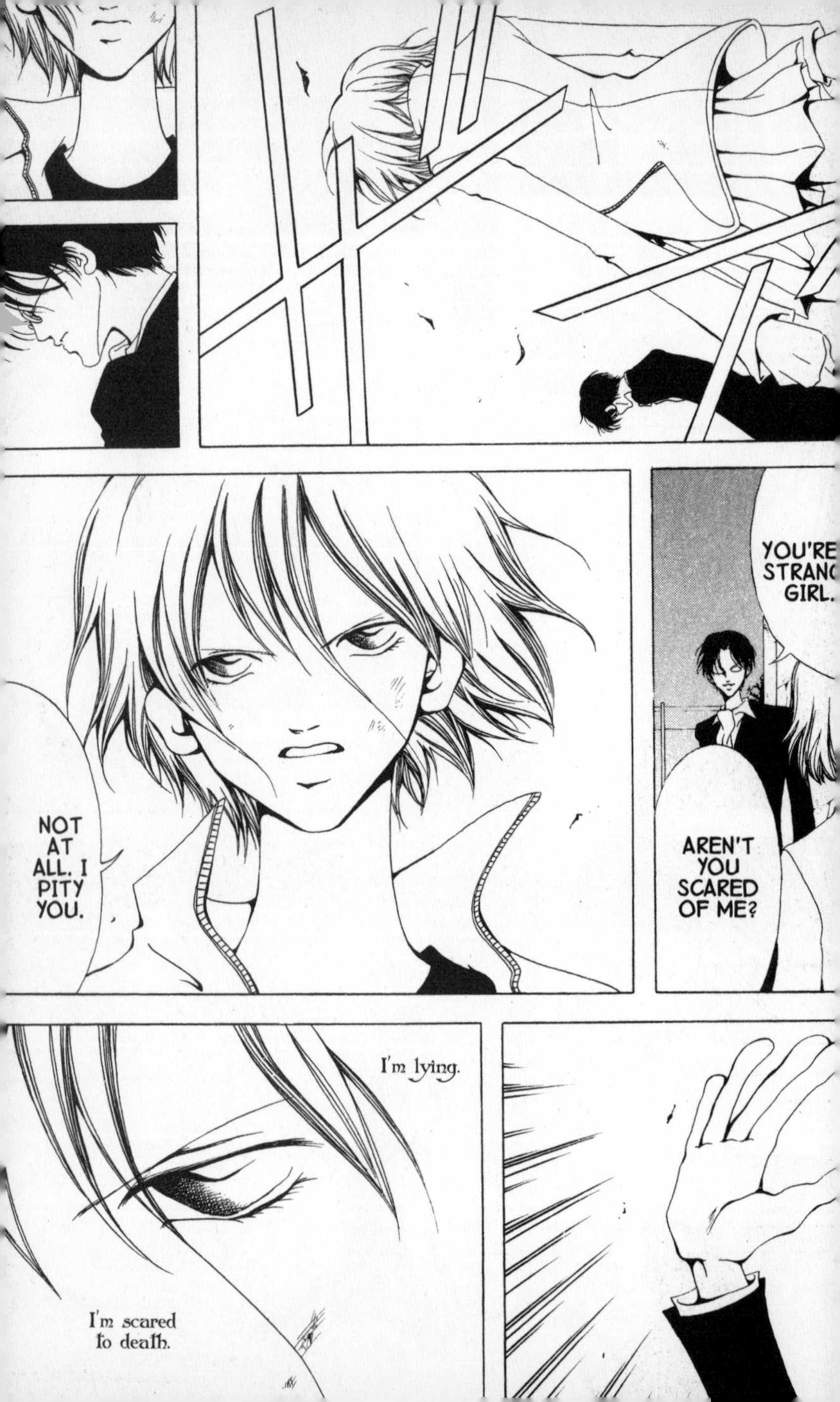
YOU'RE STRANG GIRL.
AREN'T YOU SCARED OF ME?
NOT AT ALL. I PITY YOU.
I'm lying.
I'm scared to death.

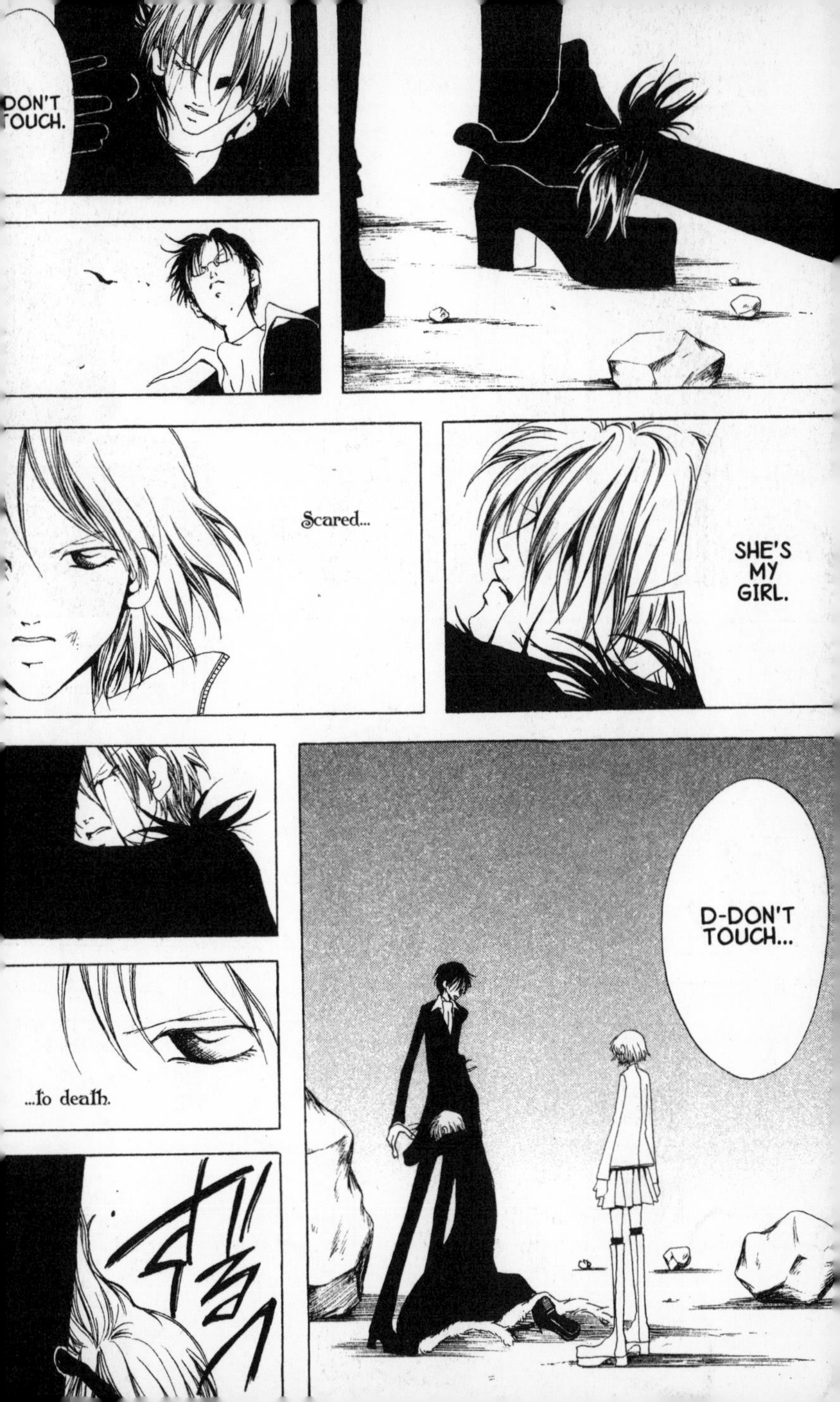
DON'T TOUCH.
SHE'S MY GIRL.
Scared...
D-DON'T TOUCH...
...to death.

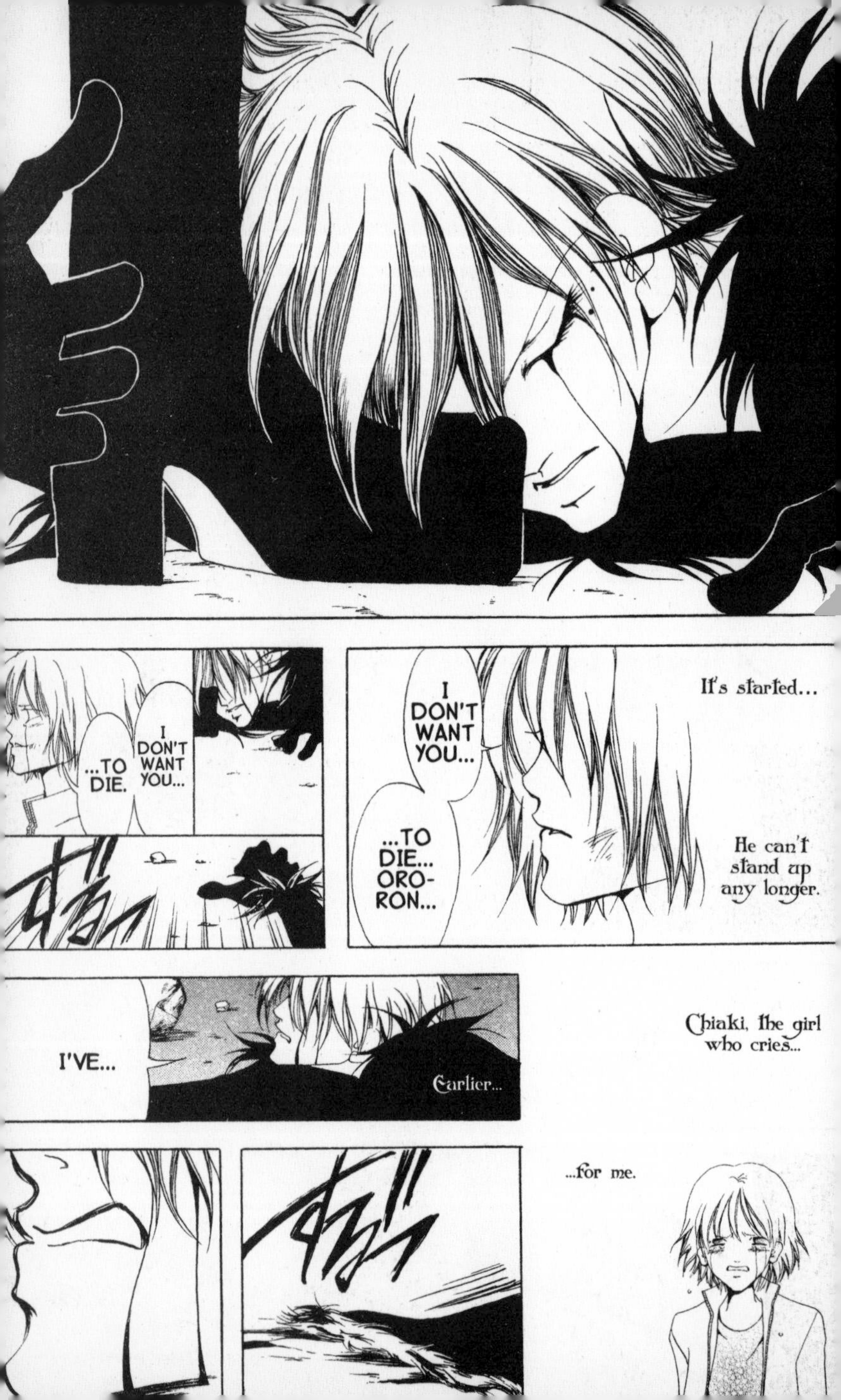
It's started...
I DON'T WANT YOU...
...TO DIE... ORORON...
He can't stand up any longer.
I DON'T WANT YOU...
...TO DIE.
Chiaki, the girl who cries...
Earlier...
I'VE...
...for me.

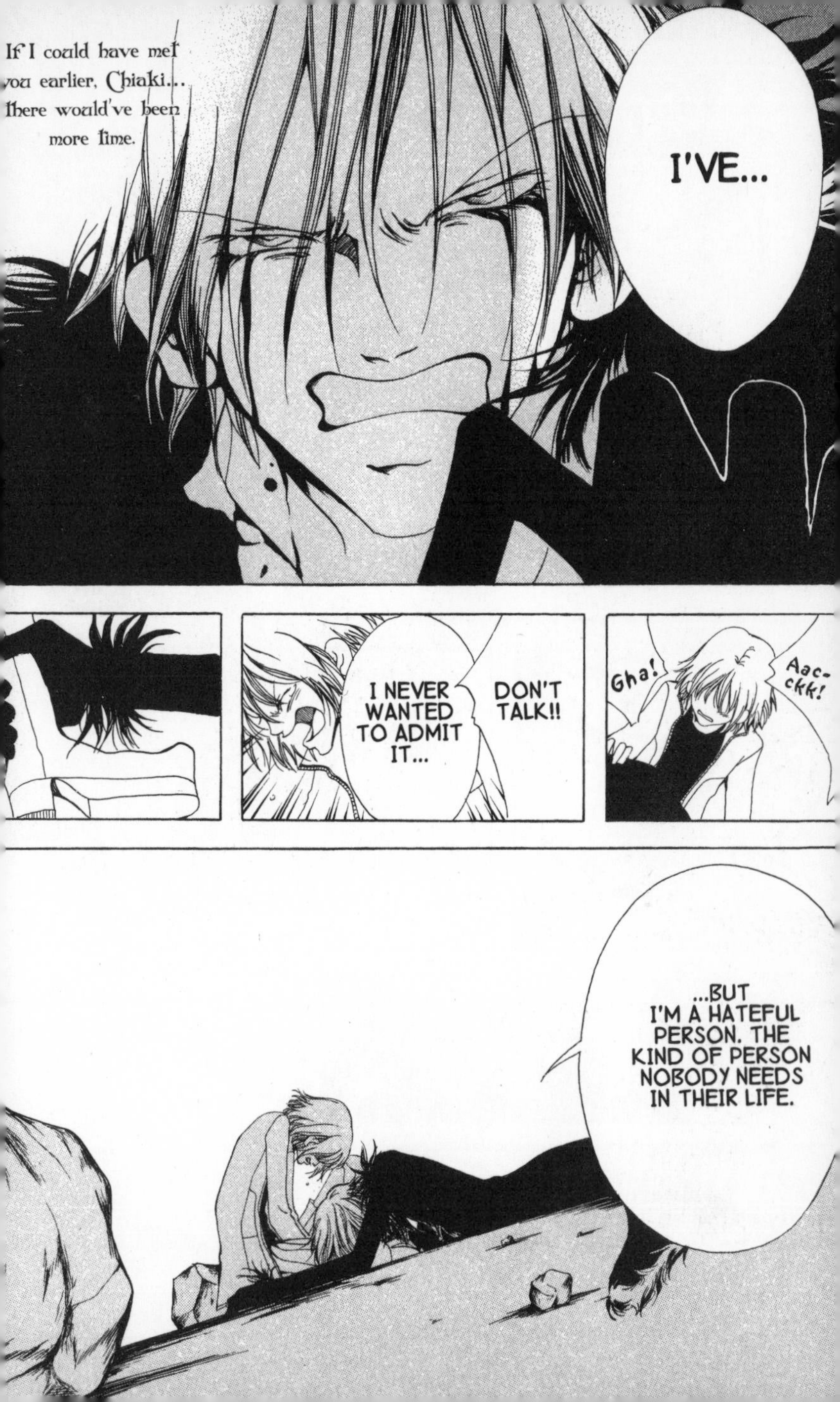
I'VE...
If I could have met you earlier, Chiaki... there would've been more time.
Aac-ckk!
Gha!
DON'T TALK!!
I NEVER WANTED TO ADMIT IT...
...BUT I'M A HATEFUL PERSON. THE KIND OF PERSON NOBODY NEEDS IN THEIR LIFE.

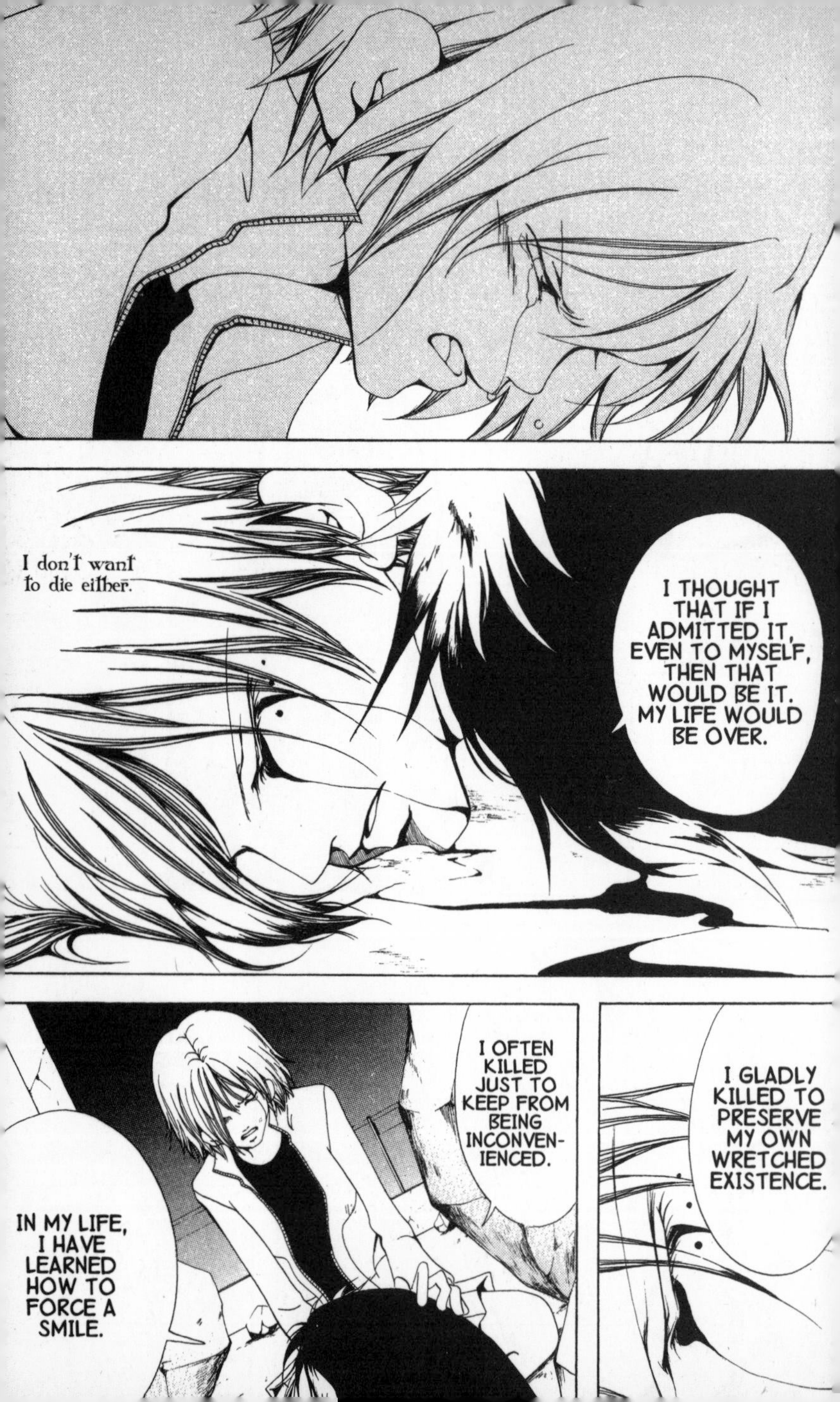

I THOUGHT THAT IF I ADMITTED IT, EVEN TO MYSELF, THEN THAT WOULD BE IT. MY LIFE WOULD BE OVER.
I don't want to die either.
I GLADLY KILLED TO PRESERVE MY OWN WRETCHED EXISTENCE.
I OFTEN KILLED JUST TO KEEP FROM BEING INCONVEN-IENCED.
IN MY LIFE, I HAVE LEARNED HOW TO FORCE A SMILE.

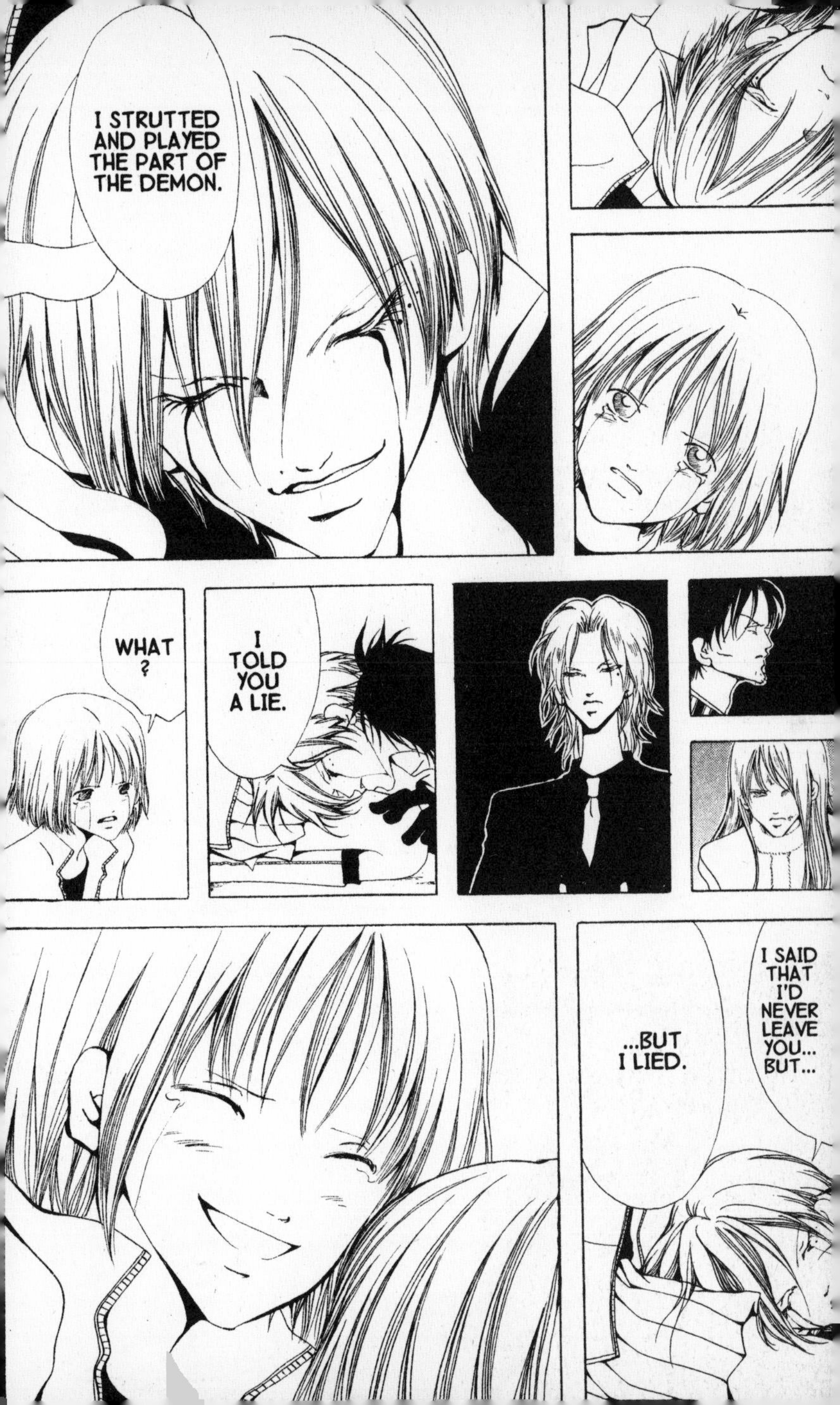
I STRUTTED AND PLAYED THE PART OF THE DEMON.
I TOLD YOU A LIE.
WHAT?
I SAID THAT I'D NEVER LEAVE YOU... BUT...
...BUT I LIED.

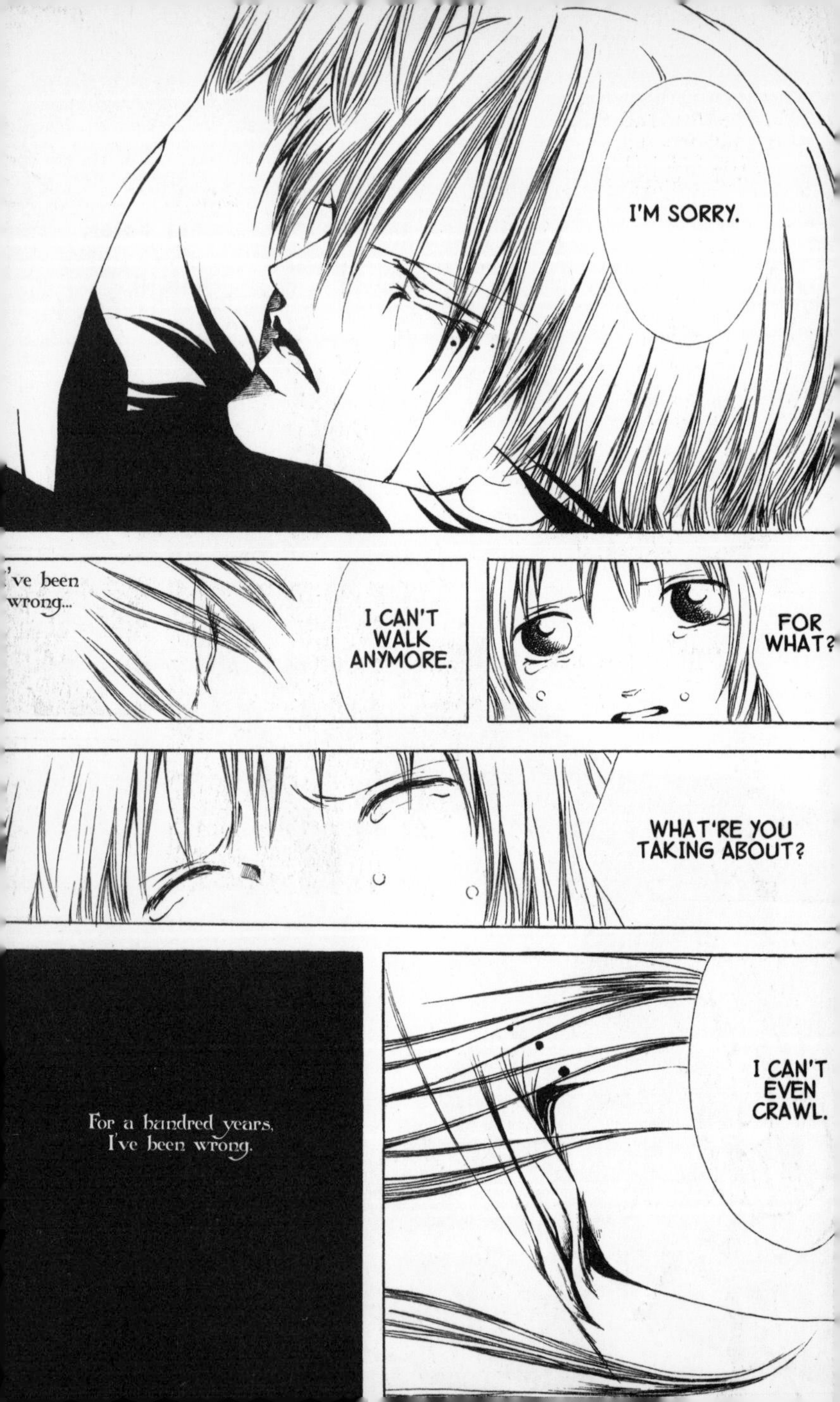
I'M SORRY.
FOR WHAT?
I CAN'T WALK ANYMORE.
've been wrong...
WHAT'RE YOU TAKING ABOUT?
I CAN'T EVEN CRAWL.
For a hundred years, I've been wrong.

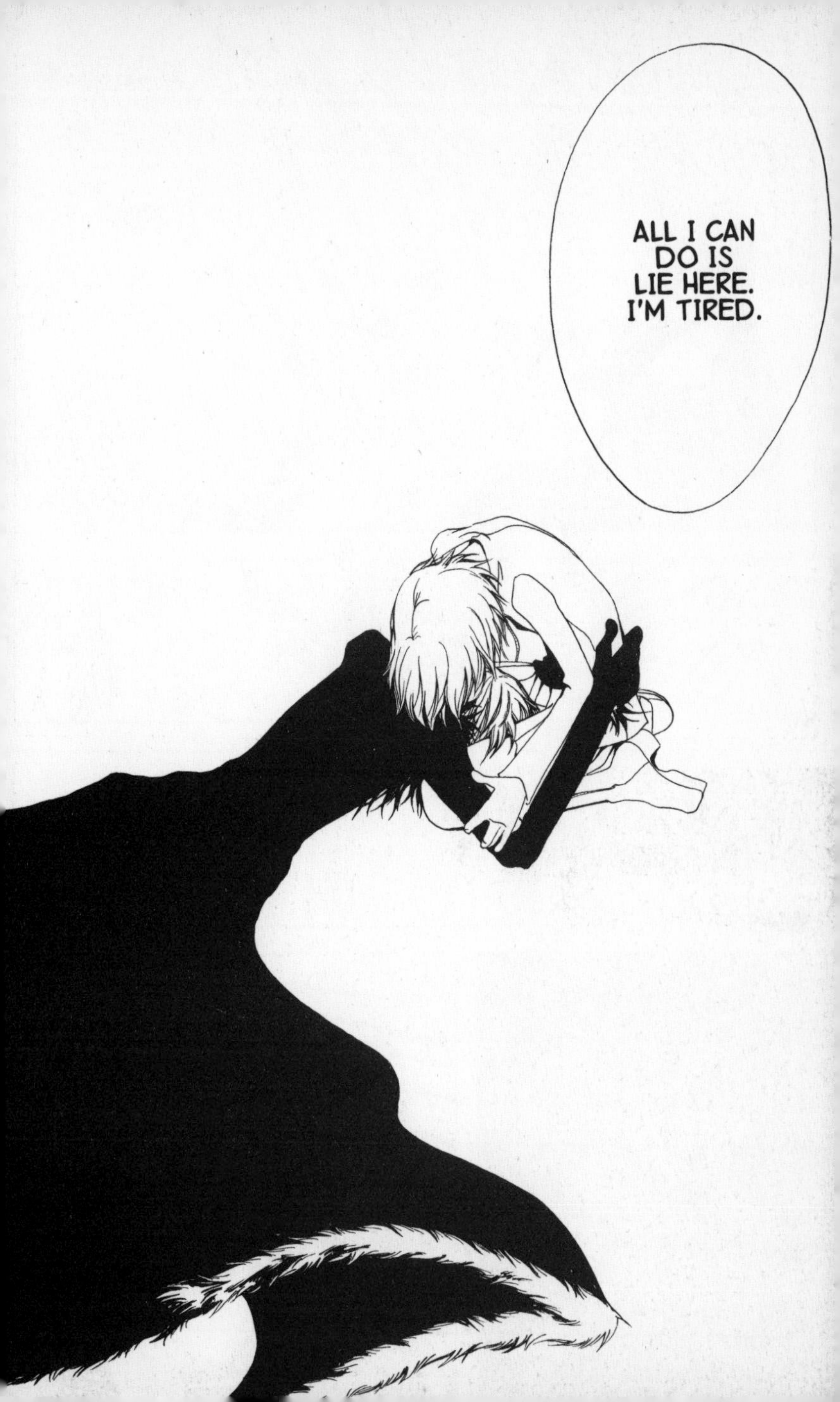
ALL I CAN DO IS LIE HERE. I'M TIRED.

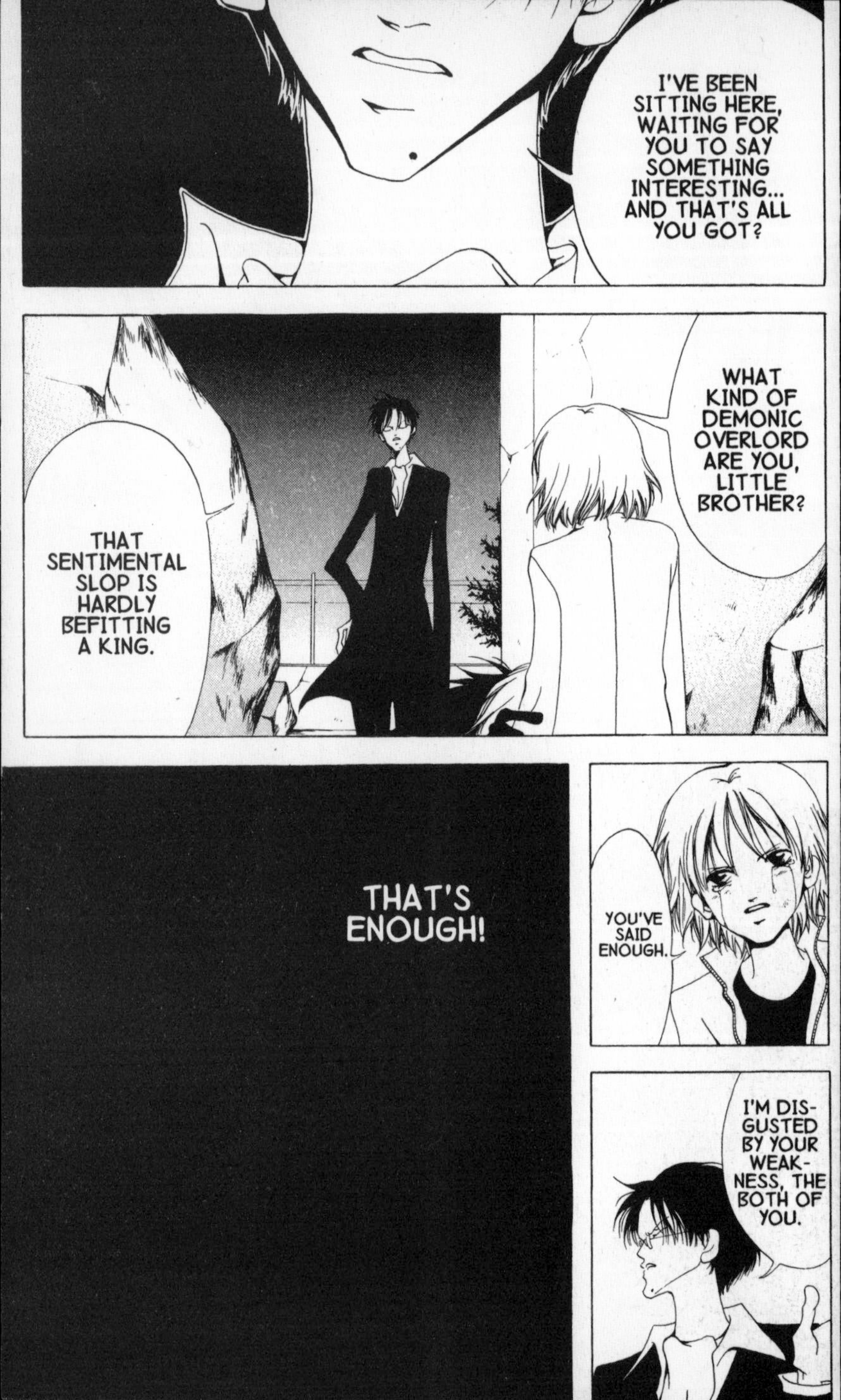
I'VE BEEN SITTING HERE, WAITING FOR YOU TO SAY SOMETHING INTERESTING... AND THAT'S ALL YOU GOT?
WHAT KIND OF DEMONIC OVERLORD ARE YOU, LITTLE BROTHER?
THAT SENTIMENTAL SLOP IS HARDLY BEFITTING A KING.
YOU'VE SAID ENOUGH.
I'M DISGUSTED BY YOUR WEAKNESS, THE BOTH OF YOU.
THAT'S ENOUGH!

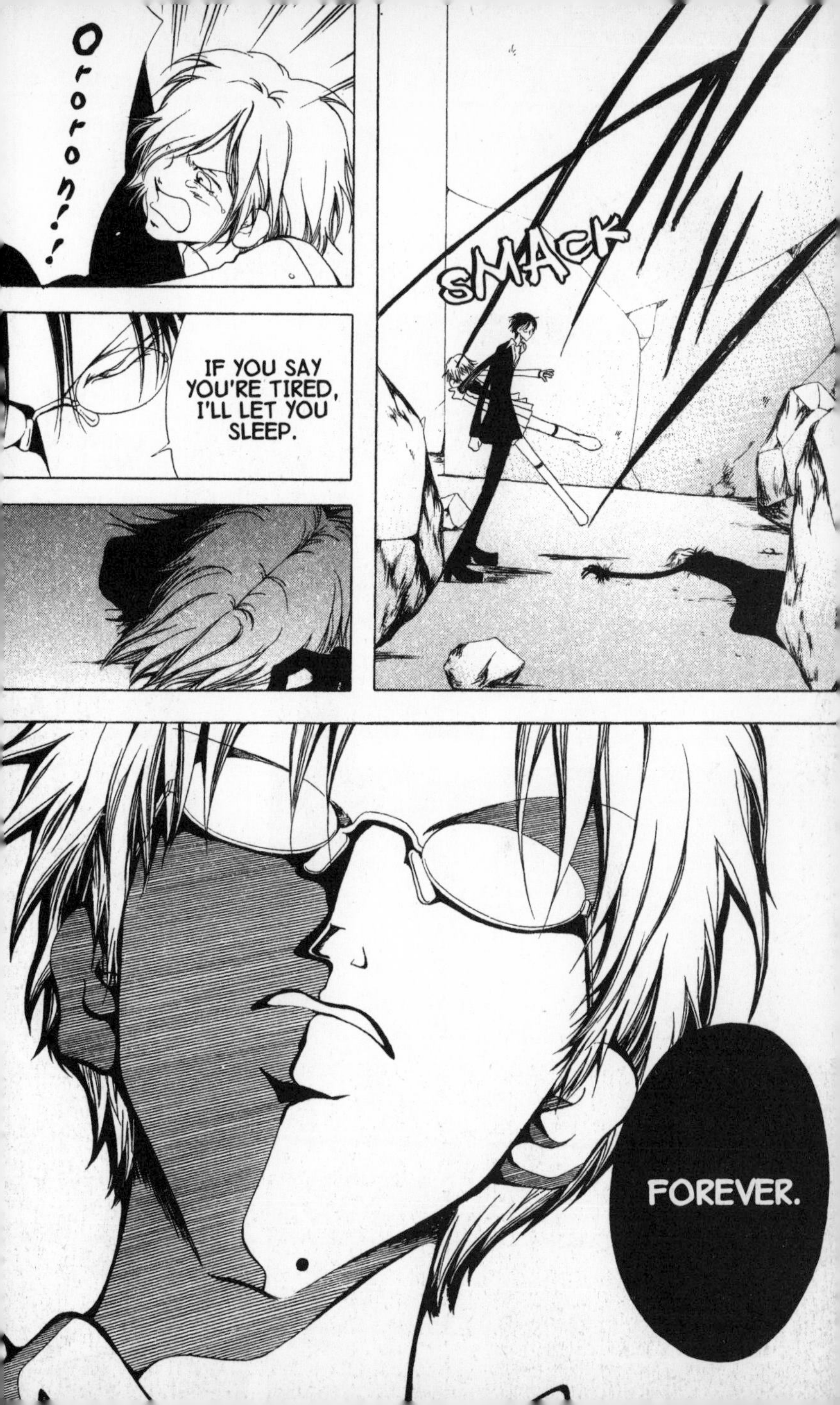
SMACK
Ororon!!!
IF YOU SAY YOU'RE TIRED, I'LL LET YOU SLEEP.
FOREVER.

-16-
LONG
NIGHT
04

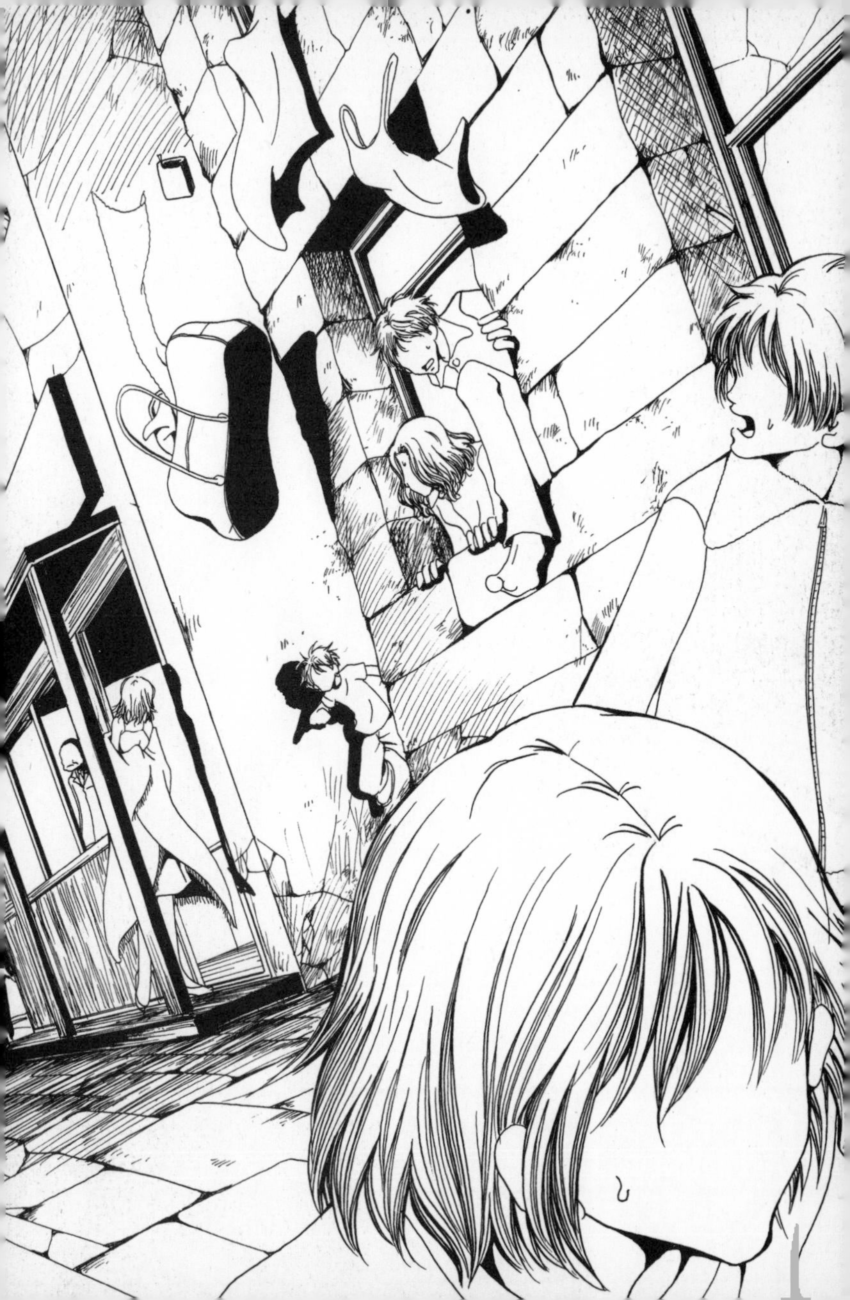

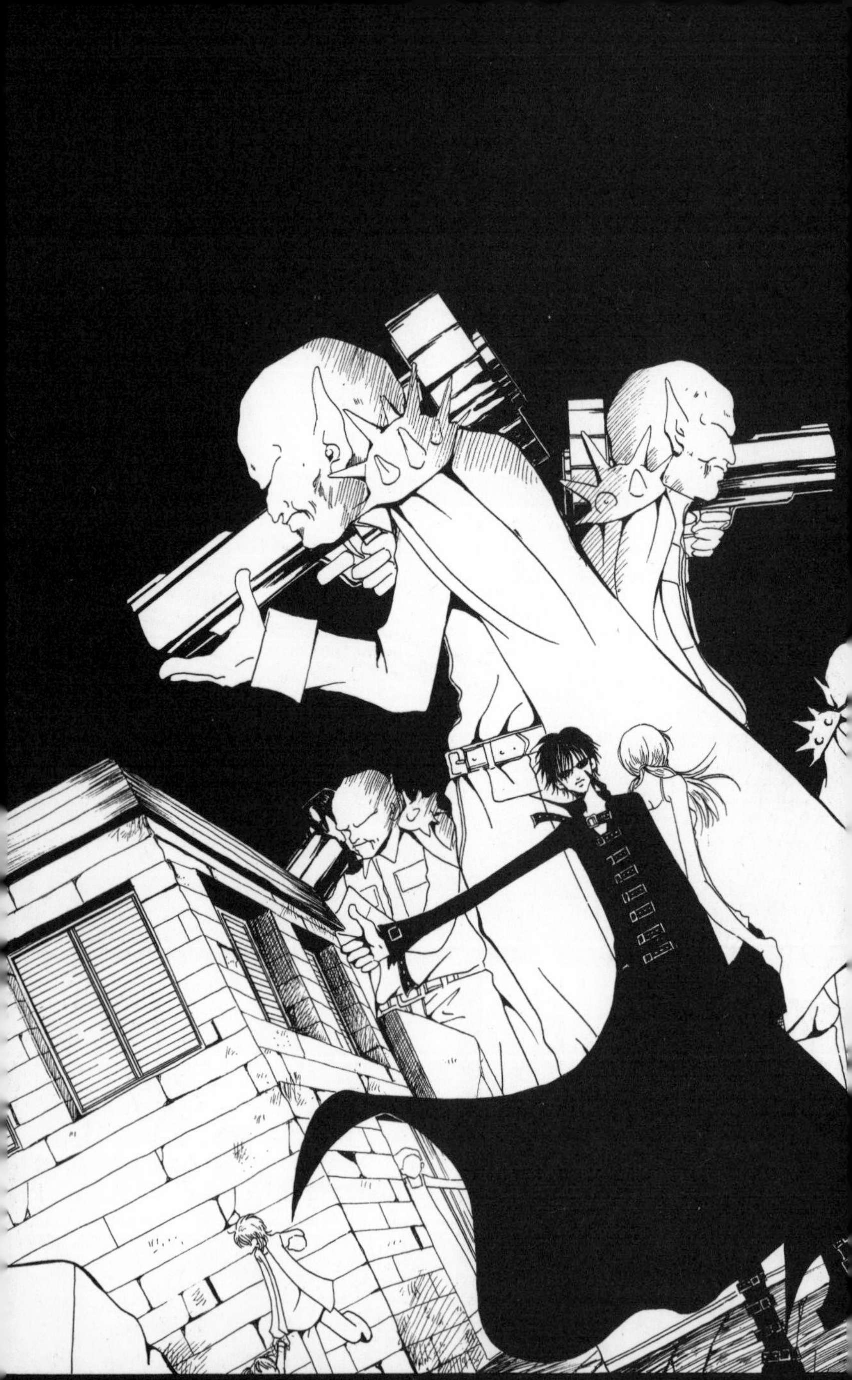

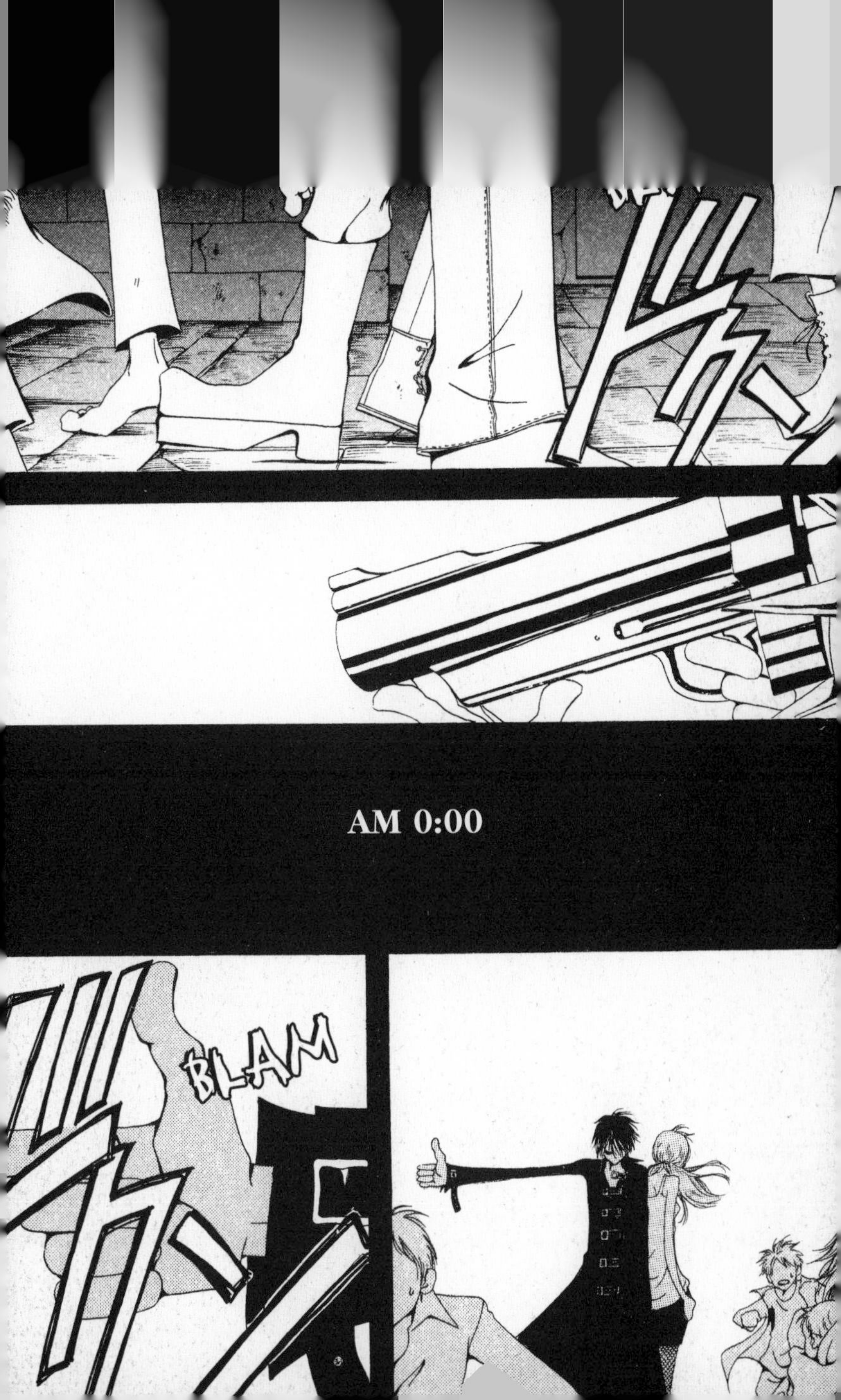
AM 0:00
BLAM

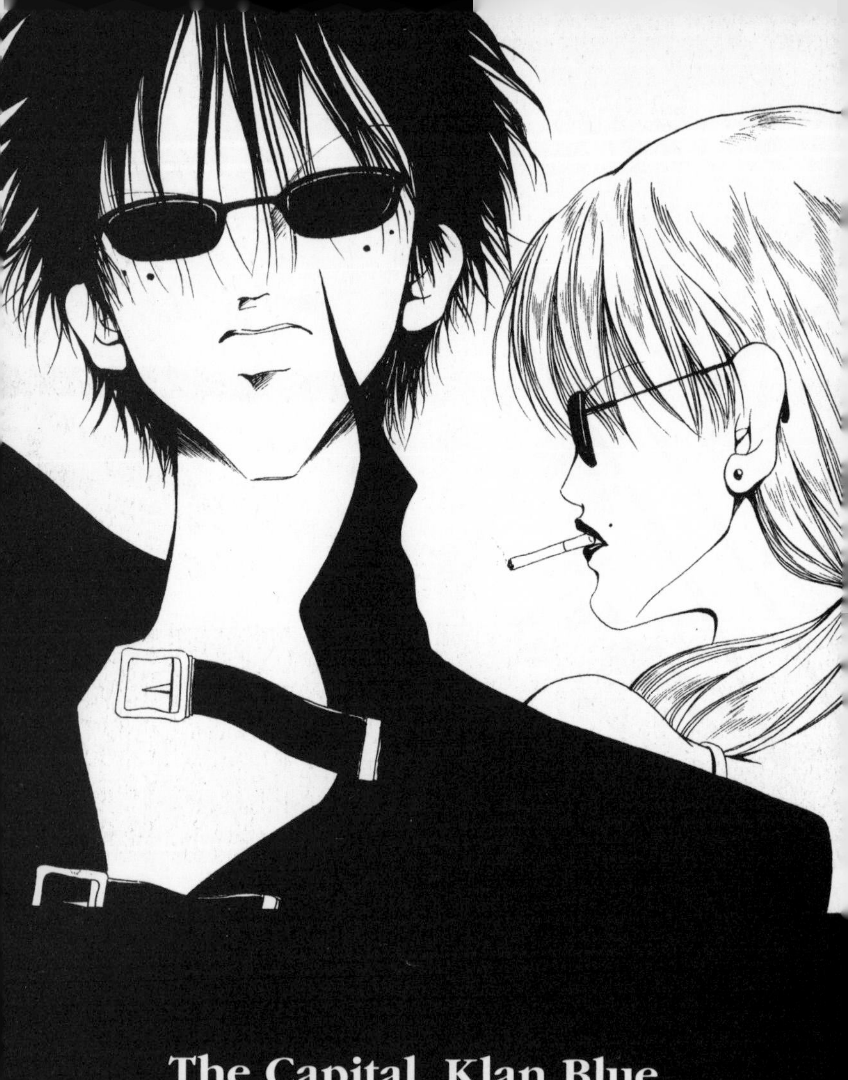

The Capital, Klan Blue

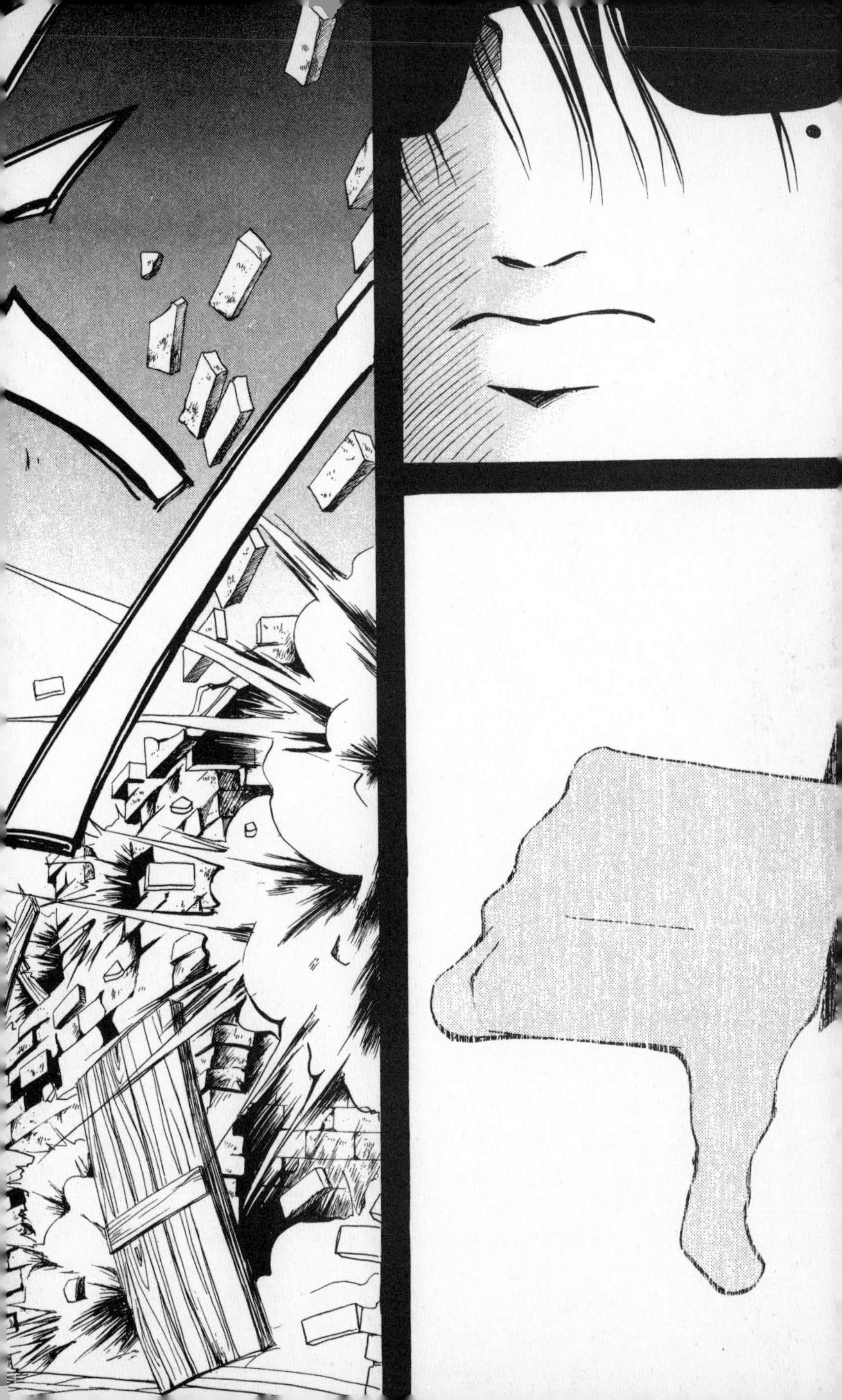

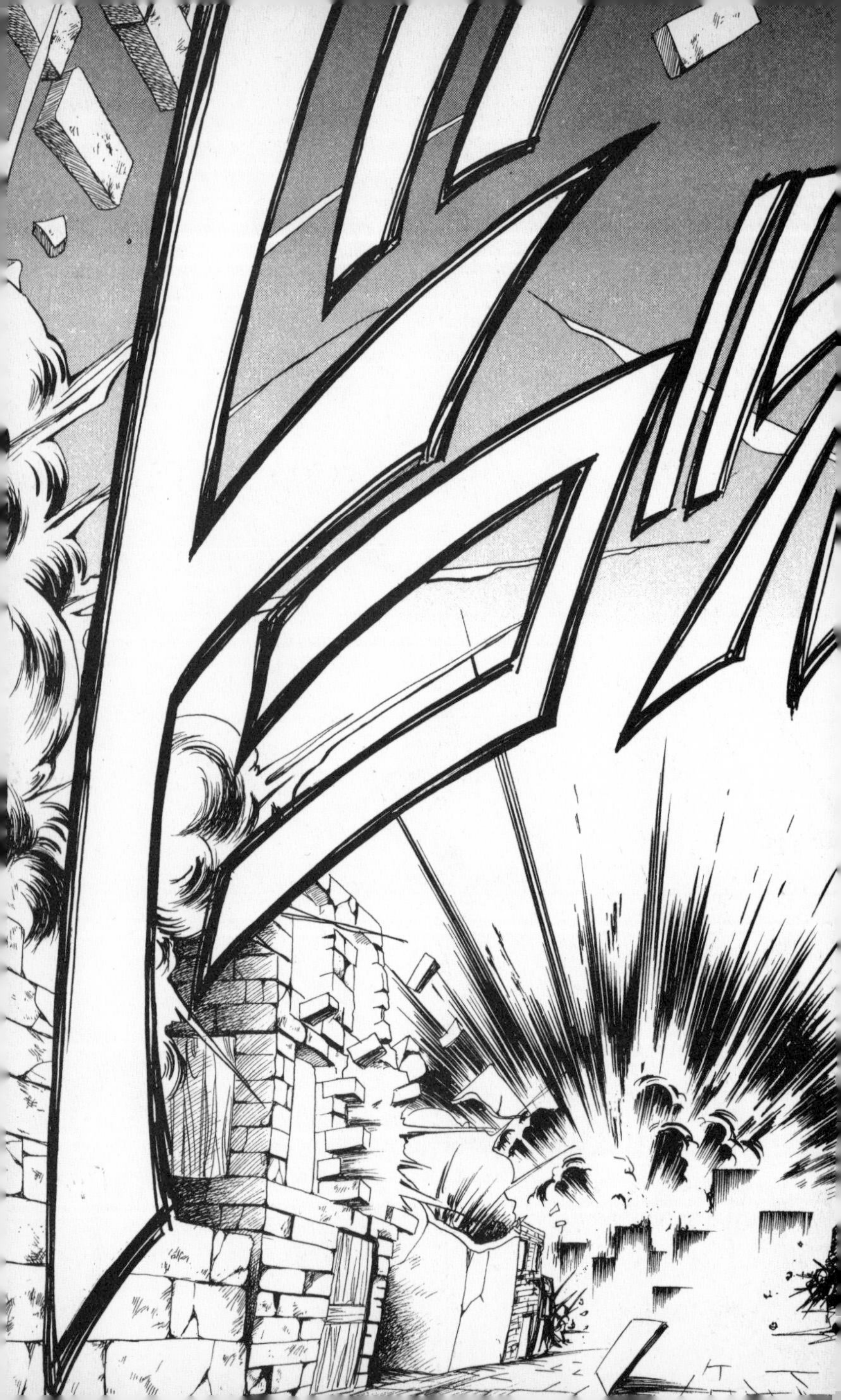

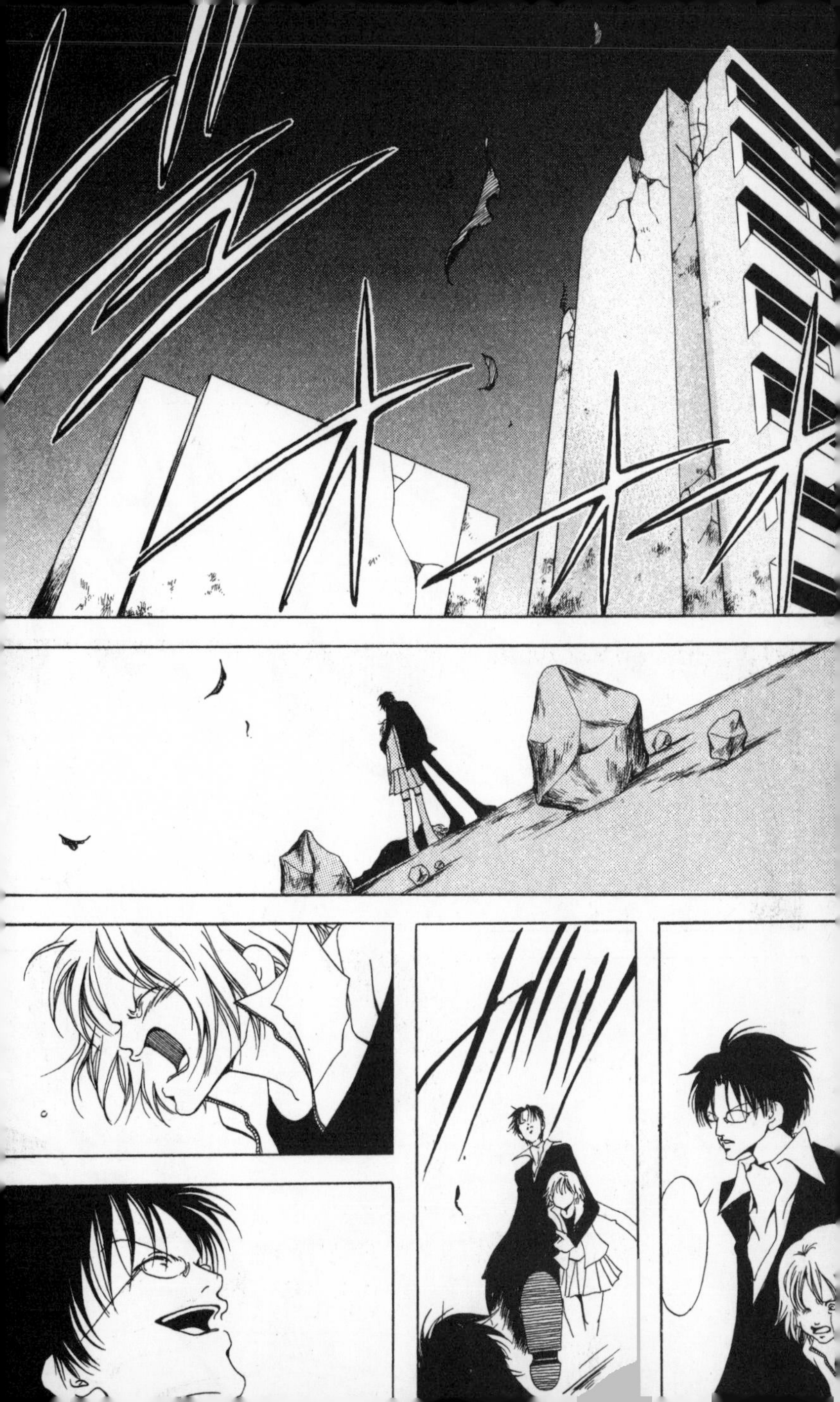

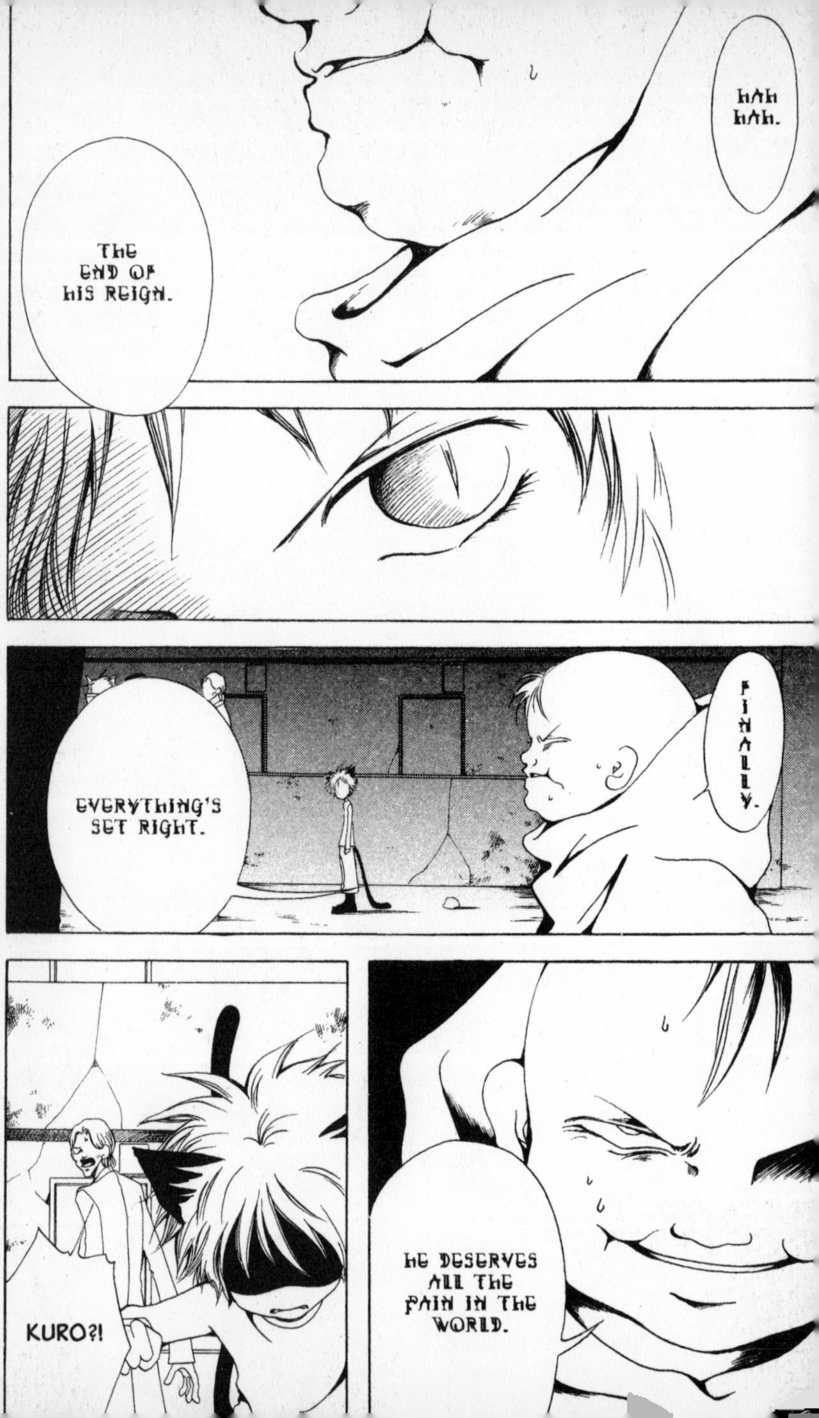
HAH HAH.
THE END OF HIS REIGN.
FINALLY.
EVERYTHING'S SET RIGHT.
HE DESERVES ALL THE PAIN IN THE WORLD.
KURO?!

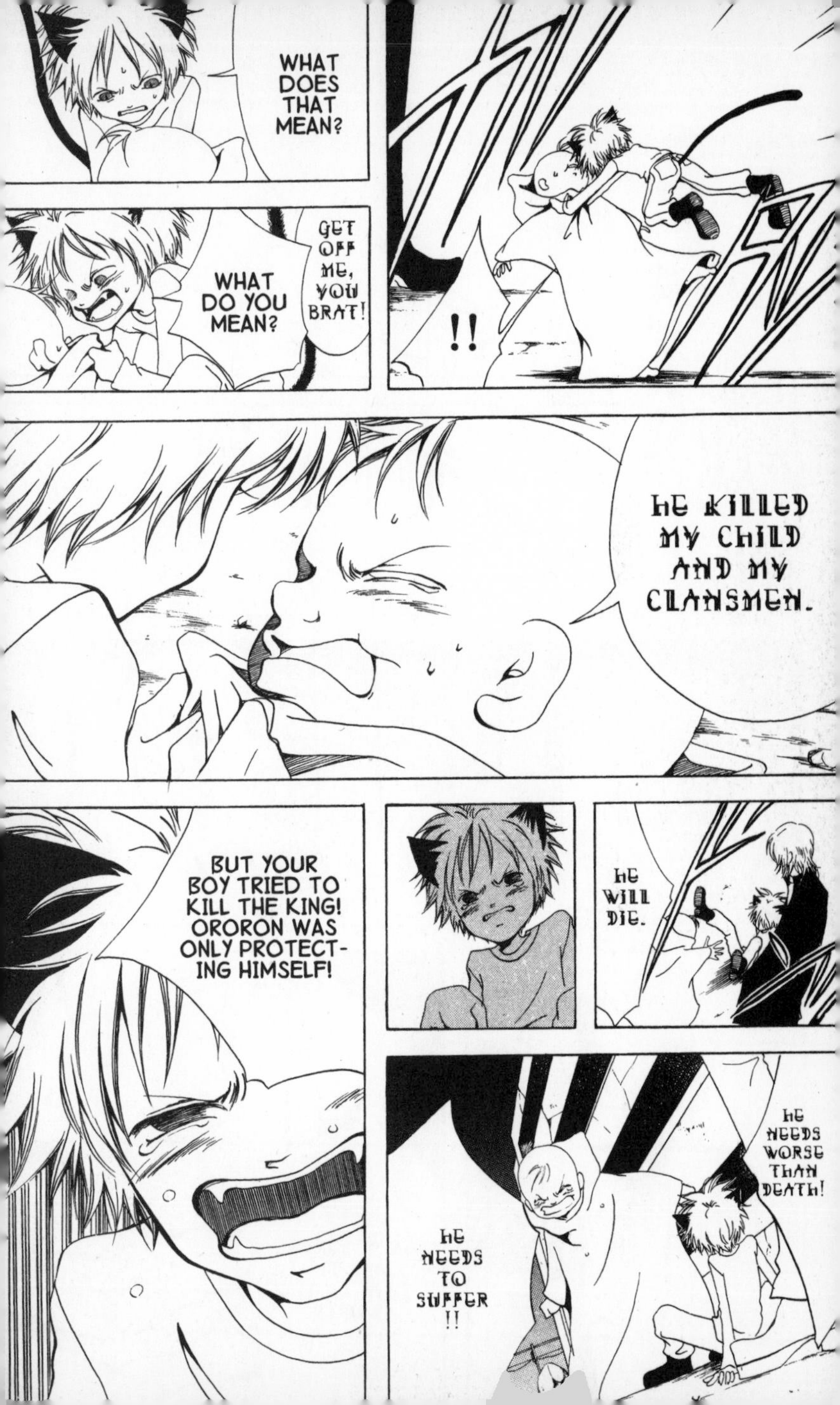
!!
WHAT DOES THAT MEAN?
GET OFF ME, YOU BRAT!
WHAT DO YOU MEAN?
HE KILLED MY CHILD AND MY CLANSMEN.
HE WILL DIE.
HE NEEDS WORSE THAN DEATH!
HE NEEDS TO SUFFER !!
BUT YOUR BOY TRIED TO KILL THE KING! ORORON WAS ONLY PROTECT-ING HIMSELF!

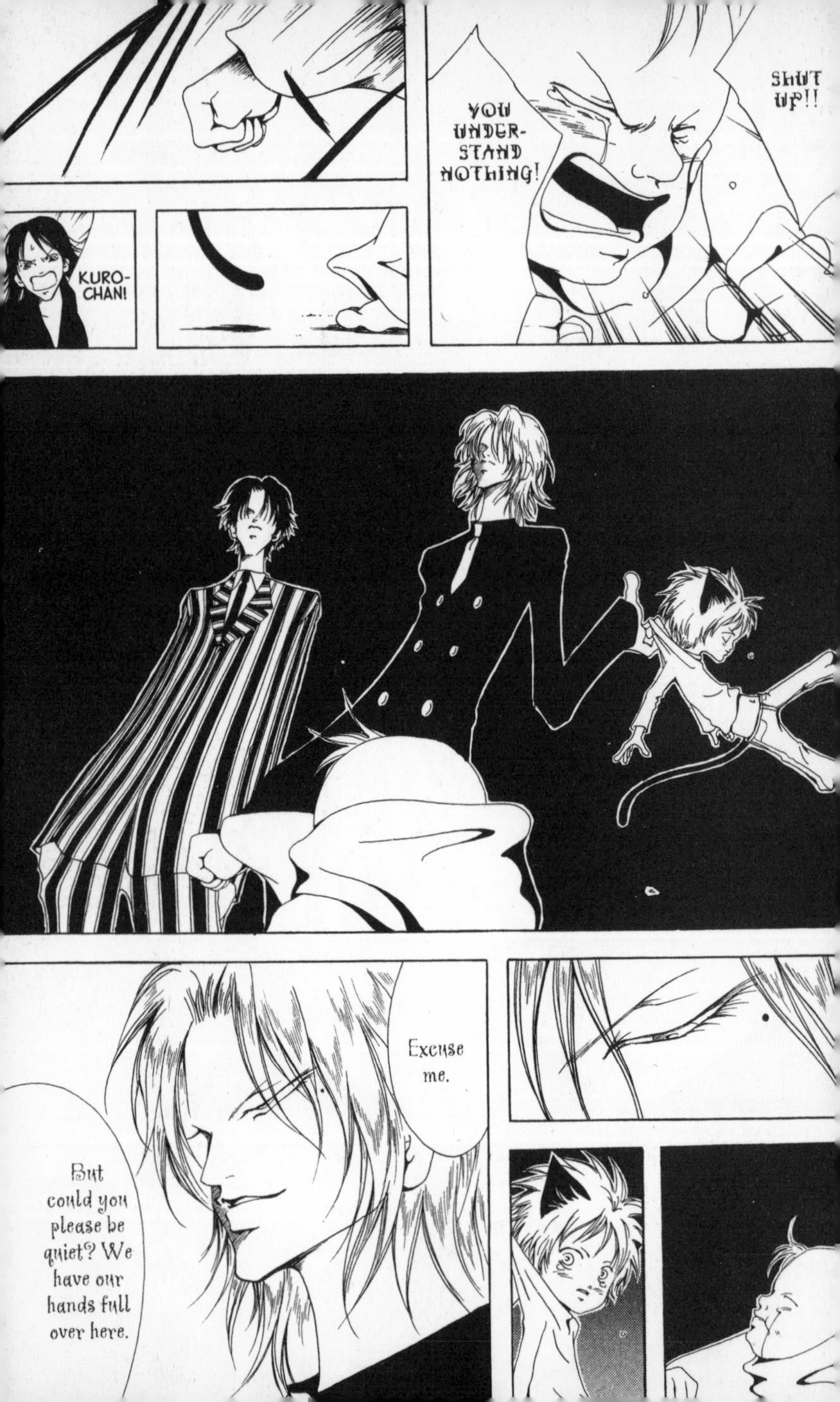
SHUT UP!!
YOU UNDER-STAND NOTHING!
KURO-CHAN!
Excuse me.
But could you please be quiet? We have our hands full over here.

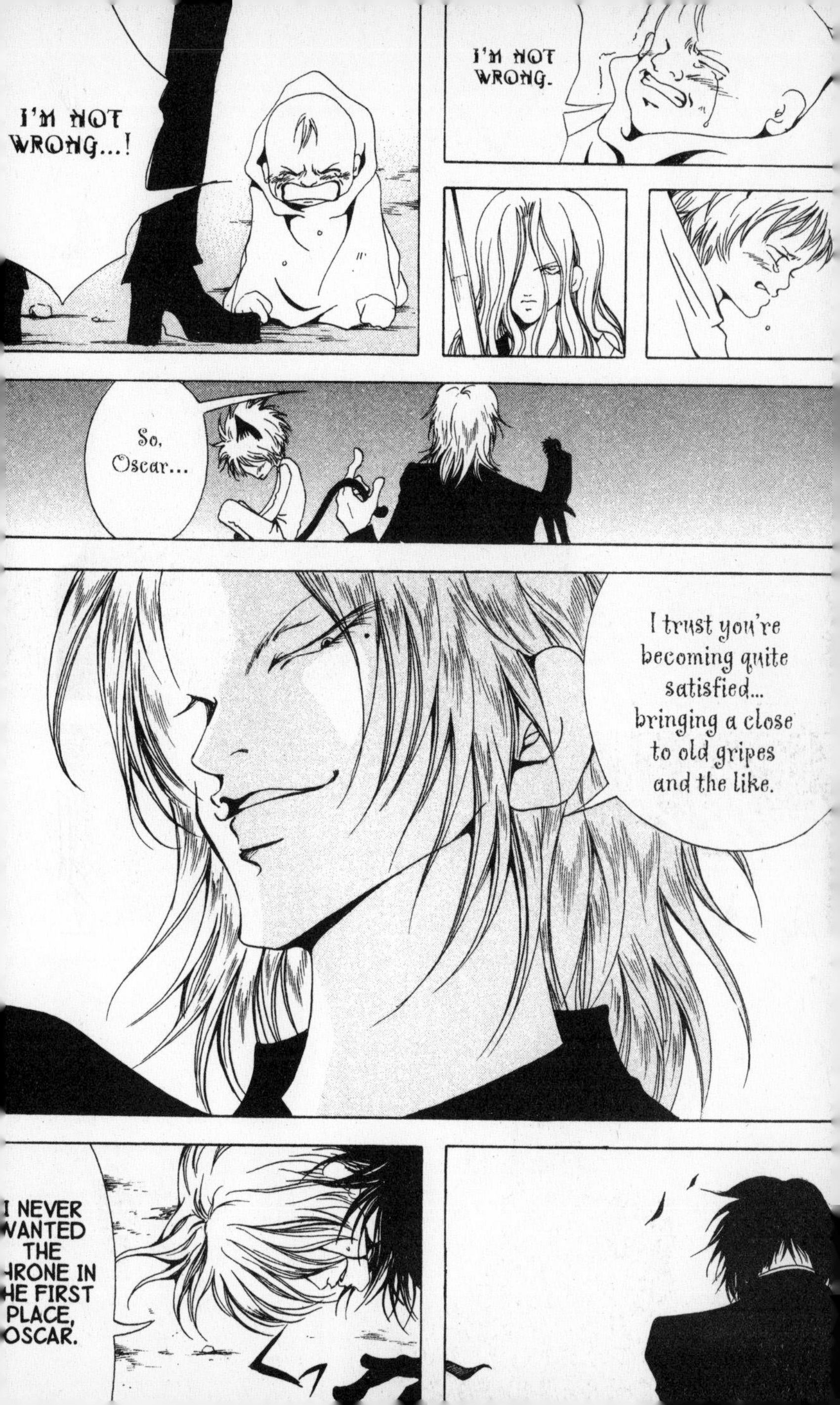
I'M NOT WRONG.
I'M NOT WRONG...!
So, Oscar...
I trust you're becoming quite satisfied... bringing a close to old gripes and the like.
I NEVER WANTED THE HRONE IN HE FIRST PLACE, OSCAR.

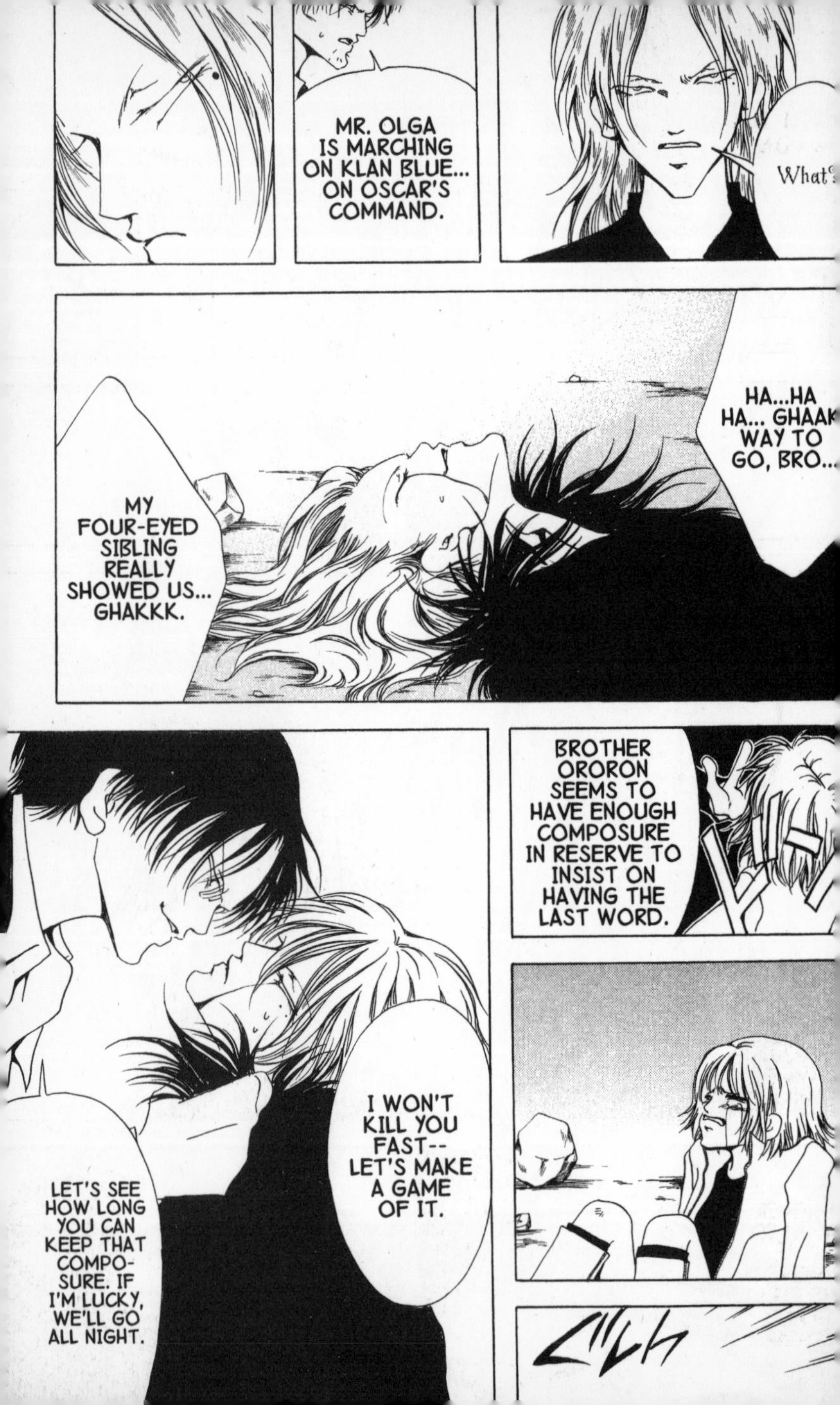
What?
MR. OLGA IS MARCHING ON KLAN BLUE... ON OSCAR'S COMMAND.
HA...HA HA... GHAAK WAY TO GO, BRO...
MY FOUR-EYED SIBLING REALLY SHOWED US... GHAKKK.
BROTHER ORORON SEEMS TO HAVE ENOUGH COMPOSURE IN RESERVE TO INSIST ON HAVING THE LAST WORD.
I WON'T KILL YOU FAST-- LET'S MAKE A GAME OF IT.
LET'S SEE HOW LONG YOU CAN KEEP THAT COMPO-SURE. IF I'M LUCKY, WE'LL GO ALL NIGHT.

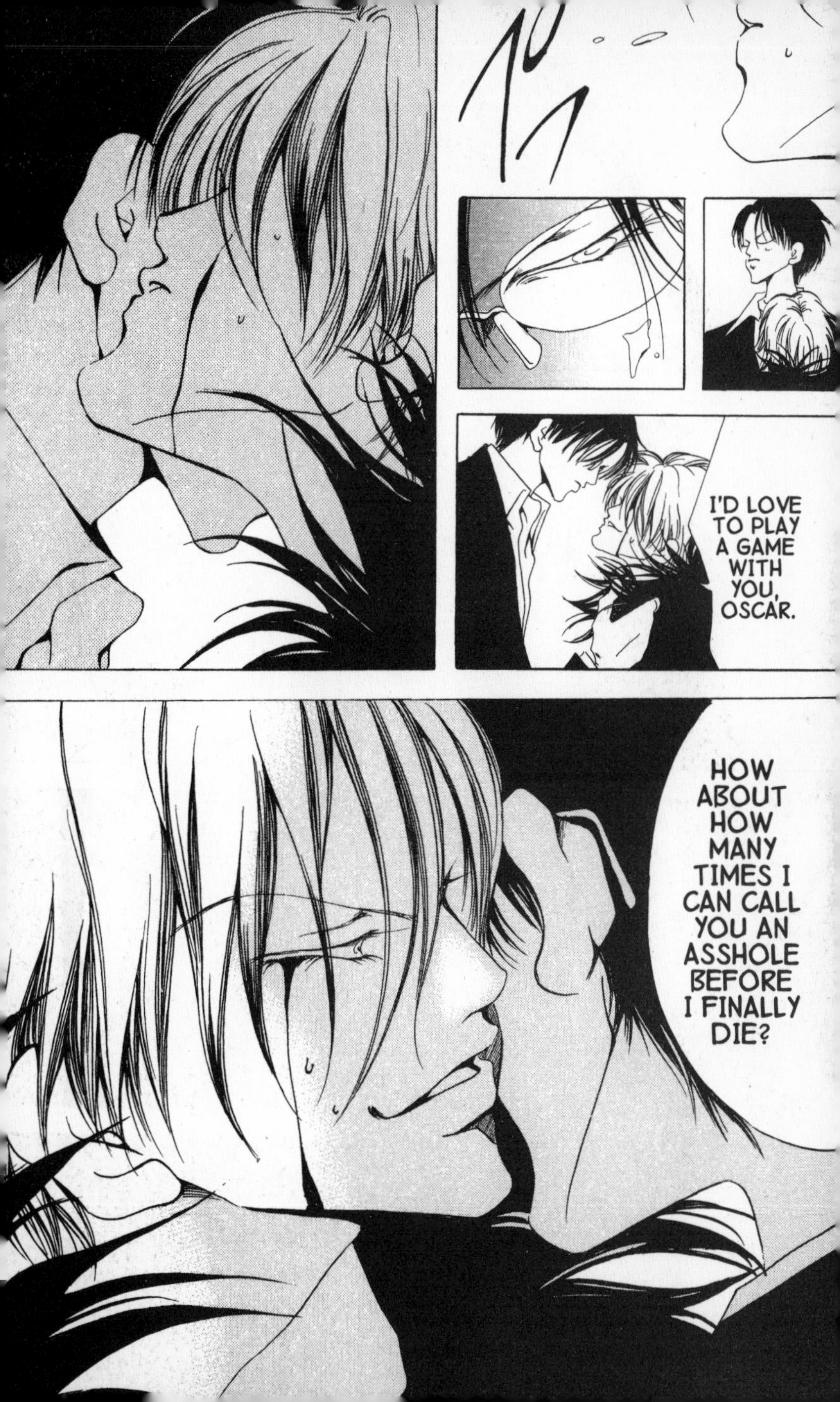
I'D LOVE TO PLAY A GAME WITH YOU, OSCAR.
HOW ABOUT HOW MANY TIMES I CAN CALL YOU AN ASSHOLE BEFORE I FINALLY DIE?

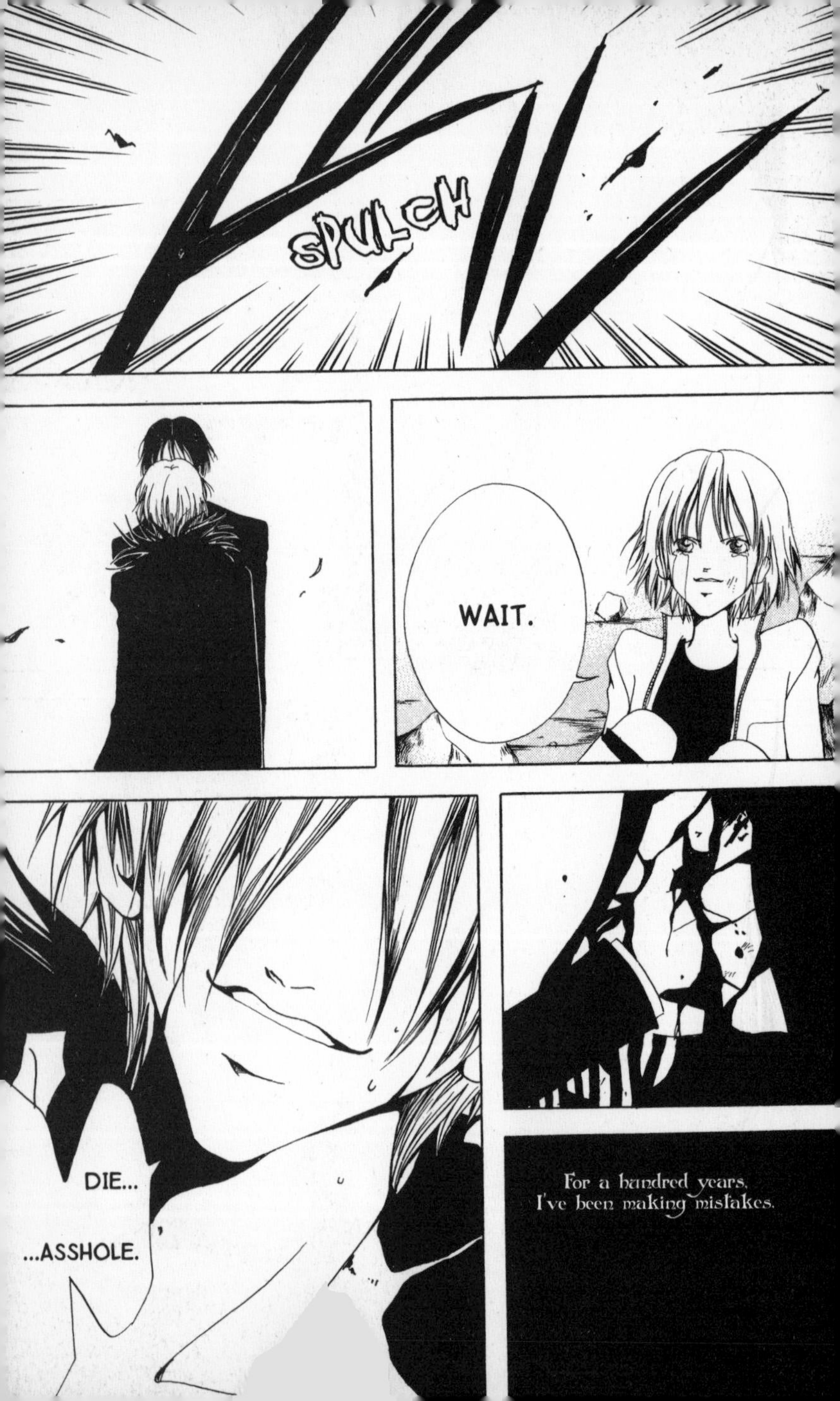
SPULCH
WAIT.
For a hundred years, I've been making mistakes.
DIE...
...ASSHOLE.

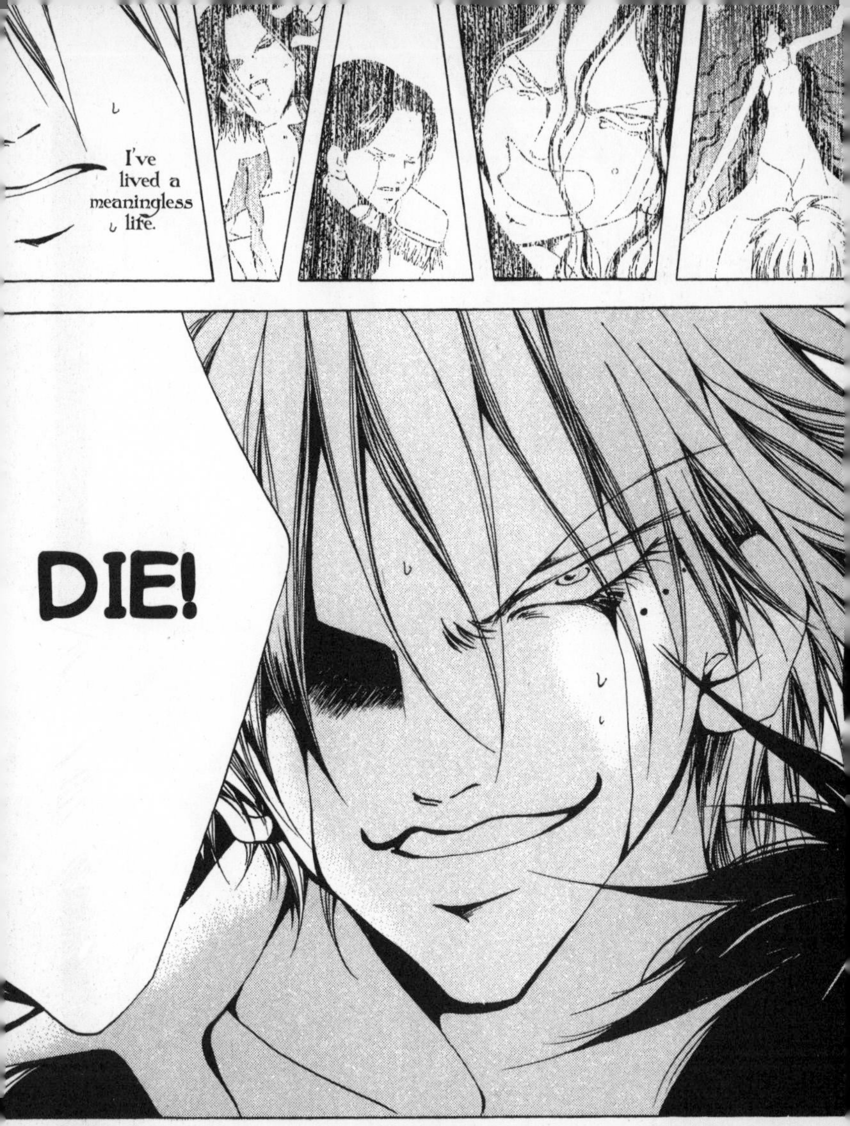

I've lived a meaningless life.
DIE!

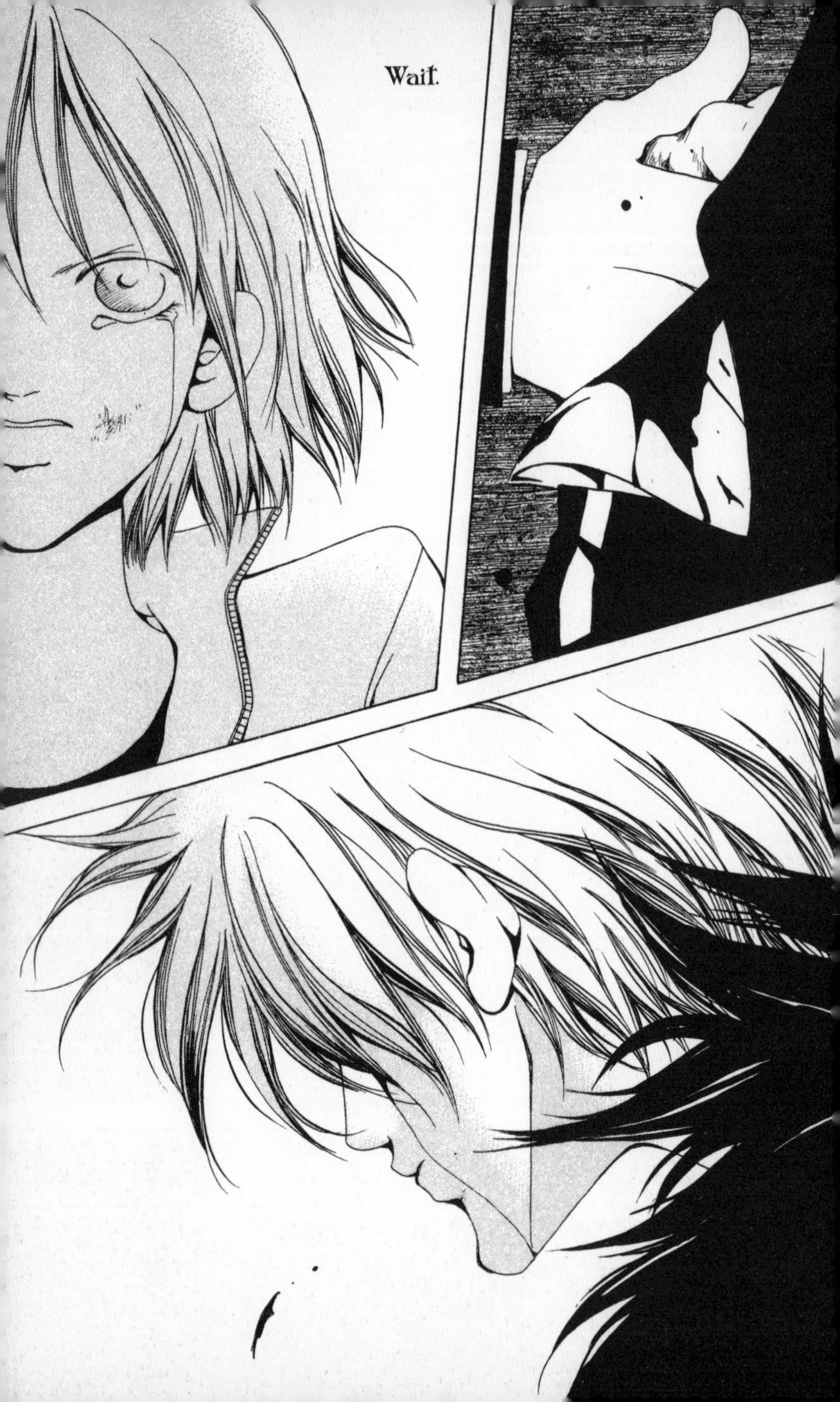
Wait.

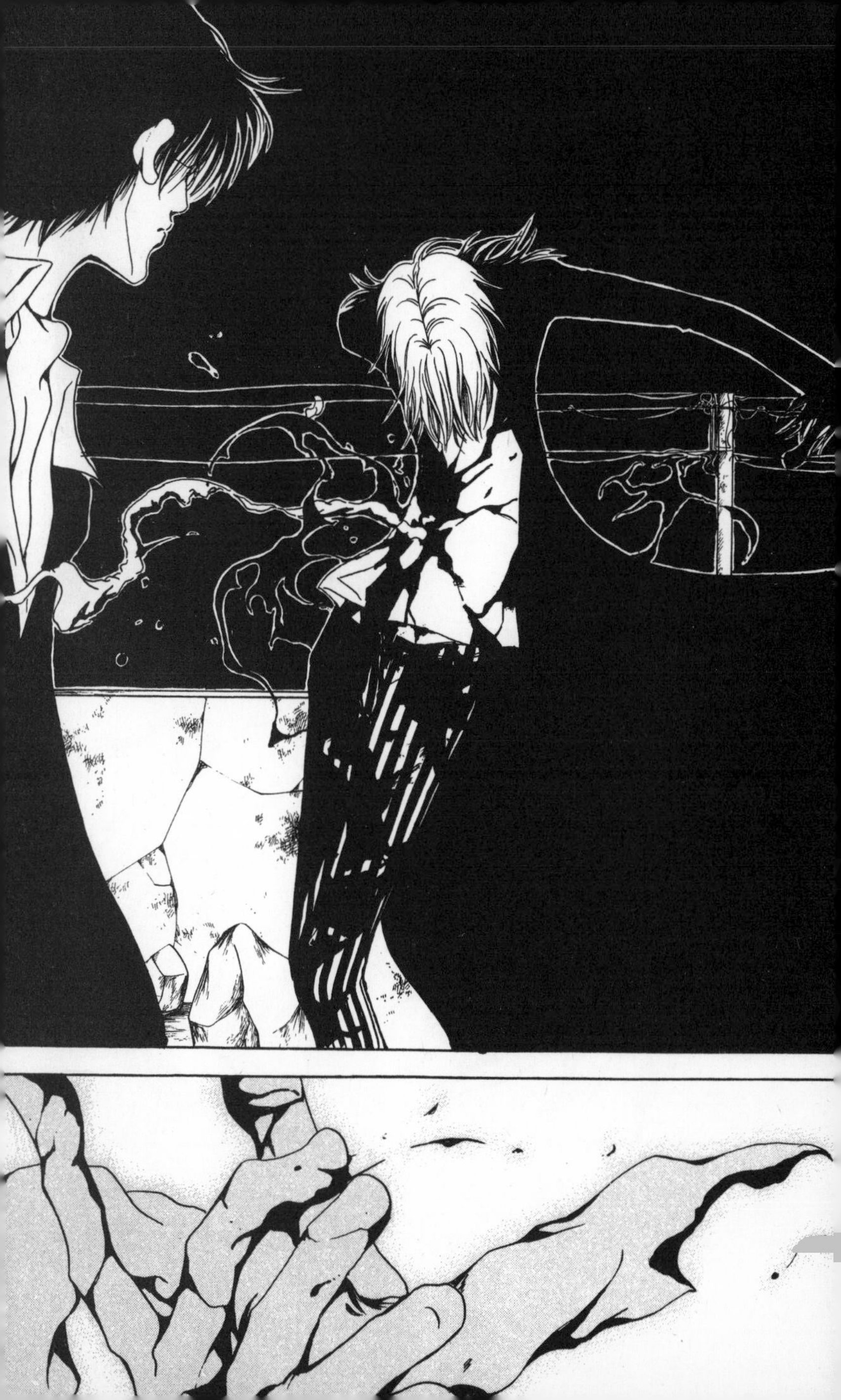

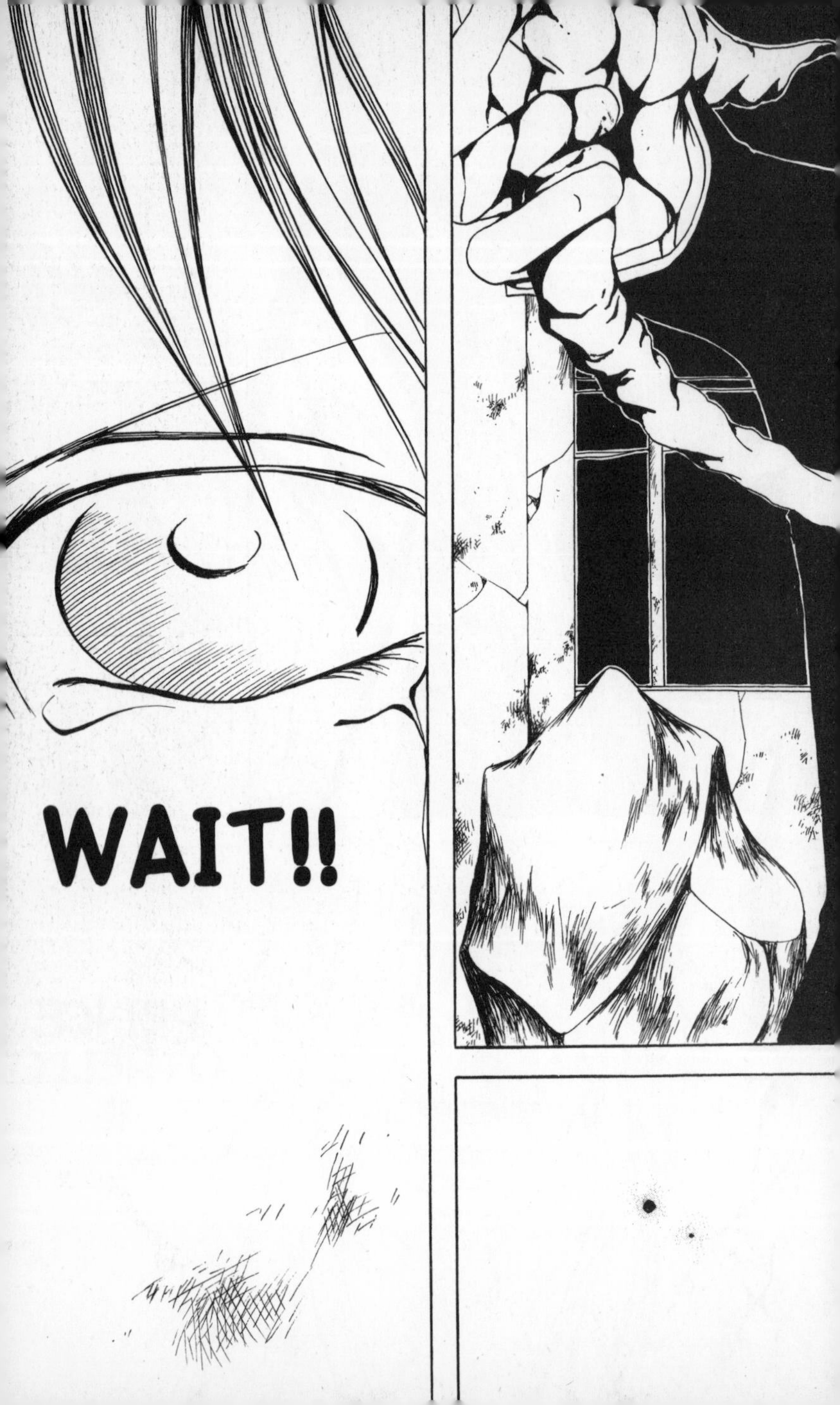
WAIT!!

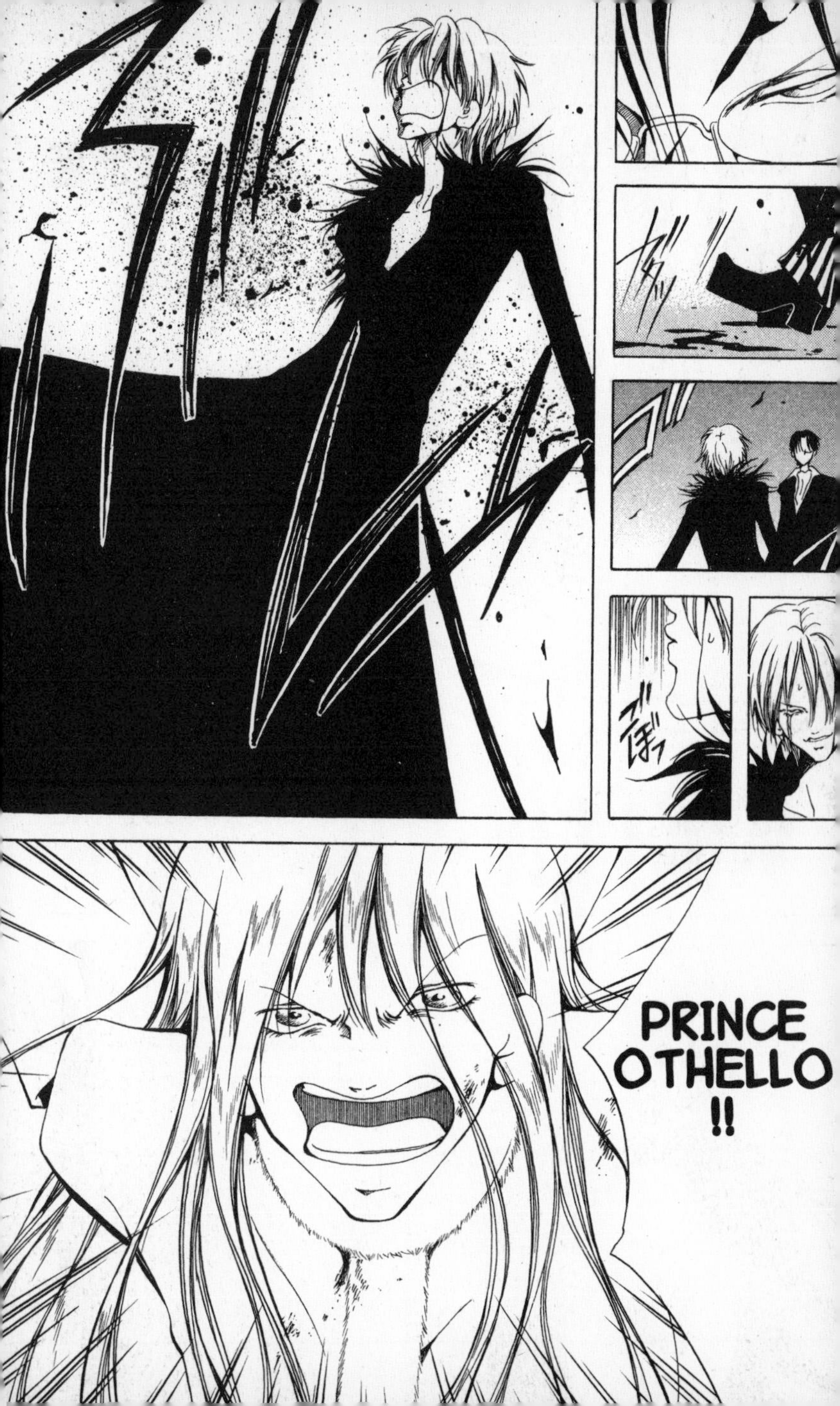
PRINCE OTHELLO !!

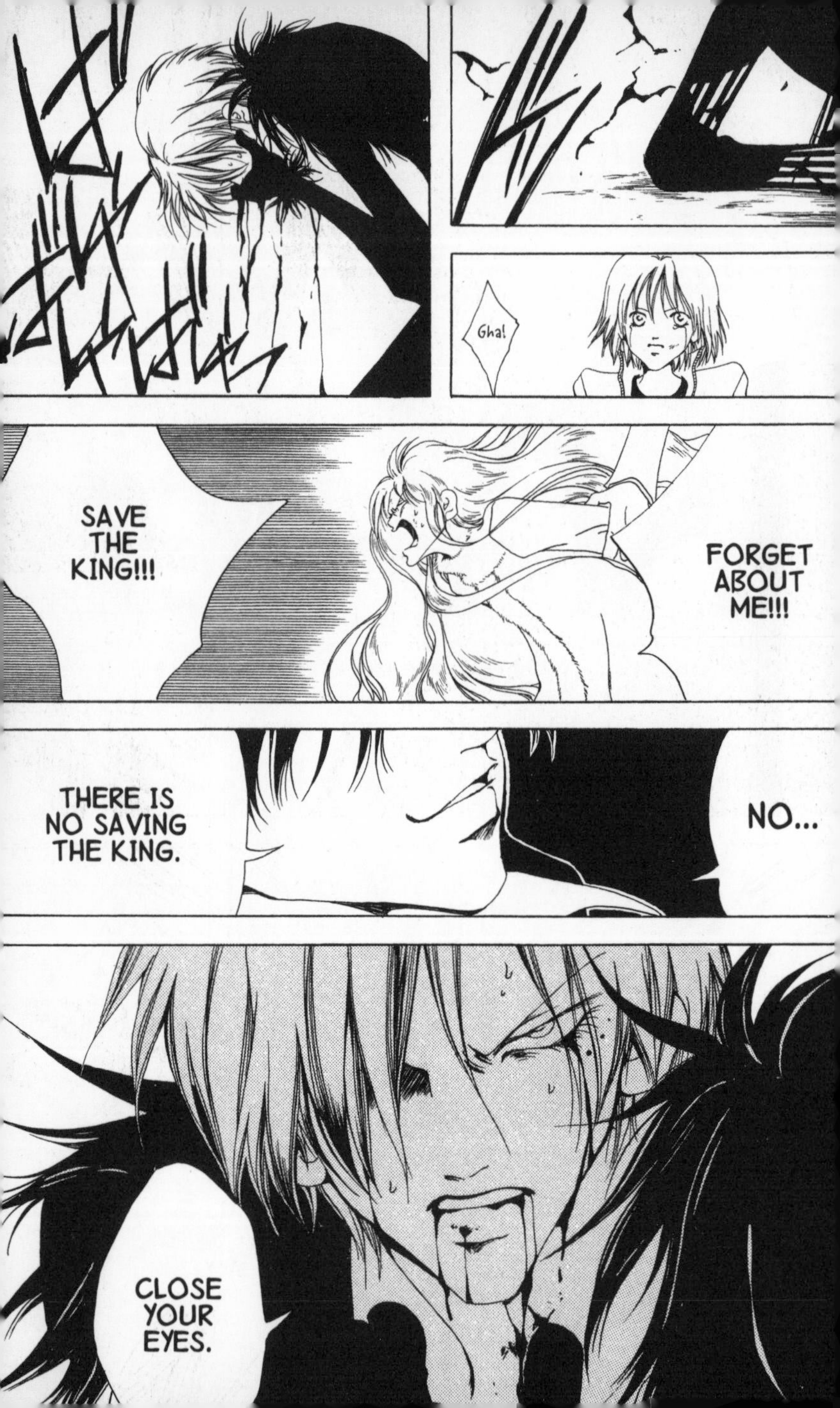
Gha!
FORGET ABOUT ME!!!
SAVE THE KING!!!
NO...
THERE IS NO SAVING THE KING.
CLOSE YOUR EYES.

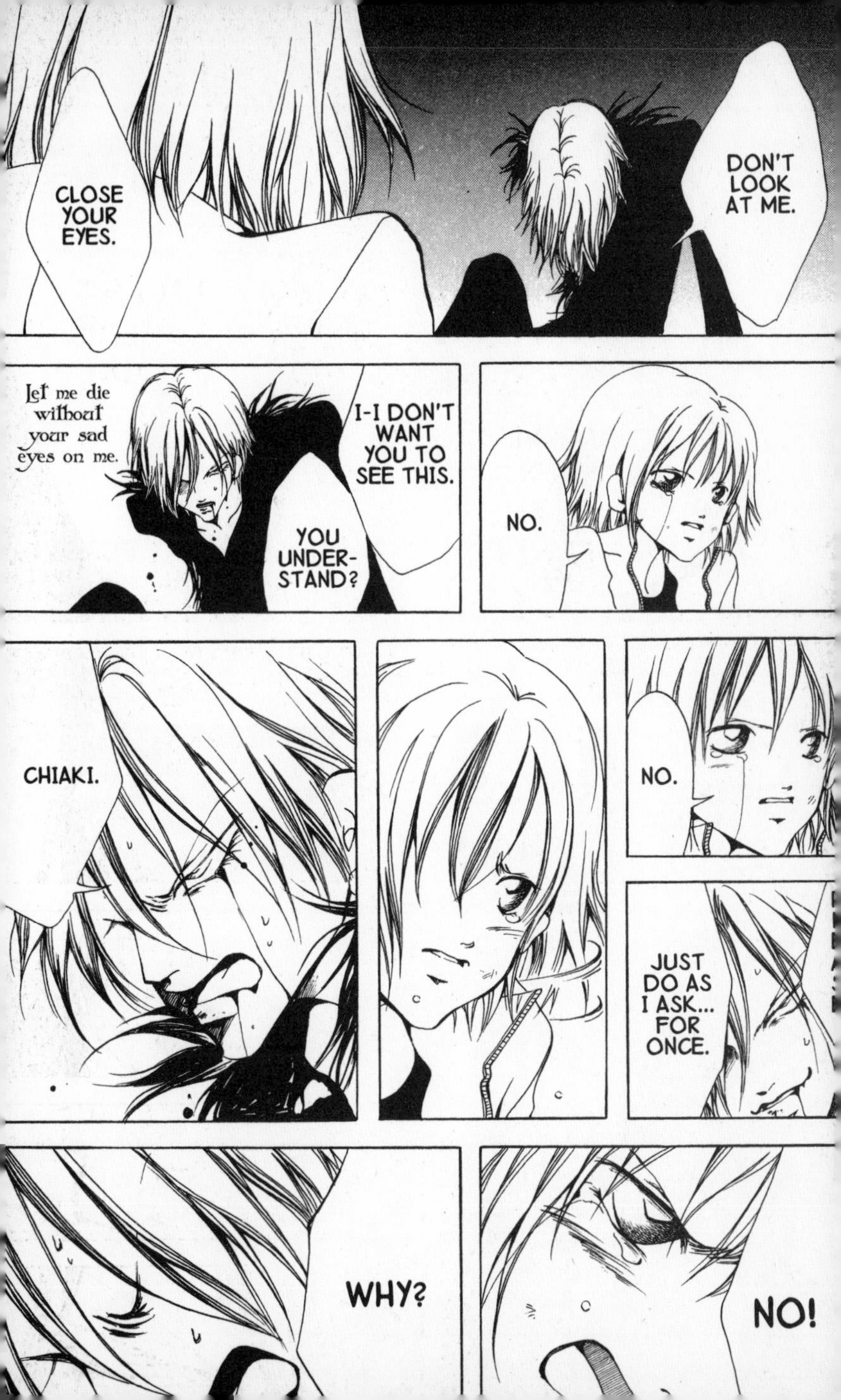
DON'T LOOK AT ME.
CLOSE YOUR EYES.
NO.
I-I DON'T WANT YOU TO SEE THIS.
Let me die without your sad eyes on me.
YOU UNDERSTAND?
NO.
JUST DO AS I ASK... FOR ONCE.
CHIAKI.
NO!
WHY?

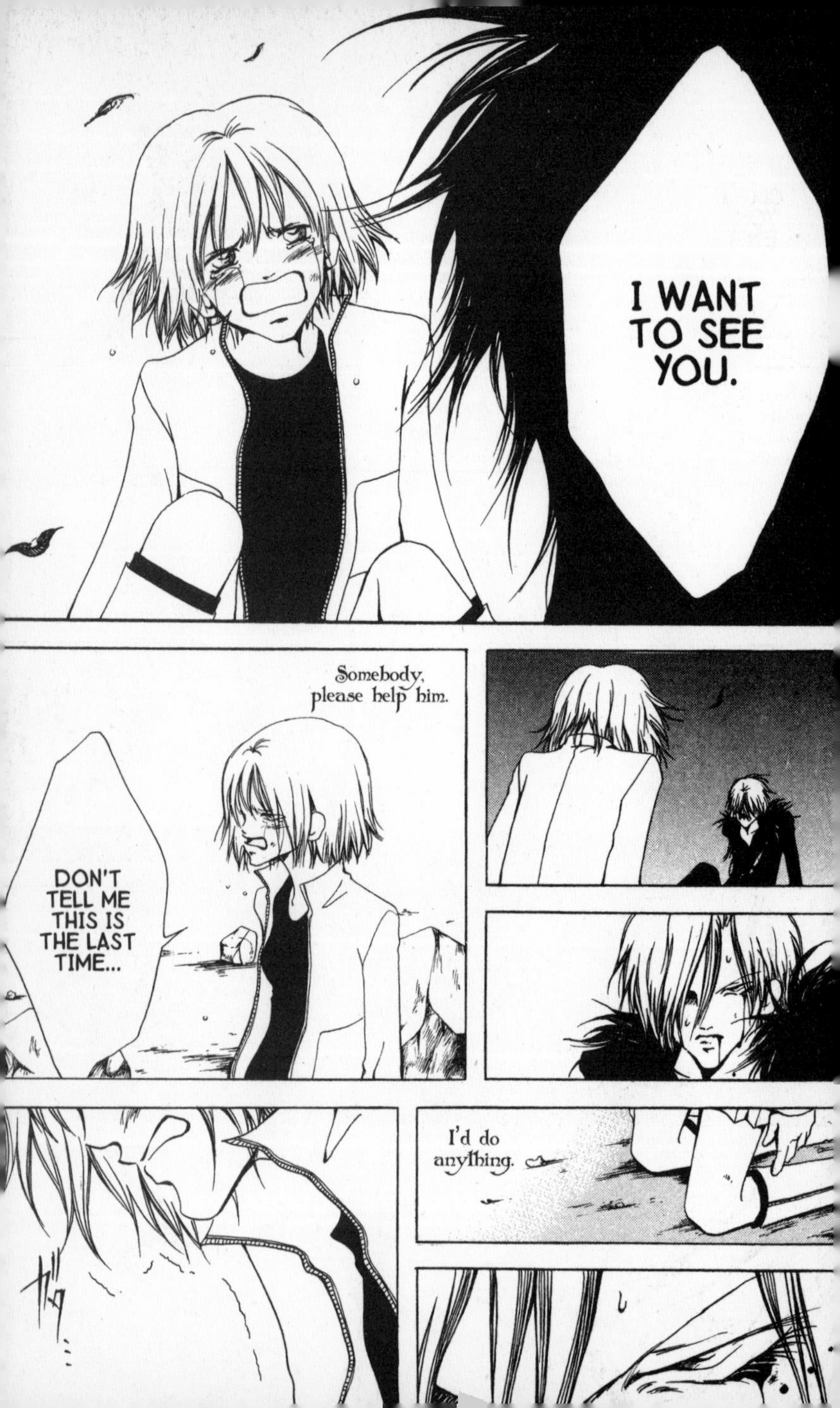
I WANT TO SEE YOU.
Somebody, please help him.
DON'T TELL ME THIS IS THE LAST TIME...
I'd do anything.

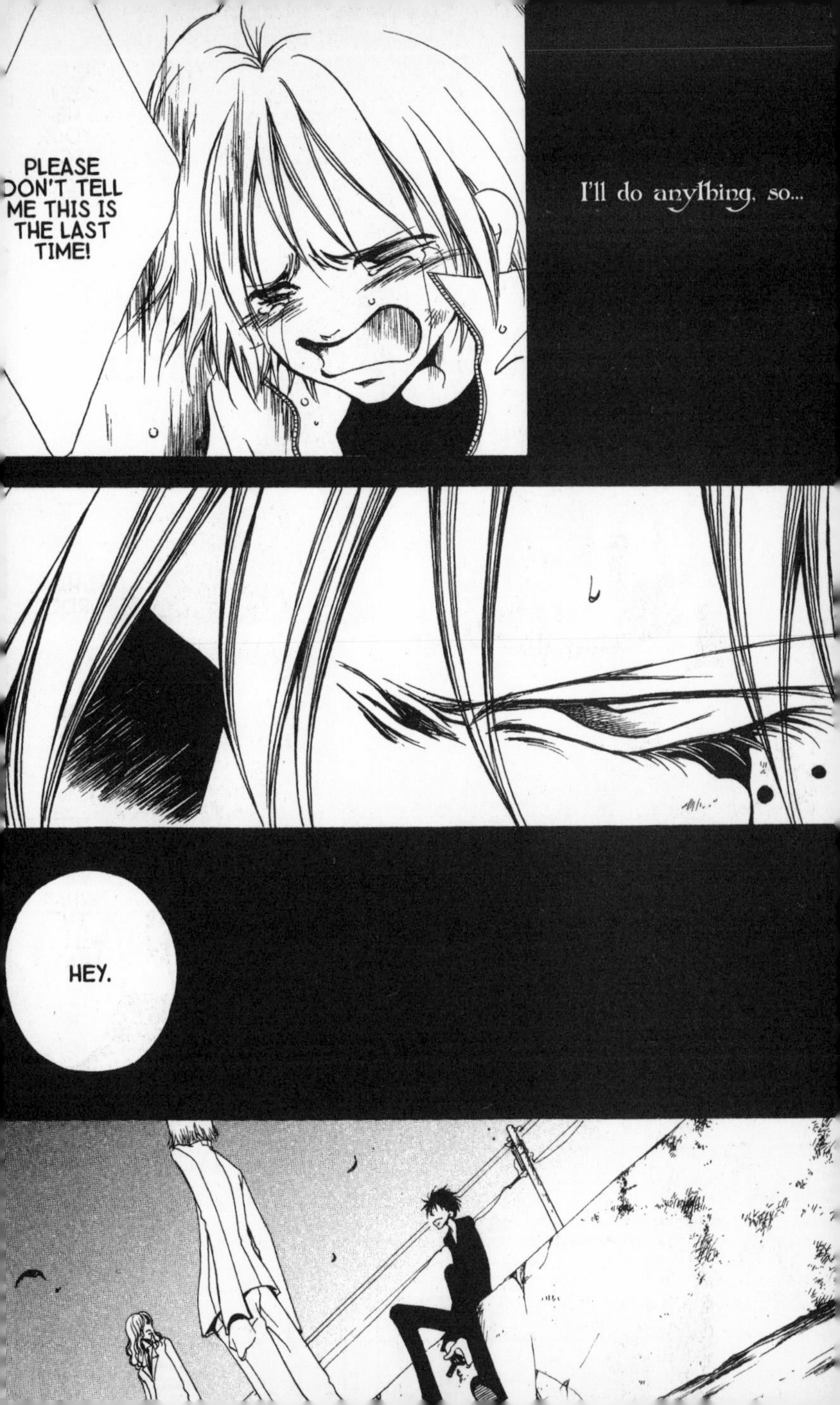
I'll do anything, so...
PLEASE DON'T TELL ME THIS IS THE LAST TIME!
HEY.

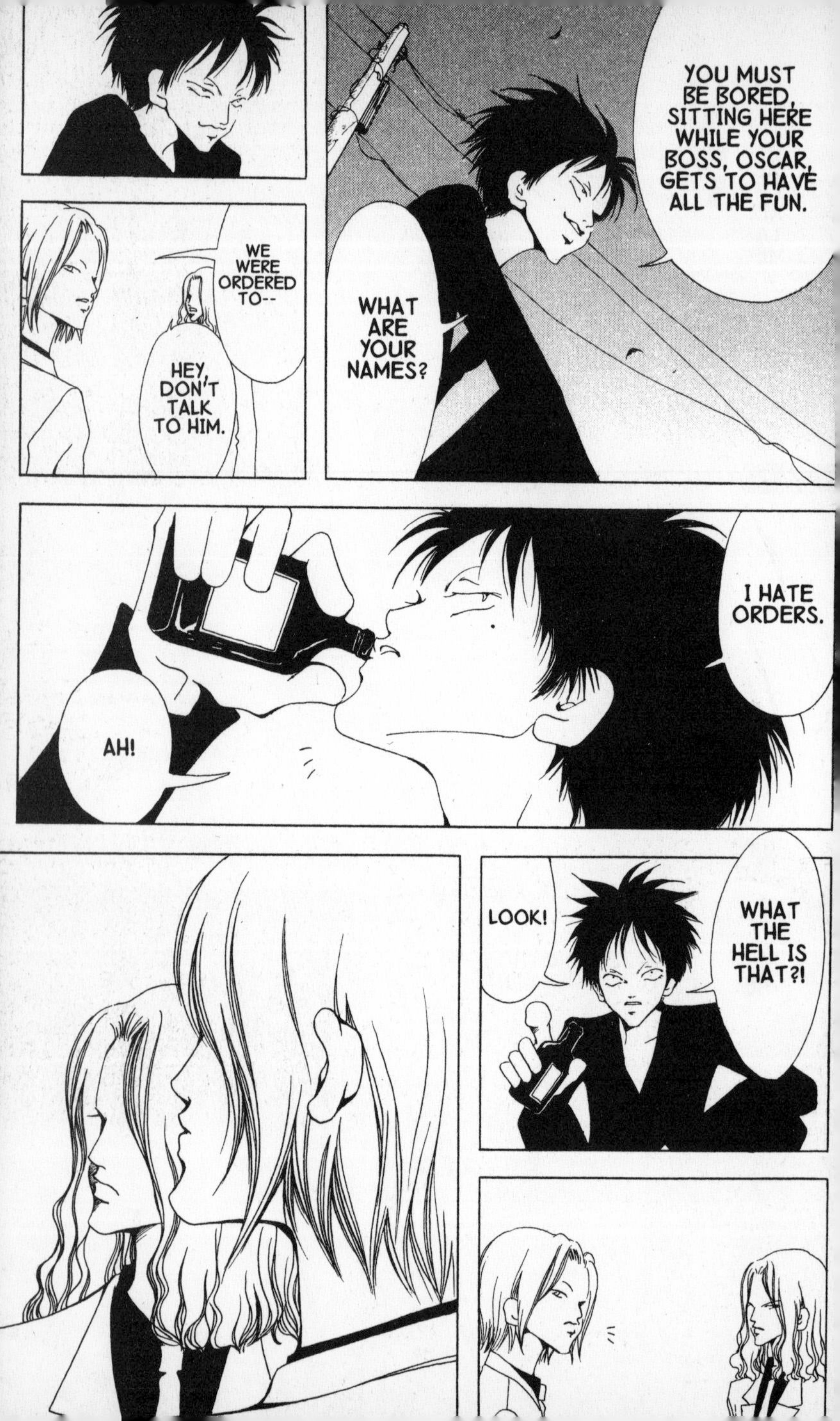
YOU MUST BE BORED, SITTING HERE WHILE YOUR BOSS, OSCAR, GETS TO HAVE ALL THE FUN.
WHAT ARE YOUR NAMES?
WE WERE ORDERED TO--
HEY, DON'T TALK TO HIM.
I HATE ORDERS.
AH!
WHAT THE HELL IS THAT?!
LOOK!

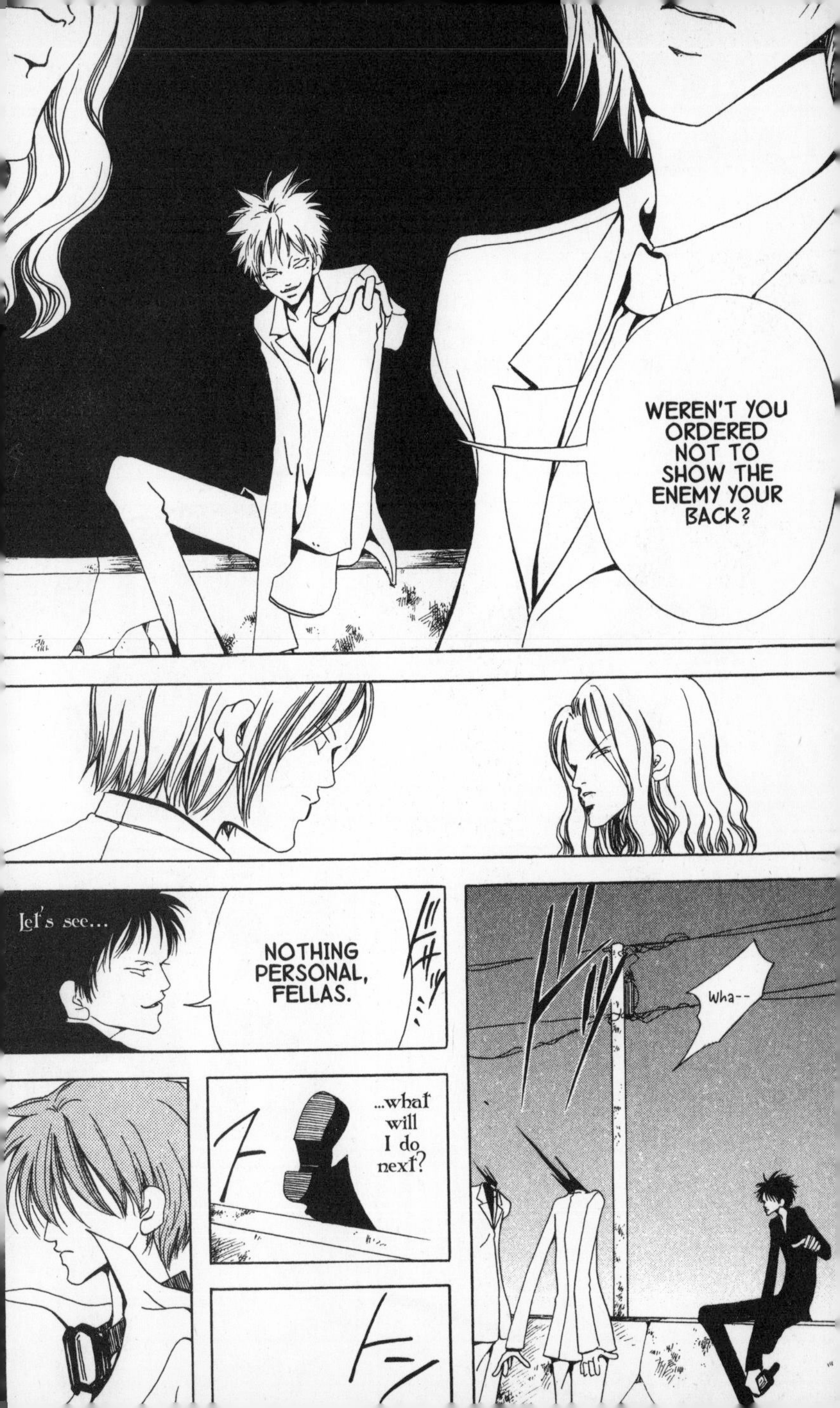
WEREN'T YOU ORDERED NOT TO SHOW THE ENEMY YOUR BACK?
Wha--
NOTHING PERSONAL, FELLAS.
Let's see...
...what will I do next?

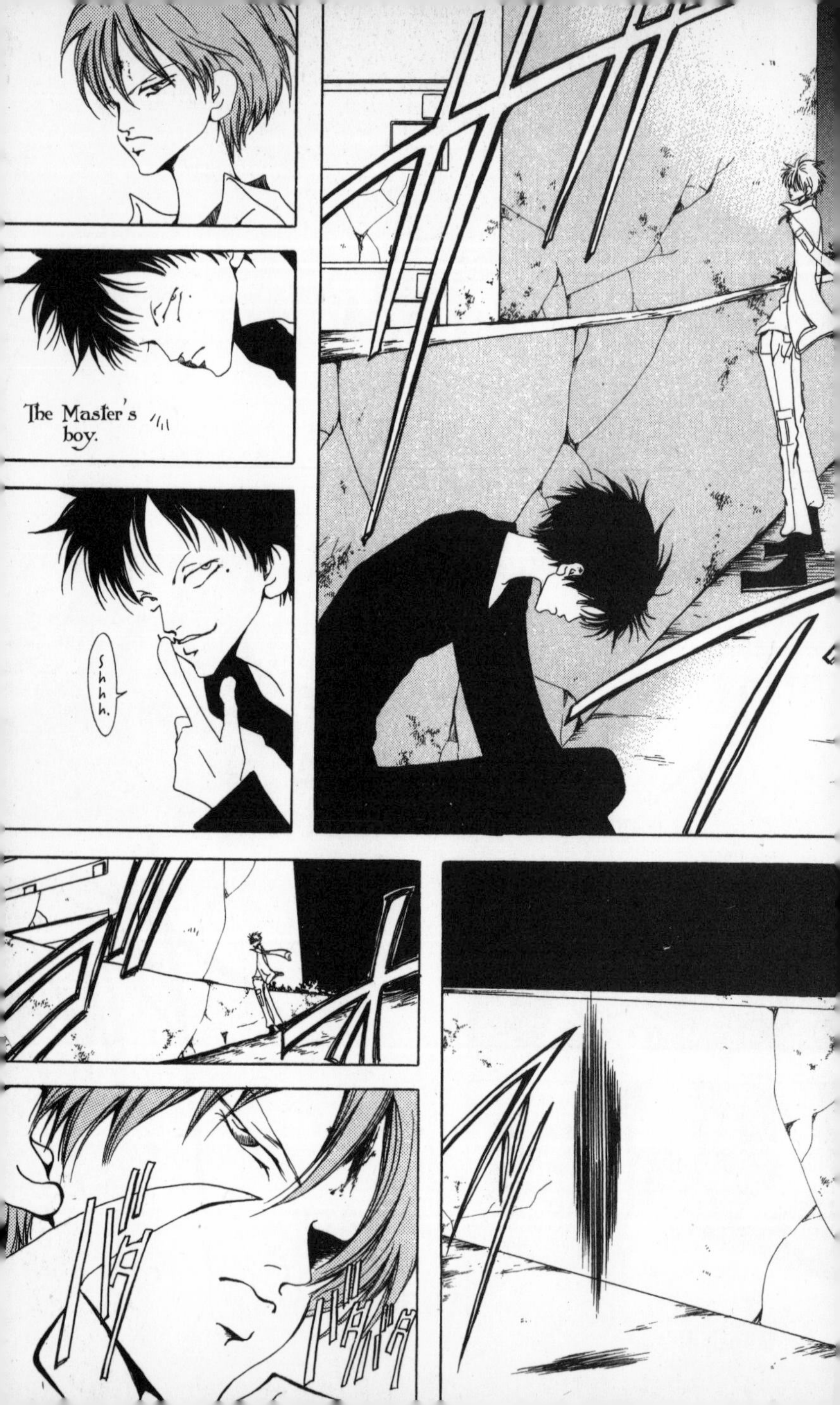
The Master's boy.
Shhh.

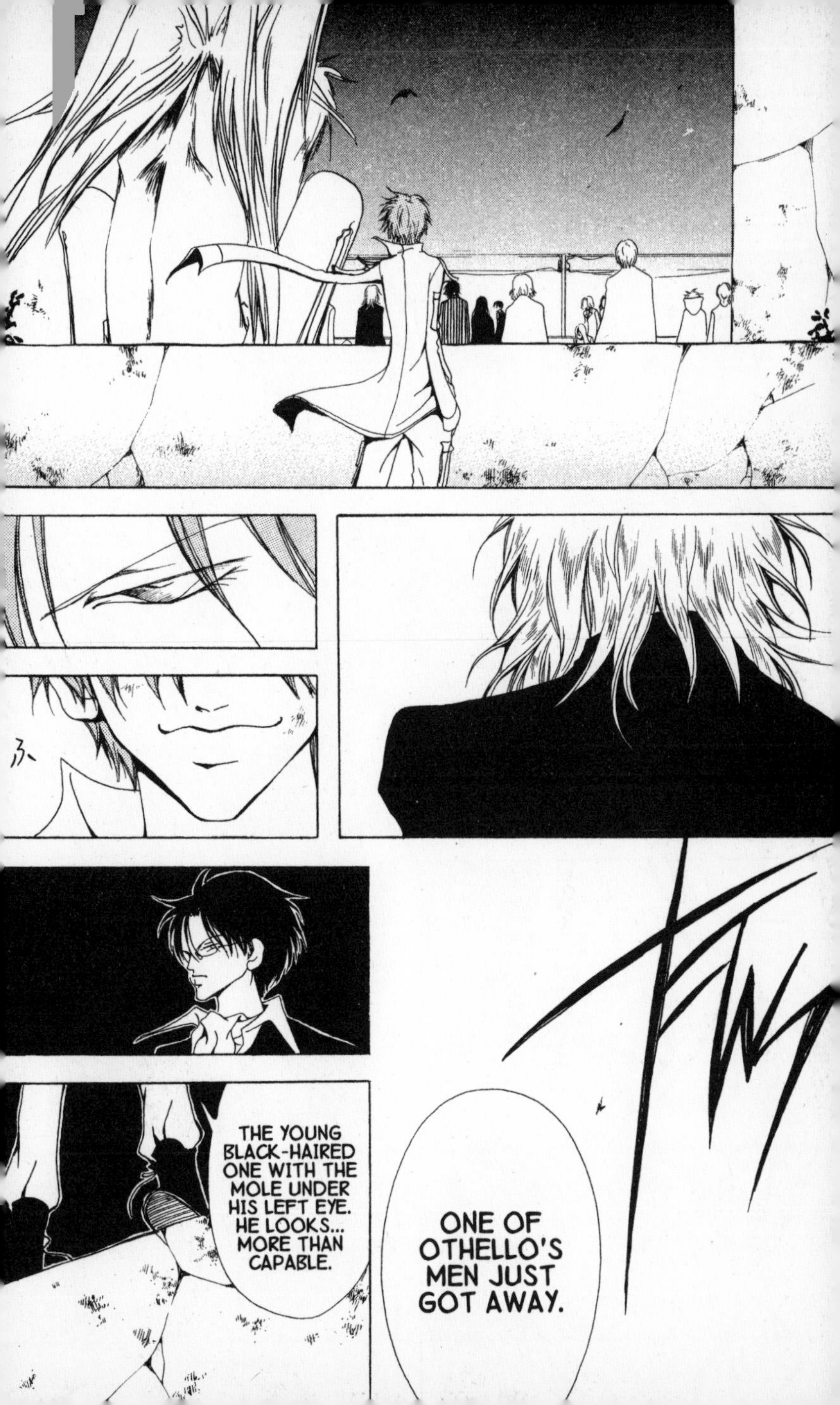
ふ
ONE OF OTHELLO'S MEN JUST GOT AWAY.
THE YOUNG BLACK-HAIRED ONE WITH THE MOLE UNDER HIS LEFT EYE. HE LOOKS... MORE THAN CAPABLE.

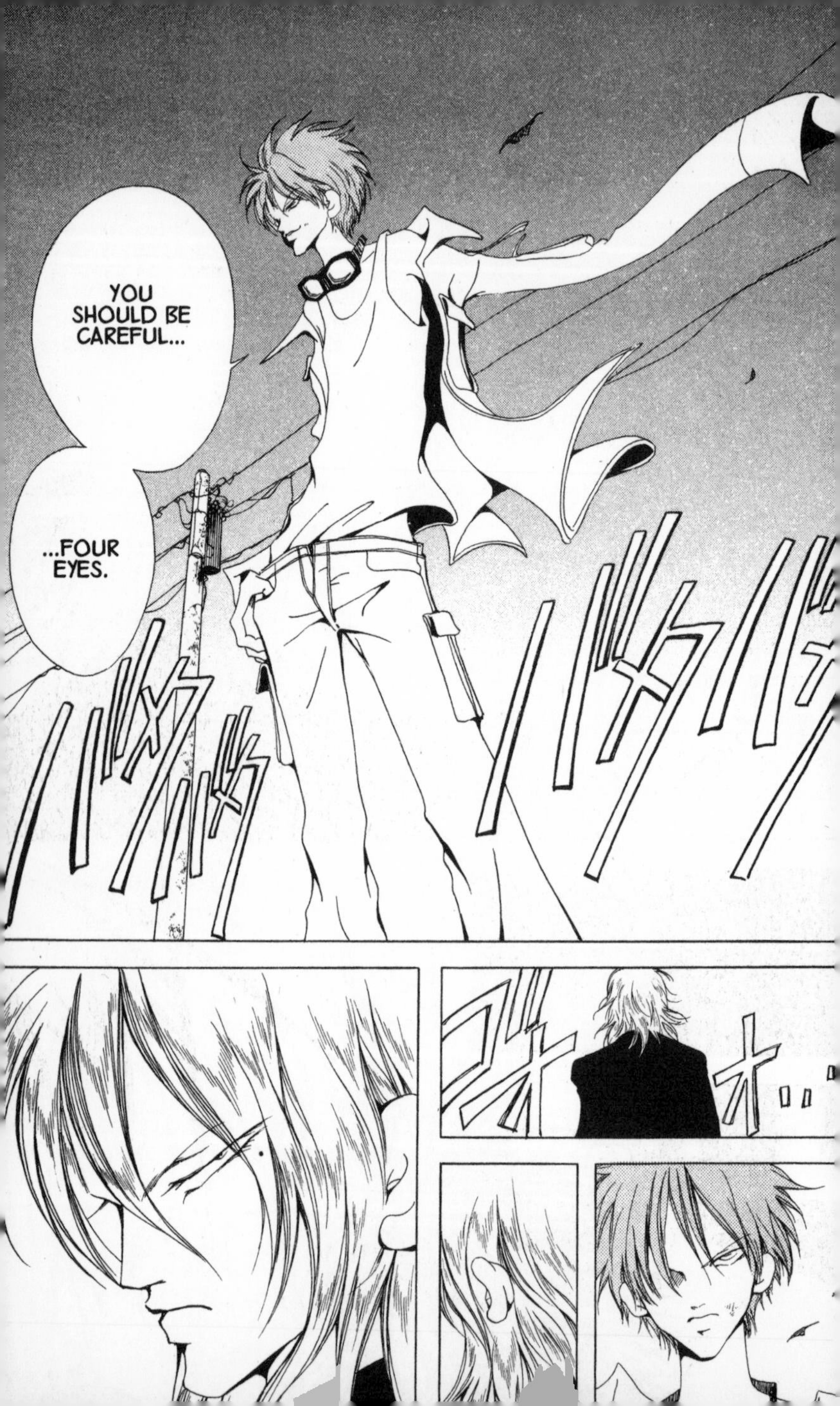
YOU SHOULD BE CAREFUL...
...FOUR EYES.

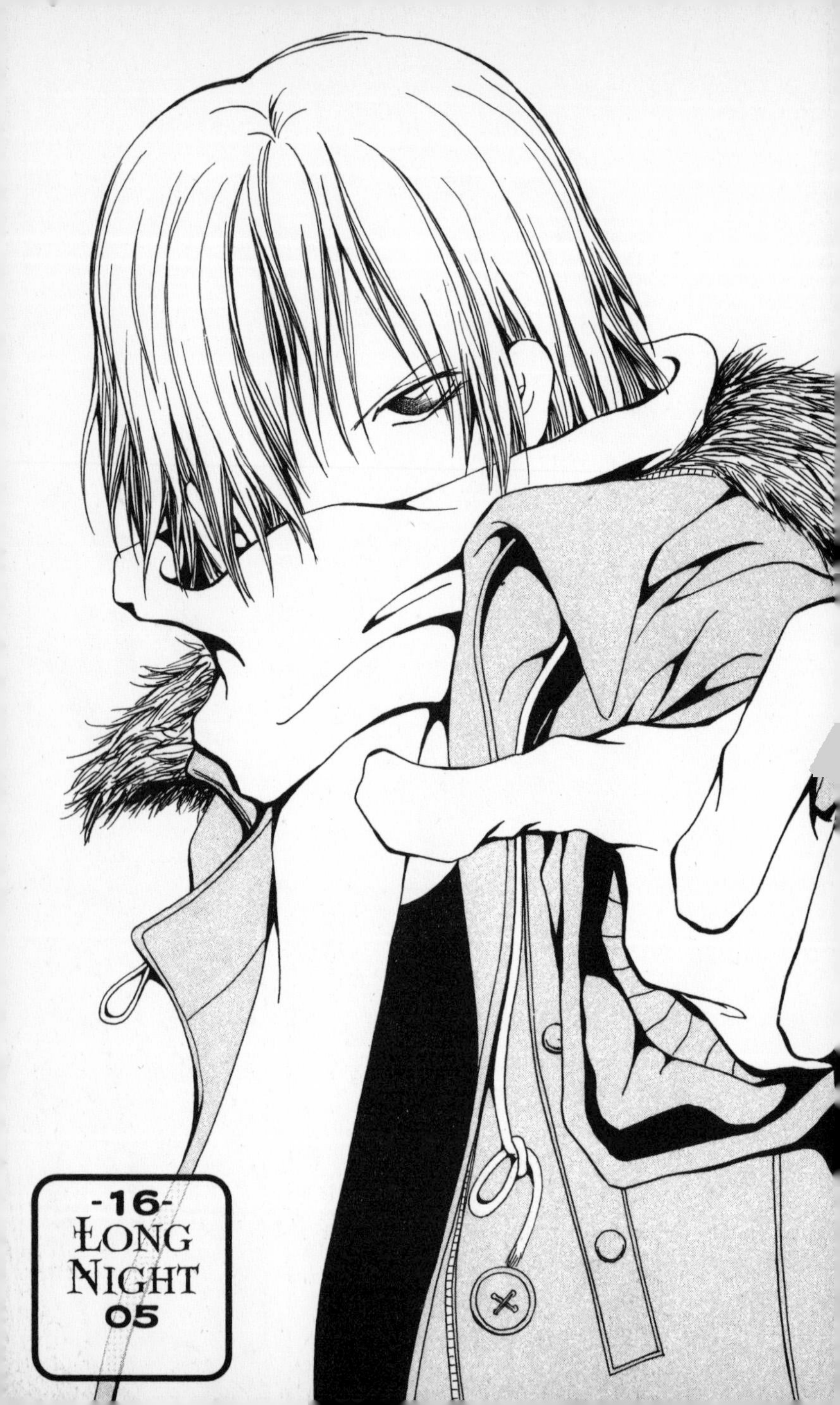
-16-
LONG NIGHT
05

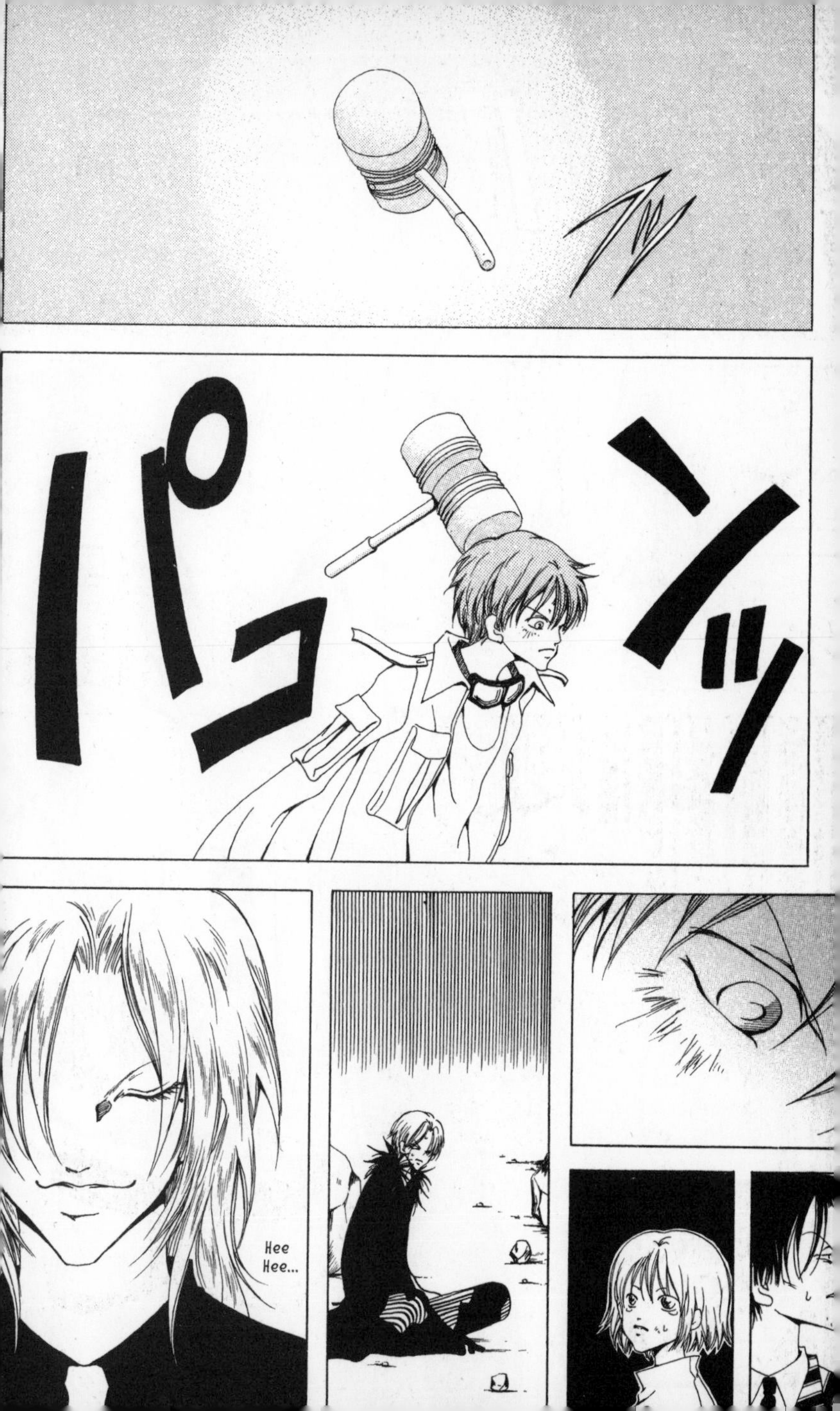
パコンッ
Hee Hee...

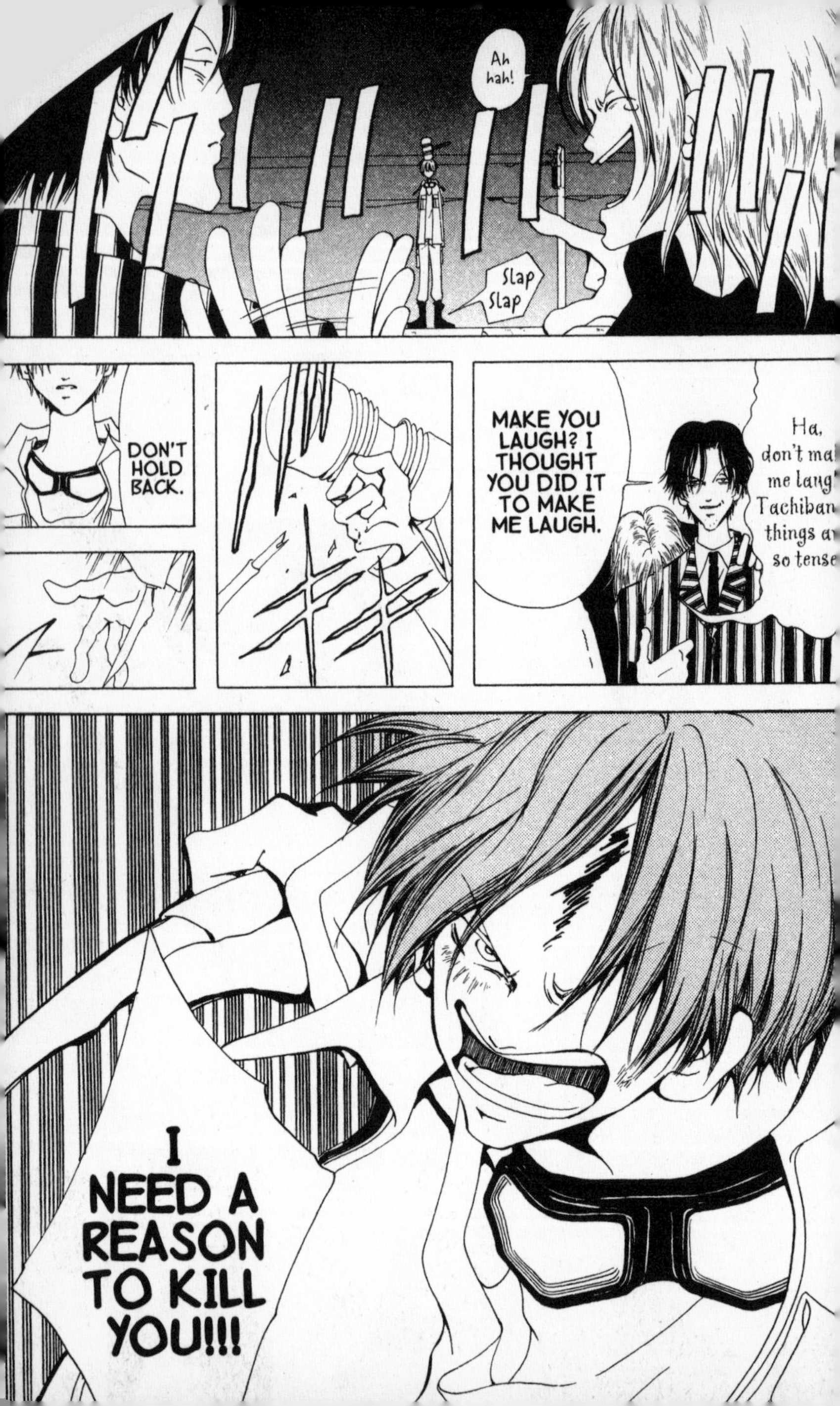
Ah hah!
Slap Slap
Ha, don't ma me laug Tachiban things a so tense
MAKE YOU LAUGH? I THOUGHT YOU DID IT TO MAKE ME LAUGH.
DON'T HOLD BACK.
I NEED A REASON TO KILL YOU!!!

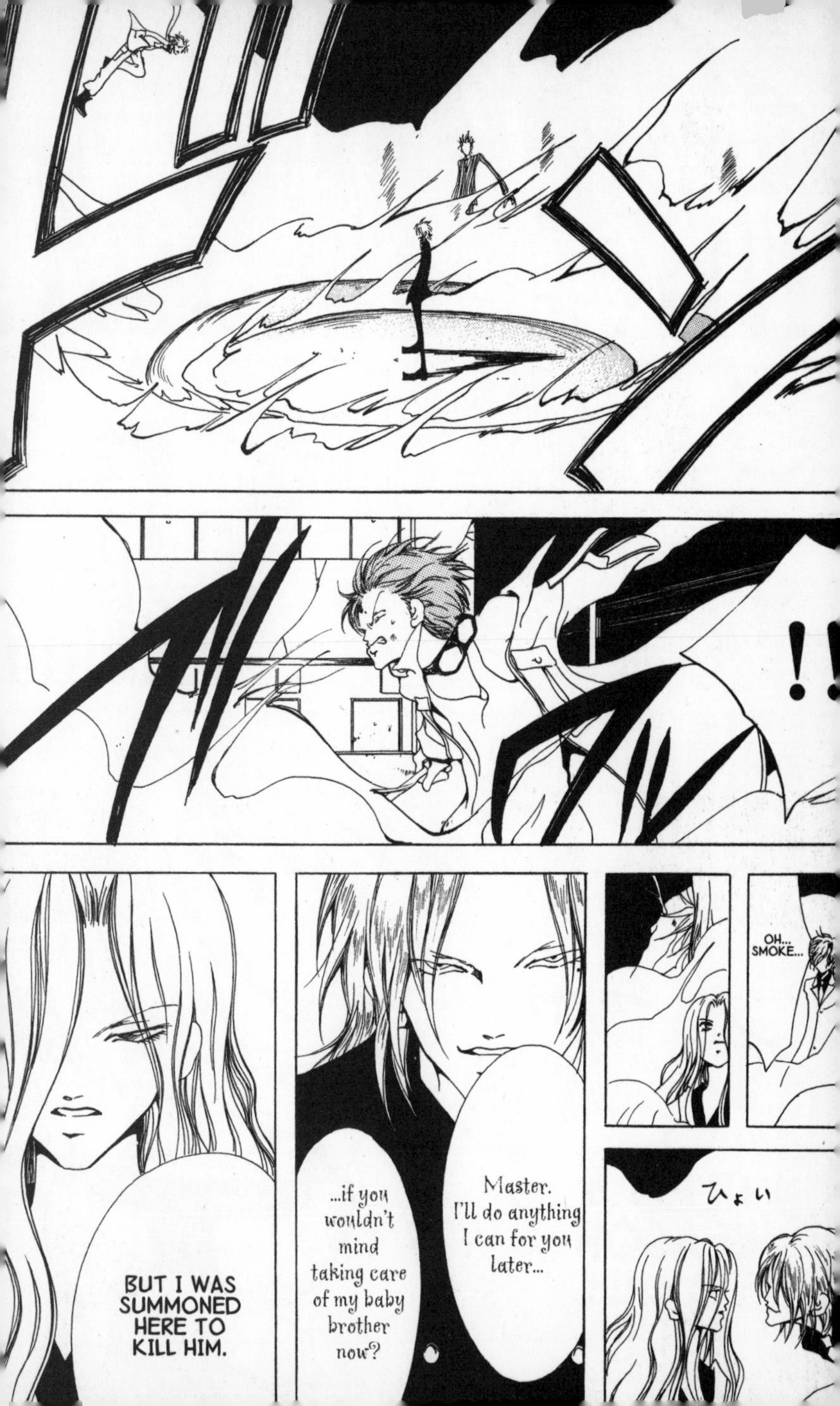
!!
OH... SMOKE...
ひょい
Master. I'll do anything I can for you later...
...if you wouldn't mind taking care of my baby brother now?
BUT I WAS SUMMONED HERE TO KILL HIM.

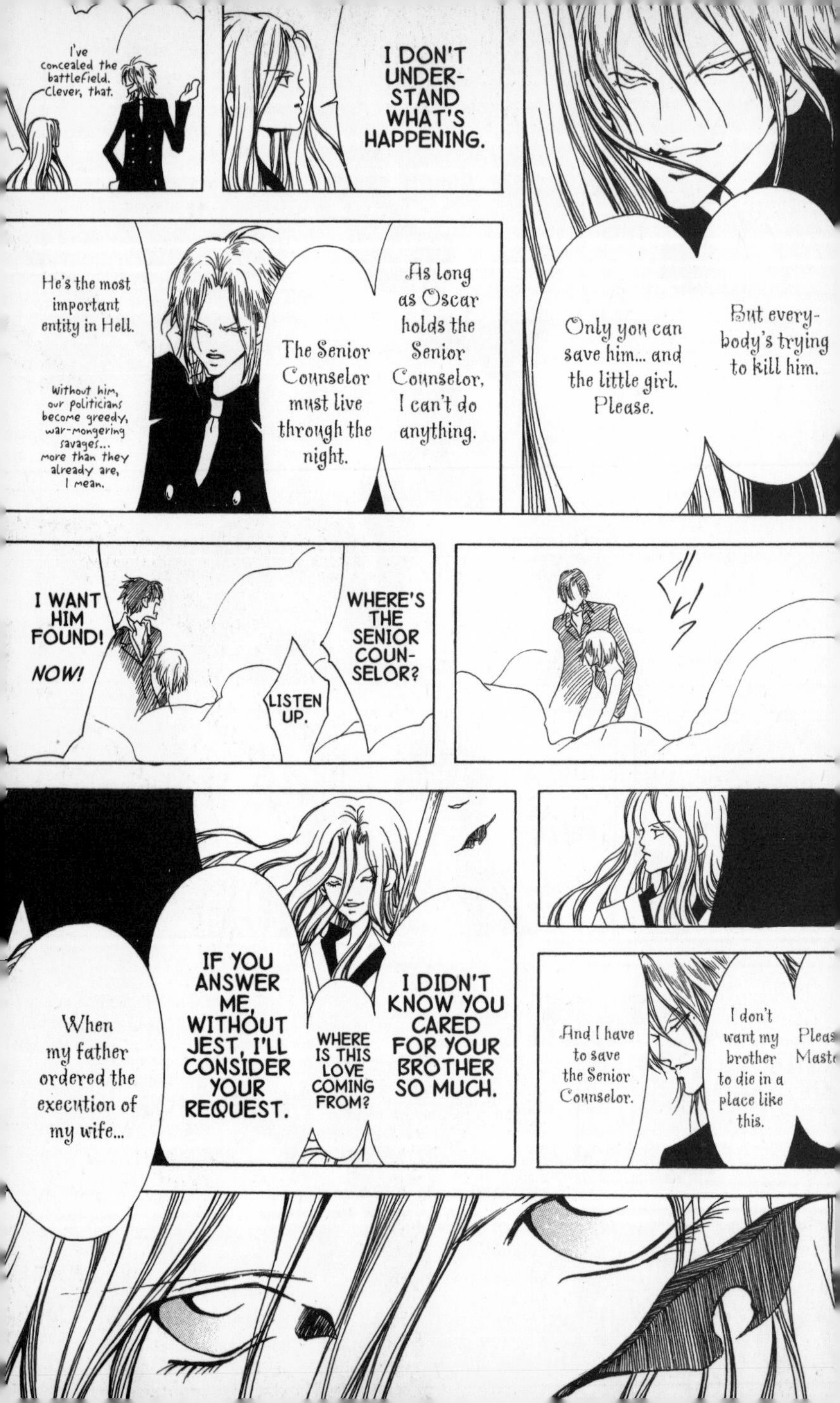

But everybody's trying to kill him.
Only you can save him... and the little girl. Please.
I DON'T UNDERSTAND WHAT'S HAPPENING.
I've concealed the battlefield. Clever, that.
As long as Oscar holds the Senior Counselor, I can't do anything.
The Senior Counselor must live through the night.
He's the most important entity in Hell.
Without him, our politicians become greedy, war-mongering savages... more than they already are, I mean.
WHERE'S THE SENIOR COUNSELOR?
LISTEN UP.
I WANT HIM FOUND! NOW!
Pleas Maste
I don't want my brother to die in a place like this.
And I have to save the Senior Counselor.
I DIDN'T KNOW YOU CARED FOR YOUR BROTHER SO MUCH.
WHERE IS THIS LOVE COMING FROM?
IF YOU ANSWER ME, WITHOUT JEST, I'LL CONSIDER YOUR REQUEST.
When my father ordered the execution of my wife...

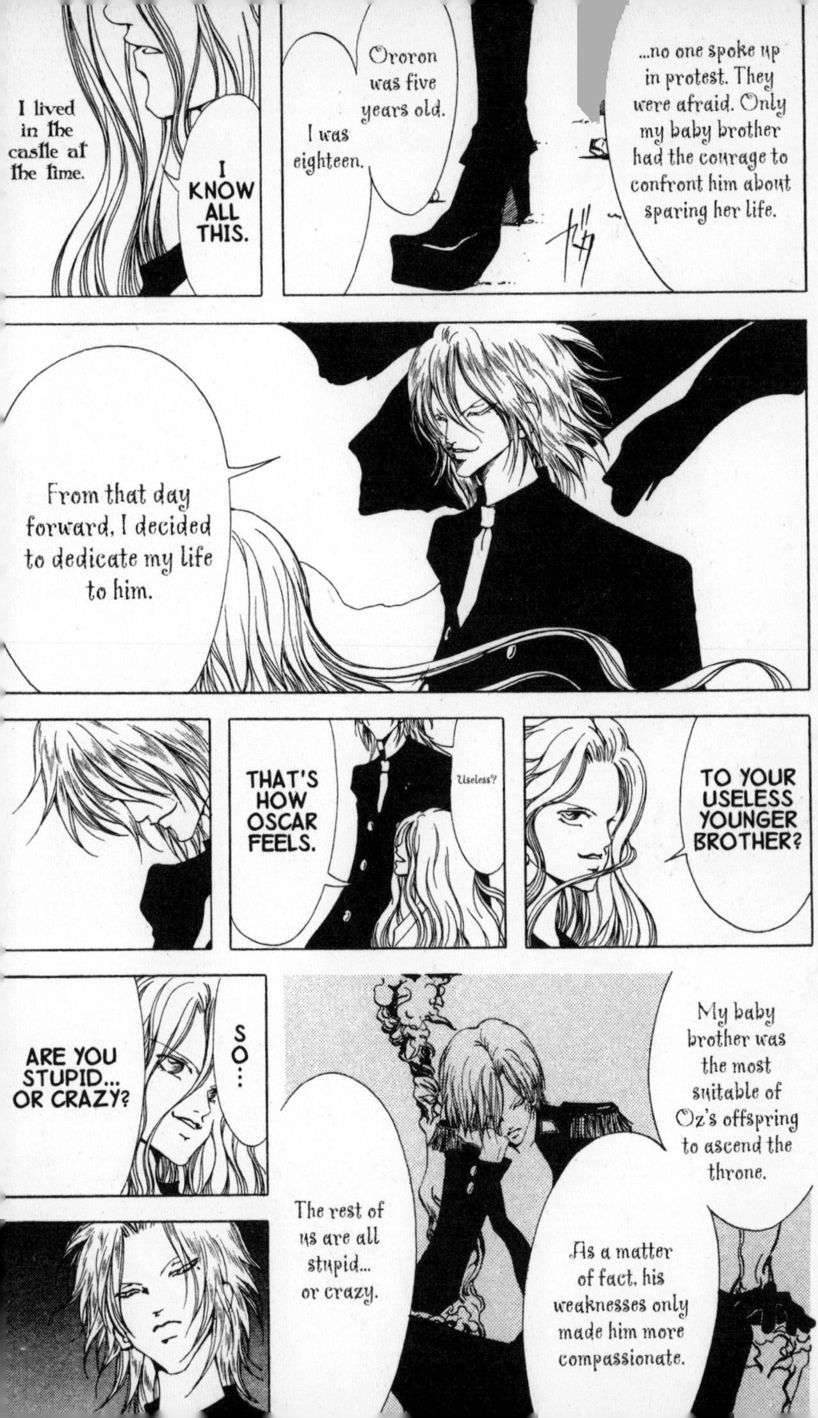
...no one spoke up in protest. They were afraid. Only my baby brother had the courage to confront him about sparing her life.
Ororon was five years old.
I was eighteen.
I KNOW ALL THIS.
I lived in the castle at the time.
From that day forward, I decided to dedicate my life to him.
TO YOUR USELESS YOUNGER BROTHER?
Useless?
THAT'S HOW OSCAR FEELS.
My baby brother was the most suitable of Oz's offspring to ascend the throne.
As a matter of fact, his weaknesses only made him more compassionate.
The rest of us are all stupid... or crazy.
SO...
ARE YOU STUPID... OR CRAZY?

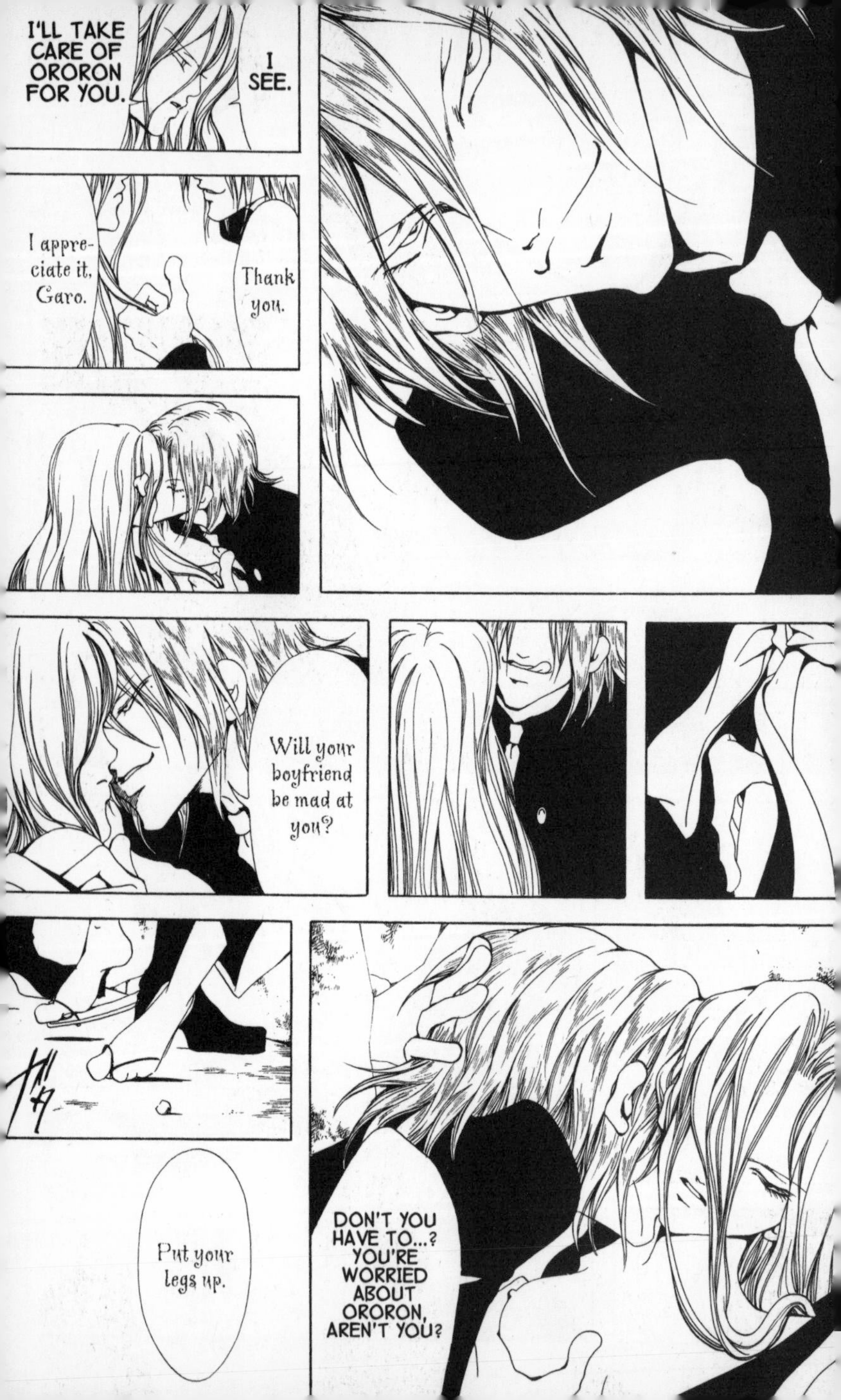
I SEE.
I'LL TAKE CARE OF ORORON FOR YOU.
Thank you.
I appreciate it, Garo.
Will your boyfriend be mad at you?
DON'T YOU HAVE TO...? YOU'RE WORRIED ABOUT ORORON, AREN'T YOU?
Put your legs up.

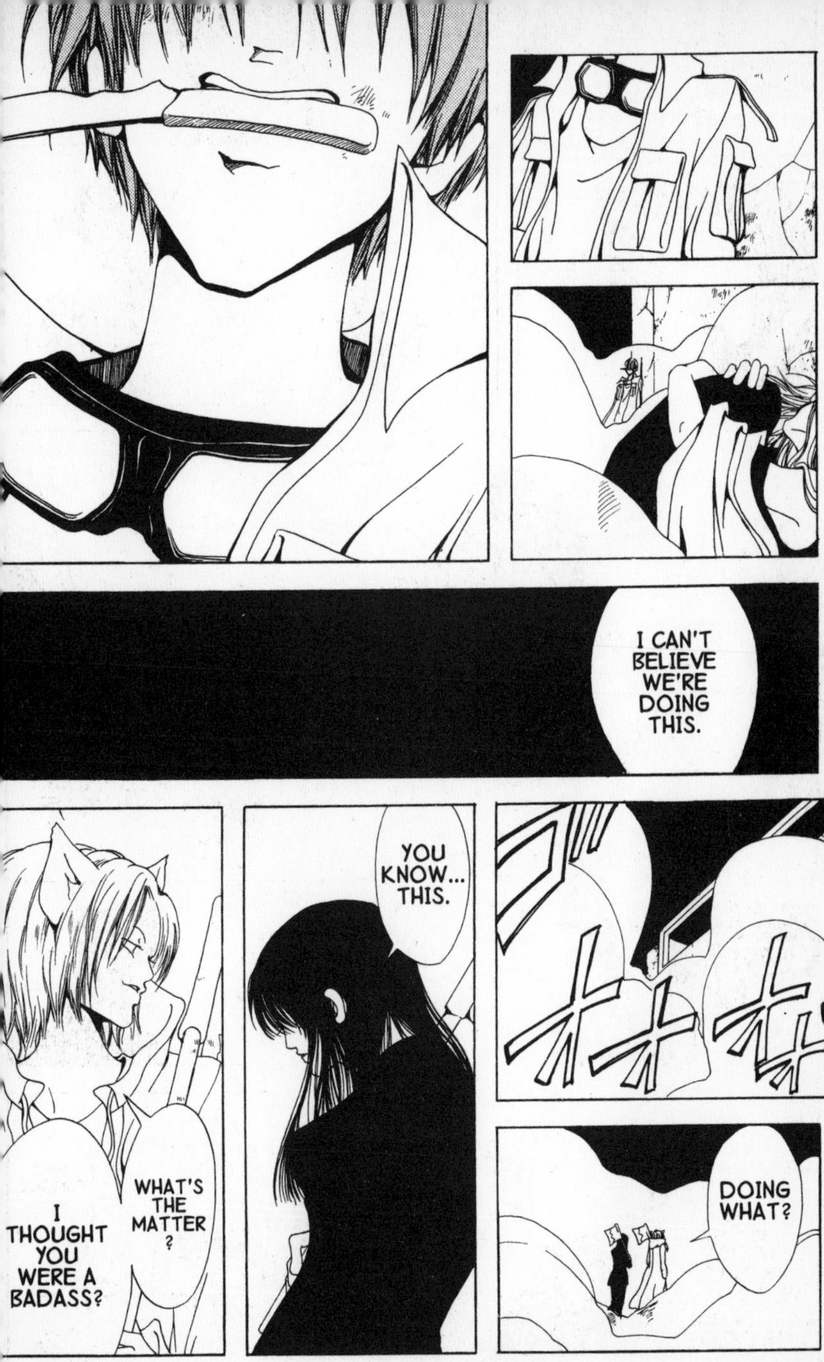

I CAN'T BELIEVE WE'RE DOING THIS.
DOING WHAT?
YOU KNOW... THIS.
WHAT'S THE MATTER?
I THOUGHT YOU WERE A BADASS?

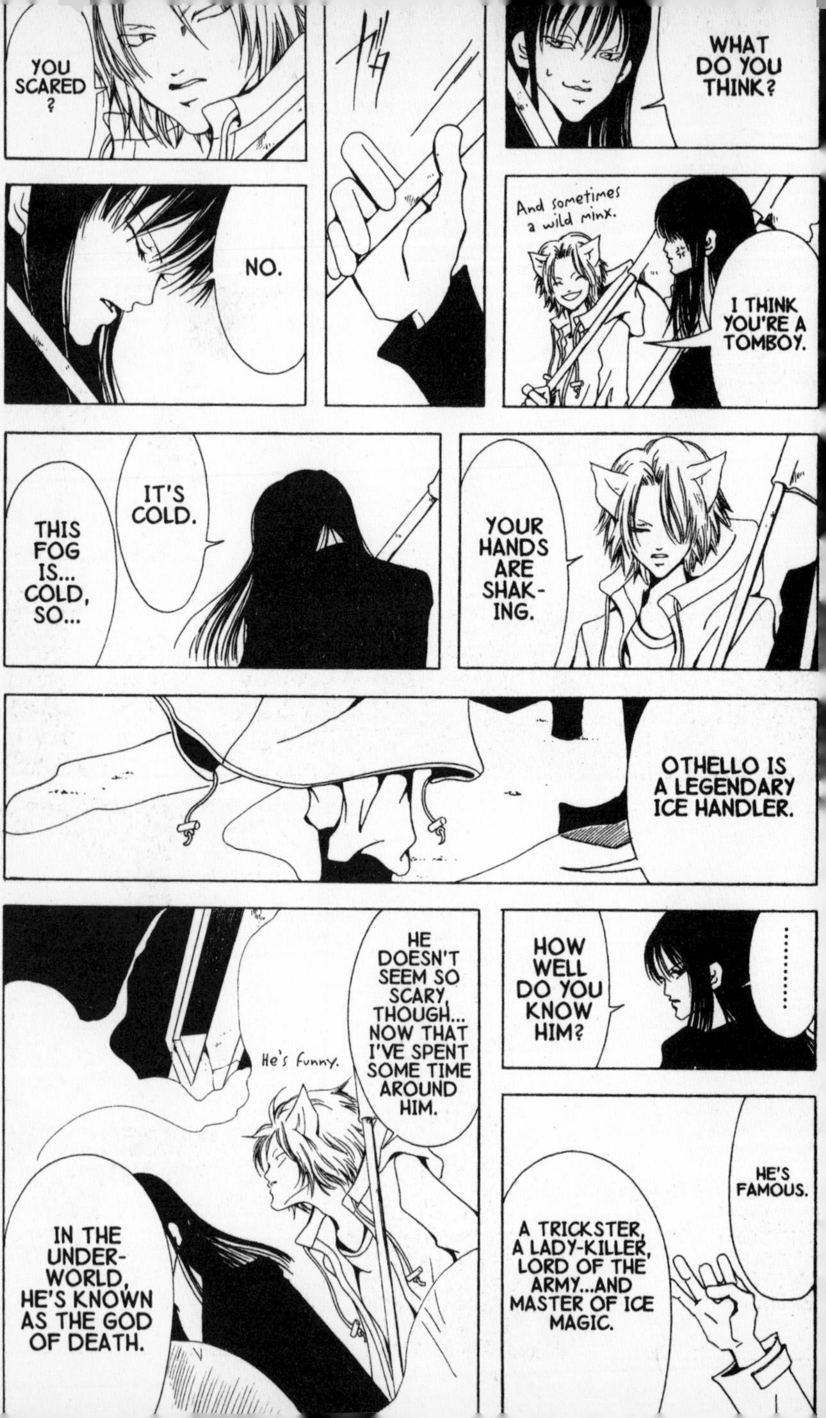
WHAT DO YOU THINK?
I THINK YOU'RE A TOMBOY.
And sometimes a wild minx.
YOU SCARED?
NO.
YOUR HANDS ARE SHAKING.
IT'S COLD.
THIS FOG IS... COLD, SO...
OTHELLO IS A LEGENDARY ICE HANDLER.
....
HOW WELL DO YOU KNOW HIM?
HE'S FAMOUS.
A TRICKSTER, A LADY-KILLER, LORD OF THE ARMY...AND MASTER OF ICE MAGIC.
HE DOESN'T SEEM SO SCARY, THOUGH... NOW THAT I'VE SPENT SOME TIME AROUND HIM.
He's funny.
IN THE UNDERWORLD, HE'S KNOWN AS THE GOD OF DEATH.

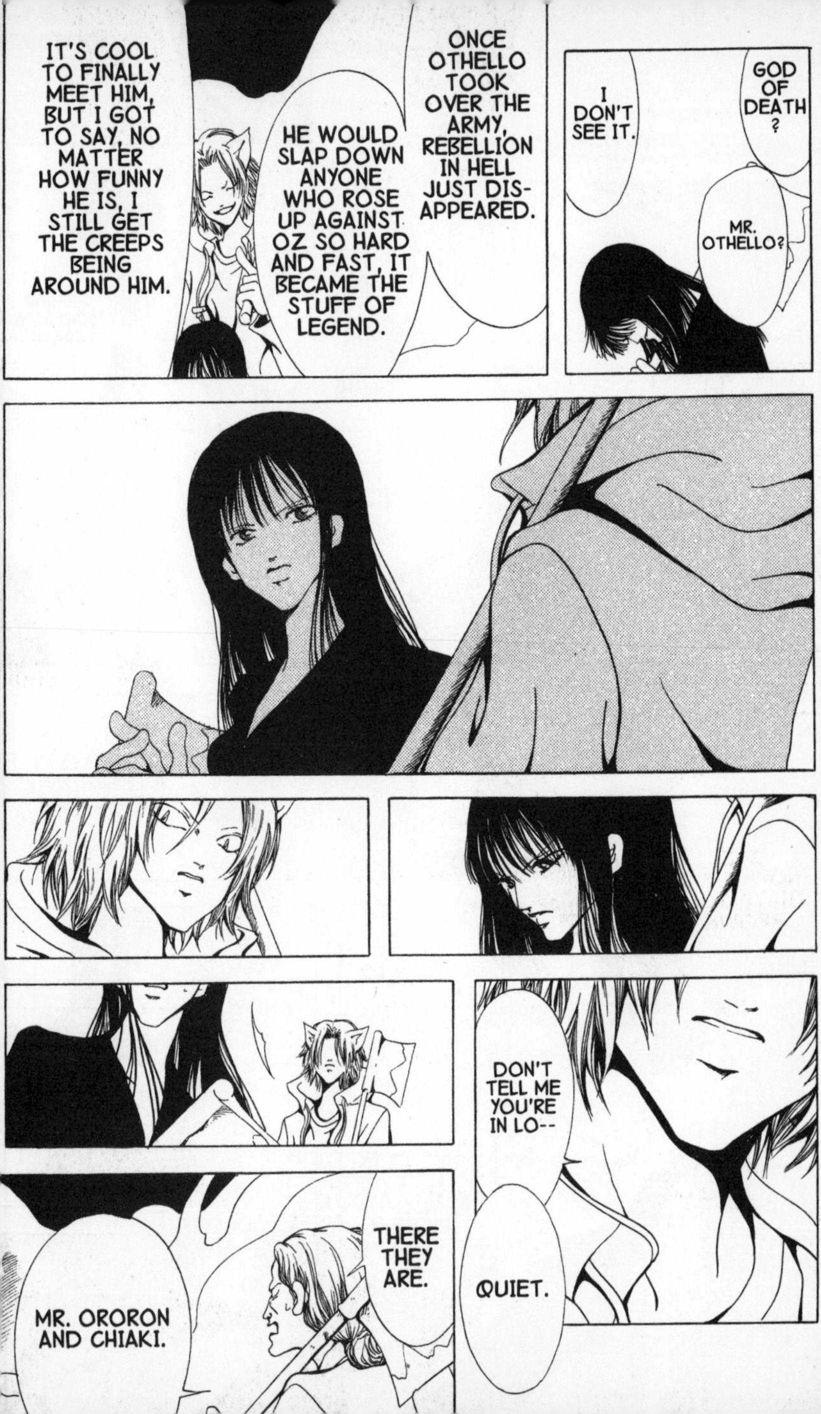
GOD OF DEATH?
I DON'T SEE IT.
MR. OTHELLO?
ONCE OTHELLO TOOK OVER THE ARMY, REBELLION IN HELL JUST DIS-APPEARED.
HE WOULD SLAP DOWN ANYONE WHO ROSE UP AGAINST OZ SO HARD AND FAST, IT BECAME THE STUFF OF LEGEND.
IT'S COOL TO FINALLY MEET HIM, BUT I GOT TO SAY, NO MATTER HOW FUNNY HE IS, I STILL GET THE CREEPS BEING AROUND HIM.
DON'T TELL ME YOU'RE IN LO--
QUIET.
THERE THEY ARE.
MR. ORORON AND CHIAKI.

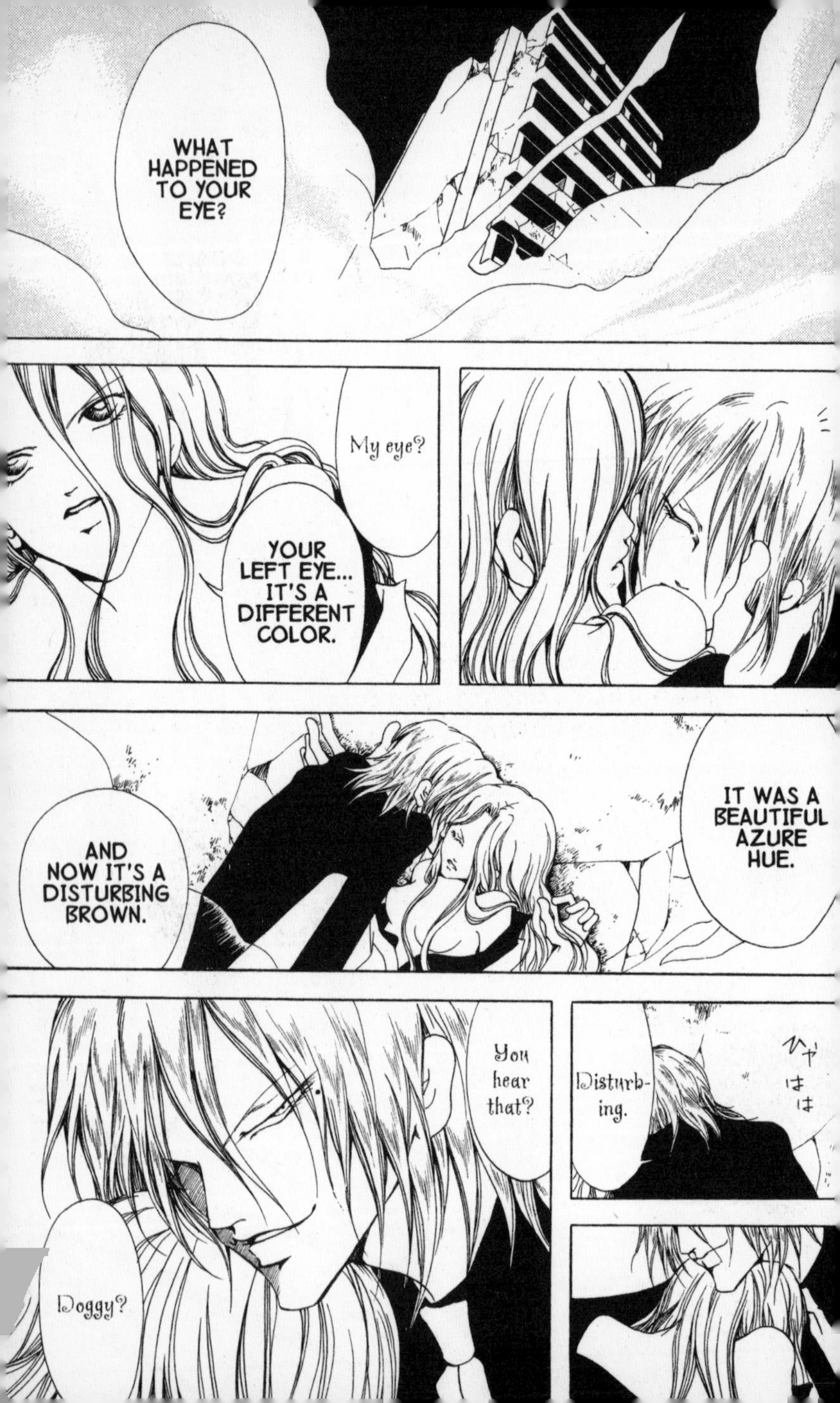
WHAT HAPPENED TO YOUR EYE?
My eye?
YOUR LEFT EYE... IT'S A DIFFERENT COLOR.
IT WAS A BEAUTIFUL AZURE HUE.
AND NOW IT'S A DISTURBING BROWN.
ひゃはは
Disturb-ing.
You hear that?
Doggy?

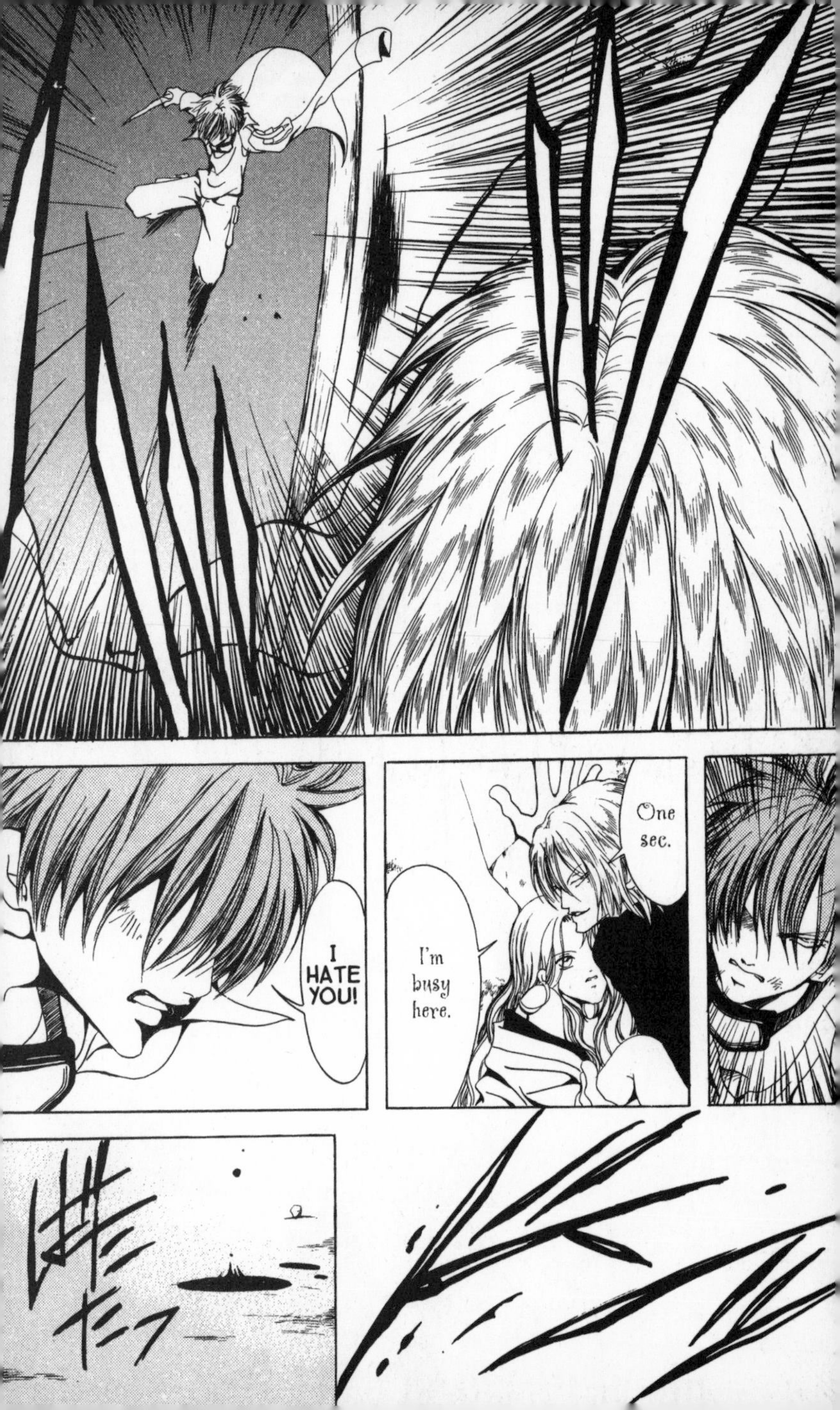
One sec.
I'm busy here.
I HATE YOU!

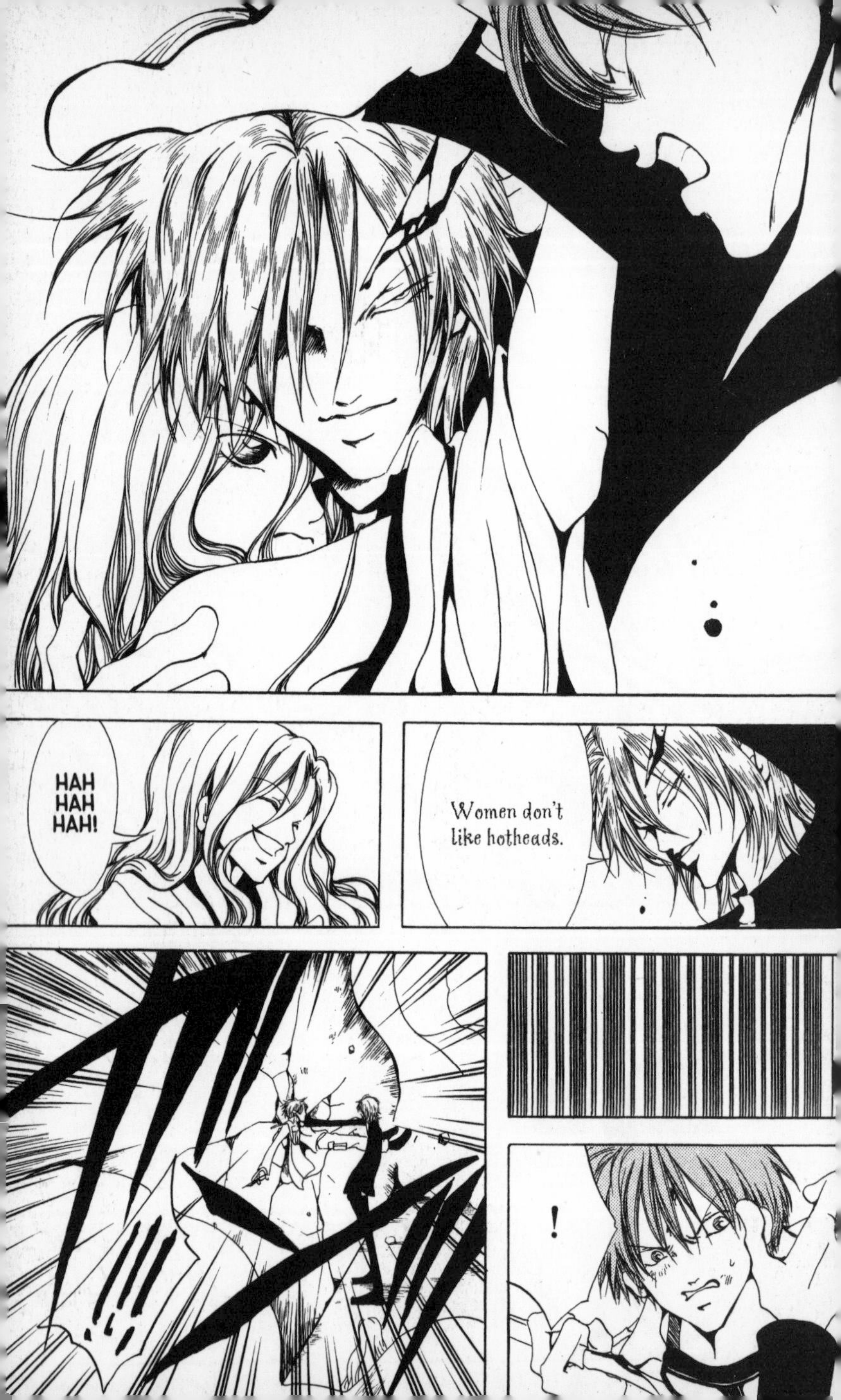
Women don't like hotheads.
HAH HAH HAH!
!
!!!

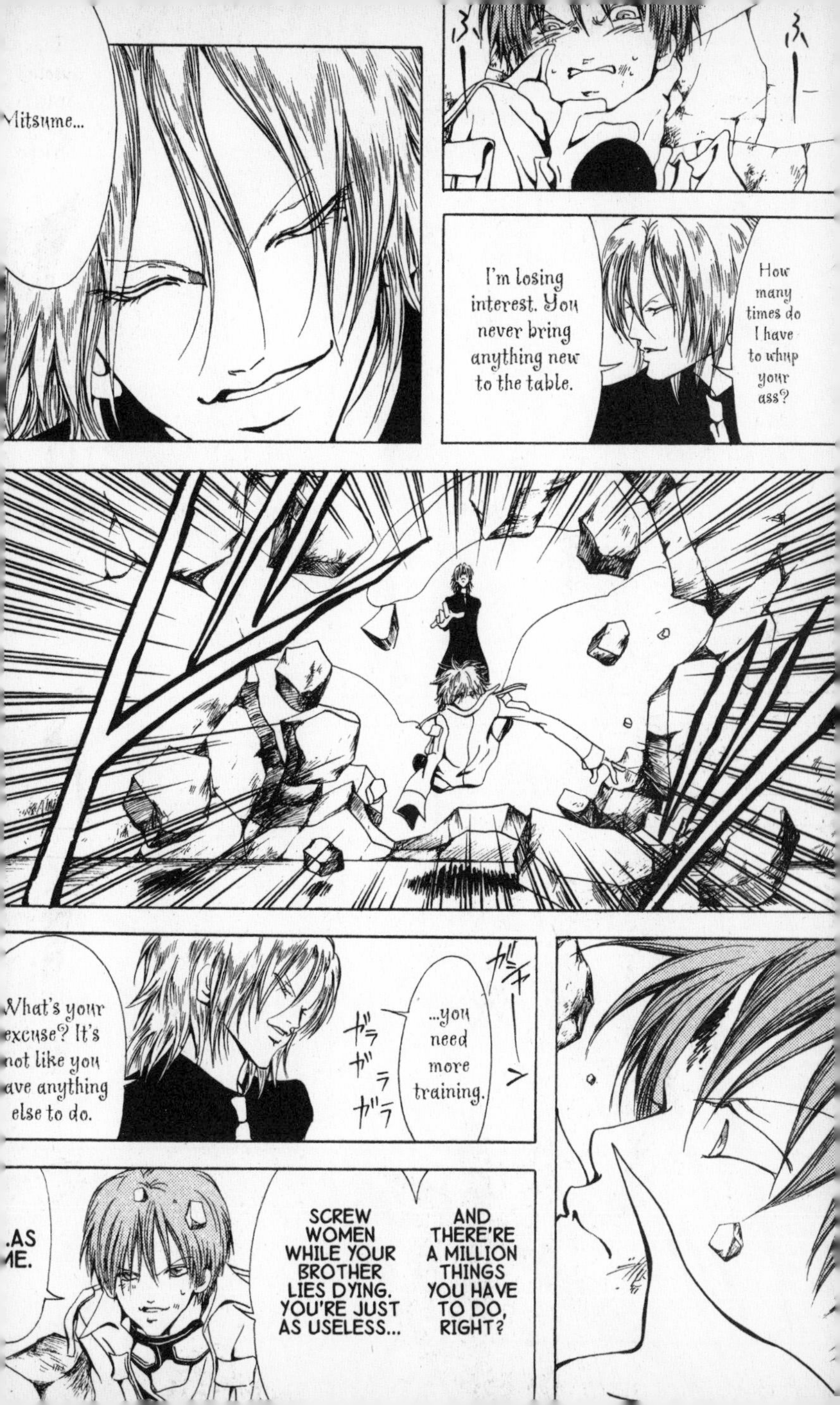

ふー
ふー
How many times do I have to whup your ass?
I'm losing interest. You never bring anything new to the table.
Mitsume...
ガチー>
...you need more training.
ガラガラガラ
What's your excuse? It's not like you ave anything else to do.
AND THERE'RE A MILLION THINGS YOU HAVE TO DO, RIGHT?
SCREW WOMEN WHILE YOUR BROTHER LIES DYING. YOU'RE JUST AS USELESS...
AS ME.

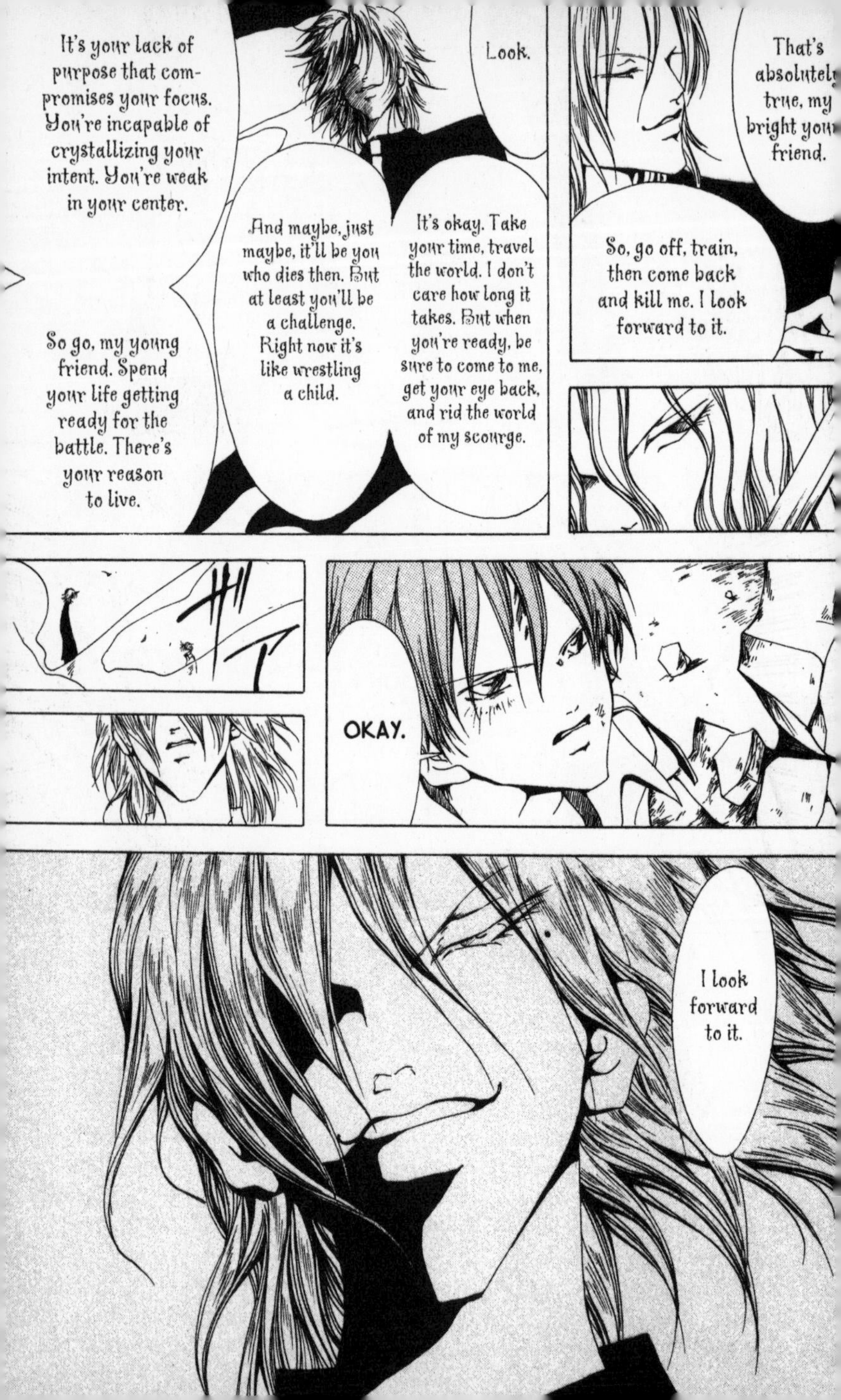
That's absolutel true, my bright youn friend.
So, go off, train, then come back and kill me. I look forward to it.
Look.
It's okay. Take your time, travel the world. I don't care how long it takes. But when you're ready, be sure to come to me, get your eye back, and rid the world of my scourge.
And maybe, just maybe, it'll be you who dies then. But at least you'll be a challenge. Right now it's like wrestling a child.
It's your lack of purpose that compromises your focus. You're incapable of crystallizing your intent. You're weak in your center.
So go, my young friend. Spend your life getting ready for the battle. There's your reason to live.
OKAY.
I look forward to it.

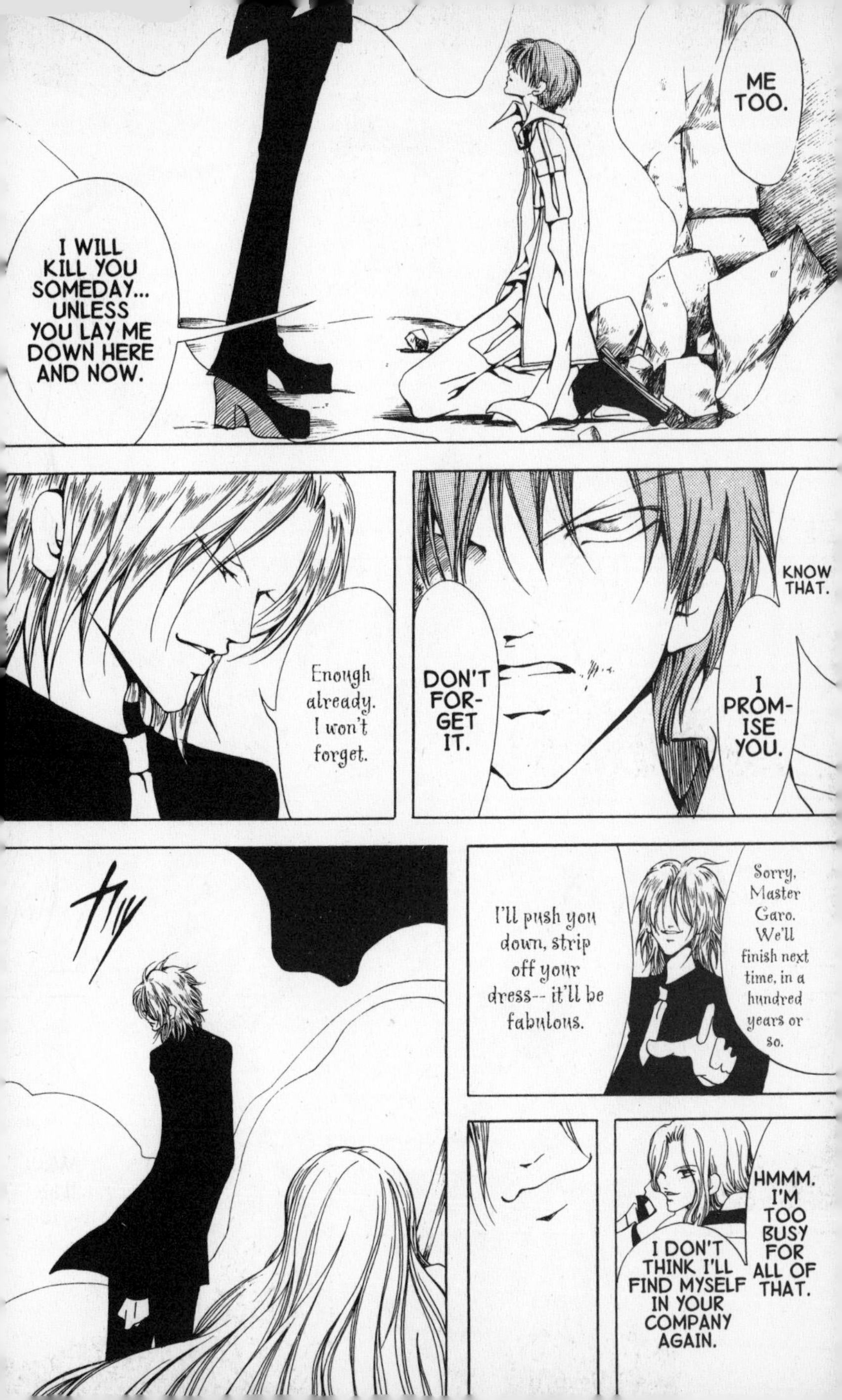

ME TOO.
I WILL KILL YOU SOMEDAY... UNLESS YOU LAY ME DOWN HERE AND NOW.
KNOW THAT.
I PROM-ISE YOU.
DON'T FOR-GET IT.
Enough already. I won't forget.
Sorry, Master Garo. We'll finish next time, in a hundred years or so.
I'll push you down, strip off your dress-- it'll be fabulous.
HMMM. I'M TOO BUSY FOR ALL OF THAT.
I DON'T THINK I'LL FIND MYSELF IN YOUR COMPANY AGAIN.

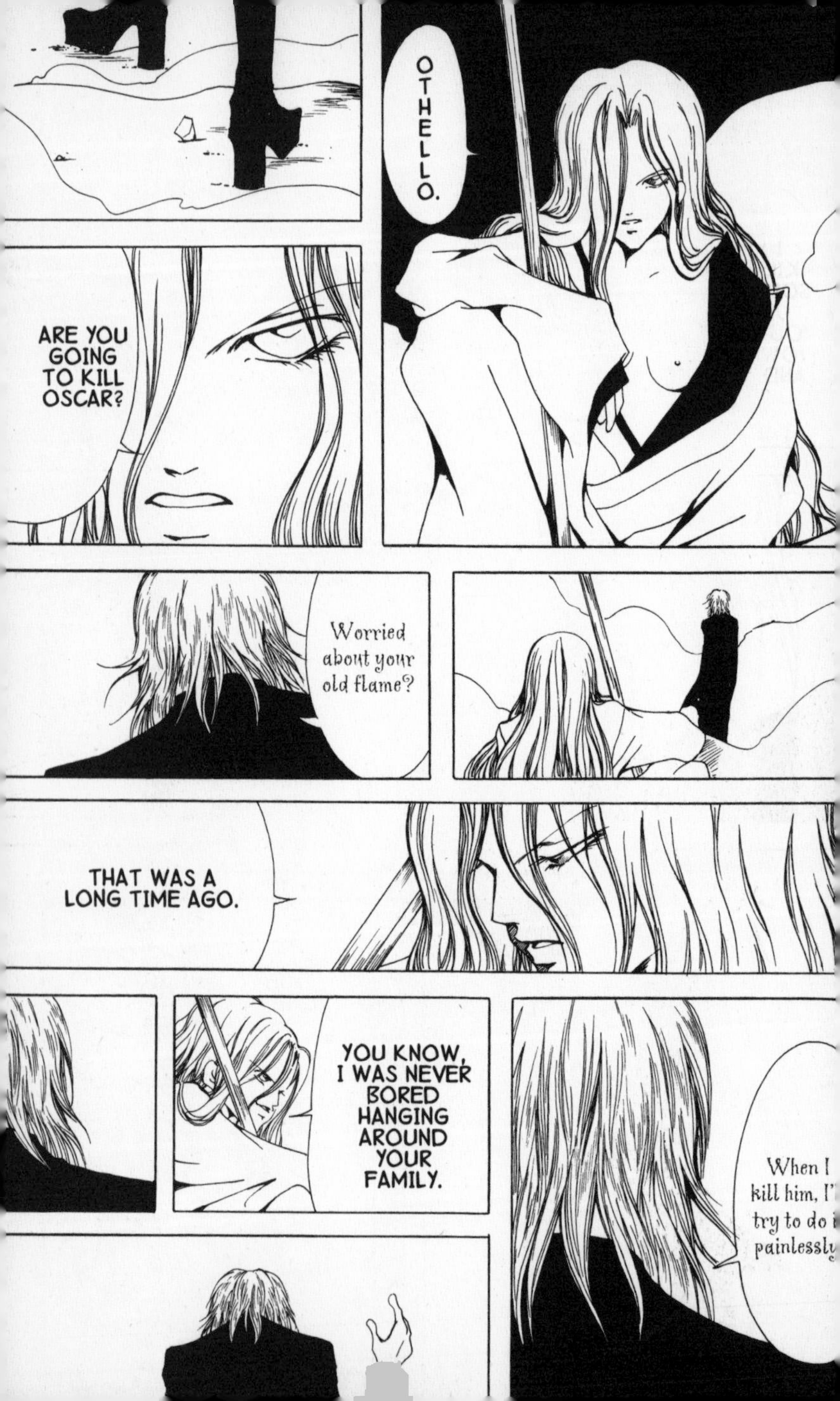
OTHELLO.
ARE YOU GOING TO KILL OSCAR?
Worried about your old flame?
THAT WAS A LONG TIME AGO.
When I kill him, I' try to do i painlessly
YOU KNOW, I WAS NEVER BORED HANGING AROUND YOUR FAMILY.

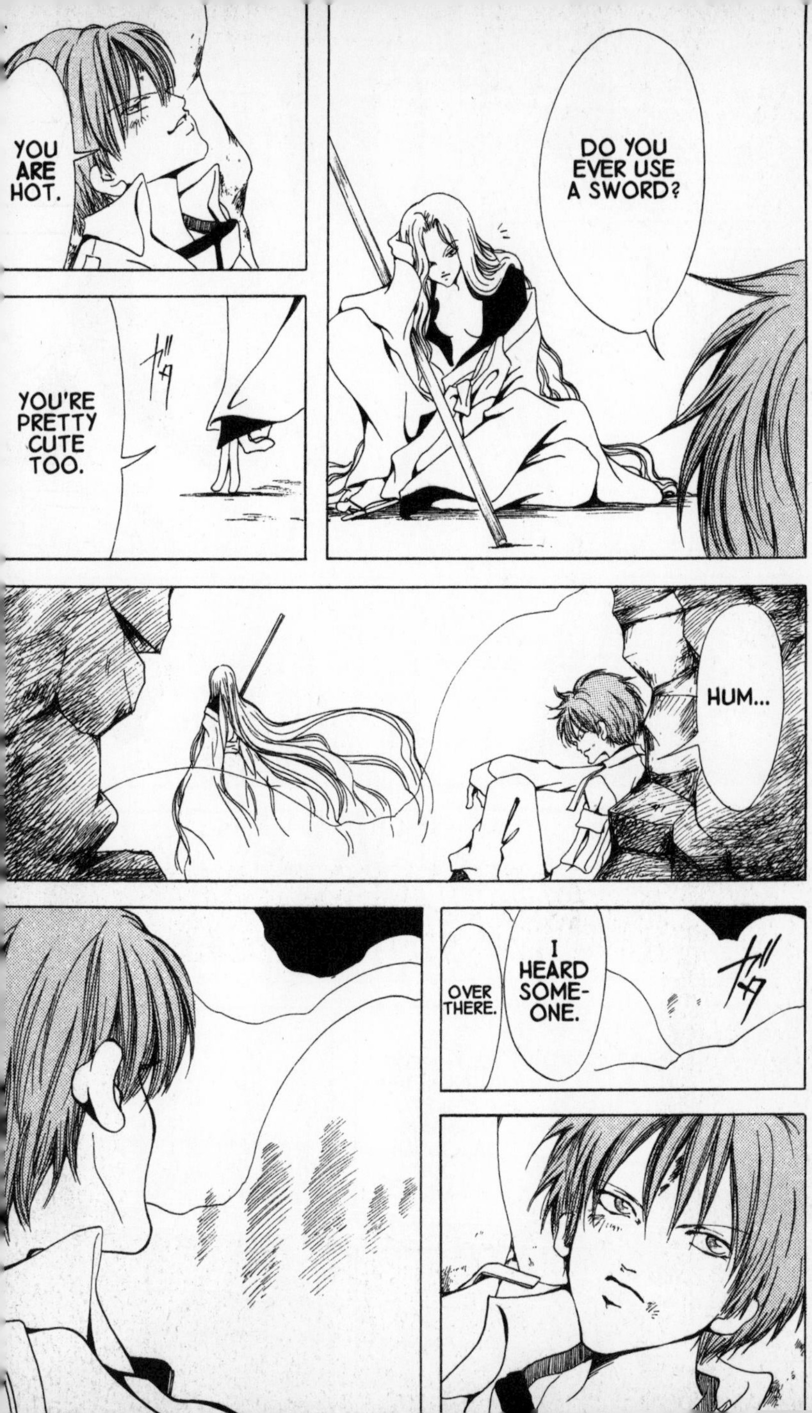
DO YOU EVER USE A SWORD?
YOU ARE HOT.
ガタ
YOU'RE PRETTY CUTE TOO.
HUM...
ガタ
I HEARD SOME-ONE.
OVER THERE.

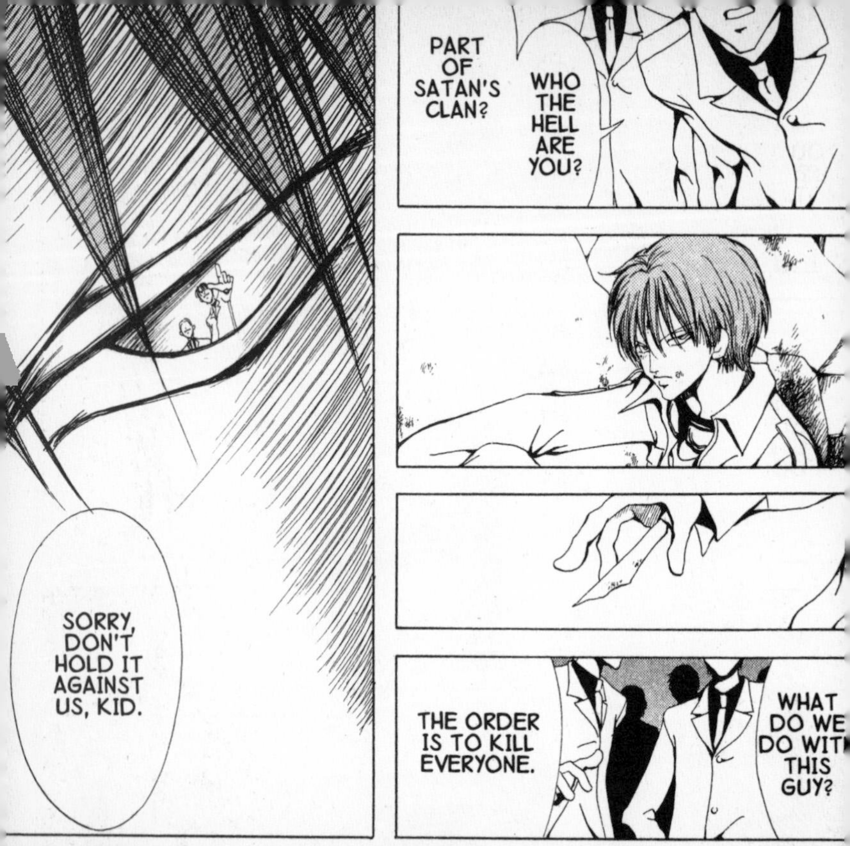
WHO THE HELL ARE YOU?
PART OF SATAN'S CLAN?
WHAT DO WE DO WIT THIS GUY?
THE ORDER IS TO KILL EVERYONE.
SORRY, DON'T HOLD IT AGAINST US, KID.
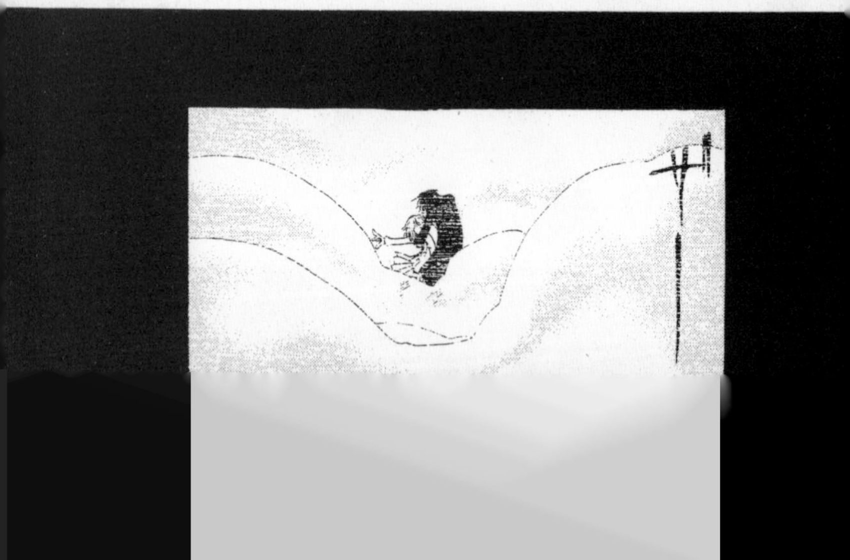

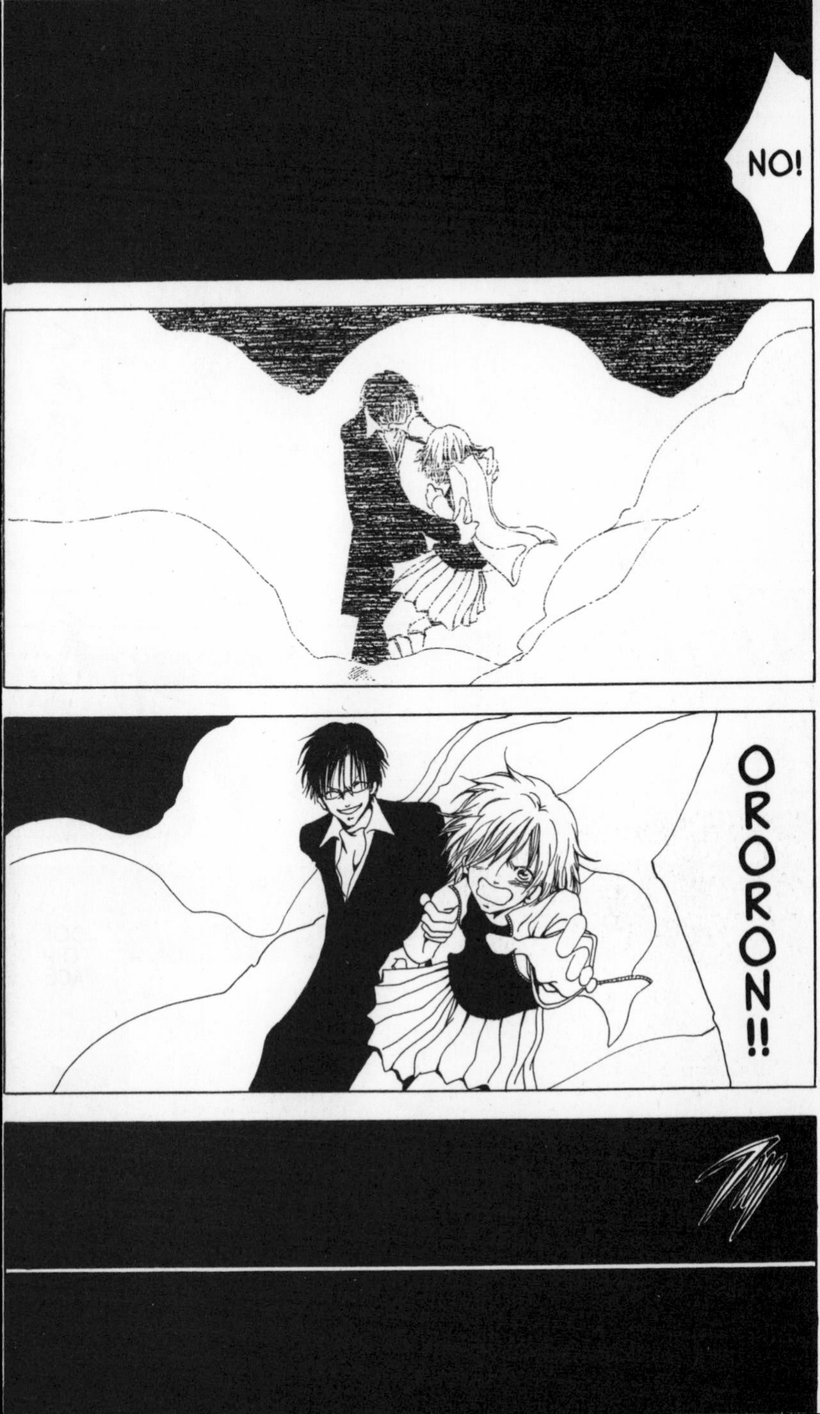
NO!
ORORON!!

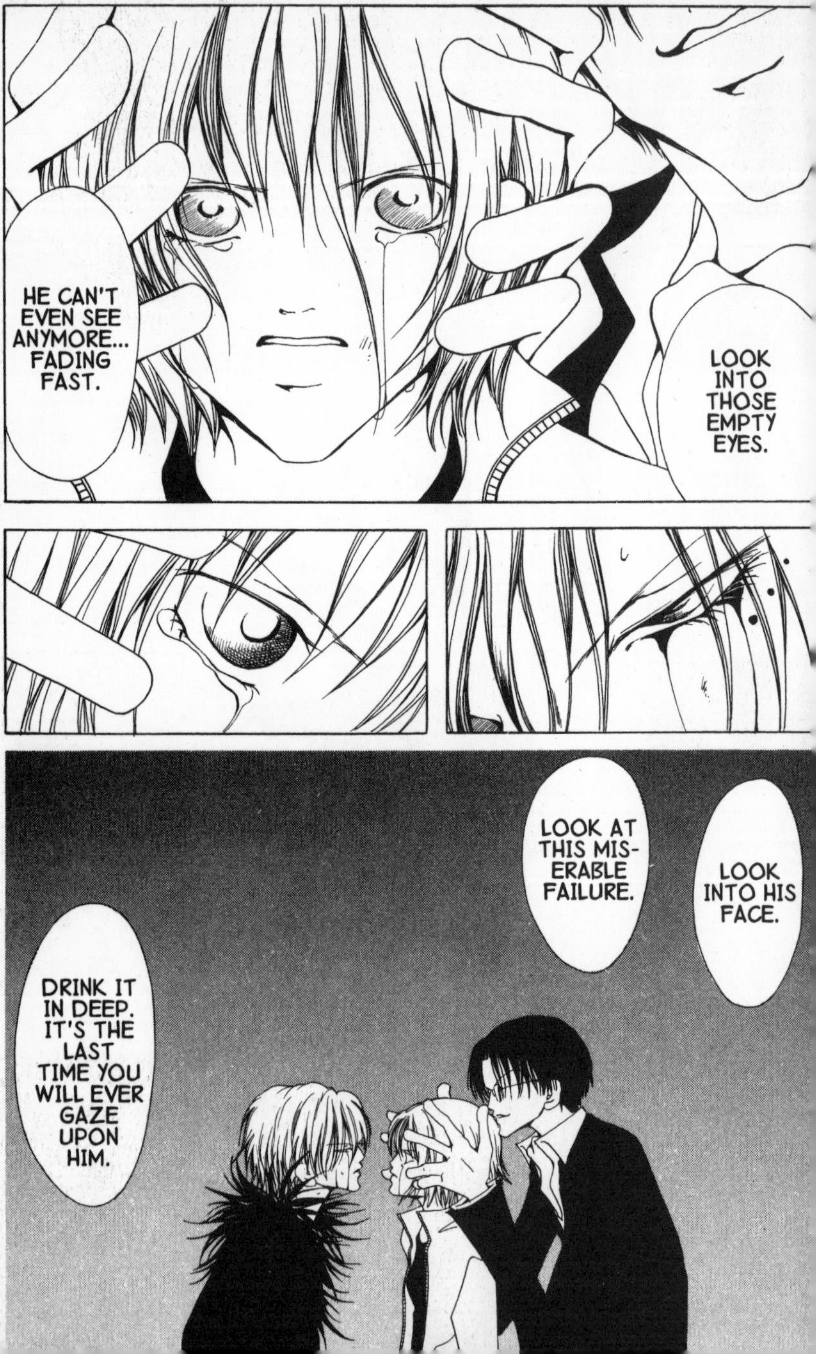
LOOK INTO THOSE EMPTY EYES.
HE CAN'T EVEN SEE ANYMORE... FADING FAST.
LOOK INTO HIS FACE.
LOOK AT THIS MIS-ERABLE FAILURE.
DRINK IT IN DEEP. IT'S THE LAST TIME YOU WILL EVER GAZE UPON HIM.

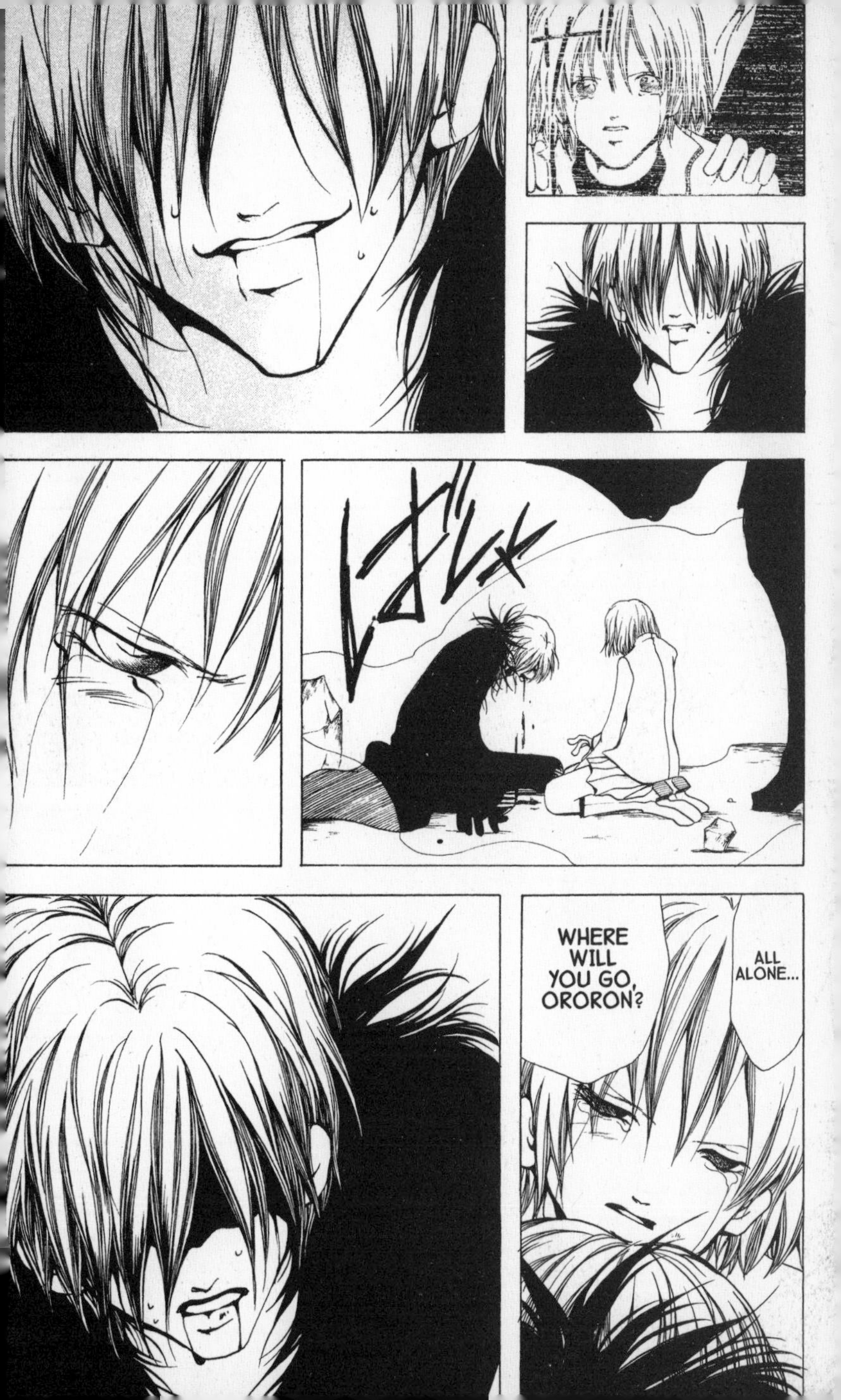
WHERE WILL YOU GO, ORORON?
ALL ALONE...

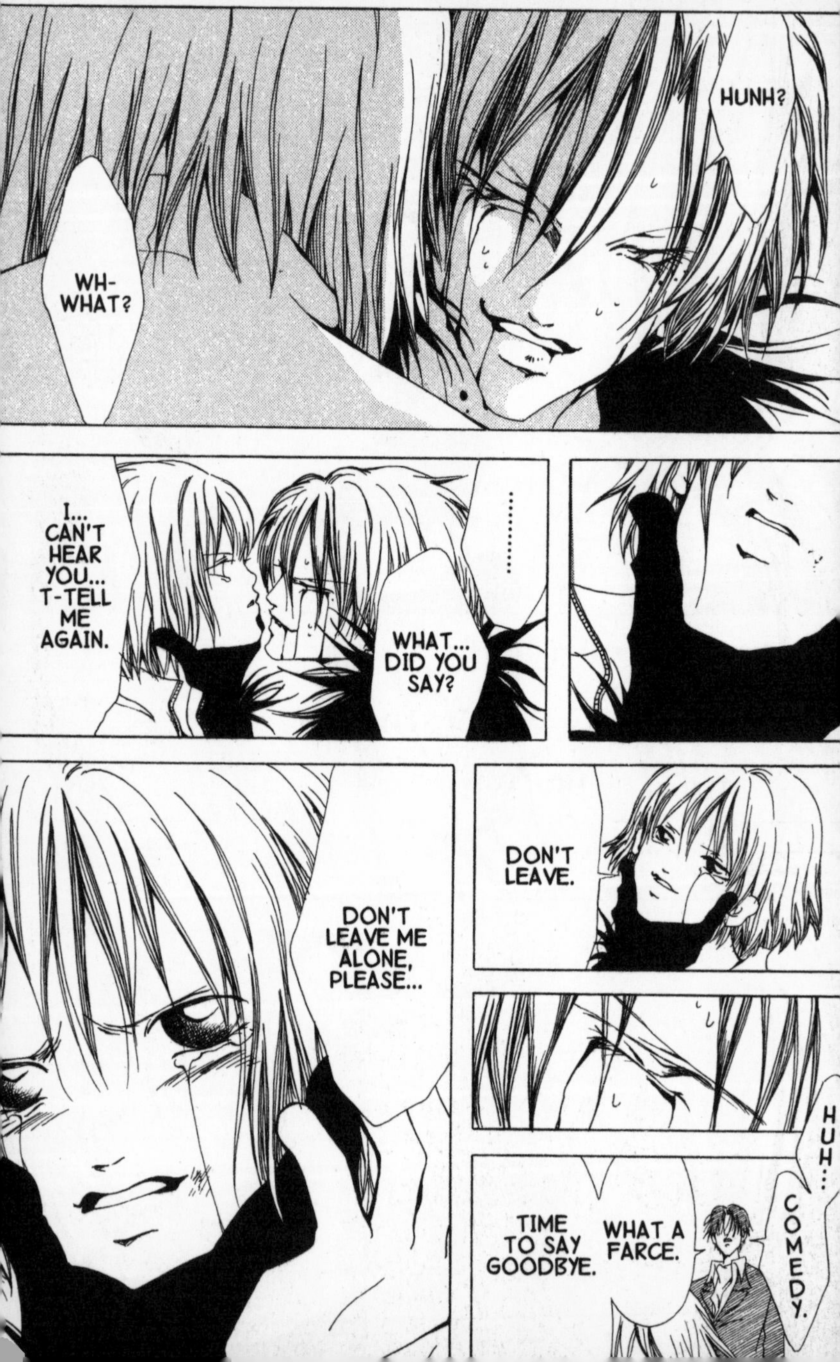
HUNH?
WH-WHAT?
......
WHAT... DID YOU SAY?
I... CAN'T HEAR YOU... T-TELL ME AGAIN.
DON'T LEAVE.
HUH... COMEDY.
WHAT A FARCE.
TIME TO SAY GOODBYE.
DON'T LEAVE ME ALONE, PLEASE...

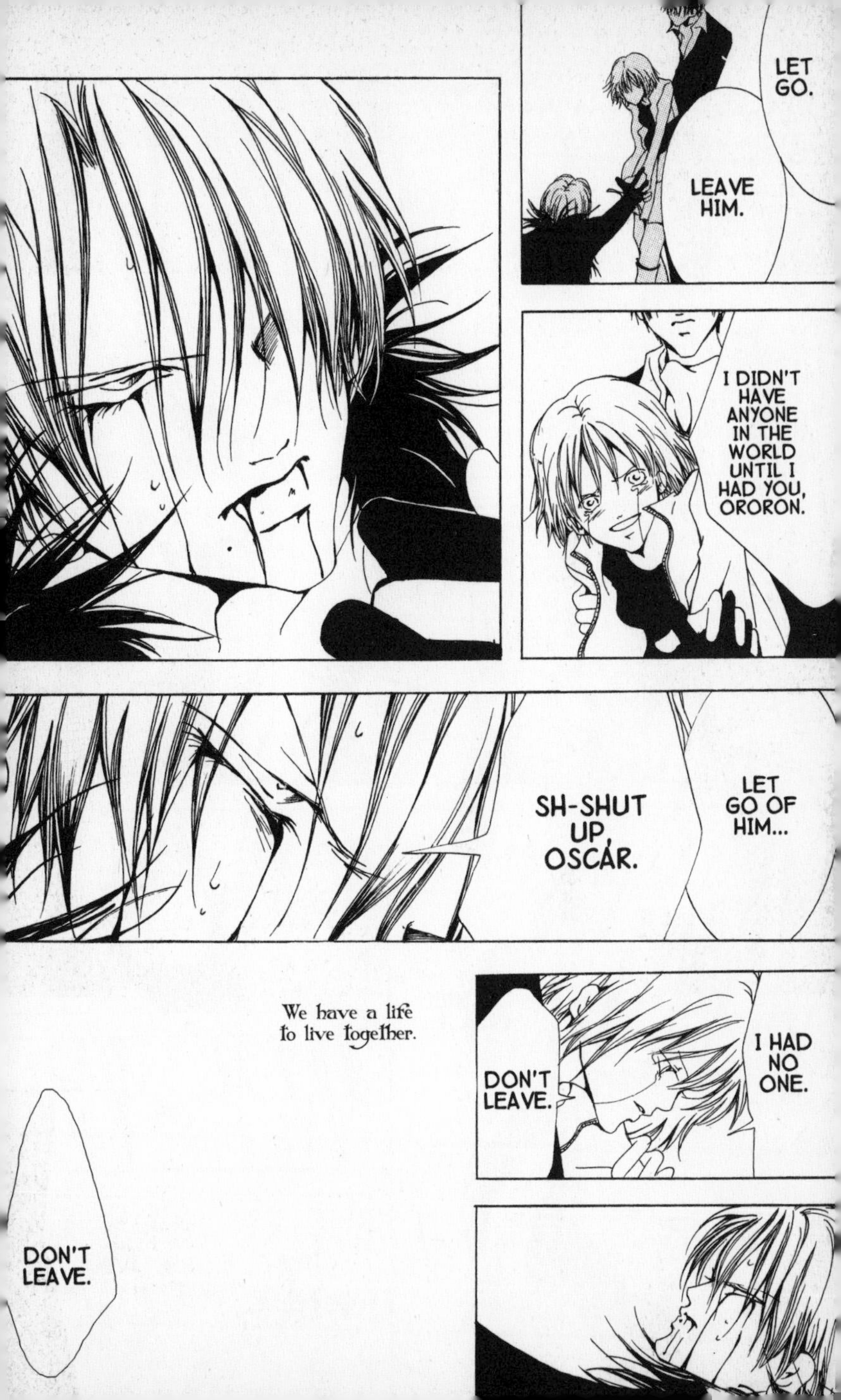
LET GO.
LEAVE HIM.
I DIDN'T HAVE ANYONE IN THE WORLD UNTIL I HAD YOU, ORORON.
LET GO OF HIM...
SH-SHUT UP, OSCAR.
I HAD NO ONE.
DON'T LEAVE.
We have a life to live together.
DON'T LEAVE.

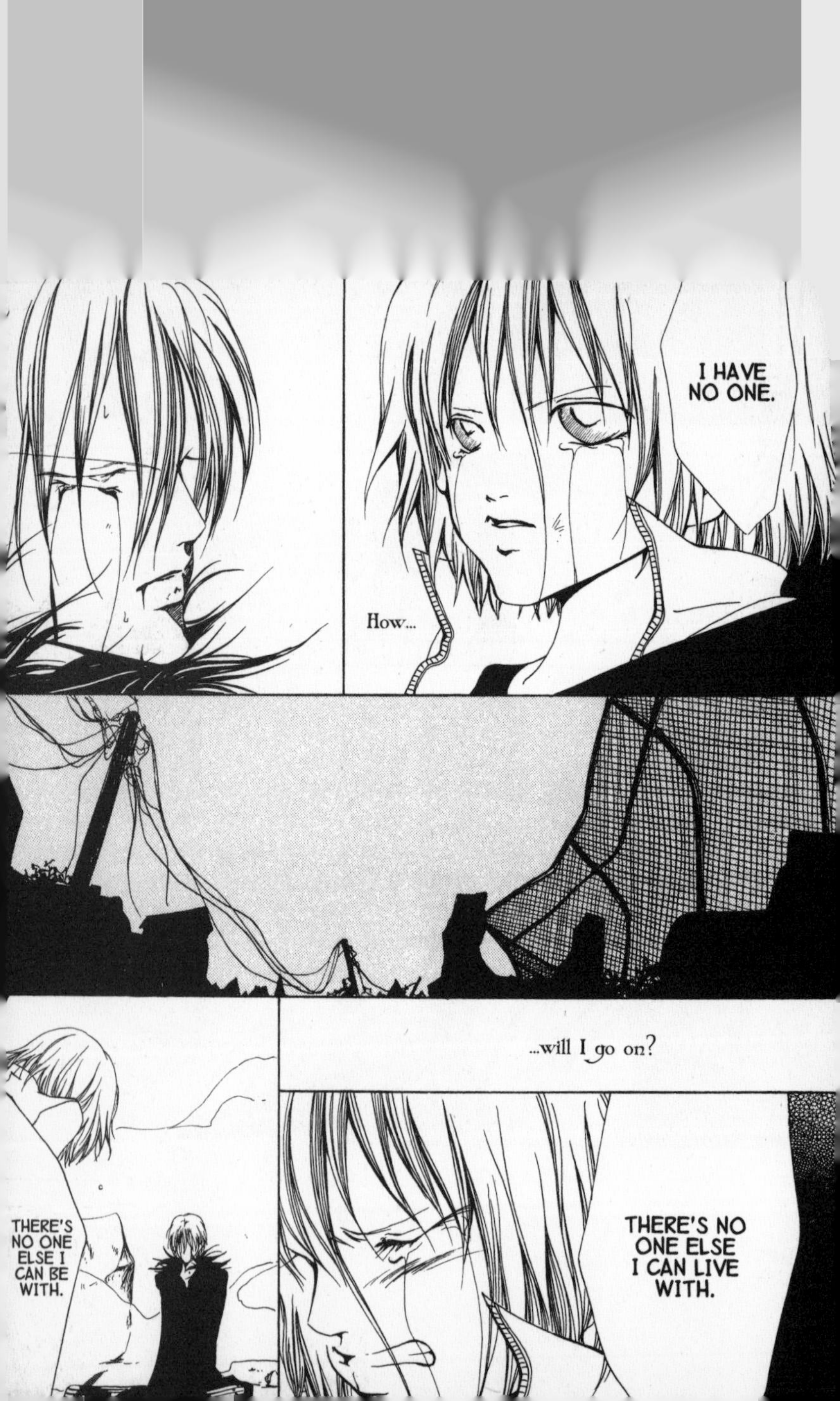
I HAVE NO ONE.
How...
...will I go on?
THERE'S NO ONE ELSE I CAN LIVE WITH.
THERE'S NO ONE ELSE I CAN BE WITH.

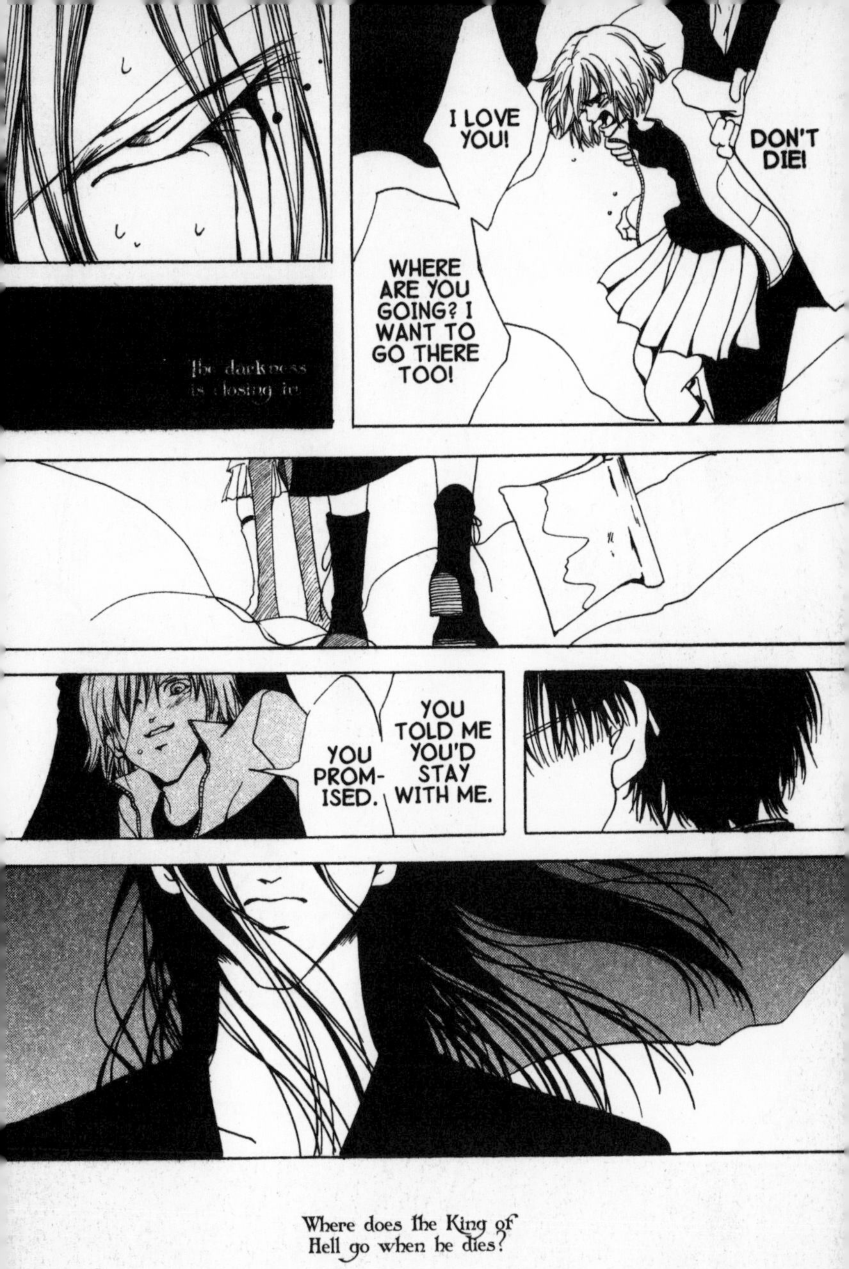
DON'T DIE!
I LOVE YOU!
WHERE ARE YOU GOING? I WANT TO GO THERE TOO!
The darkness is closing in.
YOU TOLD ME YOU'D STAY WITH ME.
YOU PROMISED.

Where does the King of Hell go when he dies?

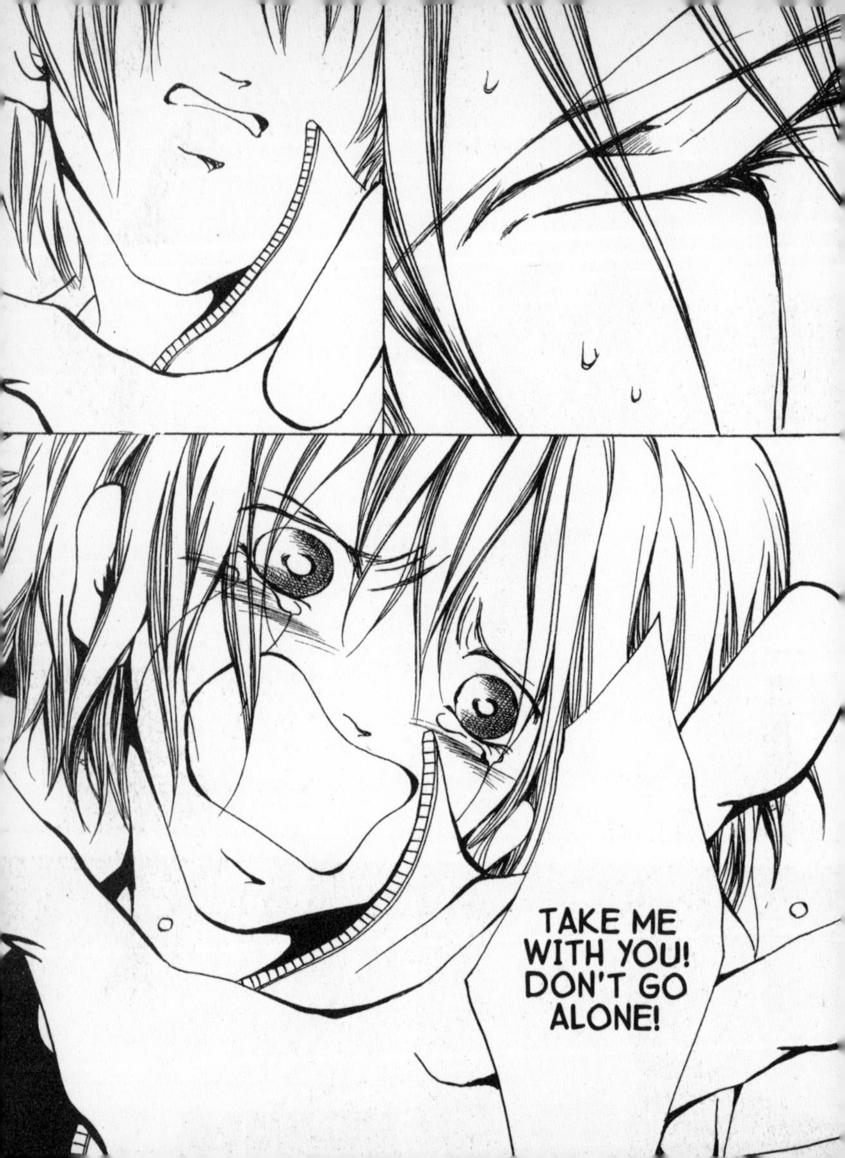
TAKE ME WITH YOU! DON'T GO ALONE!

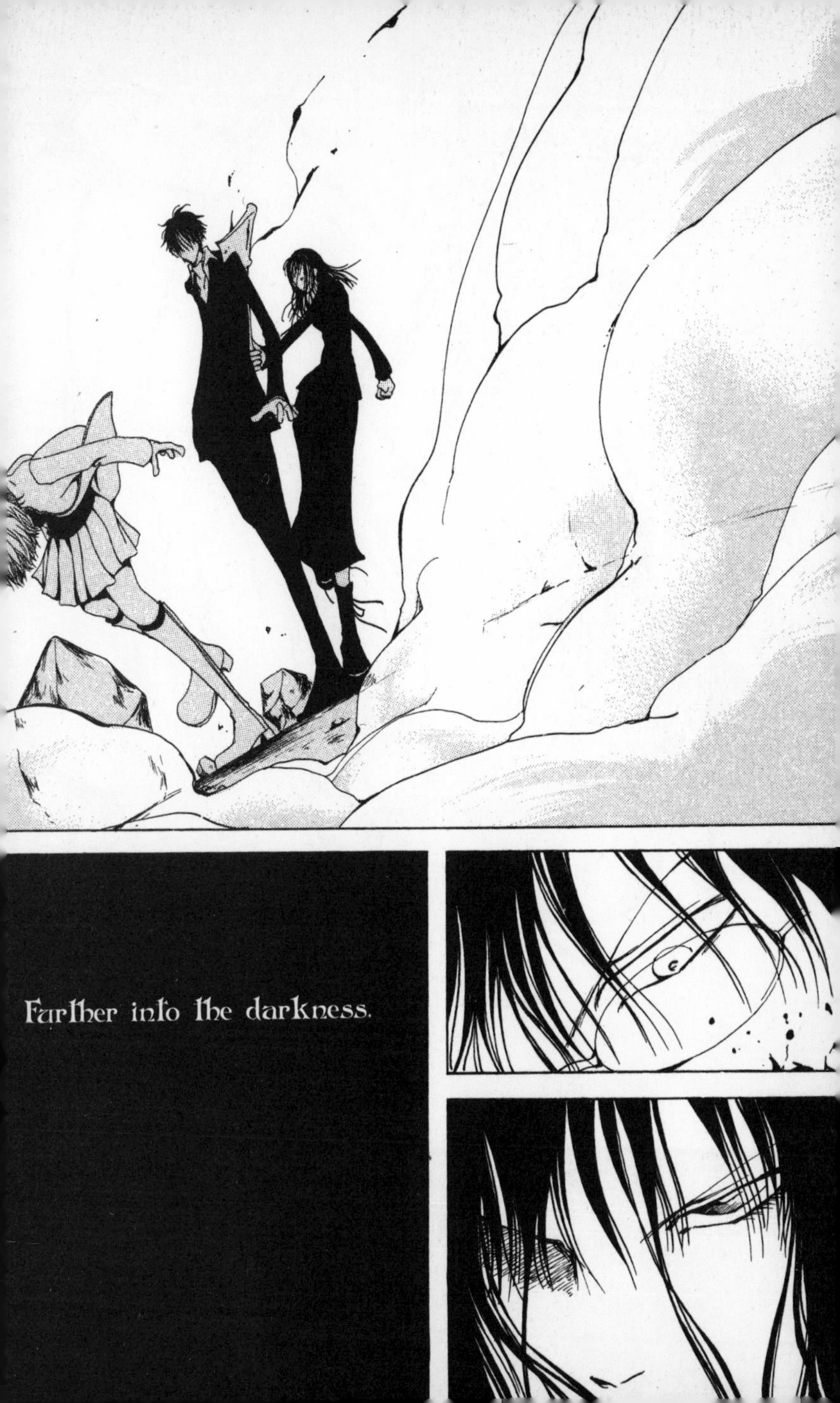
Further into the darkness.

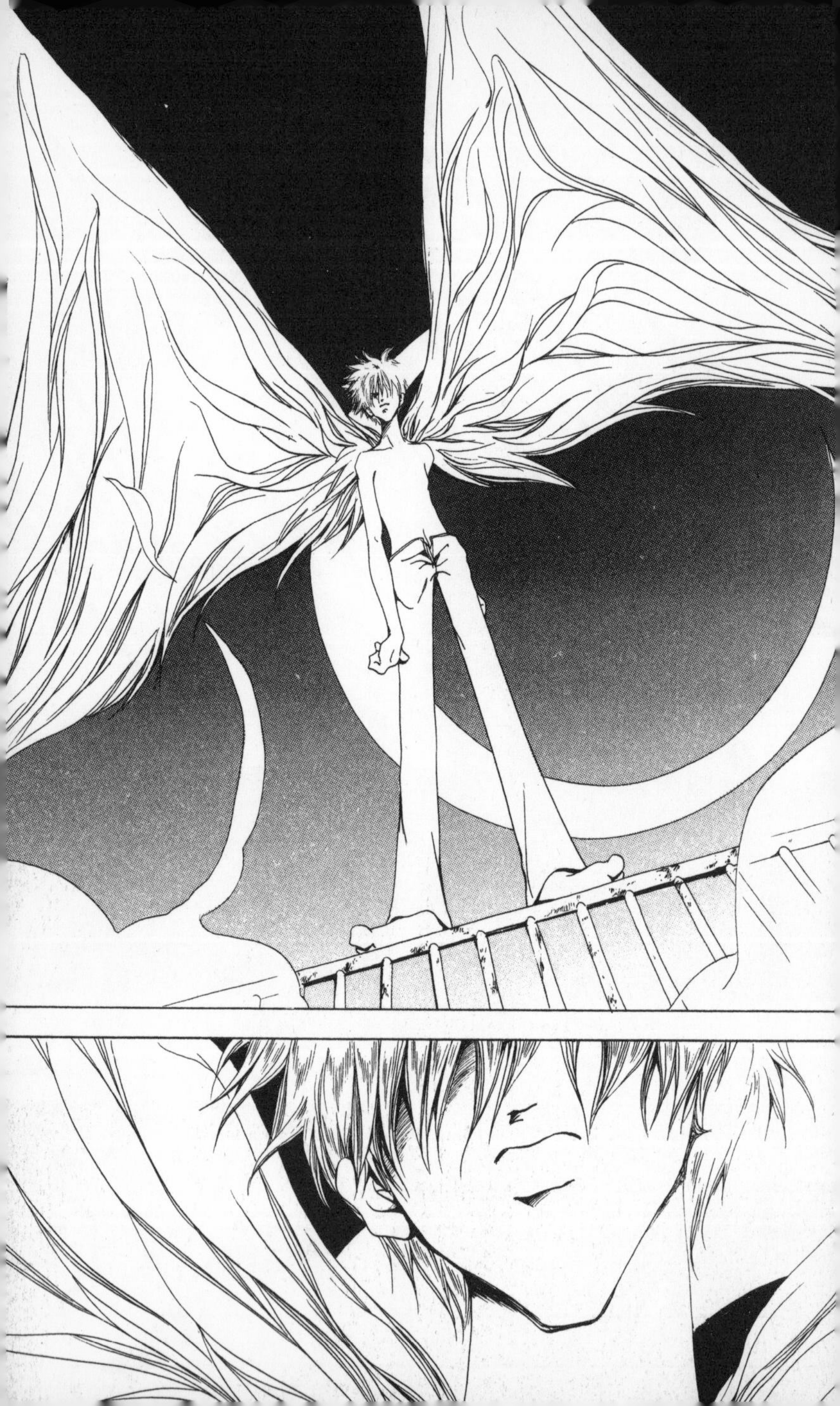

Take me with you.

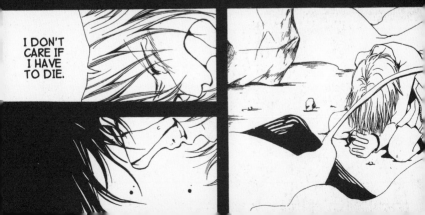

I DON'T CARE IF I HAVE TO DIE.

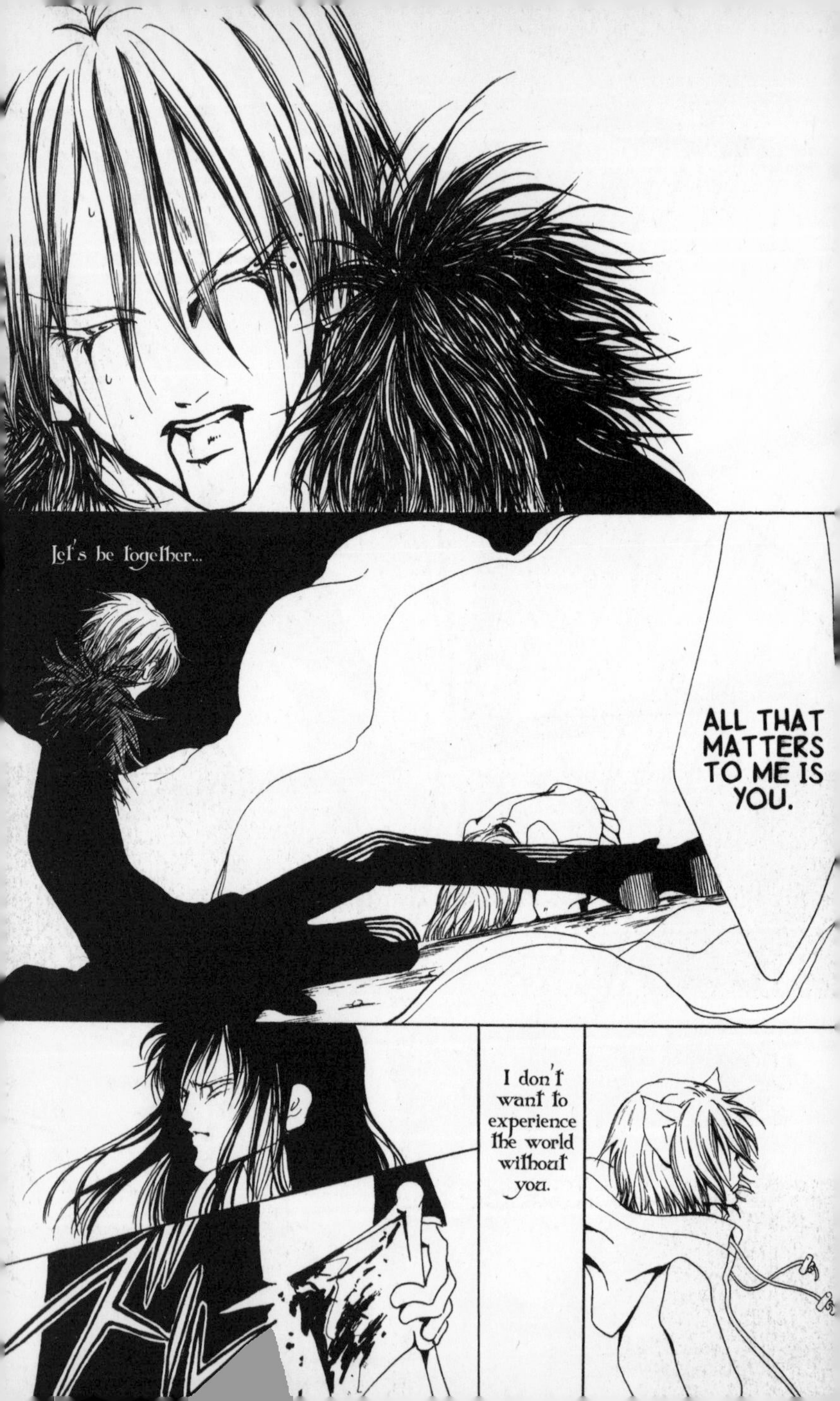
ALL THAT MATTERS TO ME IS YOU.
Let's be together...
I don't want to experience the world without you.

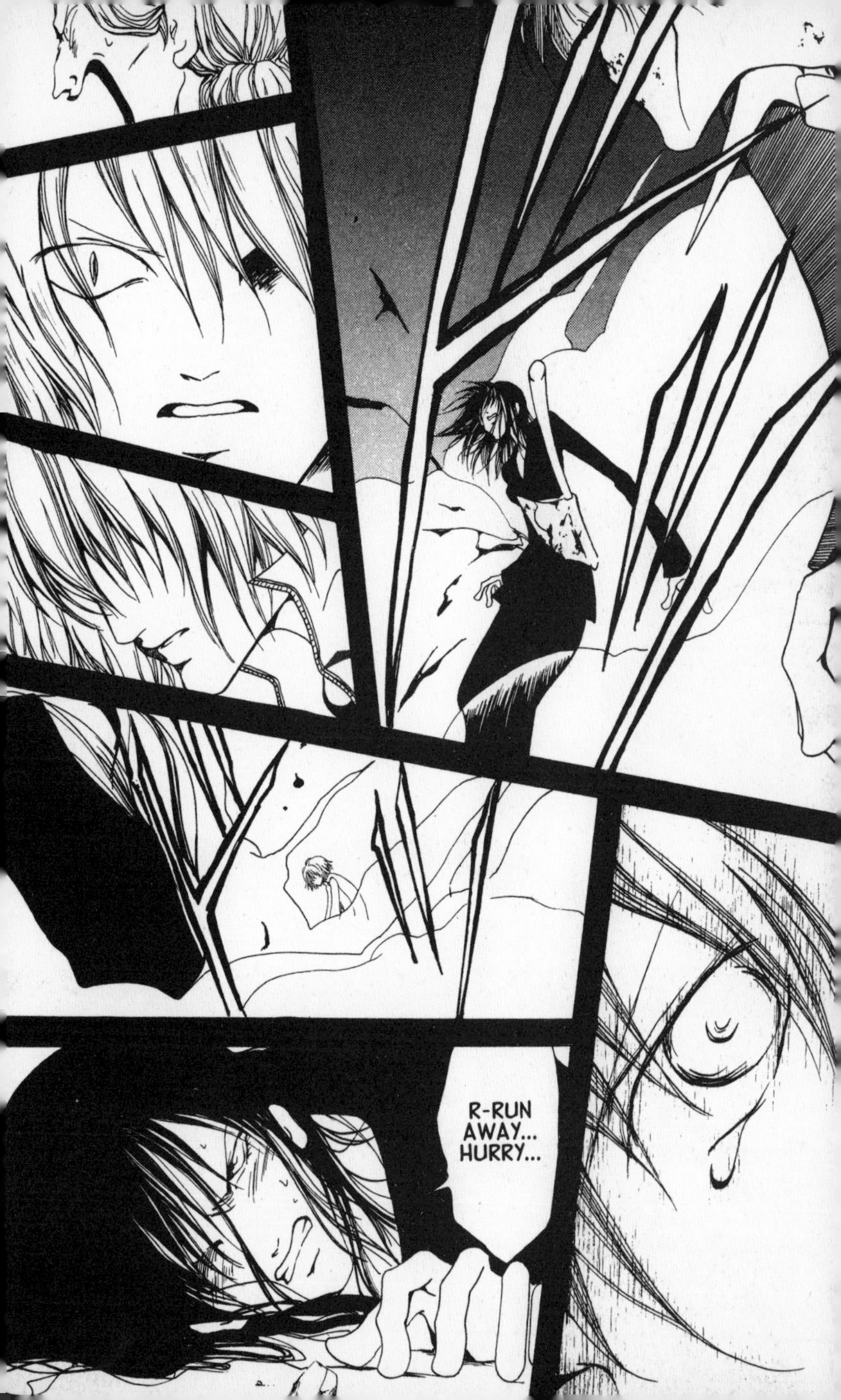
R-RUN AWAY... HURRY...

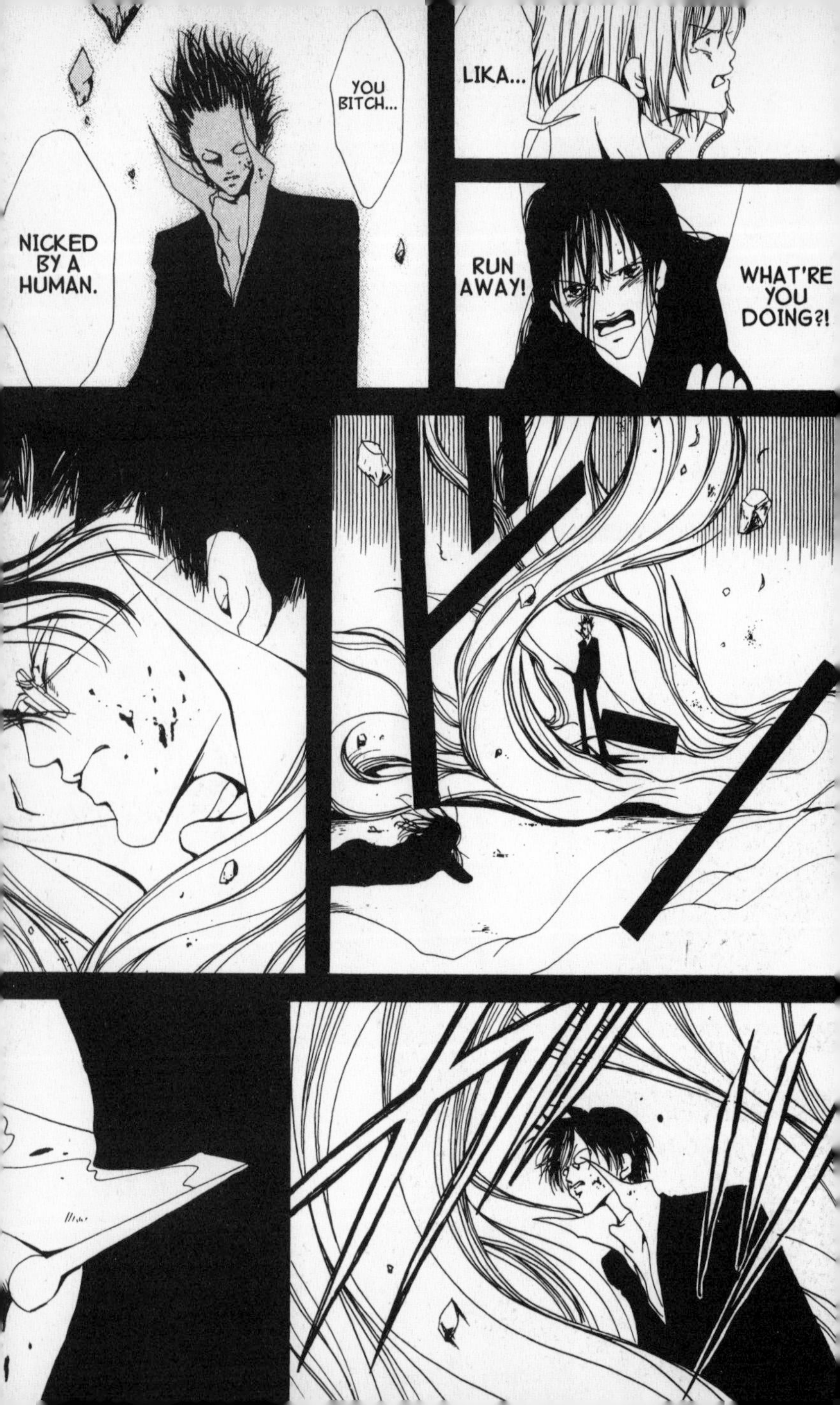
LIKA...
WHAT'RE YOU DOING?!
RUN AWAY!
YOU BITCH...
NICKED BY A HUMAN.

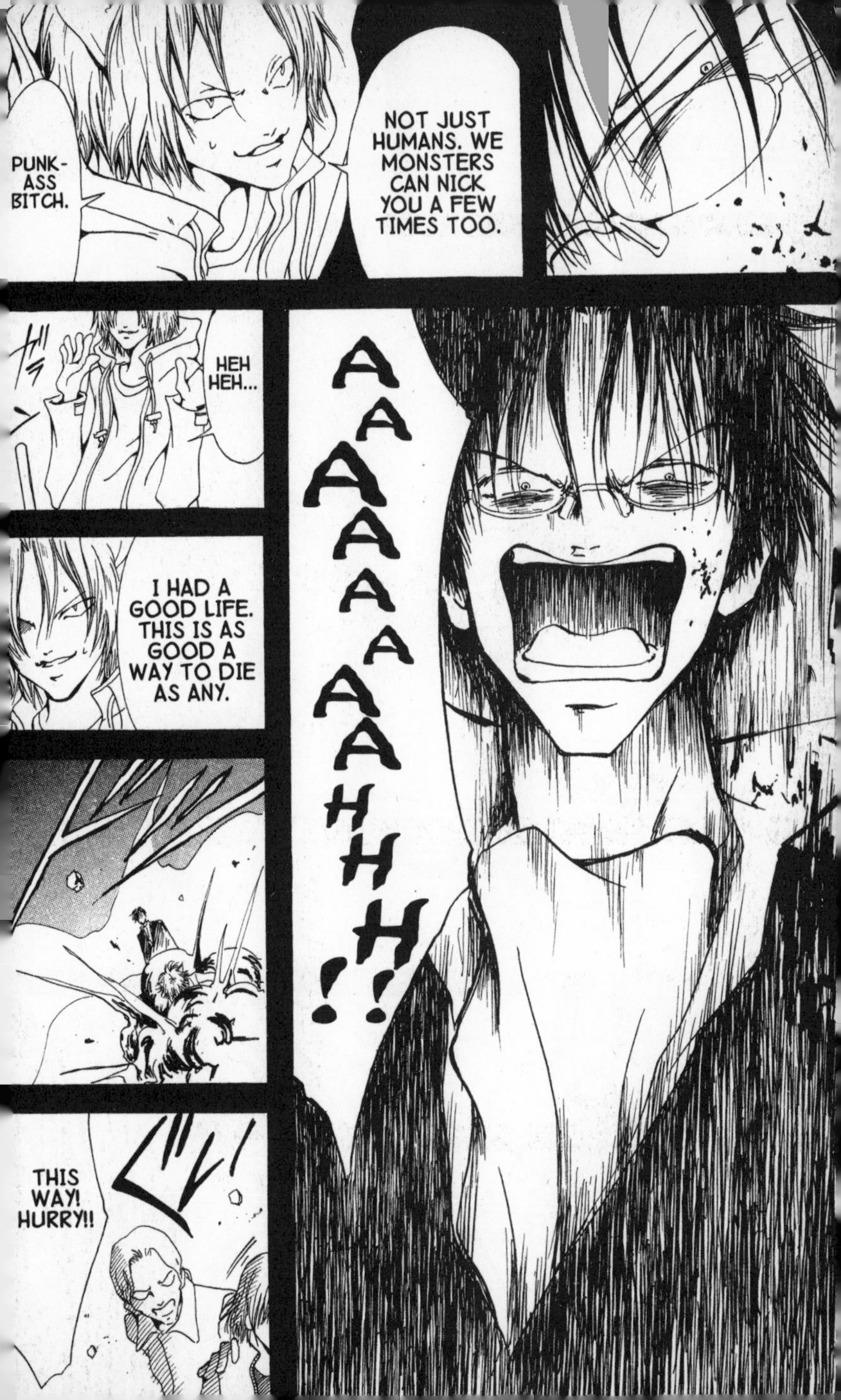
NOT JUST HUMANS. WE MONSTERS CAN NICK YOU A FEW TIMES TOO.
PUNK-ASS BITCH.
AAAAAAAAHHH!!
HEH HEH...
I HAD A GOOD LIFE. THIS IS AS GOOD A WAY TO DIE AS ANY.
THIS WAY! HURRY!!

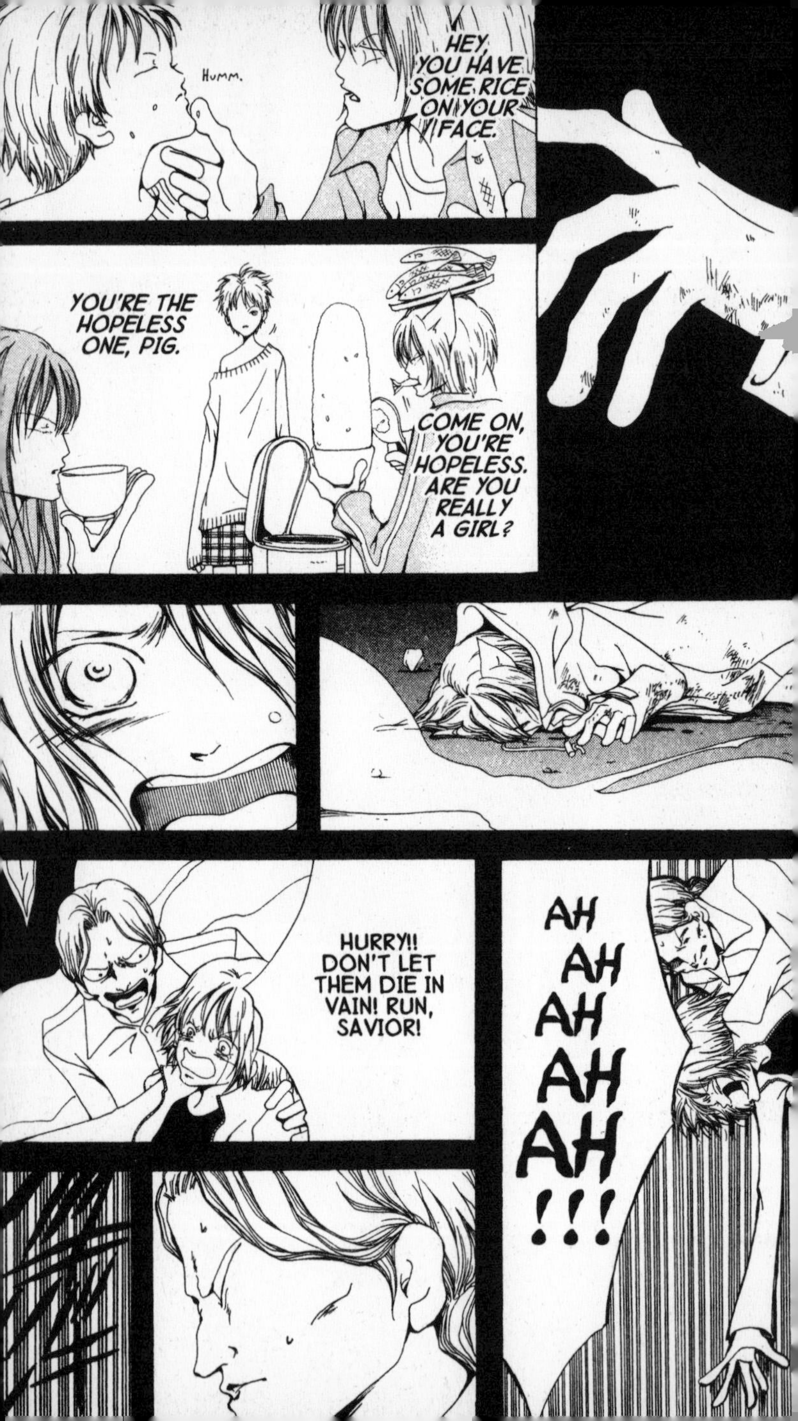

HEY, YOU HAVE SOME RICE ON YOUR FACE.
Humm.
COME ON, YOU'RE HOPELESS. ARE YOU REALLY A GIRL?
YOU'RE THE HOPELESS ONE, PIG.
AH AH AH AH AH!!!
HURRY!! DON'T LET THEM DIE IN VAIN! RUN, SAVIOR!

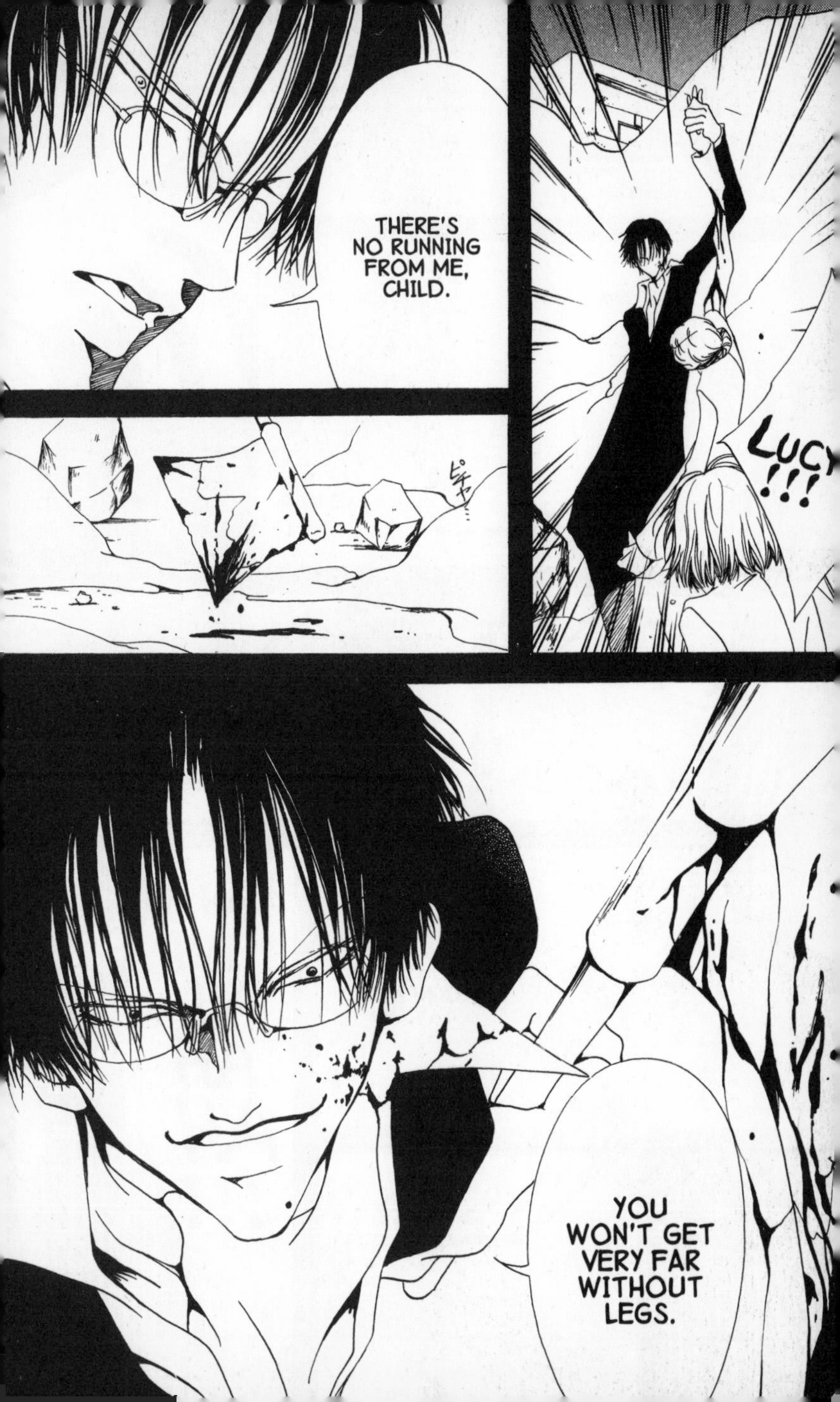
LUCY!!!
THERE'S NO RUNNING FROM ME, CHILD.
ピチャ…
YOU WON'T GET VERY FAR WITHOUT LEGS.

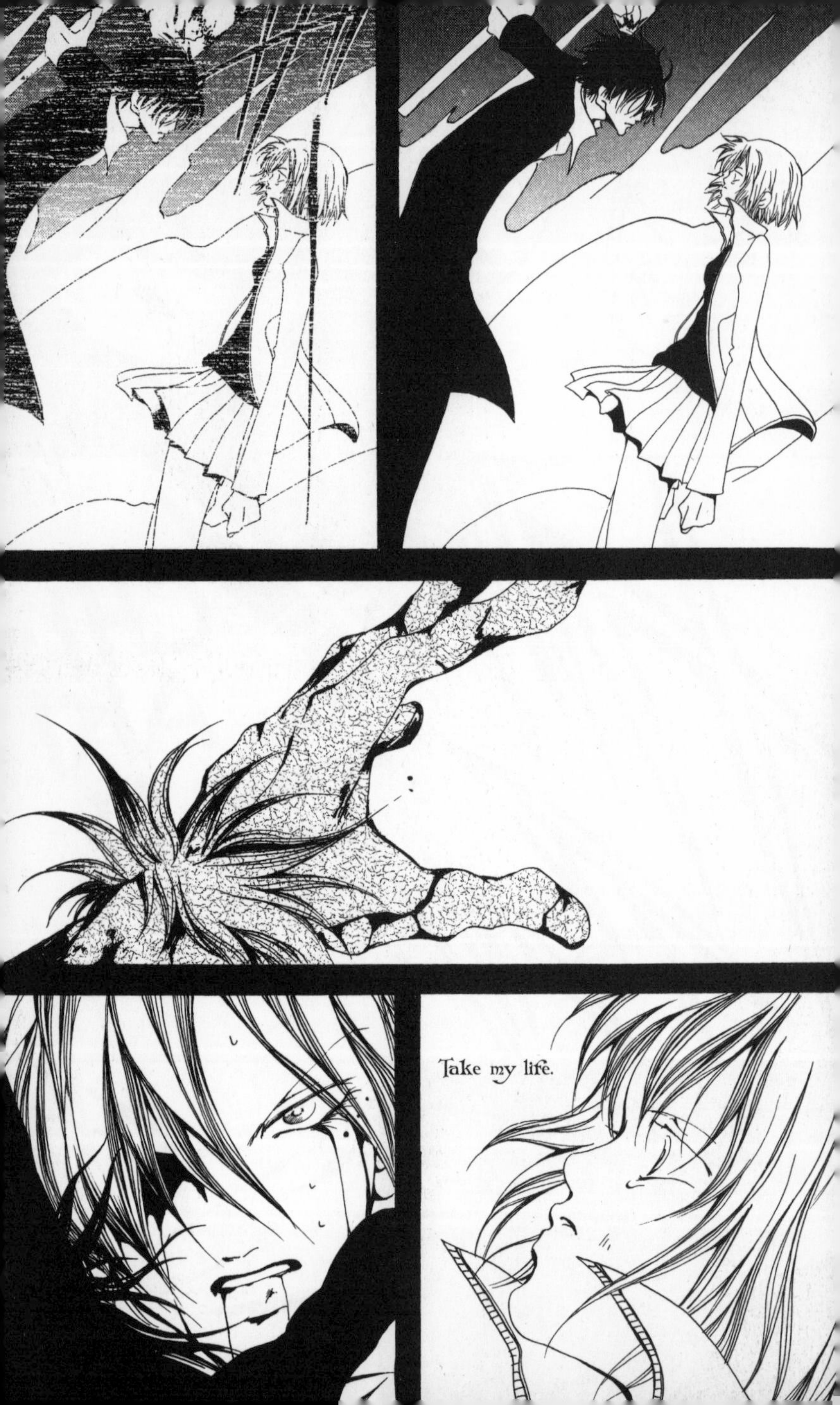
Take my life.

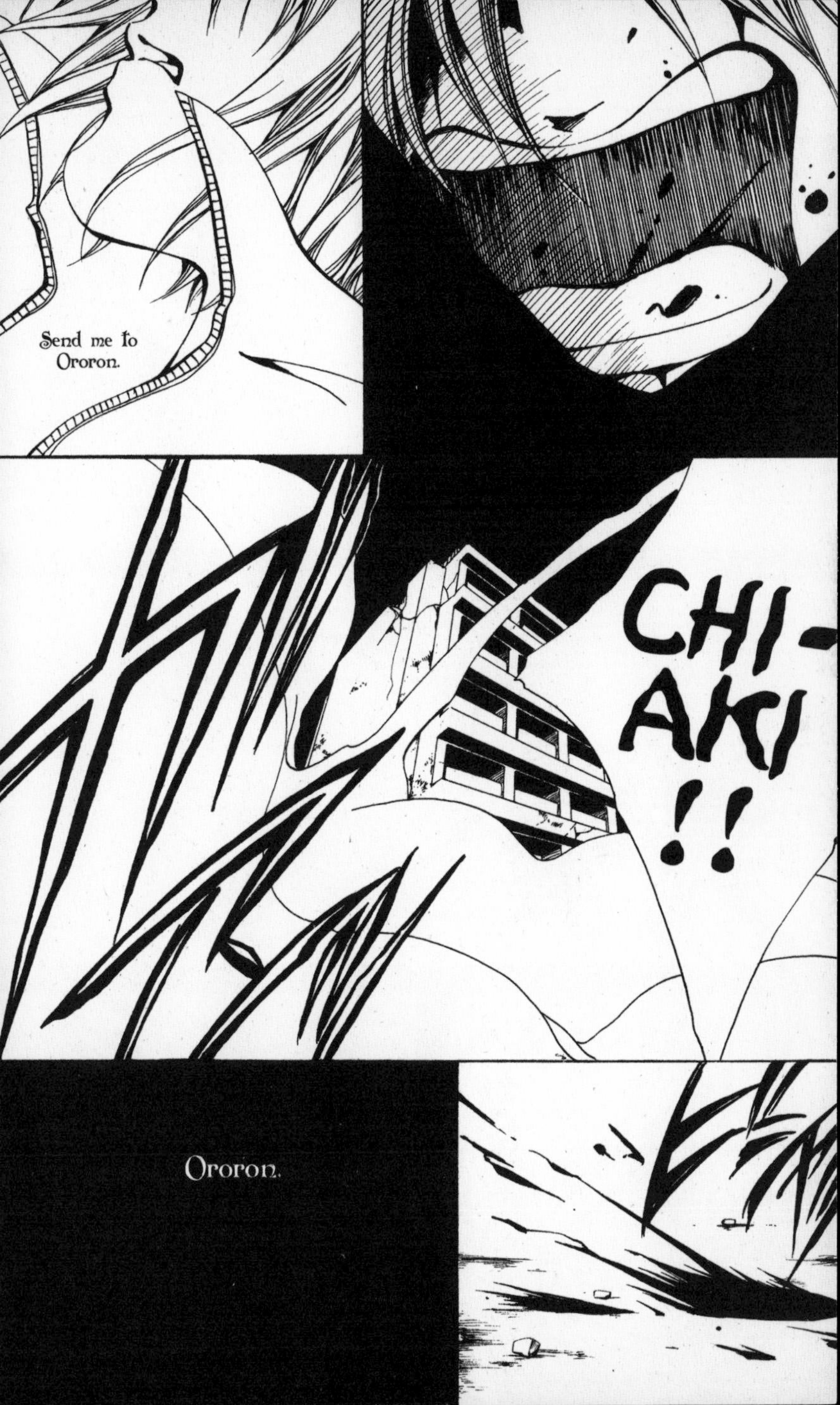
Send me to Ororon.
CHI-AKI!!
Ororon.

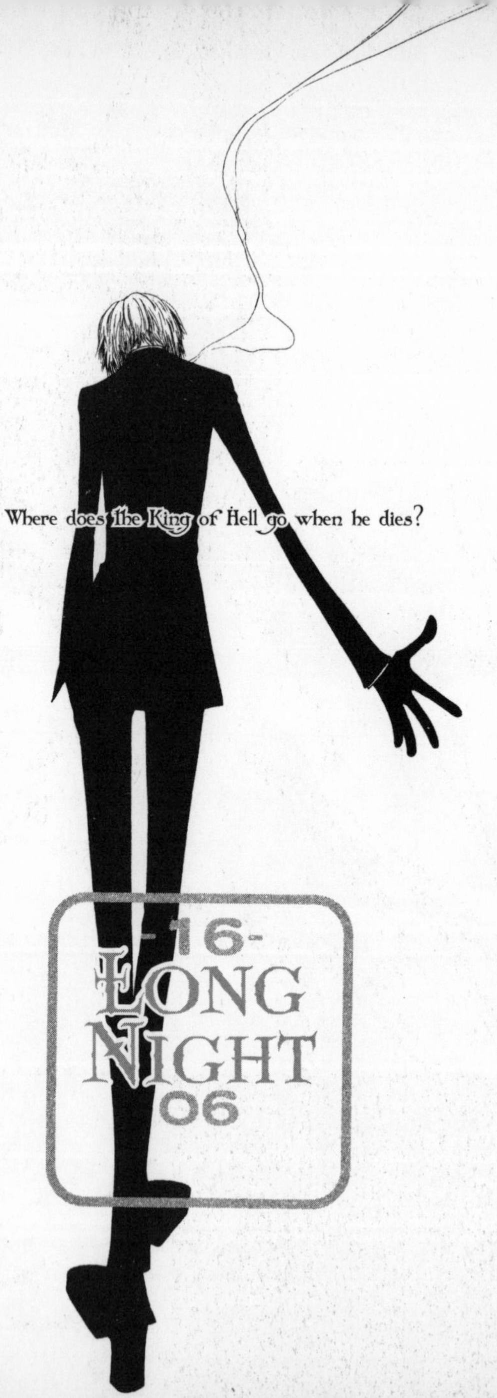
Where does the King of Hell go when he dies?
-16-
LONG NIGHT
06

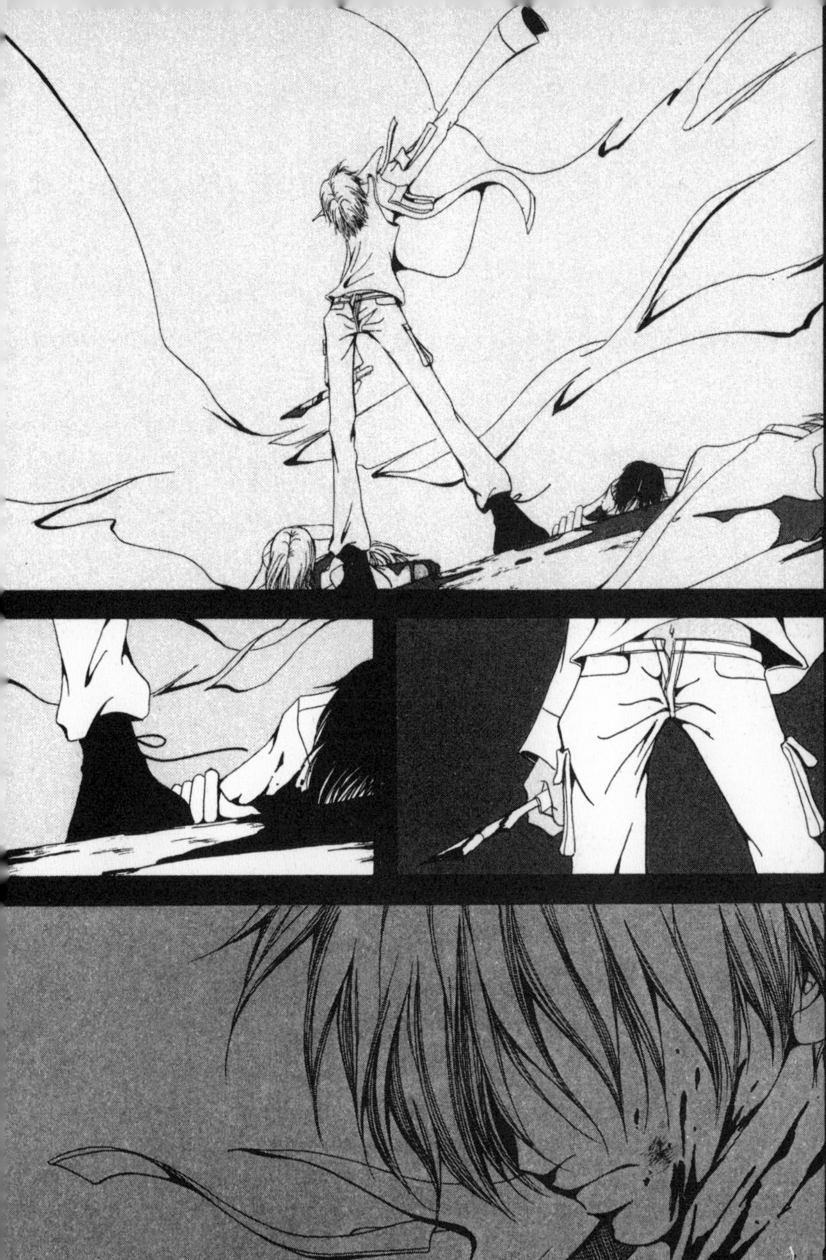

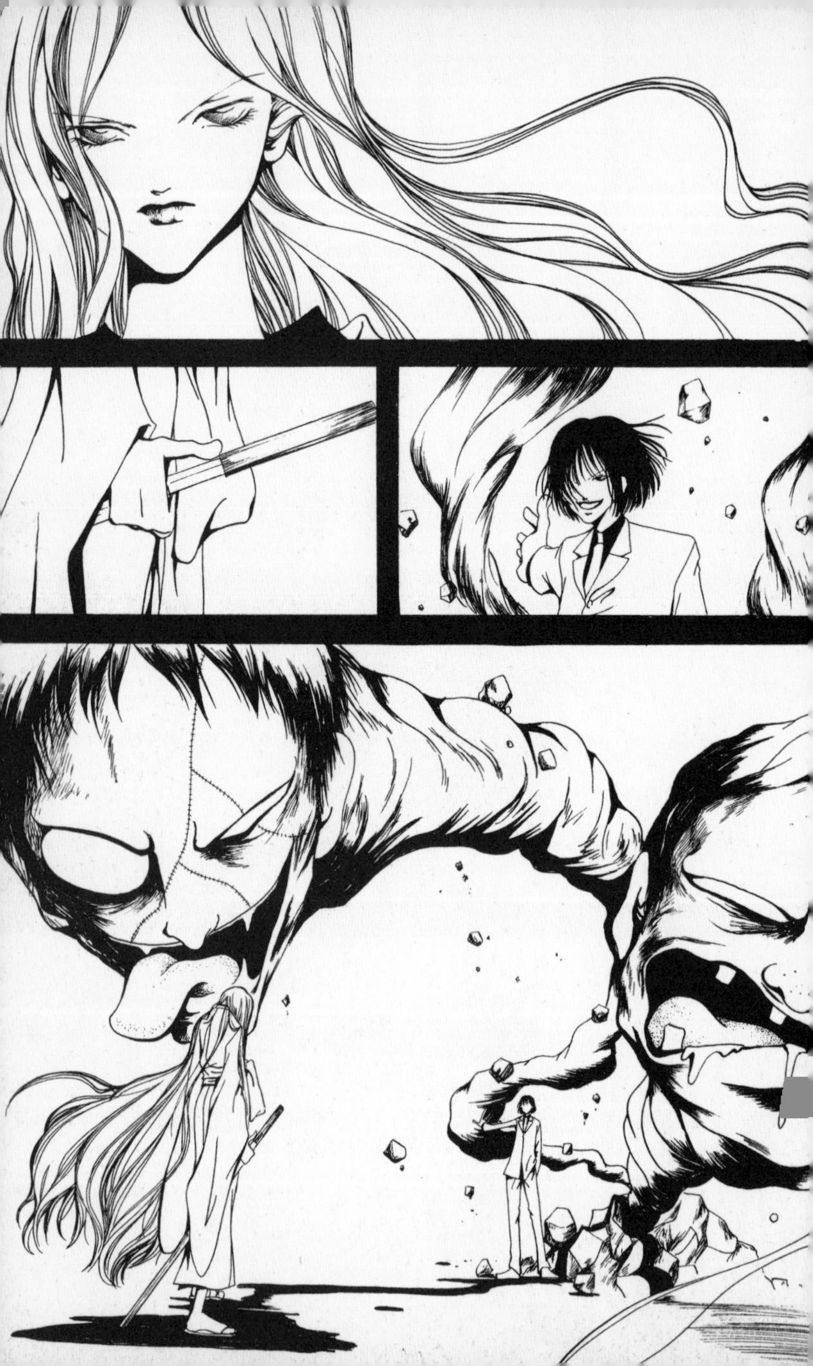

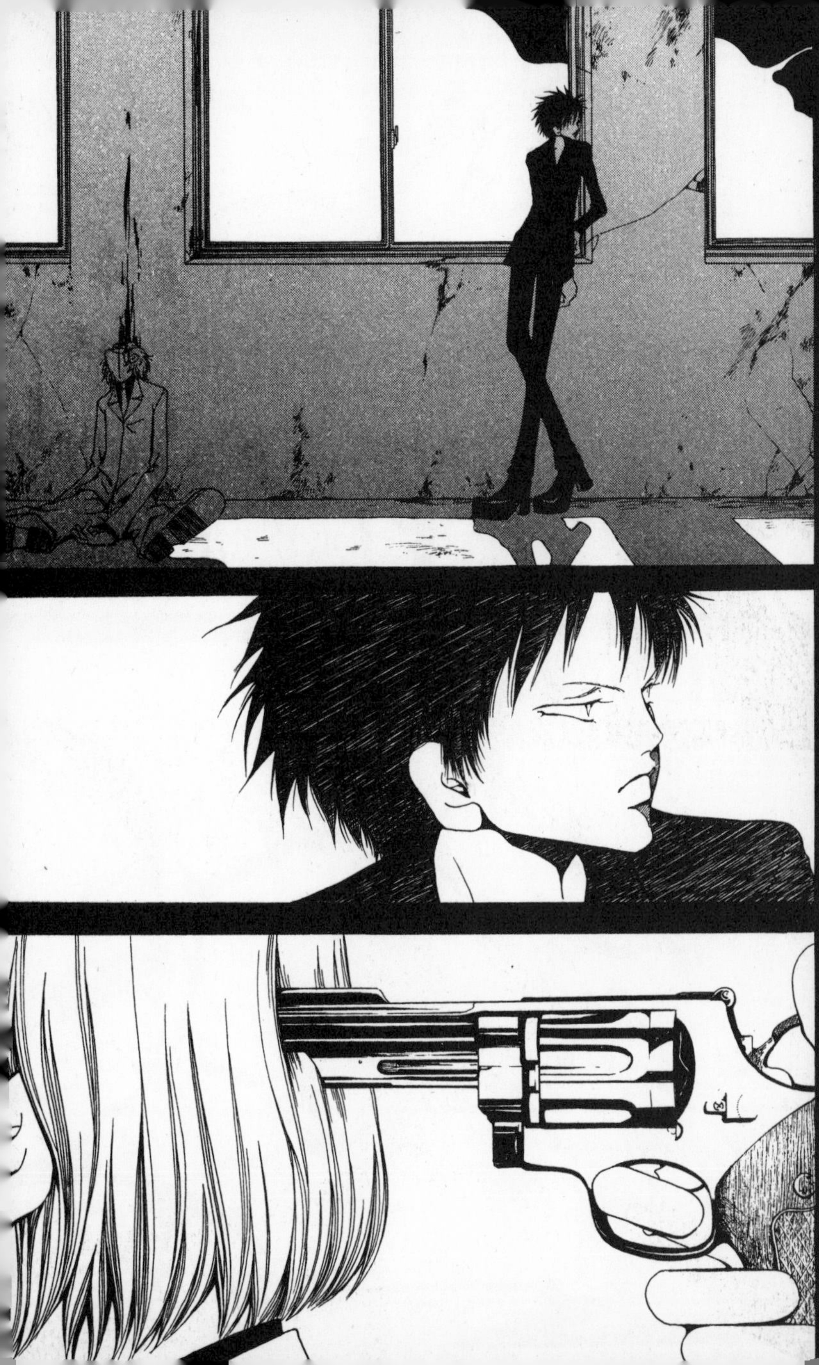

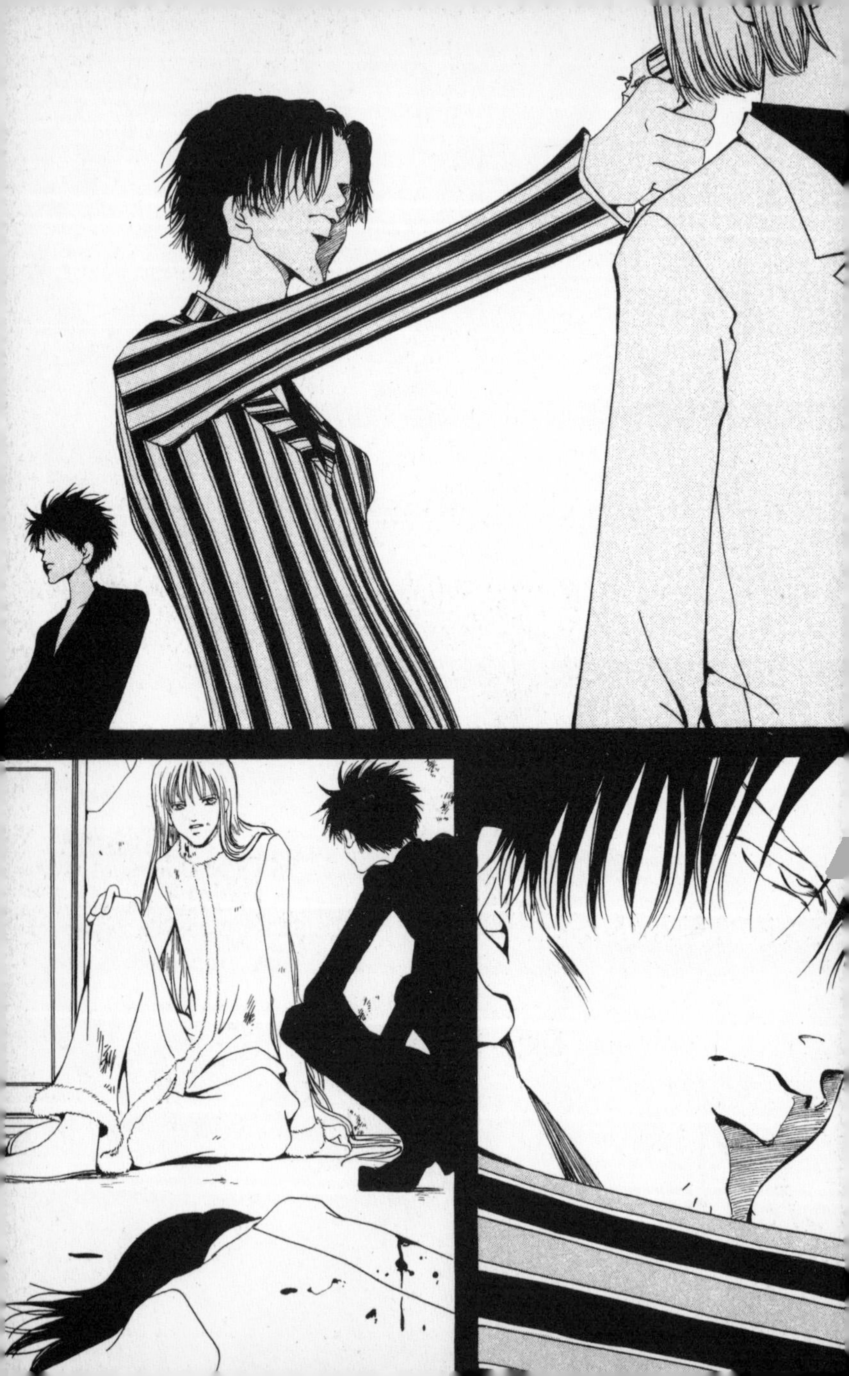

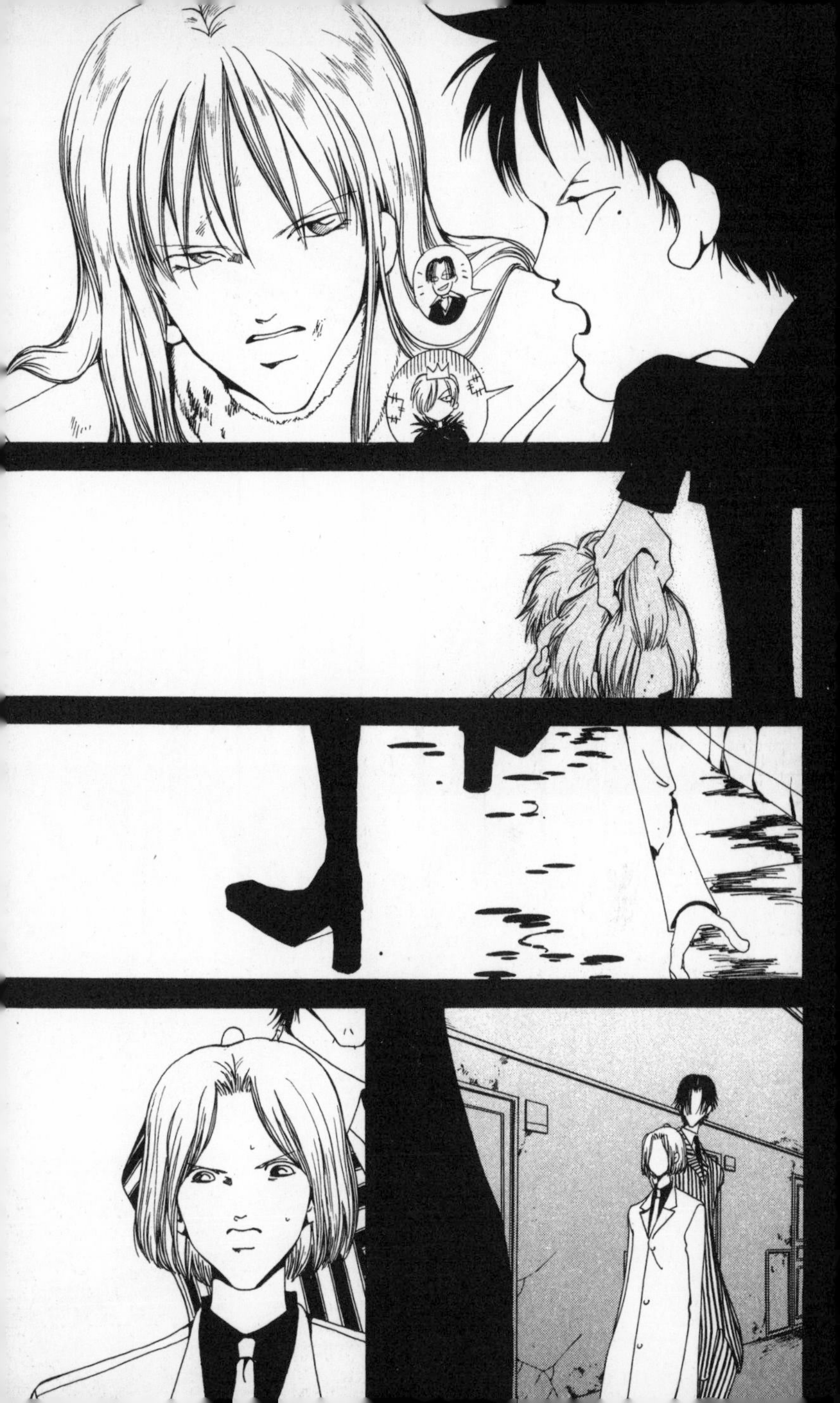

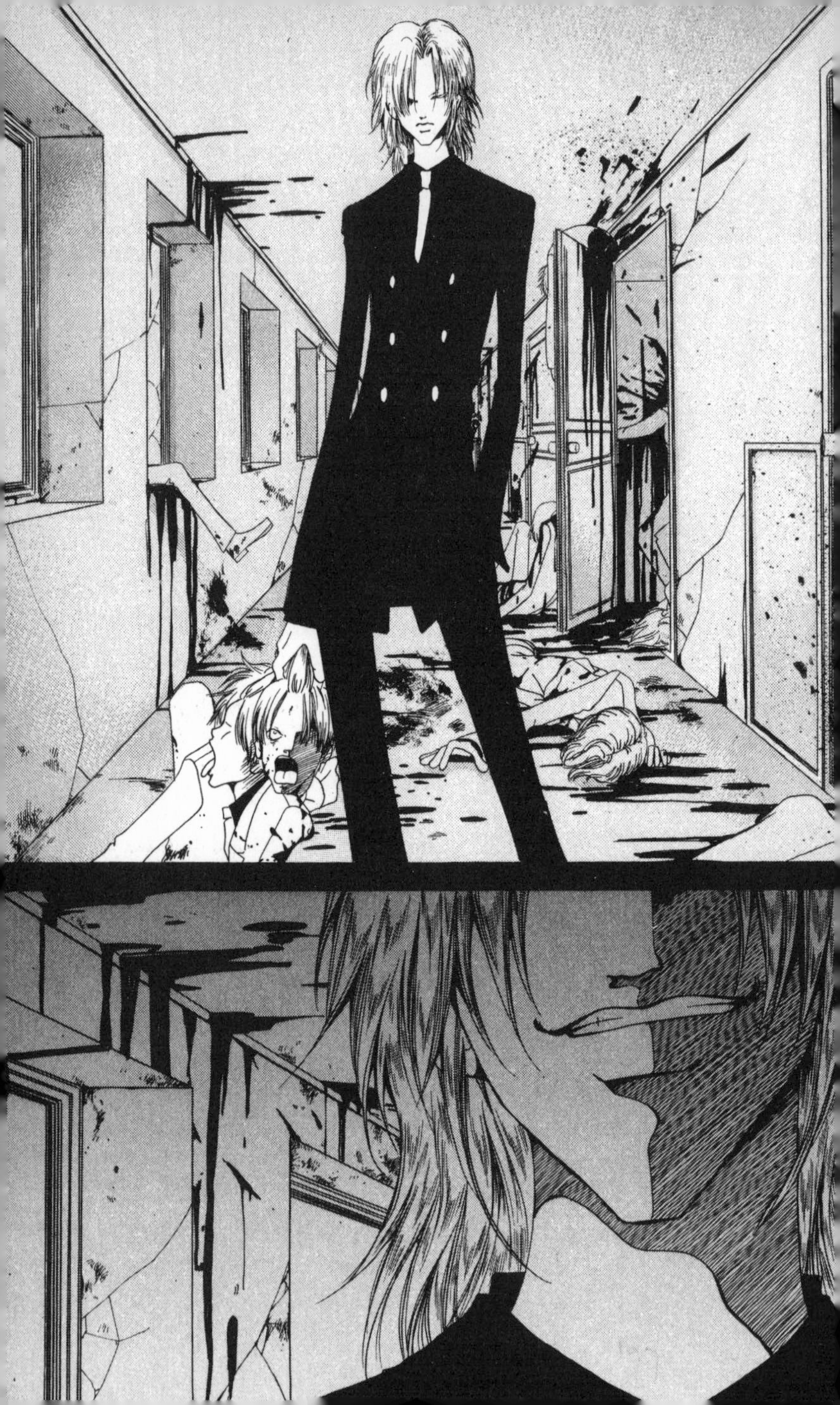

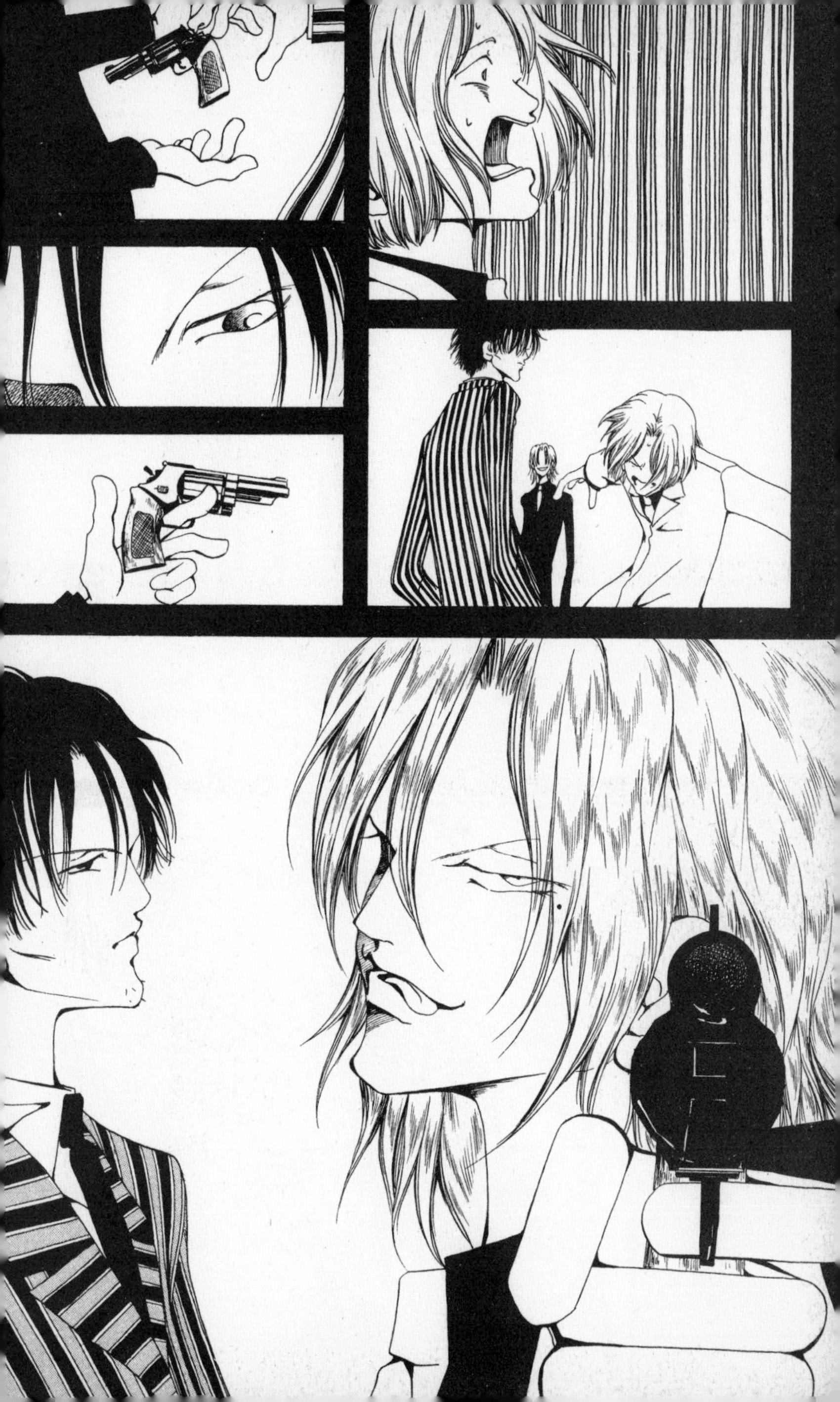

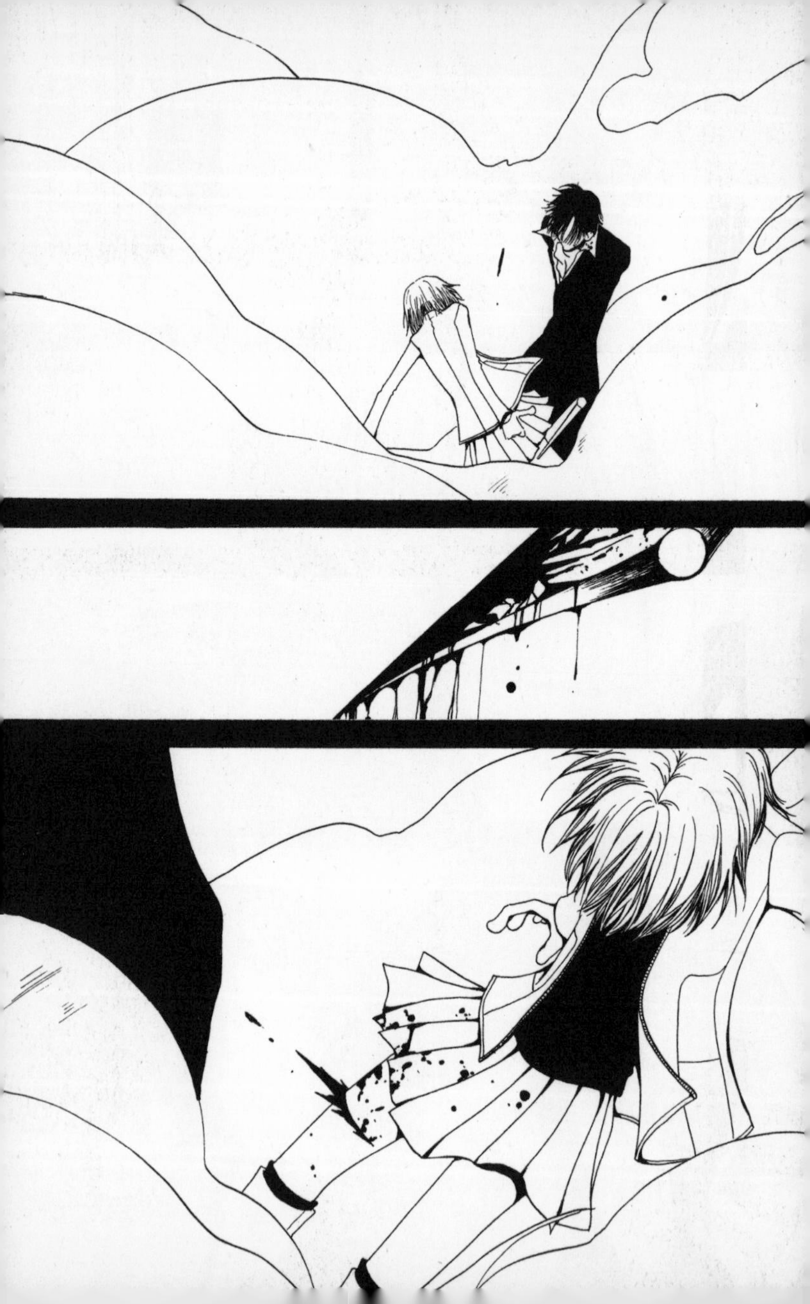

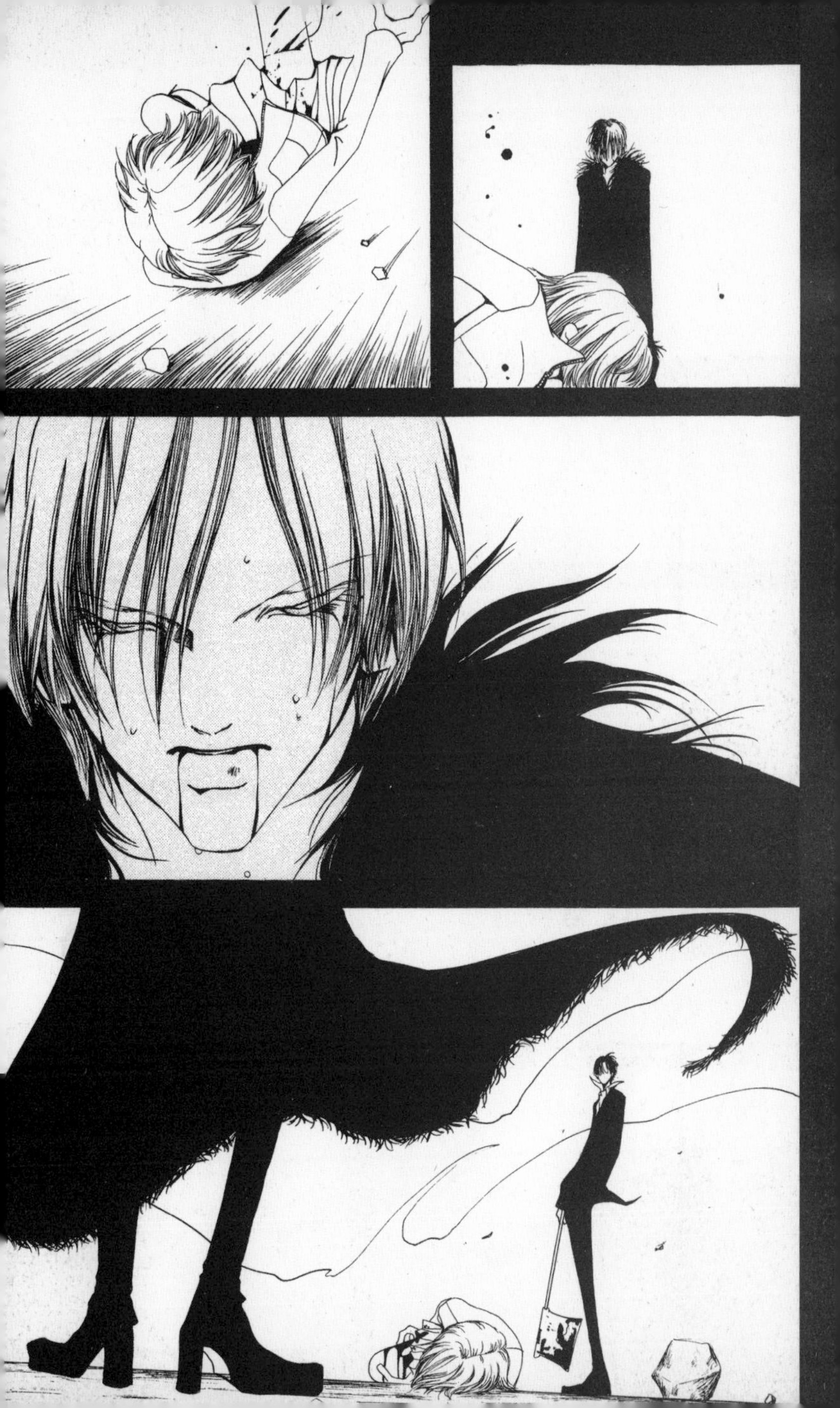

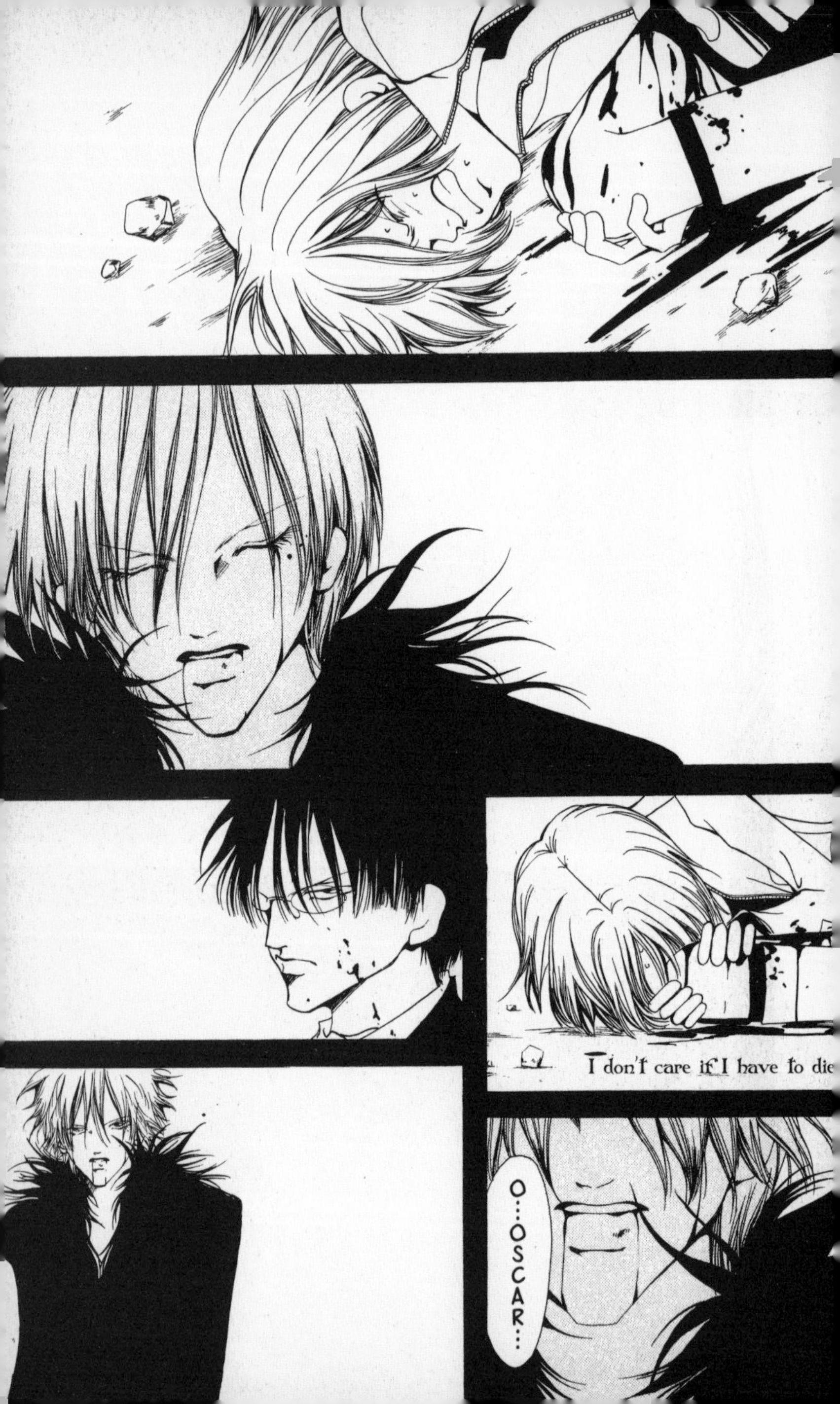
I don't care if I have to die
O...OSCAR...

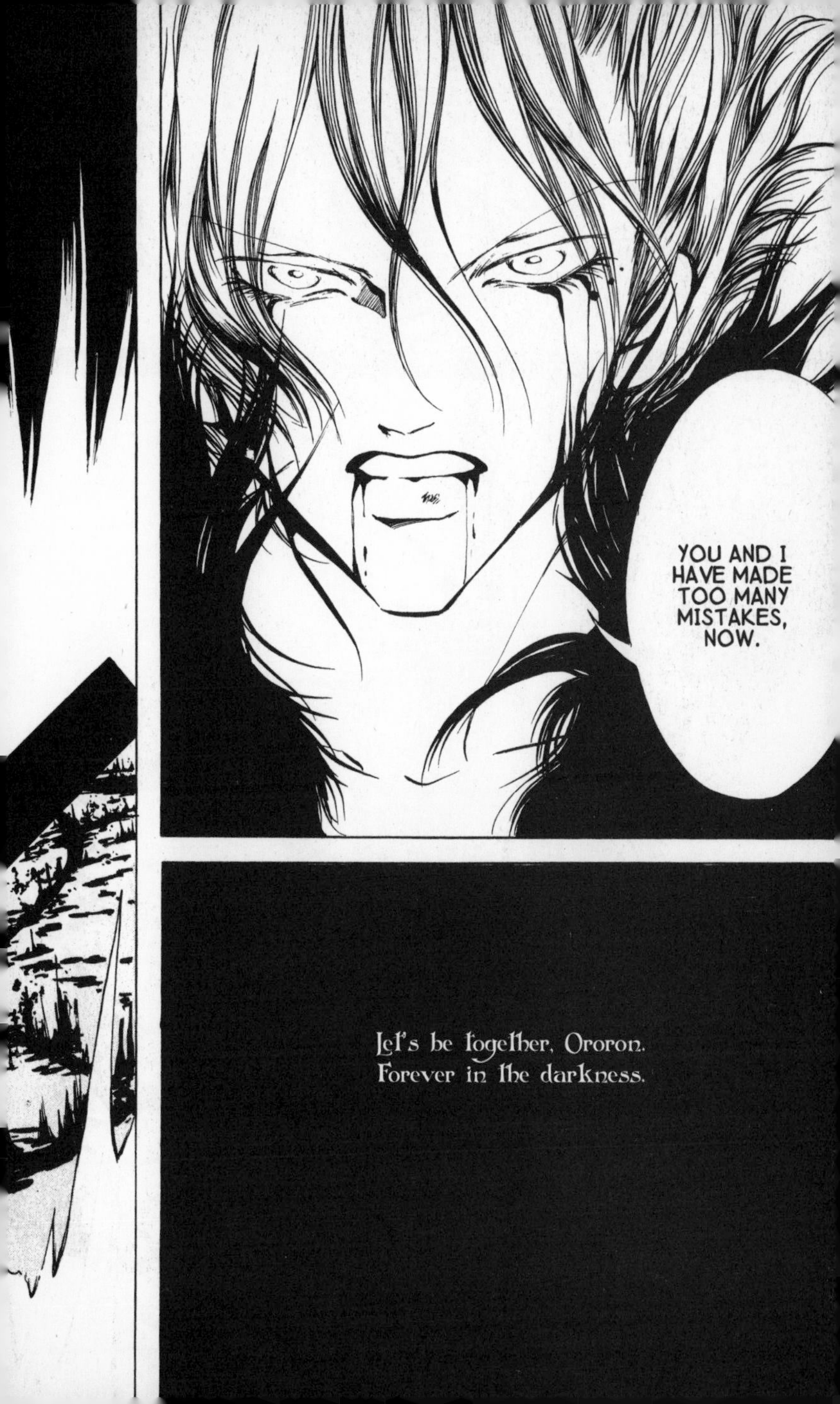
YOU AND I HAVE MADE TOO MANY MISTAKES, NOW.
Let's be together, Ororon.
Forever in the darkness.

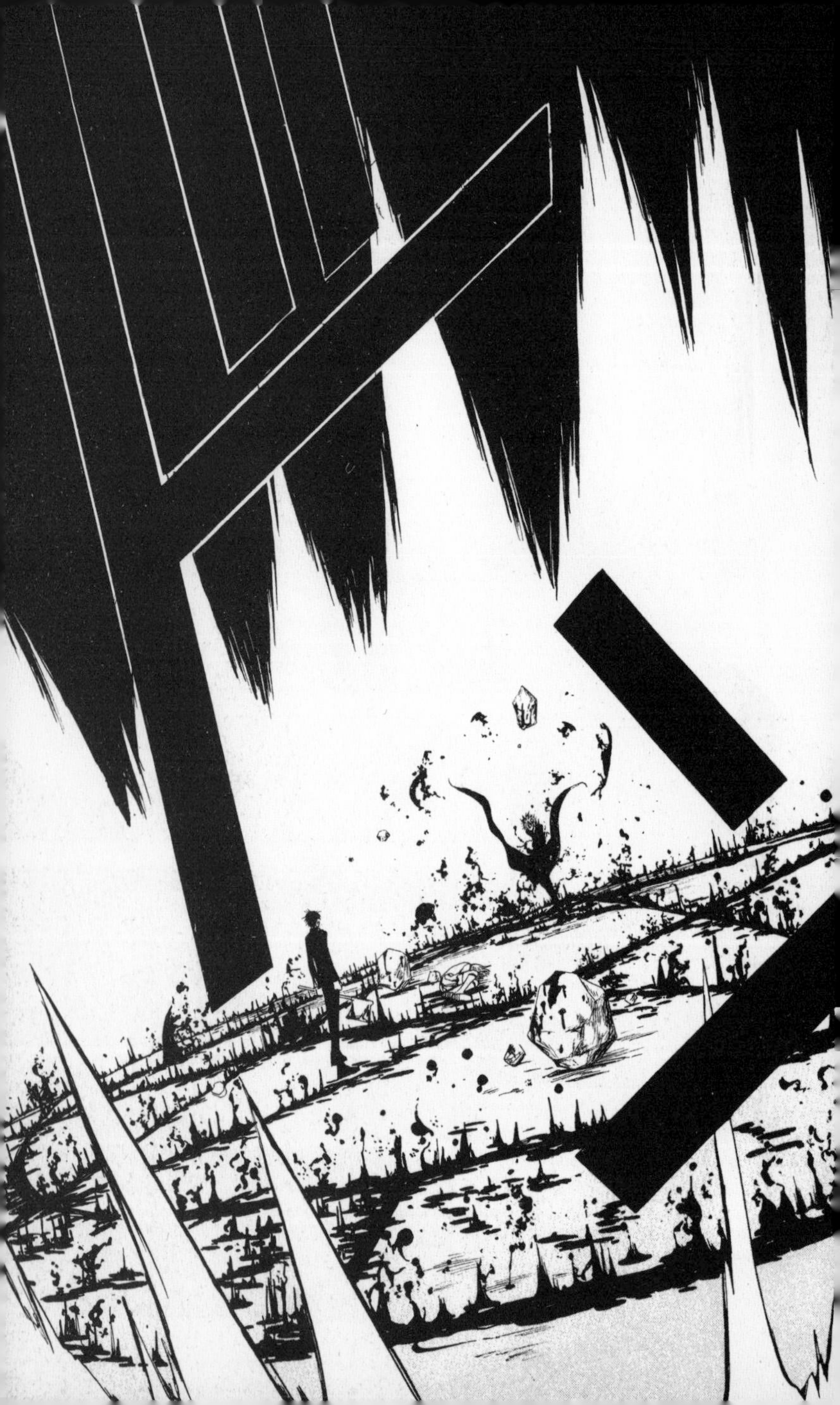
ドン

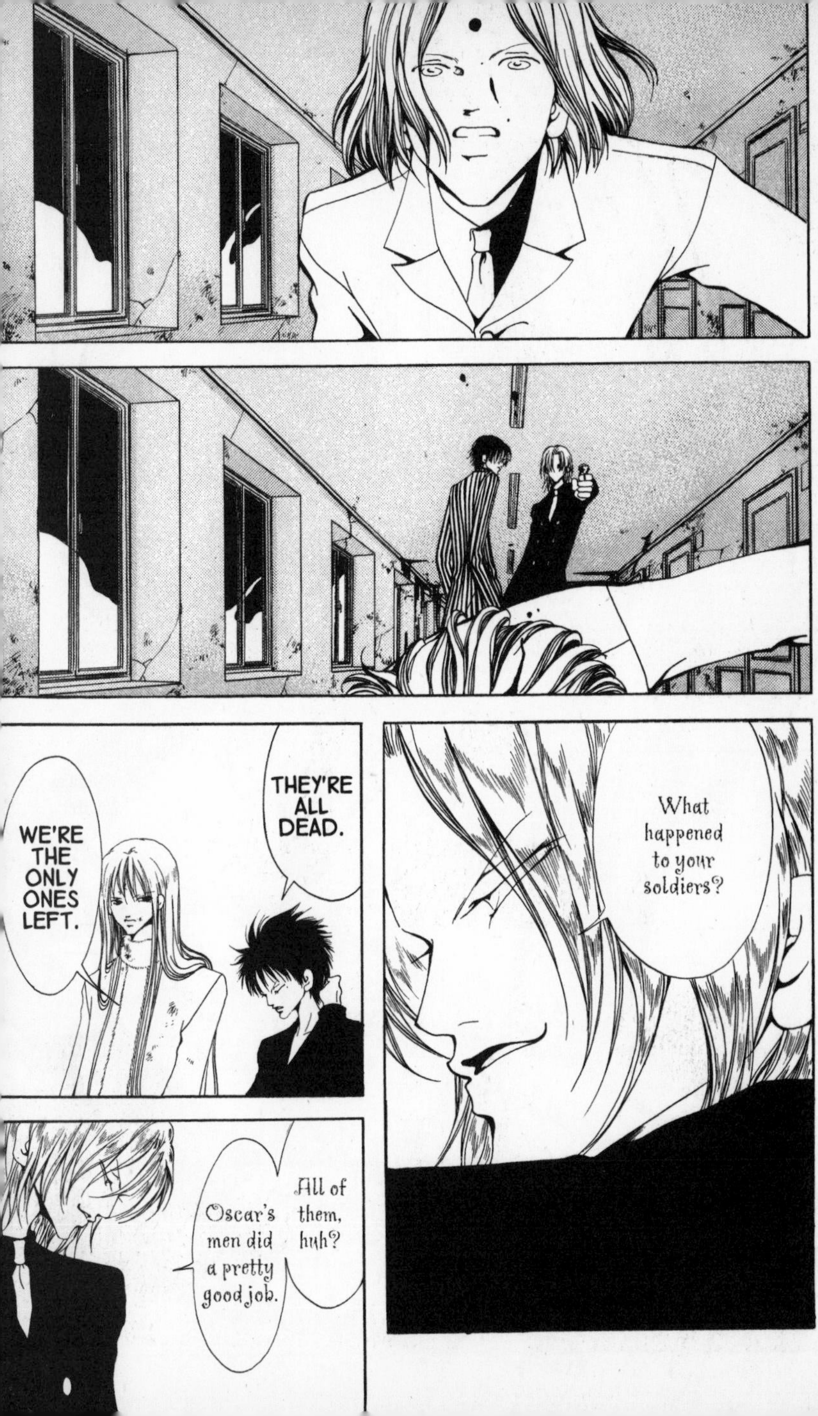
What happened to your soldiers?
THEY'RE ALL DEAD.
WE'RE THE ONLY ONES LEFT.
All of them, huh?
Oscar's men did a pretty good job.

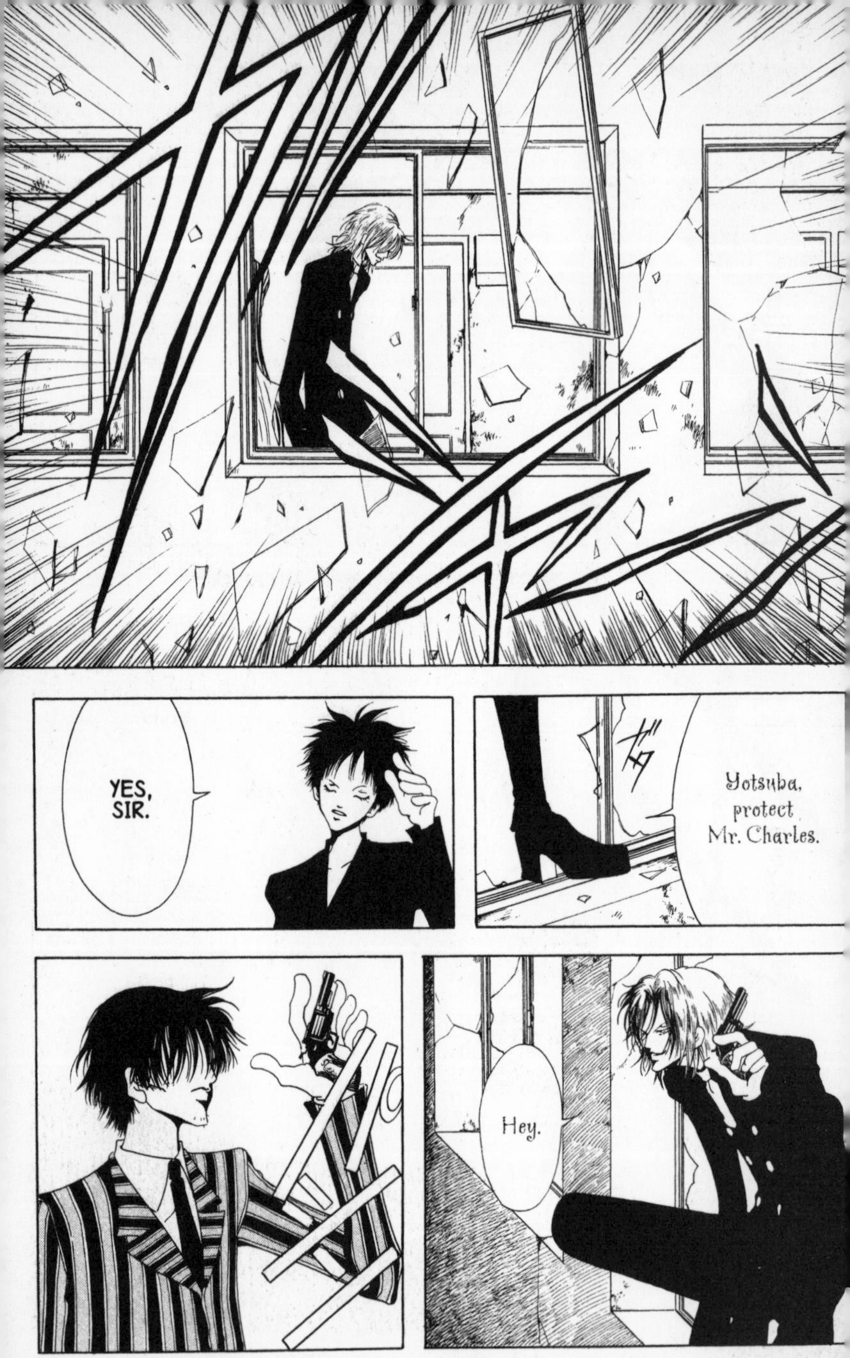
Yotsuba, protect Mr. Charles.
YES, SIR.
Hey.

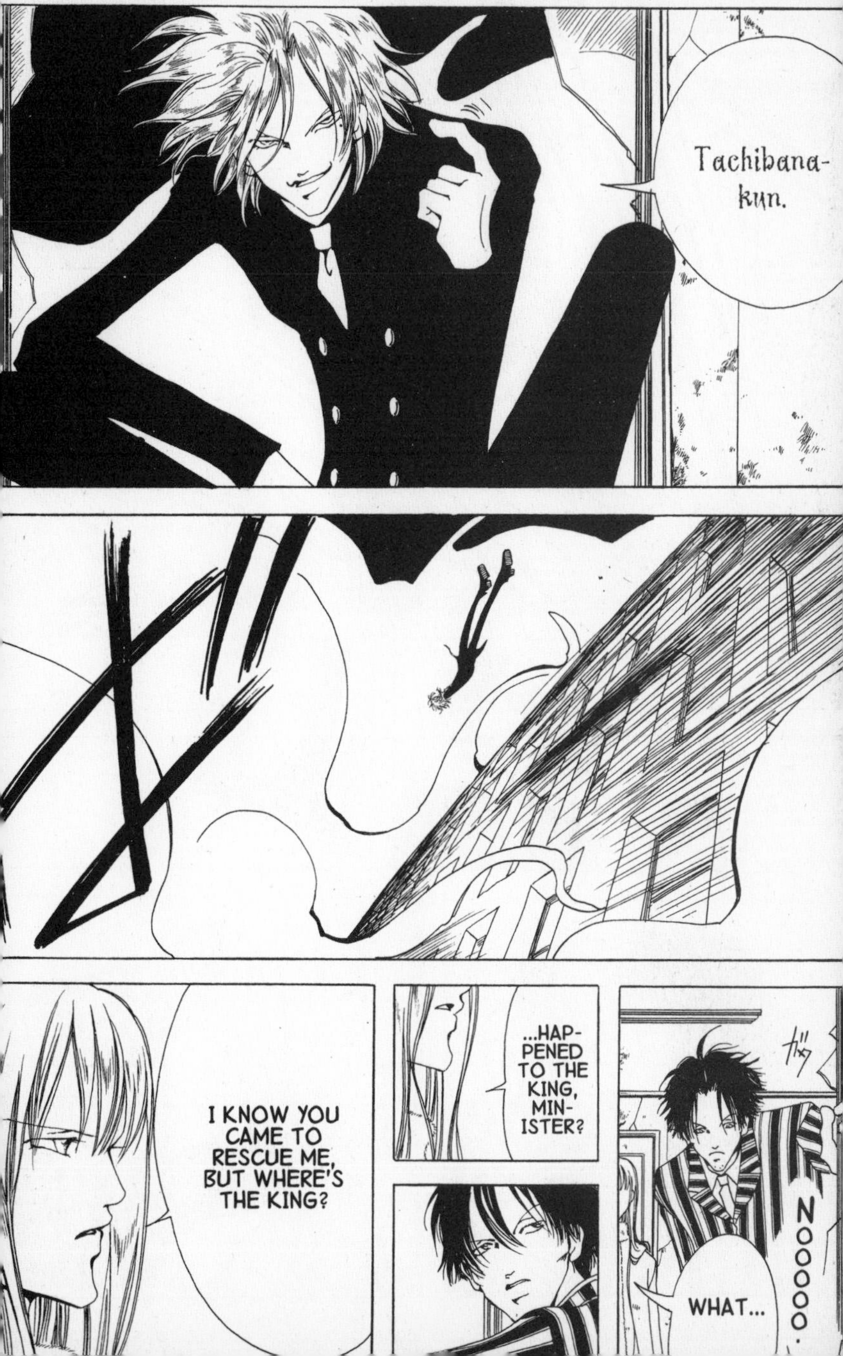
Tachibana-kun.
NOOOOO.
WHAT...
...HAPPENED TO THE KING, MINISTER?
I KNOW YOU CAME TO RESCUE ME, BUT WHERE'S THE KING?

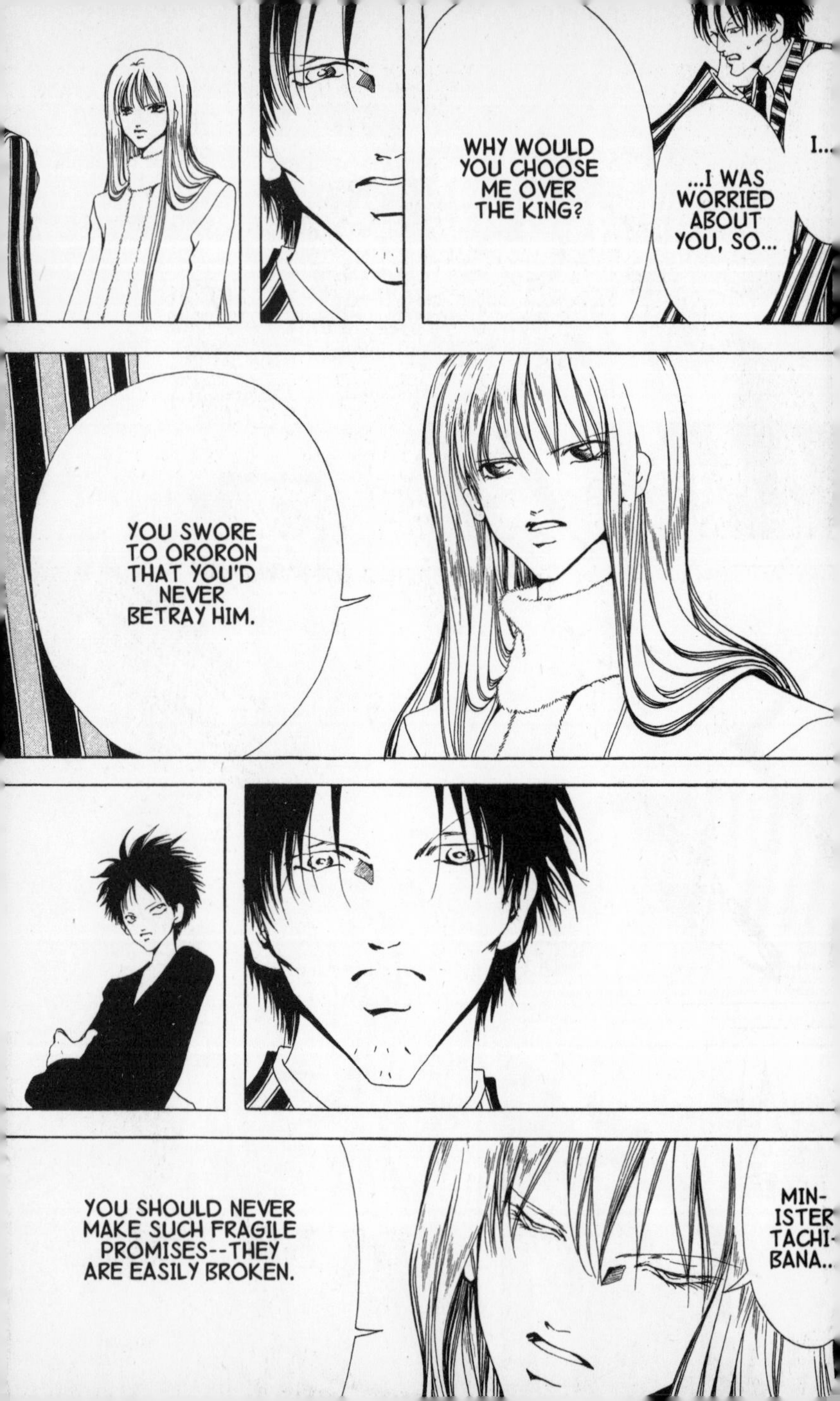
WHY WOULD YOU CHOOSE ME OVER THE KING?
I...
...I WAS WORRIED ABOUT YOU, SO...
YOU SWORE TO ORORON THAT YOU'D NEVER BETRAY HIM.
MIN-ISTER TACHI-BANA..
YOU SHOULD NEVER MAKE SUCH FRAGILE PROMISES--THEY ARE EASILY BROKEN.

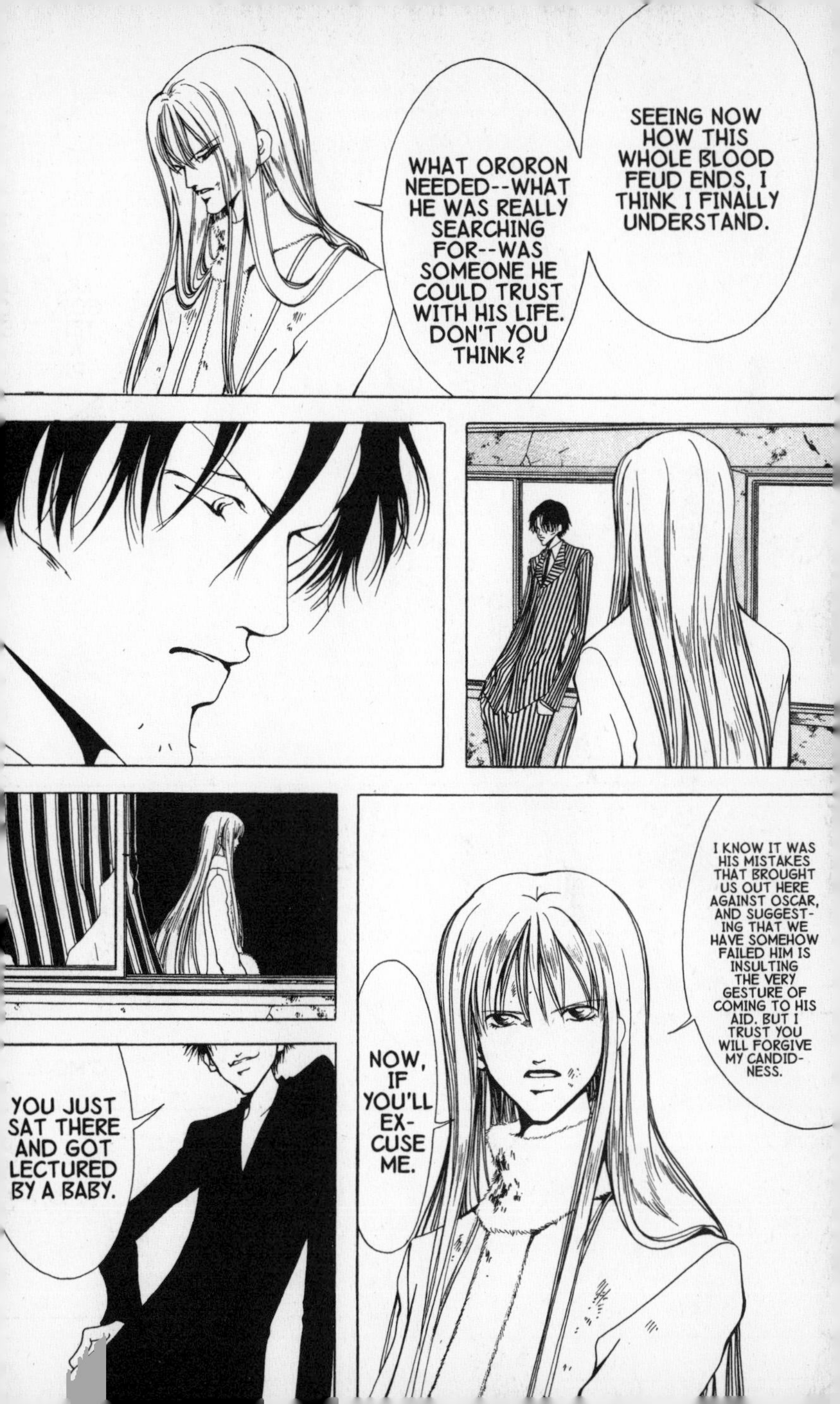
SEEING NOW HOW THIS WHOLE BLOOD FEUD ENDS, I THINK I FINALLY UNDERSTAND.
WHAT ORORON NEEDED--WHAT HE WAS REALLY SEARCHING FOR--WAS SOMEONE HE COULD TRUST WITH HIS LIFE. DON'T YOU THINK?
I KNOW IT WAS HIS MISTAKES THAT BROUGHT US OUT HERE AGAINST OSCAR, AND SUGGEST-ING THAT WE HAVE SOMEHOW FAILED HIM IS INSULTING THE VERY GESTURE OF COMING TO HIS AID. BUT I TRUST YOU WILL FORGIVE MY CANDID-NESS.
NOW, IF YOU'LL EX-CUSE ME.
YOU JUST SAT THERE AND GOT LECTURED BY A BABY.

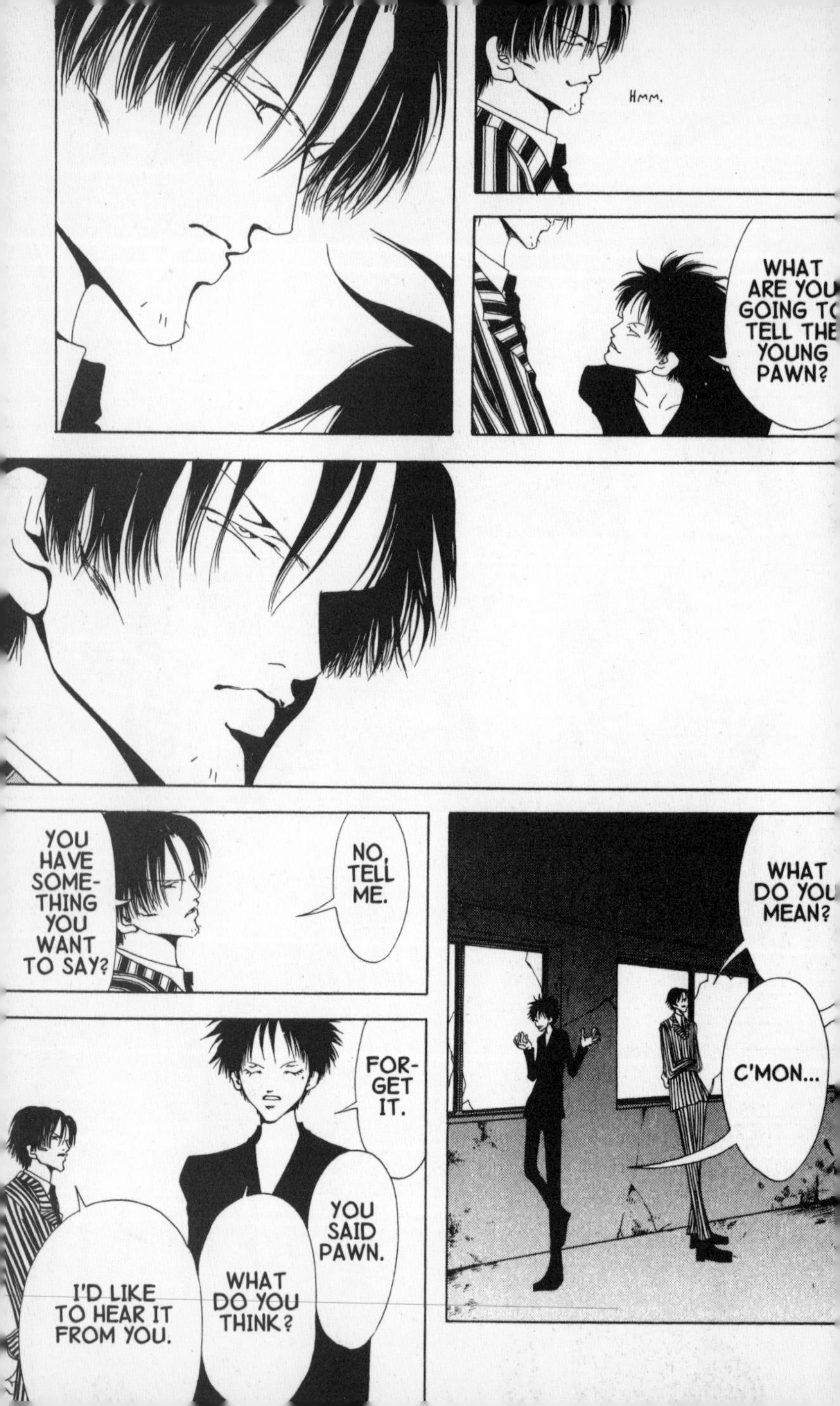
HMM.
WHAT ARE YOU GOING TO TELL THE YOUNG PAWN?
WHAT DO YOU MEAN?
C'MON...
NO, TELL ME.
YOU HAVE SOME-THING YOU WANT TO SAY?
FOR-GET IT.
YOU SAID PAWN.
WHAT DO YOU THINK?
I'D LIKE TO HEAR IT FROM YOU.

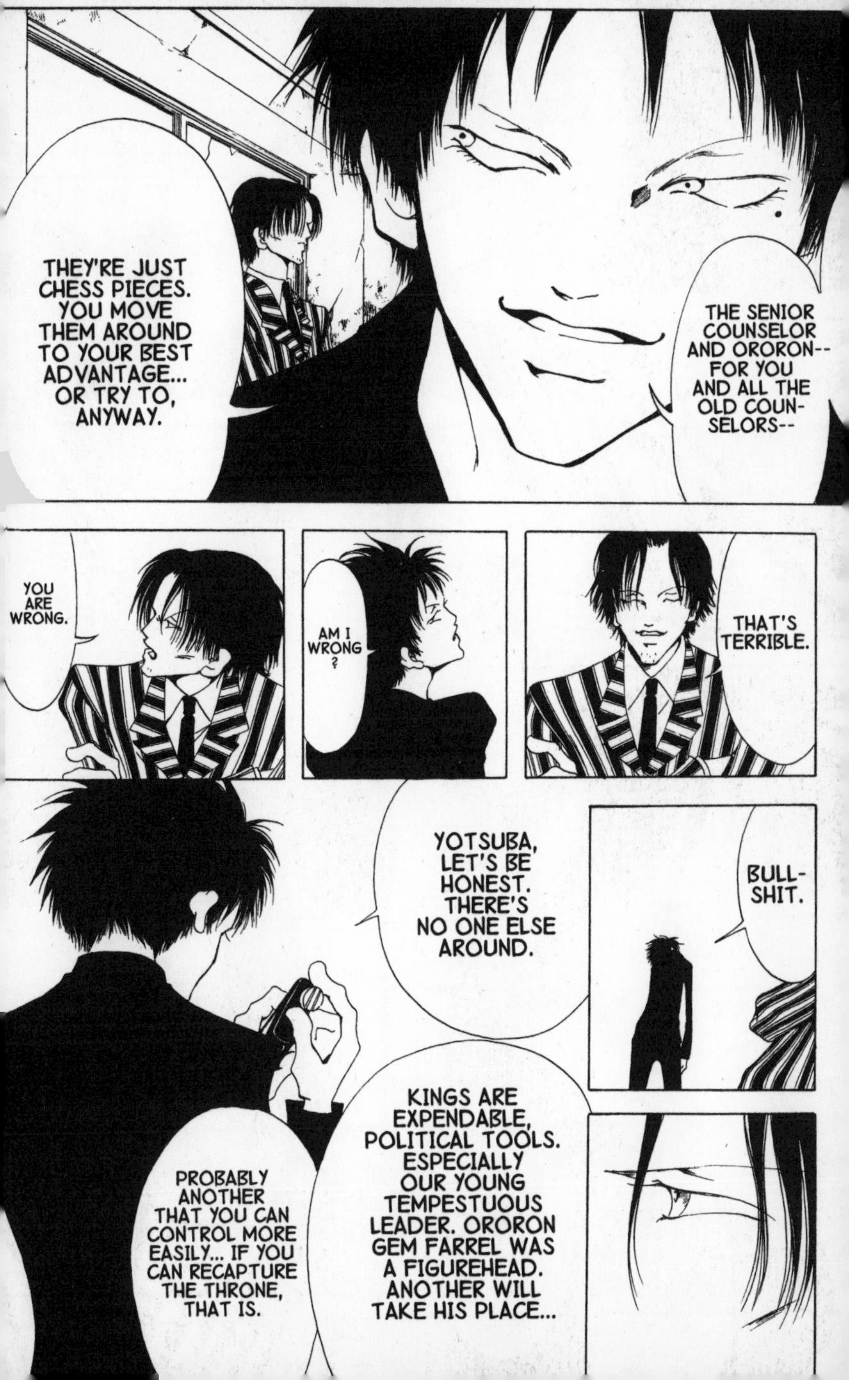
THE SENIOR COUNSELOR AND ORORON-- FOR YOU AND ALL THE OLD COUNSELORS--
THEY'RE JUST CHESS PIECES. YOU MOVE THEM AROUND TO YOUR BEST ADVANTAGE... OR TRY TO, ANYWAY.
THAT'S TERRIBLE.
AM I WRONG?
YOU ARE WRONG.
BULL-SHIT.
YOTSUBA, LET'S BE HONEST. THERE'S NO ONE ELSE AROUND.
KINGS ARE EXPENDABLE, POLITICAL TOOLS. ESPECIALLY OUR YOUNG TEMPESTUOUS LEADER. ORORON GEM FARREL WAS A FIGUREHEAD. ANOTHER WILL TAKE HIS PLACE...
PROBABLY ANOTHER THAT YOU CAN CONTROL MORE EASILY... IF YOU CAN RECAPTURE THE THRONE, THAT IS.

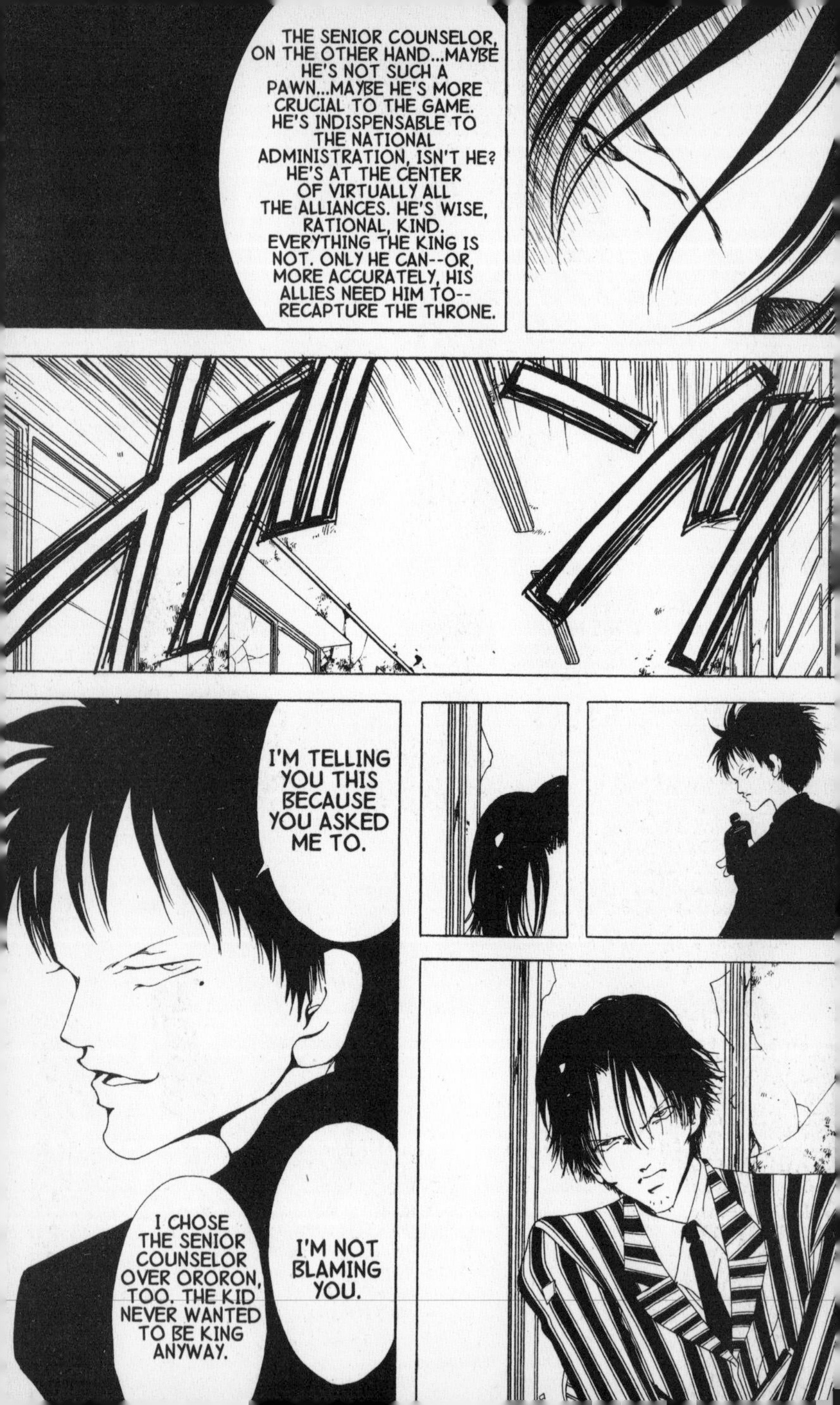
THE SENIOR COUNSELOR, ON THE OTHER HAND...MAYBE HE'S NOT SUCH A PAWN...MAYBE HE'S MORE CRUCIAL TO THE GAME. HE'S INDISPENSABLE TO THE NATIONAL ADMINISTRATION, ISN'T HE? HE'S AT THE CENTER OF VIRTUALLY ALL THE ALLIANCES. HE'S WISE, RATIONAL, KIND. EVERYTHING THE KING IS NOT. ONLY HE CAN--OR, MORE ACCURATELY, HIS ALLIES NEED HIM TO--RECAPTURE THE THRONE.
I'M TELLING YOU THIS BECAUSE YOU ASKED ME TO.
I'M NOT BLAMING YOU.
I CHOSE THE SENIOR COUNSELOR OVER ORORON, TOO. THE KID NEVER WANTED TO BE KING ANYWAY.

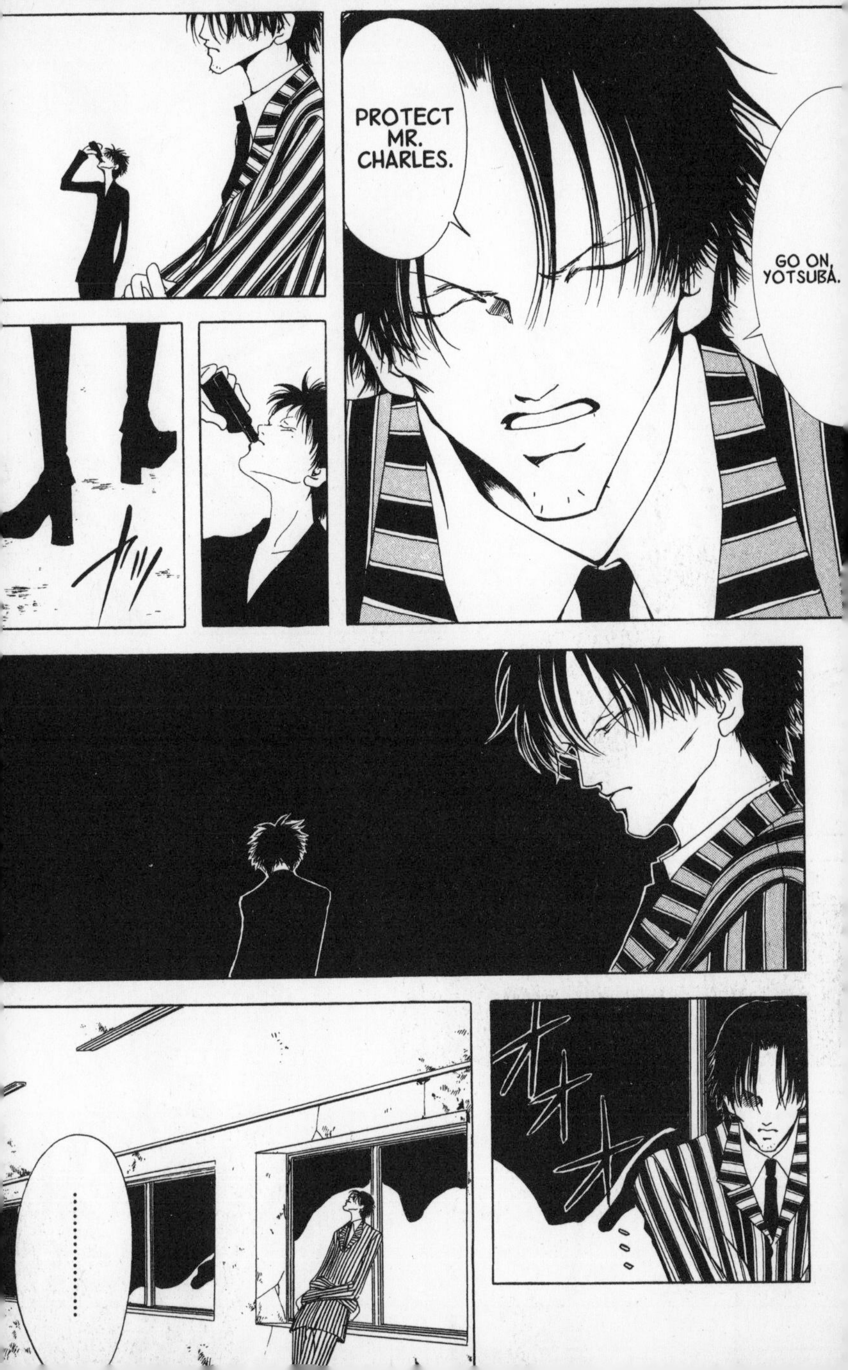
GO ON, YOTSUBA.
PROTECT MR. CHARLES.
....

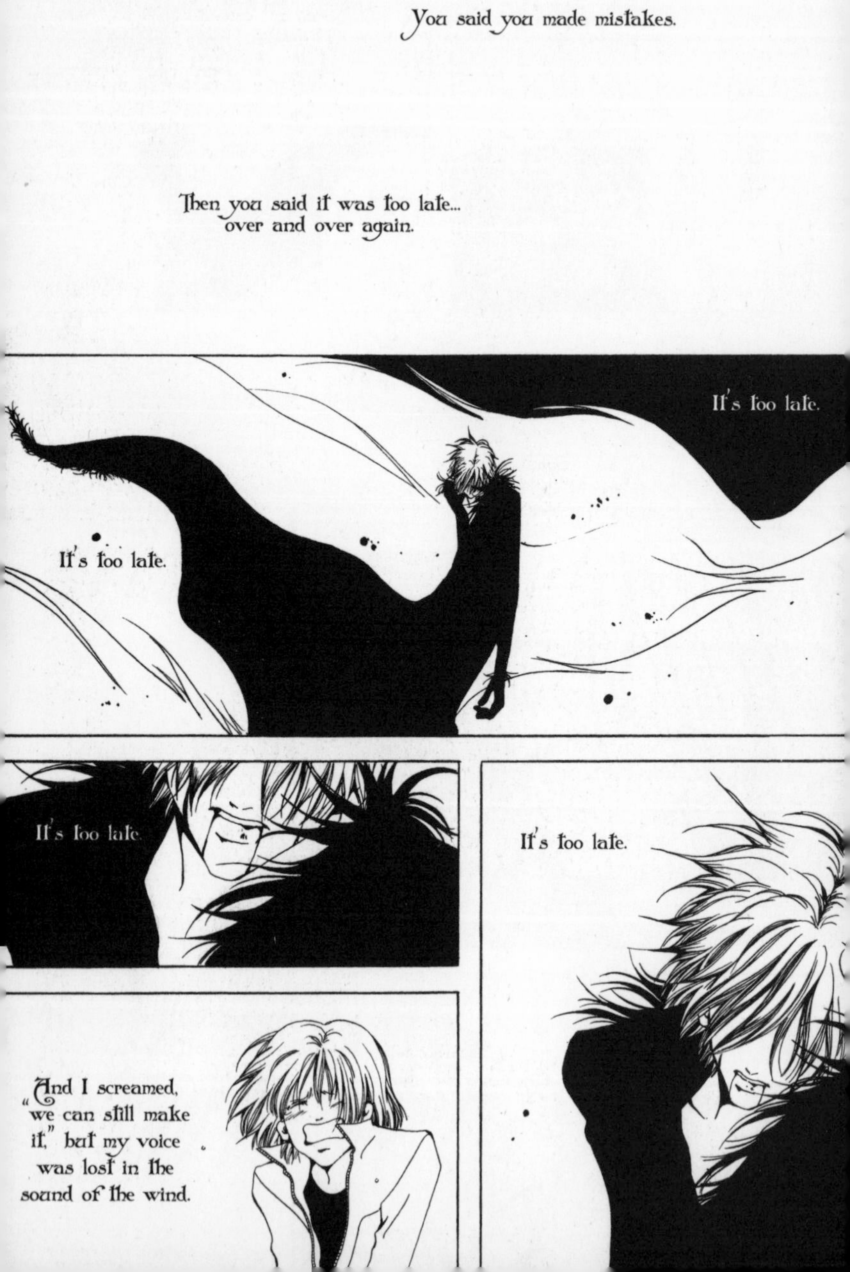
You said you made mistakes.
Then you said it was too late... over and over again.
It's too late.
It's too late.
It's too late.
It's too late.
"And I screamed, "we can still make it," but my voice was lost in the sound of the wind.

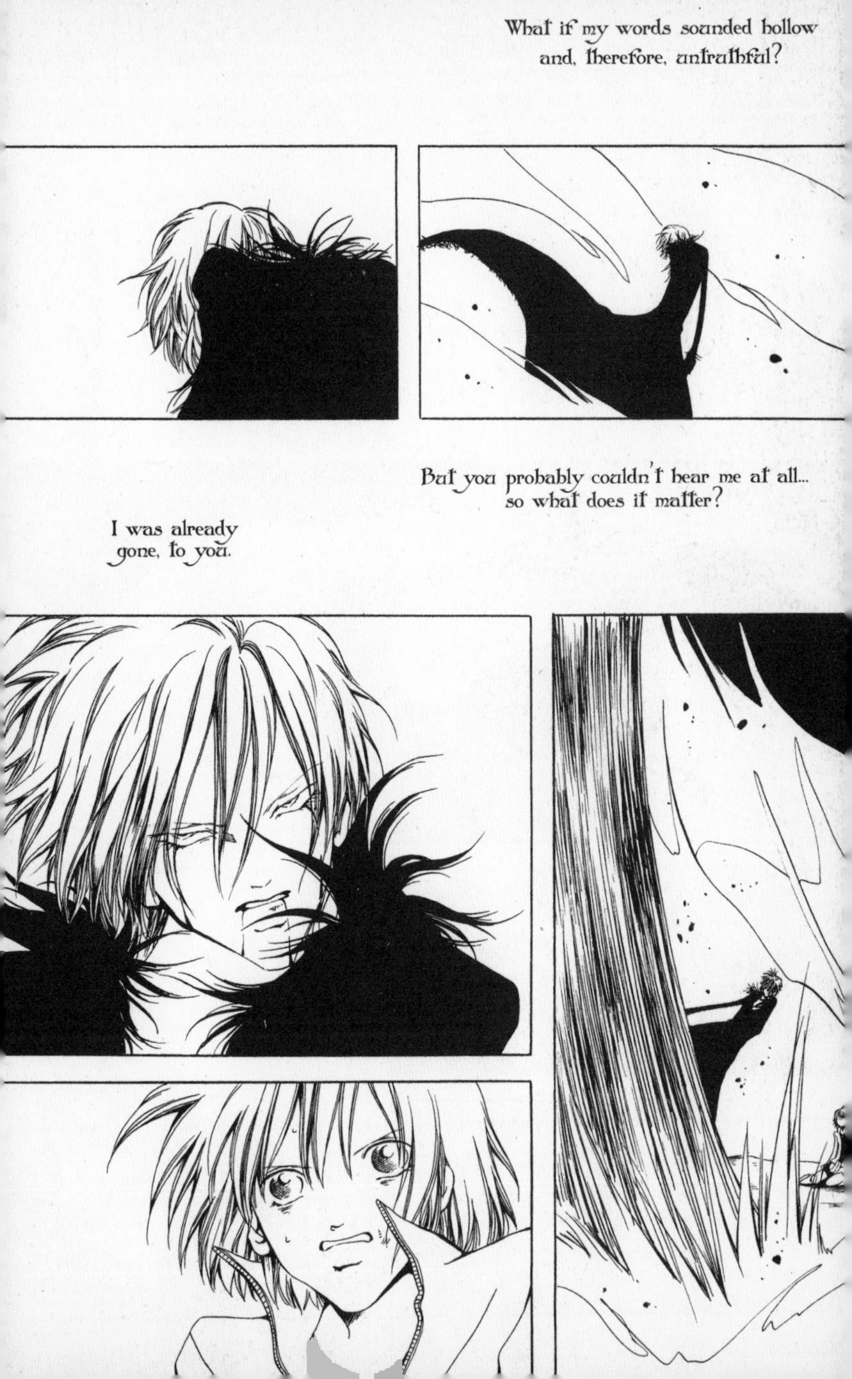
What if my words sounded hollow and, therefore, untruthful?
But you probably couldn't hear me at all... so what does it matter?
I was already gone, to you.

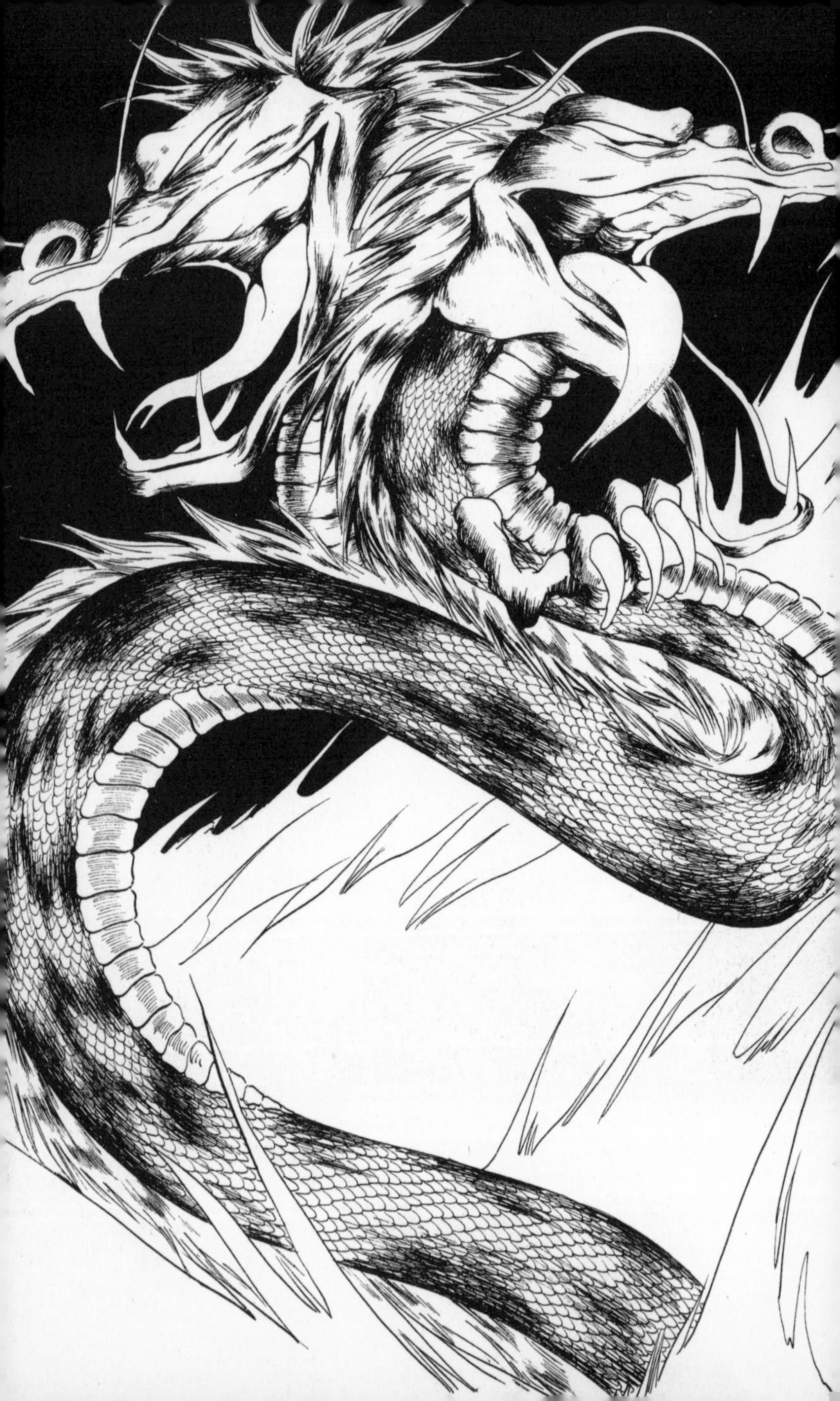

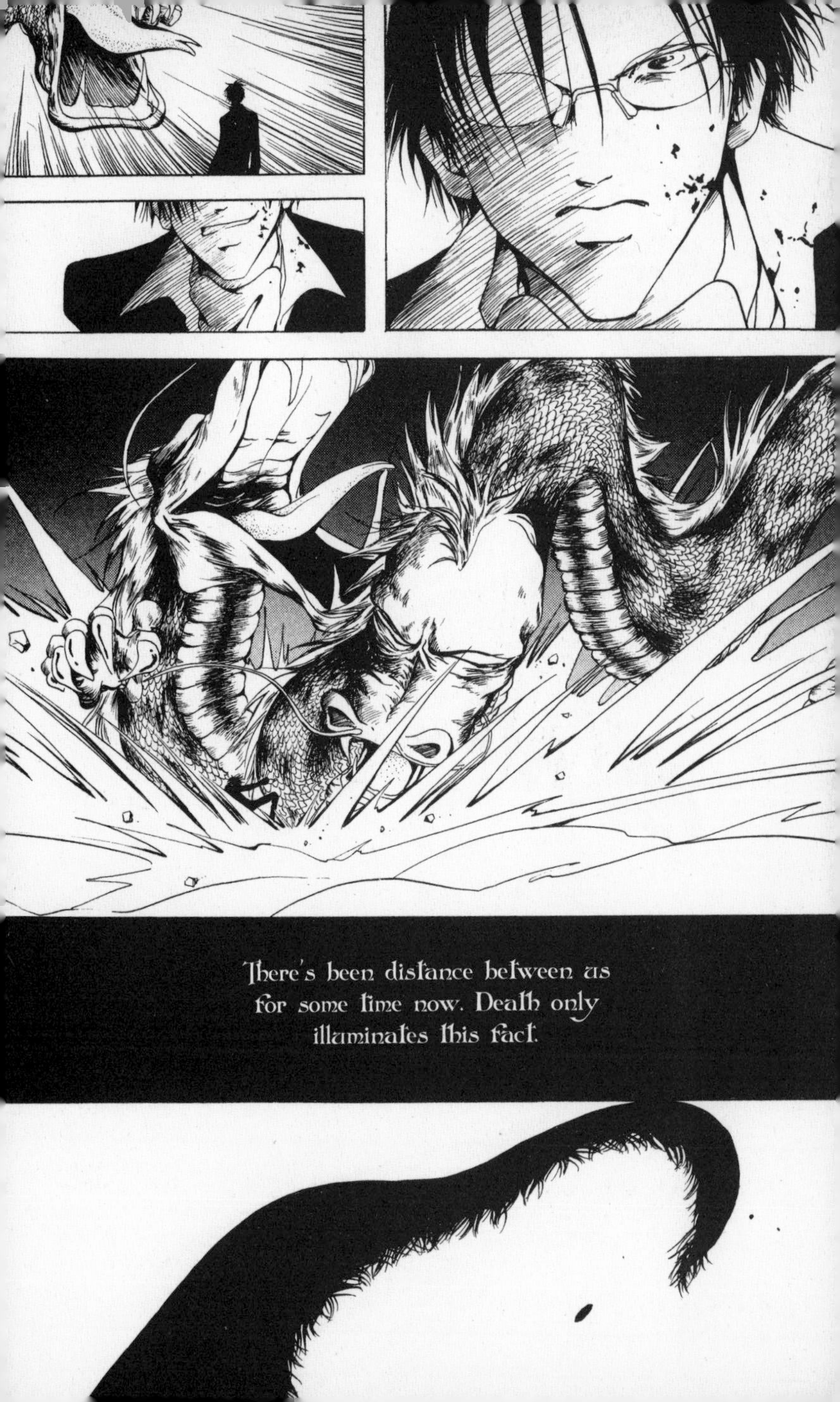
There's been distance between us for some time now. Death only illuminates this fact.

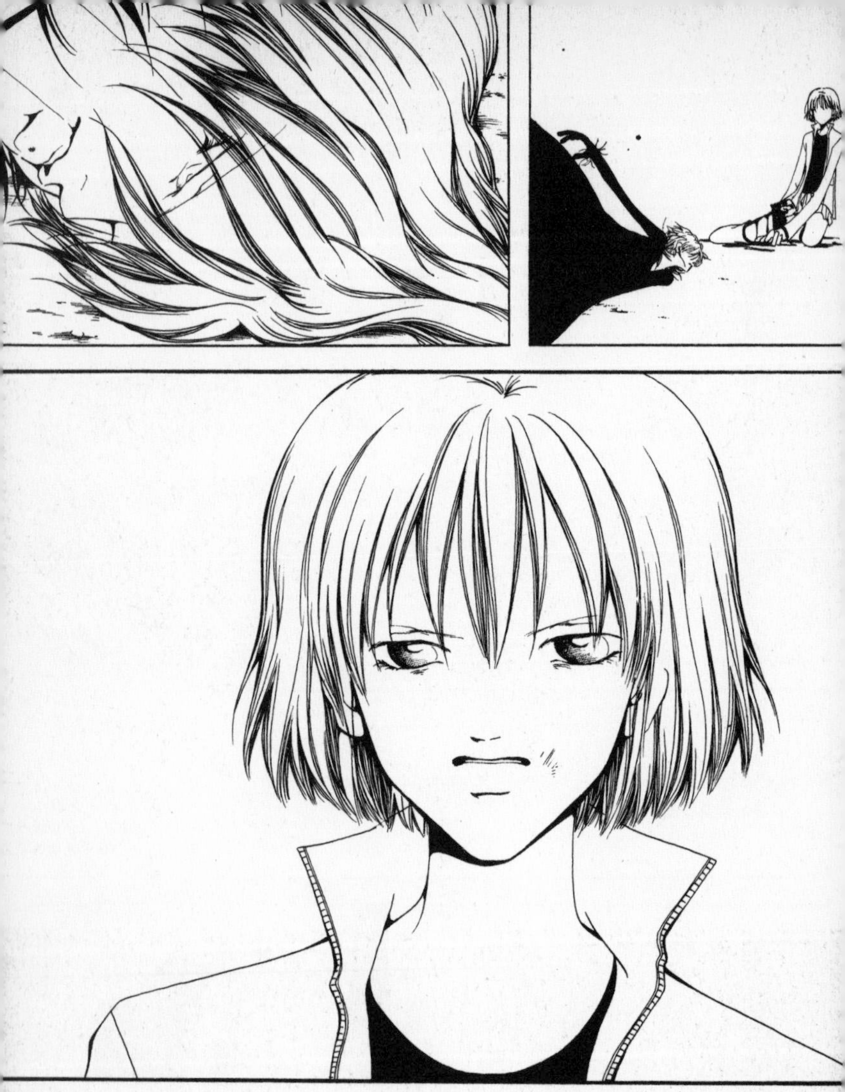

I've been useless to you.

During our last conversation,
I was lost, confused, terrified.

I should have tried communicating
more and crying less.

No, it wasn't the tears that
were at fault. I should have
just stayed beside you.

I should've just held
your hand.

By the time Garo and Othello came to the rescue, it was too late. I was angry~~where had they been all this time? Was I the only person that loved you enough to be here when you died?

Just like you said, Ororon...too late.

Othello laughed.

But through his laughter, he quaked with anger.

A black~haired boy I've never met closed your eyes. Then everything was done.

Right.

So it was in the fall of my fifteenth year...

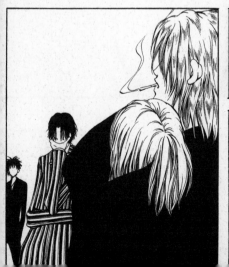

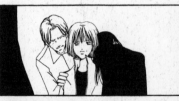

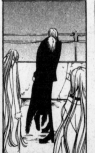

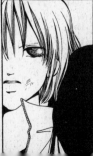

...that my first love died.

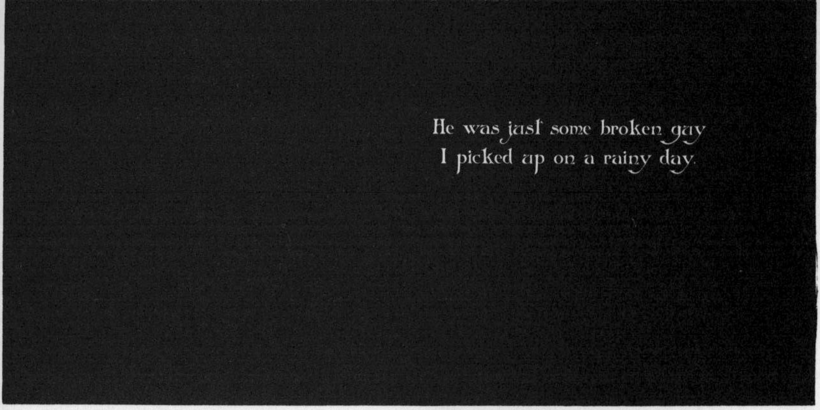
He was just some broken guy
I picked up on a rainy day.

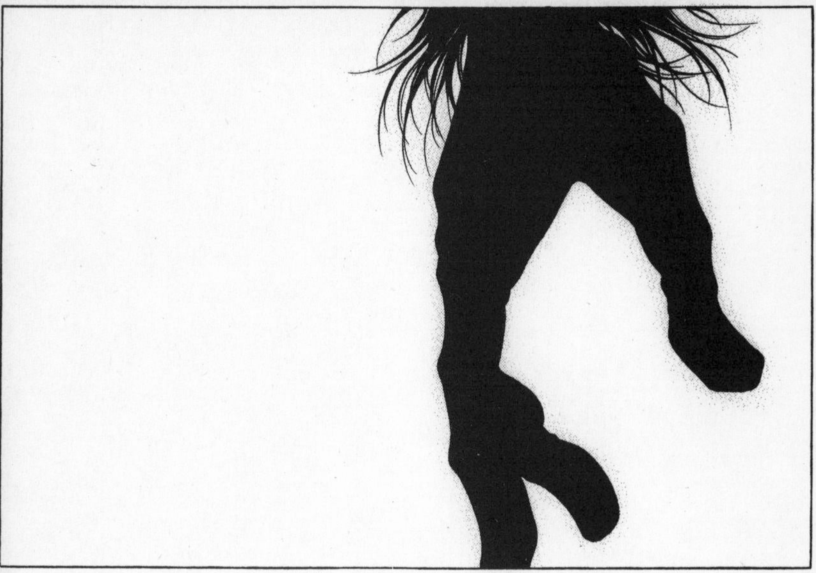

Some lonely devil...

...who had beautiful dark gray eyes....
and smelled like blood.

THE DEMON ORORON THE END